LIAM MELLOWS
AND THE IRISH REVOLUTION

In Memoriam
P. A. G.

LIAM MELLOW

LIAM MELLOWS

AND

THE IRISH REVOLUTION

by

C. DESMOND GREAVES

LAWRENCE & WISHART
LONDON 1971

ACKNOWLEDGMENTS

The materials used in compiling this biography have been found widely dispersed; in general histories of the revolutionary period; biographies of Mellows' contemporaries; references in periodicals; reminiscences held privately in manuscript; reports in the press; and above all in personal recollections by his associates.

Those who provided or indicated sources, or gave their valuable time in discussion, are too numerous to acknowledge separately. At the risk of invidiousness I would nevertheless like to thank specially for their help and encouragement, Mrs. Rita Brady, Miss Maire Comerford, Mrs. Nora Connolly-O'Brien, Messrs. R. J. Connolly, Padhraig Fahy, George Fleming, Frank Hynes, Stephen Jordan, Joseph MacHenry, Eamon Martin, Ernest Nunan, Peadar O'Donnell, Cormac O'Malley (who allowed me to examine his father's papers), Frank Robbins, and Tony Woods (whose mother's papers are a mine of information); also the late Ailbhe O'Monnchain who placed his valuable papers at my disposal, and the late Rev. Norman Thomas. None of these is to the slightest degree responsible for opinions expressed or errors committed.

To these must be added the staffs of the Irish National Museum, National Library, Dublin City Library and Sligo County Library, and that of the British Museum Newspaper Library at Colindale, together with many State and City Libraries in the U.S.A. A special word of appreciation must be said of Mrs. Fiona Connolly-Edwards who prepared the manuscript for the press in a critical manner, making many useful suggestions.

The map opposite page 302 is based on one contained in *No Other Law* by Florence O'Donoghue, Irish Press, Dublin, 1954.

C. D. G.

Birkenhead, March 1971

Printed in Great Britain by
The Camelot Press Ltd., London and Southampton

CONTENTS

INTRODUCTION

THE IRISH REVOLUTION

"My business is revolution."—James Connolly

JAMES CONNOLLY coined the phrase "The reconquest of Ireland by the Irish people". By this he meant the total process of replacing imperialist property relations by those of Irish democracy. The elimination of externally imposed backwardness, isolation, dependence and poverty may be called "The Irish Revolution" in its broadest sense. But the expression may be used in a narrower sense also, of the great political upheavals aimed at this object. The most noteworthy of such marked the years 1782–98 and 1912–22.[1] During this last period the impinging of the world imperialist crisis on the Union, already in a state of advanced crisis, led to its disruption and the emergence of an Irish national State. The purpose of this introduction is to show how the failure of the first revolution rendered the second inevitable and how the form of the second depended on the legacy left from the first.

The legislative Union which came into effect on 1st January 1801, represented the end-point of the political counter-revolution which began in 1795. The victors, the Irish landlords and the English oligarchy, shared the spoils between them. The heroic last stand of 1798 had failed to halt the march of reaction. The United Irishmen and their followers were dispersed, disorganized and dispirited. The desolation of the dreadful year 1799 emerges in the void hopelessness of such songs as *The wind that shakes the barley*. In 1800 the play was over, the curtain seemingly rung down on "the rights of man in Ireland". The Irish Parliament was extinguished. With it lapsed the short-lived power to impose tariffs and negotiate commercial treaties. The peasantry had been tamed by the whip and the pitch-cap. Now the bourgeoisie that had incited them against the aristocracy was delivered defenceless to its competitors. The landlords enjoyed privileged access to the English market, and an exclusive right to the jobberies and emoluments of Parliament.

---

[1] Professor Alison Phillips speaks of the Irish Revolution of 1906–23, William O'Brien of 1916–21, Erskine Childers of "the revolution that began in 1918", Erhard Rümpf of "Die irische Revolution seit 1918", and Frank Gallagher's "Four glorious years" are the years of armed struggle 1918–21. It is clearly a question of different conceptions and different stages of the one thing.

The Union was challenged before it had subsisted three years when Robert Emmet led the artisans of Dublin in a well-planned but unsuccessful attempt to overthrow it by force. The aim was to separate Ireland once again from England and to resume the democratic advance interrupted in 1795. Throughout the ensuing century this purpose was never wholly forgotten, though sometimes obscured by force of immediate necessities. The result was a resistance movement of a progressive character, in which the masses gained confidence with experience, in each generation preferring more advanced demands, and improvising the most daring and ingenious forms of struggle.

Three great strategic principles were the legacy of the United Irishmen, and these have served to the present as tests of the seriousness of any movement. These are:

1. The unity of the Irish people, irrespective of religious belief, around the demands of the most numerous exploited classes. For the greater part of the nineteenth century these were the peasants and landless men, later the proletariat.
2. Mutual solidarity with the forces of democracy in Britain—at first the radicals, then the Chartists, finally the socialists.
3. Orientation towards those countries which stood in the van of political progress—for most of the period France or the United States, later Soviet Russia.

They were opposed by principles of imperial domination no less clear-cut and logical, namely:

1. The maintenance of an economic garrison class in Ireland able to attract the support of a proportion of the population.
2. The encouragement among the British people of chauvinism directed against both Irish national aspirations and the persons of Irish immigrants in Britain.
3. The systematic isolation of Ireland from international contact and exchange, especially from countries undergoing progressive developments.

The application of these principles was facilitated by the constitutional forms adopted. The two countries were not merged. The "partially shared executive" through which Britain had controlled Ireland during the years of legislative independence was retained, subject to modification as necessity required. A Lord Lieutenant or Viceroy, complete with satrapal court and all appurtenances of nepotism and corruption, stood at the pinnacle of a caste system whose basis was the robbery of the tillers of the soil. His machinery set in motion legislation passed at Westminster from headquarters in Dublin Castle. By 1914 there had been established twenty-nine distinct Irish departments of State, and eleven branches of United Kingdom departments.[1] This combination proliferated "enough Boards to make Ireland's coffin".

The financial Union was delayed until 1817. In the preceding sixteen years the Irish National debt had been encouraged to rise from £28 million to £113 million. Now the pillage could begin in earnest. It is of some interest to estimate its total magnitude. Ireland was taxed on a basis twice that of its real capacity to pay. Consequently by 1896 the Financial Relations Commission was able to report that the country had been mulcted of £325 million. Sums ranging from £2 million to £6 million were withdrawn each year by landlords resident in Britain, to say nothing of the mortgages of those who lived at home. Railway and cross-channel freight charges were manipulated so as to subsidise British exporters at the expense of goods consigned in Ireland. The well-known disparity between agricultural and industrial prices told increasingly if incommensurably against Ireland.[2] The greater part of the deposits of the Joint Stock Banks, standing at the turn of the century at about £40 million, was invested in Britain, and represented a capital transfer from Ireland.

British investment in Ireland, apart from ground leases, was largely confined to railways, but spread into shipbuilding, textiles, brewing, milling, banking and insurance. The total sum extracted from Ireland through all forms of rent, interest, profit and taxation cannot have fallen far short of £1,000 million during the period of the Union, and may well have exceeded it. What price indeed can be put on the loss by emigration of the entire natural increase of the population? Let us suppose, by way of an estimate, that the Irish economy was compelled to support half a million children who would never add anything substantial to the national product. If their annual maintenance

[1] MacDowell, *Irish Administration*, p. 29.
[2] This is not an easy subject. If 1840 prices are taken as 100, then 1910 prices of wheat, oats, mutton, wool and store cattle are respectively 62, 111, 146, 98 and 275 (O'Donovan, *Economic History of Livestock in Ireland*, p. 210). It seems surprising that no satisfactory study of prices within Ireland in the nineteenth century seems to be available. It has been held that thanks to the customs union, British indices may be used, except perhaps in the case of heavy imports like coal and iron. This is by no means free from doubt, and a thorough examination of the subject is badly needed. The British indices show a marked trend against agriculture. Taking the 1840 price level as 100, the agricultural price index fell to 62 in 1900, thereafter recovering to 67 in 1910. The corresponding figures for "principal industrial products" were 100, 82·6 and 87. But in Ireland the different price movements in different sectors of agriculture would be of vital significance.

"including rags" amounts to no more than £10 per head, the loss to the country by their emigration would amount to £350 million over the period 1845 to 1915. A substantial proportion of these emigrants would spend their entire productive life in Britain. The consequences of this massive outflow of wealth were seen in the low standard of living of the people, the chronic agrarian crisis, and the stunting and distortion of industrial development.

The history of the Union falls naturally into four periods, each opening with its special crisis. These were:

1. From its inception to the fiscal Union of 1823.
2. From the fiscal Union to the great clearances, that is from 1823 to 1846.
3. The period of clearance up to the great land agitation and the Gladstone Act of 1881.
4. From the Gladstone Act to the crisis of 1912, and the onset of revolution.

The first period was characterised by a specious prosperity due in great measure to the wars with France, and the fact that the economic Union was not consummated. The full blast of British industrial competition was felt after the introduction of steam navigation in 1824, and under the influence of the commercial crisis of 1825. In the ensuing period Irish industry suffered severe contraction, accelerated as United Kingdom tariffs were reduced in pursuit of the principle of international free trade.

The old established Dublin silk trade, for example, which employed 6,000 workers in 1824, had lost all but a few hundred by 1838.[1] Cotton, leather, woollen and hat manufactures underwent reductions of comparable scale. In their efforts to continue in production, employers made repeated assaults on wage levels, which the workers defended in a series of unsuccessful rearguard actions. In 1836 a prominent iron-founder testified that his output had only been maintained thanks to the reduction of the weekly wage of his operatives from 50s. (in 1825) to 12s.[2] The numbers of the working class declined through starvation and emigration, and there were many empty houses in the Liberties of Dublin.

For the time being agriculture escaped the economic decay that affected manufactures. The reason was the insatiable demand for food in Britain's growing industrial centres. Thus Ireland exported 580,000

[1] J. J. Webb, *Industrial Dublin since 1698*, p. 167.
[2] E. J. O'Riordan, *Modern Irish Trade and Industry*, p. 35.

bushels of wheat in 1805, but 2,724,000 in 1822. Allowing home consumption constant, about 350,000 acres of pasture must have been ploughed up, and labour was consequently in demand. Holdings were subdivided, and bog and mountain were reclaimed with spade, crowbar and gunpowder. In 1841 the census showed that Ireland had attained the highest population in her history, 8,175,124. That year there was recorded the lowest cattle population, 1,863,000.[1]

The crisis of the Union, which became apparent in the thirties, was by no means an exclusively Irish phenomenon. Its intimate connection with the rise of English Chartism is often overlooked, and with it the significance of the inclusion of "Repeal of the Union" in the Chartist programme. The matter may be put in the following way. To reimpose feudalism upon Ireland had demanded only military force and average statesmanship. But to maintain a constant increase in agricultural production on a feudal basis was fundamentally impossible. The ruling class of Britain must either force its workpeople on to a potato diet, or introduce free trade in grain and let the Irish landlords bear the consequences.

In Ireland the crisis took its corresponding form. Either the intensifying land-hunger of the peasants must be assuaged at the expense of the landlords' fine estates (in the Tithe War at the expense of the established Church) or there must be an industrial revolution to provide them with a livelihood apart from the land. Neither solution, and indeed the two are complementary and amount to the revolution that was strangled in 1795, was compatible with the survival of the Union. This blocked every avenue of progress, and since in the event it endured, brought about "the common downfall of the contending classes".

It is against this background that the tremendous mass struggles of the thirties and forties must be seen. Daniel O'Connell's role was that of the small Catholic landowner trying to harmonise the unharmonisable, like Griffith three generations later. He used the threat of insurrection to wring Catholic emancipation from the Iron Duke, but allowed him to lop 174,000 names from the Irish electoral register of 200,000. Having as he thought assured landlord hegemony in any

[1] That a contrary process was beginning, particularly in Leinster, is illustrated by the increase in live cattle exports from 27,994 in 1801 to 98,150 in 1835. These figures compare with 700,000 at the end of the century and 900,000 in 1924. The export of provisions, notably from Munster, had also increased by 1835, but more modestly and irregularly. The agricultural division of labour between different regions of Ireland was showing its first signs of development. See references in T. W. Freeman, *Pre-famine Ireland*, under cattle in various provinces, pp. 168 and 207.

restored Irish Parliament, he spent thirteen years seeking repeal of the
Union "by a dexterous succession of political combinations, first with
one English party, then with another".[1]

During this period the social convulsions of the 'Tithe War'
endangered his cautious policy. This struggle was the complement of
Chartism, and was enthusiastically supported by Bronterre O'Brien.
Among the advanced forms of struggle which arose was the institution
of popular arbitration courts to eliminate competition between tenants.
A compromise was reached in 1838, thanks largely to the determination of Under Secretary Drummond, one of the few who filled his
post with credit. His programme of "Justice for Ireland" was tolerated
by the government as a means of "killing Repeal with kindness" while
the Chartist menace was at its height.

Drummond died in 1840, and the Whig Ministry resigned.
O'Connell must now lead the people or lose them. The Repeal
agitation of 1843 became one of the greatest mass movements in the
history of these islands. Attendances at open-air meetings were counted
in hundreds of thousands. Everywhere the scent of victory was in the
air. But O'Connell had no sympathy with the strategic principles of
the United Irishmen. He dropped the agrarian demands of previous
agitations; he scorned proffered aid from the New World; he rejected
the overtures of the English Chartists and persecuted their Irish
representatives.[2] The English Government saw no reason to yield. A
Government Proclamation, without even a whiff of grapeshot, and his
final meeting at Clontarf was tamely abandoned, and himself illegally
imprisoned.

This need not have ended matters. The crisis was still unresolved, the
people undefeated. Under all normal expectations the exposure of
O'Connell's inadequacy would have taught the peasants to choose
leaders who were not entangled with landlordism. Let a few years go
by and another effort would be made, perhaps under the leadership of
the bourgeoisie, whose alternative political centre already existed in
"Young Ireland", so named from a fancied parallel with the Italian
Risorgimento. Among its most talented adherents were Thomas Davis,
John Mitchel and Fintan Lalor. But the Union was saved at the last
moment by a *deus ex machina*, the European potato blight borne far and
wide by the newly invented means of communication.

The special dependence of the Irish peasant on the potato was the

[1] T. A. Jackson, *Ireland Her Own*, p. 212.
[2] E.g. Hoey who was drummed out of his native Drogheda by an O'Connellite mob,
after which he returned to Barnsley.

dietetic consequence of Ireland's national dependence on Britain. It arose because the Irish landlord had been assigned the role of supplying Britain's industrial population. The peasant was harnessed to the chariot in the following manner. The labour necessary for his own subsistence and that which he performed free for the landlord, had come to be incorporated in two distinct crops, potatoes and corn. Let us suppose the corn crop failed. The land would produce no rent. The peasant would, however, remain in possession of his subsistence which was of little use to the landlord. Indeed an eviction merely forfeited the prospect of a future payment of arrears. Suppose on the other hand the potato crop failed. Again the land would produce no rent, but the landlord would be in a position to claim what customarily belonged to him, though what had formerly been a surplus product was now the peasant's necessary means of subsistence. And to separate him finally from this all that was required was eviction.

The great potato failure of 1845–47 provided the British Government with the opportunity to initiate the most grotesque act of expropriation in the history of Europe. What was immediately required was the prohibition of food exports so as to restore to the peasant his means of subsistence and put the rent on the long finger. Following this there should have been agrarian revolution. Instead the British Government repealed the corn laws, achieving at a blow the emasculation of the Chartist movement by cheap grain imports,[1] and the transformation of Ireland from a granary into a ranch.

The potato blight was the heaven-sent opportunity to begin "clearing the estate of Ireland". The process was well under way in Scotland and a succession of theorists, drawing inspiration from Malthus,[2] had advocated its application to Ireland. It has been argued for the British Government that its policy merely reflected the theories of political economy fashionable at the time. All decisions by which a ruling class aims to enrich itself give expression to "laws of political economy". By the same token burglars speak of "jobs", swindlers of "deals" and prostitutes of "love". It is not always wise to judge sin by the sinner's consciousness of it. The British ruling class saw an advantage and pursued it with single-minded ruthlessness. But lest the eternal laws of political economy were not strong enough to stand up by themselves, Ireland was flooded with soldiers to support them.

The soldiers dealt with "riots" and "murders" which unfortunately

---

[1] Th. Rothstein, *Chartism to Labourism*, p. 264, suggests that the immediate effect was to ease the economic burden on the lower middle class and thus isolate the workers who were defeated. But the further cheapening of consumption affected the working class directly.

[2] See *Essay on the Principle of Population*, Everyman edition, Vol. I, pp. 277–8.

were not co-ordinated into a general campaign of resistance. It is an exaggeration to claim, as landlord sycophants have done, that the peasants voluntarily starved rather than defraud the landlord of the rent the land did not produce. The problem was one of leadership. O'Connell spoke, and was disregarded, in Parliament, and "Young Ireland" could only watch impotently from Dublin, outside which the bourgeoisie was in a state of total enervation. According to the estimate published in the 1851 census, 985,366 persons died of starvation and typhus, and about 1,500,000 are said to have emigrated— nearly a third of the population was lost in five years. And apart from the crow-bar brigade with its enforced evictions, the Government made the granting of relief conditional on the relinquishment of all land in excess of a quarter of an acre. The policies and their results speak for themselves. No argument will ever justify this crime.

Some might congratulate themselves that the potato blight averted revolution. But the less robust landlords were saved only for the pot. When the corn laws were repealed in their hour of paralysis, the sustenance of which they were stripping the country shrivelled in their hands. World prices ruled the London Market.[1] In the ensuing era of free trade Britain entered on its greatest industrial expansion. But by 1849 the London financiers who had advanced loans on the security of Irish estates were clamouring for Government protection.[2] The landlords' entails were swept away by the Encumbered Estates Act, and many a big house noted in the annals of local aristocracy was knocked down to a village bailiff. In the next thirty years one fifth of the superficies of Ireland changed hands at an average price of £10 an acre. The purchasers included land agents, the more substantial tenants and capitalist speculators. These were "owners who were prepared to manage their estates upon strictly business principles".[3]

The repeal of the corn laws reduced the value of the crops that paid the rent. To meet his commitments the surviving landlord must either demand a higher rent, which was difficult to produce even from enlarged holdings, or go into stock-raising where prices were rising. The result was an agrarian revolution spread over a number of years. There was a transition to capitalist farming, but it was superimposed upon feudal exploitation and extortion. In the years 1847–52 the number of families who lost their holdings by writ of ejectment was 84,123. The 1851 census records the loss of 355,689 dwellings of the

[1] The price of wheat fell 20 per cent between 1845 and 1850, but thereafter partially recovered, moving erratically before plunging in the eighties.
[2] See Strauss, *Irish Nationalism and British Democracy*, p. 136.
[3] Professor Pomfret, *The Struggle for Land in Ireland*, p. 45.

"fourth class", that is, mud cabins occupied by landless labourers who paid rent for tiny holdings as a deduction from wages during such times as work was available. The number of holdings of less than an acre fell from 135,314 to 37,728. The numbers between one acre and five fell from 310,436 to 88,083. But the number of those above fifteen acres rose from 127,967 to 290,401. The typical holding became that between five and fifteen acres.

No event in Irish history was so devastating as the economic war launched on the Irish people under cover of the potato blight, and none ever impressed itself so deeply on the memory of the people. Without the "famine" in mind it is impossible to understand the tenacity of the Irish separatist movement expressed in Fenianism, and twentieth-century Republicanism. The very magnitude of the material destruction made it visible for half a century and remembered for a half-century more. The facts were written on the face of the country, and travellers recorded them.

Thus, Friedrich Engels who toured Ireland in 1856 wrote:[1]

The whole of the West, but especially the neighbourhood of Galway, is covered with these ruined peasant homes. Whole villages are devastated, and there among them lie the splendid parks of the lesser landlords, who are almost the only people still living there, mostly lawyers . . . the country has been ruined by the English wars of conquest from 1100 to 1850.

A half-century later a French visitor, the liberal Jean Paul Dubois, described the grandchildren of the survivors:

There are still in the west of Ireland half a million inhabitants who are unable to make a living on the remnants of land left to them since the clearances. But from their place of exile they sometimes look down on the valley and see the fields from which their fore-fathers were driven, and the ruined hearth-stone, still black with smoke, of the house where they were born.[2]

And a half-century later again, as recently as 1952, one of the leading ideologists of the revolution, P. S. O'Hegarty, could write:

My mother was born in 1851, and sometimes she would talk of how in her native place of Kilmurry, Co. Cork, an estate belonging to the Beamish family was cleared for sheep in the fifties, and the farmers, well-to-do farmers who had never been behind in their rent, and whose people had had the land for generations, were

---

[1] Adoratsky (ed.), *Correspondence of Marx and Engels*, tr. Dona Torr, p. 93.
[2] J. Paul Dubois, *Contemporary Ireland*, p. 301.

evicted and thrown by the roadside, some of them having to be torn by force from the gateposts.

If in the consciousness of the people the "famine" and the clearances continued to symbolise British Imperialism, so the political controversies of the revolution that never took place provided the starting point for the later generation. O'Connell's capitulation at Clontarf was partly to be explained by his having promised a bloodless revolution. The horrors of 1798 had been the work of counter-revolution. A successful revolution would have made them impossible. But in ruling-class mythology revolution was equated with violence. After his release O'Connell sought an alliance with the Ulster "Federalists", forerunners of "Home Rule", who sought a two-tier system separating Irish from imperial functions. Despite growing impatience on the part of the younger men he held his control of the Repeal Association until his retirement at the end of 1846.

At this point bourgeois initiative became possible. Young Ireland established the Irish Confederation not, it is true, to effect a democratic revolution, but to restore to the cause of repeal the virility it had possessed before Clontarf. The bourgeoisie was not the power it had been seventy years previously. The overwhelming proportion of the national wealth passed through landlord hands, and the balance was not immediately redressed. At the very outset its purposes were challenged by the lawyer son of a farmer of Laois, James Fintan Lalor, who quickly showed himself the possessor of the keenest intellect of his age.

He argued that repeal would be the consequence of agrarian revolution not its indispensable precursor. The immediate task was to preserve the Irish people from extinction. The fundamental principle he asserted was the right of the people to possess the soil. They should "refuse obedience to usurped authority" and declare a state of "moral insurrection" (that is to say defensive non-co-operation) in which they should "take quiet and peaceable possession of all the rights and powers of government, and proceed quietly to exercise them". If there was anything utopian in the conception he dispelled it by adding what in effect amounted to "until attacked". The principle of the clearances was expropriation. The principle Lalor announced was re-appropriation.

His arguments weighed heavily with John Mitchel, the son of a dissenting clergyman of the County Derry who had been a United Irishman. But the appeal to the most numerous and exploited classes did not recommend itself to the city men, least of all to those with landlord connections. Six months were lost and Lalor then resigned from the Confederation. In doing so he stated his views more precisely. His purpose was not merely to repeal the Union but to repeal the conquest. In other words not only the colonial status, but the colonial system must go. In any case the system had broken down and was being replaced by another equally vicious. The landlords? "I never recognised the land-owners as an element, as a part or portion of the people. I recognised them as 'aliens and enemies' when I solicited them to join with us and become a part of us, and of a new Irish nation." To landlords prepared to accept the supremacy of that nation he was prepared to grant new titles from the State.

For a further six months Mitchel fought against the tenacious class prejudices of the landlord element in the Confederation. He had become converted to Lalor's programme of *holding* the harvest and *obstructing* the export of foodstuffs. But he does not appear to have understood how, given the right conditions, this could pass over into armed insurrection. This he regarded as an independent development seemingly without a social base. Resigning from the Confederation early in 1848 he launched the "United Irishman" and in doing so founded what may be termed the "party of physical force".

Mitchel's journalism was unsurpassed. Yet he lacked the intellectual resolving power of Lalor. Lalor could see clearly that the fundamental weakness of O'Connell, whose policies he contemned to the centre of his being, was his acceptance of the necessity of landlordism. Mitchel grasped this, but more diffusely. He directed his attack against O'Connell's tactics, his pacifism and reliance on Parliamentary com-binations. Where O'Connell had cold-shouldered the English Chartists, Mitchel bade boldly for their support. Their movement was delivering its last flash of light before economic changes extinguished it. But for the moment Feargus O'Connor led the Repeal movement at West-minster. The agitation in England, above all the French Revolution of 16th February 1848, combined to revive the sentiments of 1797 when "the French were in the bay", and the British navy was paralysed by the mutiny at the Nore.

The split in the Confederation was hastily healed. There were proposals to embody a "militia" or "National Guard" on the model of the Volunteers of 1782. As the government reinforced its garrisons, drilling and pike-making began. T. F. Meagher was despatched to Paris, and returned with an Orange, White and Green tricolour, proclaiming the unity of Protestant and Catholic communities through the equalising principle of Republicanism.

Mitchel has been blamed for underestimating the exhaustion of the people.[1] But his proposition was that an uprising should be undertaken only after the harvest. It was his incautious expression of his intentions that precipitated matters, and led to his arrest in March 1848, and his transportation in May. A new crime, "treason felony", was specially invented for dealing with him. The remaining leaders went south and organised a short-lived insurrection with the aid of the very classes whose interests they had refused to espouse—the agricultural workers and mill-hands of County Kilkenny, and the coal-miners of Slieve Ardagh, County Tipperary. At Callan a significant incident took place. The insurgents were greeted with bonfires in the streets. Troops of an Irish cavalry regiment, the 8th Hussars, publicly fraternised with them. Next year Lalor, Luby, Savage and Brenan attempted another insurrection in Tipperary and Waterford. This also was unsuccessful. The landlords proceeded with the decimation of the Irish nation.

The third period of the Union discloses a new "law of motion" in Irish affairs. A colonial system of a new type was imposed. Other parts of the world performed what had previously been allotted to Ireland, as British commercial policy developed the international connections which paved the way for modern imperialism. The production of food crops in Ireland fell steadily until the early sixties. Thereafter followed a long stagnation, which gave way to a slow revival. Even at the turn of the century production was but 80 per cent of that in 1851, and the full level was not reached at the height of the tillage campaign of the First World War.

Ireland was saddled with a perverse mode of capital accumulation which was described by Marx in a celebrated section of *Capital*.[2] The paradoxical situation was that rent, interest and profit increased despite a general reduction of economic activity. The producers starved or emigrated. Their means of production became capital in the hands of others. Figures covering twenty-six counties, published in 1928, illustrate the principle.[3] The average annual product of all food crops in the quinquennium 1851–55 was 2,661,000 starch tons. The corresponding figure twenty years later was only 2,043,000 starch tons. There was thus a decline of 618,000 starch tons, about 25 per cent. But the 1851 population of 5,111,557 had been reduced over the same period to 4,053,187, a decline of about a million or 20 per cent. Assume the

[1] See Denis Gwynn, *Young Ireland and 1848*, p. 149.
[2] Marx, *Capital*, Vol. I, Chapter XXV, section 5 (f): "Ireland".
[3] Department of Industry and Commerce, Dublin, *Agricultural Statistics*.

emigrants represented an impoverished section consuming not more than 2,000 calories a day, then it is possible to estimate that they would have consumed about 1,645,000 starch tons had they remained at home.[1] Thus about a million starch tons per annum became available for consumption by cattle. This and other factors contributed to the increase in the number of beef cattle from 2,326,743 in 1851 to 3,198,547 in 1871. Ireland thus ceased to produce the staple diet of the English masses, and instead provided higher class foodstuffs for the expanding middle class and "aristocracy of labour". Through the growing practice of purchasing Irish store cattle for profitable fattening on English farms, the Irish industry was converted into a specialised department of British agriculture. In the process England's dependence on Ireland diminished, while that of Ireland on England was accentuated.

The division of labour between Irish regions became more marked. Thus the north-west became the land of stockbreeding. In 1851 County Leitrim, for example, held 18,175 cattle over a year old and 16,732 not yet a year old. In 1871 it held 27,990 under a year old, but only 18,799 over. What had happened to last year's calves? They had been sold off the farm. They were feeding in the grazing lands of Leinster or the dairy lands of Munster.[2] The province of Ulster on the other hand, thanks to its more favourable land tenures and the development of industry, escaped the regional straitjacket, although there developed a comparable differentiation between east and west within the province.

The old organisation of fairs and markets was now supplemented through a new class of cattle dealers whose function it became, for a consideration, to distribute round the differentiated regions the offspring of all-purpose cows, and to get the surplus out of the country. With the general increase in movement went the growth of a money economy. Foodstuffs were increasingly sold off and bought on to farms. Animal feed was purchased by larger farmers to supplement a bad harvest. Merchants pushed their way from the rail-heads with an ever-increasing assortment of English manufactures. The language of this commerce penetrated all but the remotest parts of the west. Irish-speaking districts became separated by ever-widening swathes of anglicisation. In vain might a later generation of bourgeois bemoan the extinction of the old tongue. It was their class, in expressing the necessities of its economic position, that was the means of it.

The cottier class and the dispersed landless labourers were cleared

---

[1] Potatoes containing about 25 per cent starch produce about 1 calorie per gramme.
[2] Slaughtering for veal declined during this period.

from the land. There accumulated pools of reserve agricultural labour in the country towns, but not uniformly throughout the four provinces. At the same time the growth of large holdings was accompanied by a corresponding development of wage labour, the extent of which can be judged roughly by the great increase in the numbers of the very smallest, kitchen-garden, holdings. In sum the Irish economy, despite its overall contraction, assumed an increasingly capitalist character, and the question was bound to arise of whether this was compatible with the continuance of feudal tenures.

This issue was raised as early as 1852. The Irish land system was a perfect recipe for rural decay. The three main grievances were the right of the landlord to vary the rent at will, to evict at discretion, and in doing so to appropriate the capital sunk by the tenant in his holding. The former Young Irelander, Gavan Duffy, began an agitation for fair rent, fixity of tenure and freedom of sale[1] (of a tenant's interest in his holding). The principle of "tenant right", involving the doctrine of joint ownership of the soil, was known as the "Ulster custom". It was said to be derived from the survival in Ulster, the last province to come under English domination, of the Gaelic system of communal land ownership. As a result of unusual historical circumstances it had been transmuted not as elsewhere into the feudal principle of feofdom but into the capitalist principle of saleable goodwill. The agitation engaged the energies of the famous Callan curates, who mobilised the veterans of the Tithe War and their children. But the campaign remained in County Kilkenny and failed to move the nation. It encountered hostility from the higher clergy, who now for the first time separated themselves from the people and identified themselves with the merchants, dealers and new Catholic landowners of bourgeois origin. For a quarter of a century cattle prices remained stable. Evictions bore heavily only on the smallest tenant. And he replied by taking himself abroad. Irish resistance expressed itself in the political movement of Fenianism.

Great exile communities were established in the cities of the United States. To these the land question no longer seemed the point of attack. With bitter clarity the emigrants discerned the fount of their misfortunes in t   British connection, the essential precondition for the whole process of capital accumulation amid social decay. Here Irish nationalism was separated from its social base, becoming a movement of pure separatism, whose tactics worked by military analogy, and whose theory was Irish history. To an extent its interests coincided

[1] The "Three Fs".

with those of ascendant American capitalism in competition with the
"workshop of the world". But at the same time, after such experiences
as the Irish people had suffered, the ideology of separatism inevitably
became a force in its own right, maintained over the generations.

Articulate leaders were to hand in the emigrant Young Irelanders.
Some of these, as Emmet had done in 1803, sought to re-enact with
better success the last act in the tragedy of 1845–49. They found a
leader in James Stephens, the young Kilkenny man who had been aide
to Smith O'Brien at Ballingarry. He had escaped to Paris where, before
proceeding to the United States, he had broadened his outlook by
contact with the French revolutionaries. It is said he was influenced by
Blanqui, from whom he may have borrowed the plan of a revolutionary secret society. But he must be acquitted of "the fantasy that it is
possible to turn over a whole society by the action of a small conspiracy". His conspiracy was to cover all Ireland. It was to be durable
and to strike when the renewal of the European revolution (or alternatively the outbreak of war between England and America) brought the
prospect of success.[1] Returning to Ireland he recruited the members of
O'Donovan Rossa's "Phoenix Society", the majority of the secret
agrarian societies who meted out rough justice to landlords who went
too far, and large numbers of shop assistants and skilled workers in the
towns. There was also a formidable membership in the British Army.

A detailed scientific study of Fenianism is badly needed. That its
ranks were filled with members of the Irish proletariat is certain. That
this proletariat had various points of origin and had not yet amalgamated as a class also seems clear. Hence Fenianism represented
plebeian interests in a generalised, almost rarefied manner. On all
local and sectional interests it superposed the grand conception of a
people in permanent revolt, a land occupied but unconquered. The
object of the Fenian organisation, the "Irish Revolutionary Brotherhood", was the establishment of an "Irish Democratic Republic" and
the means was force of arms. The oath of loyalty to the organisation
was later given to "The Irish Republic, now virtually established" and
the fiction was created that the Supreme Council of the Brotherhood
was "in fact and law" the government of that Republic. At some
point in its evolution the name "Revolutionary Brotherhood" became
"Republican Brotherhood", possibly on the establishment of the
fiction of an existing "Government". The value of the fiction was that
it personified Fenianism's total rejection of the gigantic process of

[1] So T. A. Jackson (*Ireland Her Own*, p. 263) explains Stephens' delaying tactics which
lost him his leadership of the movement.

robbery taking place under English law and with the protection of English arms. And it made the Fenians soldiers, not *franc-tireurs*.

In Dublin, Cork and among exiles in London, Fenian circles were in contact with the First International. Marx discerned in Fenianism "a socialist tendency, in the negative sense, directed against the appropriation of the soil, and by the fact that it is a movement of the lower orders". British policy in Ireland was based on the principle of profit. The country was regarded as an estate to be managed for the enrichment of its owners. Fenianism rejected this principle utterly. Ireland was being consumed by a plundering army. Its people must return force with force. Ireland would then exist for the use of its people. Two opposing philosophies were evident and Marx was justified in ascribing to the second a socialist tendency. This was just after he had made his classical analysis in *Capital*.

The misfortune of the Fenians was that though they prepared for revolution with courage and skill, objective conditions were not mature. Britain remained prosperous. Chartism had collapsed into a congeries of radical and republican clubs. The policeman's empire in France offered no premonition of the catastrophe that was to engulf it in 1871. The American Fenians (now calling themselves *Clann na Gael*) grew impatient. An insurrection was attempted when no revolutionary situation existed. This is the reason for the failure of 1867. It has been argued that different tactics or better luck might have brought a more favourable result. When objective conditions are ripe it is as if a force akin to gravity is applied to social developments, so that things must move the one way. This was not so in 1867.

After a temporary disorganisation the I.R.B. was reconstituted in 1873 and new rules were adopted. The "Republic now virtually established" seems to have gone temporarily into abeyance. And Rule Three stated that "the I.R.B shall await the decision of the Irish nation as expressed by a majority of the Irish people as to the fit hour of inaugurating a war against England and shall pending such an emergency lend its support to every movement calculated to advance the cause of Irish independence consistently with its own integrity".

The precise significance of this rule may be open to dispute. Possibly it was intended to give protection against transatlantic impatience which had forced the pace in 1867 and thus conceivably lost an opportunity in 1871. At the same time it subjected the Brotherhood to the democratic control of the Irish people and foreshadowed the "new departure", a transition to public agitation on a scale that rivalled O'Connell's.

Out of the movement for the amnesty of Fenian prisoners taken during the rising of 1867 grew the Home Rule Association, founded in 1870 by Isaac Butt, the one time Conservative barrister who had defended many of them. It did not attempt to revive the demand for repeal, but adopted Sharman Crawford's aim of "Federalism" with which O'Connell had dallied in 1843. This represented the barest minimum any self-respecting Nationalist could ask for. Yet it was the agitation for this modest relief that was to shake the British constitution and make separation ultimately inevitable.

The great land agitation which brought about the "fall of feudalism in Ireland" began in 1879 when following two poor harvests and in face of a third the former Fenian prisoner Michael Davitt founded the Land League in County Mayo. The fall in agricultural prices now included those of cattle. Thus if the price index for the year 1840 is taken as 100, that of two-year-old store cattle reached its maximum of 280 in the year 1874. It then fell steadily to reach a minimum of 174 in 1887, thereafter slowly recovering.[1] Landlords adopted their time-honoured remedy, rent increases and writs of ejectment. But now they were faced with mass refusals to pay the rent the land had not produced, and an agitation for the transfer of the ownership of the soil to the tillers. The leadership was now taken by Charles Stewart Parnell whose candidates swept the country at the 1880 election. The Fenians supported the rising mass movement, and within a few years Parnell was the "uncrowned king of Ireland". The Gladstone Act of 1881 conceded the three principles of Tenant Right.[2] The landlords' monopoly was broken and the final period of the Union saw their gradual retreat and the steady transfer of land ownership to the people.[3]

This fourth period was dominated politically by the issue of "Home Rule", that is to say federation. It is essential to grasp its intimate connection with the process of land reform. Land reform progressively eliminated the landlord garrison class. The Union, if it was to survive, must now rest on consent. This Gladstone saw clearly and proposed to bring in Home Rule simultaneously with land purchase. The Tories prevented him, and by refusing a political arrangement that in some measure corresponded to the new economic conditions contributed their mite to the cause of revolution.

The first Home Rule Bill, Gladstone's Government of Ireland Bill of 1886, provided for the establishment of a bicameral legislature in

[1] See Barrington, *Statistical and Social Enquiry Society of Ireland*, 1927, p. 252.
[2] See Leet and McCutcheon, *Law of Property in Land in Ireland*, p. 28 et seq.
[3] Pomfret, *Struggle for the Land in Ireland*, pp. 306-7, states that by 1909 more than half the soil of Ireland had passed to former tenants at about £10 an acre.

Dublin. This was to pass laws in relation to exclusively Irish affairs. Certain powers were reserved to the imperial Parliament, although Irish representation in it was to cease. These included the Crown, peace and war, army, navy, treaties, tithes, treason, naturalisation, trade, navigation, lighthouses, coinage, copyrights, patents, and the Post Office without Ireland. The Irish legislature was excluded from favouring religion or impairing "the rights or property of corporations" without an address from both Houses and consent of the Crown. Customs and Excise were to be levied by the imperial Parliament, but all other taxes within Ireland were to be under Irish control. Subject to instructions from Westminster the viceroy was to have a power of veto on all Irish legislation, and Ireland was to pay annually an imperial contribution of £3,242,000.

Gladstone's proposals met with great opposition in the original home of federalism, north-east Ulster. It was deliberately stirred up by Randolph Churchill and it was he who consciously appealed to religious sectarianism in the mixed populations of the area. It is important to distinguish the motives of the British statesman from those of his Irish supporters. The crowds who screamed "Home Rule is Rome Rule" at Unionist meetings were far from an understanding of what was really at stake. Catholic emancipation had been confined to the political field. The economic inferiority remained. Throughout Ireland the largest landowners, the wealthiest merchants, the most distinguished professional men, were Protestant. In the mixed communities of the north the Protestant planters and settlers held the fertile valleys while the Catholic aborigines scratched out a living on the hills. In working-class Belfast skilled hands were mostly Protestant, unskilled Catholic. Undoubtedly there was a system of freemasonry which served the purpose of maintaining the inequality of the two sections, and widespread discriminatory practices. To important sections of the Protestant population, the establishment of a Dublin Parliament, notwithstanding the strict veto on discriminatory legislation (i.e. legislation calculated to redress the balance), seemed to threaten the security of every twopence-halfpenny that was looking down on twopence. Hence the revival of the moribund Orange Order on the basis of class collaboration and sectarian hatred.

But the real objections were a different matter, and revealed the imperialist aspect of Gladstone's Bill. The bourgeoisie of the north had no reason to sympathise with the landlords and cared little if they lost all their land. But the possibility of having to find some £250,000,000 out of Irish taxation was a different matter. The sole industry to survive the Union, the linen industry, was established exclusively in the north. Ship-building was centred in Belfast where it encouraged a host of ancillary activities. The most urgent agrarian need was in the south-west. The maximum taxable capacity was in the north-east. To the north-eastern capitalists the imperial financing of land purchase was a vital interest. So the Union must be retained. Gladstone's parsimony split the Irish bourgeoisie. Tariffs of course did not enter into it at this stage, but there was nevertheless some fear that if fiscal independence were ever to be restored, the taxation of imported raw material (e.g. flax) might become a method of financing land purchase.

Finally from Randolph Churchill's standpoint, apart from the sympathy of an aristocrat for landlords, the most important considera-tion would probably be imperial. It would go against the grain to start dismantling the Empire near its heart just when its fingers were making grabs at Africa. Labouchère raised with Parnell a proposal to "annex the area round Belfast to England". It was one of the first feelers towards partition. Naturally Parnell was not interested. The Bill was lost in the Commons and Gladstone resigned.

The result was an agitation in which Parnell acquired an ascendancy comparable with O'Connell's. It was remarked that Parnell unlike O'Connell did not hesitate to co-operate with radical elements both in the English population and among Irish emigrants. The fear that an alliance between Irish nationalism and British Labour might con-tribute to social revolution in England no doubt played its part in determining Gladstone's decision to free himself from dependence on Parnell. The famous divorce case provided the opportunity. After the fall of Parnell the Irish party was split for ten years. Gladstone's second Government of Ireland Bill was introduced in 1893. It added to the reserved powers the Lord Lieutenant, Volunteers, Extradition, the Post Office within Ireland and Land Legislation for a period of three years. But trade within Ireland was to be controlled from Dublin, and eighty Irish members were to sit at Westminster, but with votes on Irish and imperial matters only.[1] This Bill passed the Commons but was rejected by the Lords.

The new Conservative administration then set about "killing Home Rule with kindness". The "kindness" consisted of social and economic reforms which merely added to the absurdity of refusing Home Rule. The process of land purchase was speeded up. Under the Wyndham Act of 1903 the Land Commission was empowered to acquire whole estates for distribution. In 1898 the Conservatives introduced the Irish

[1] See John Redmond, *The Home Rule Bill*, Appendix, p. 171.

Local Government Act which replaced the system of Boards by elected County, Urban and Rural Councils, thus ending the landlords' political monopoly in the countryside. The failure of the Conservatives to broaden their base arose from the fact that the agrarian reform set in action forces which generated fresh demands.

It has been noted that even by 1911 only half the land of Ireland was subject to agrarian reform. The agitation did not therefore die away. The sight of their neighbours as peasant proprietors whetted the appetities of the remaining tenants. But thanks to the saleability of their goodwill these now had every motive for improving their holdings. The diligence with which they set about it was reflected in the increased agricultural production that followed the turn of the century. Thus the total yield of all crops averaged over the quinquennium 1881–85 was 1,992,500 starch tons; over the quinquennium 1909–13 the corresponding figure was 2,339,400, an improvement of about 17 per cent. Since the land reform retarded but did not halt consolidation, the improvement in rural capital formation must have been represented by a yet higher figure. The result was the revival of rural industry, among other things through the establishment of co-operative societies to market and process farm produce.

The population of the towns began to rise again. Belfast had of course never ceased to expand. Despite its acceptance of displaced population from the countryside Dublin had declined until 1871, thereafter resuming its growth. After 1891 the process of recovery spread to Cork, Limerick, Waterford, Sligo, Killarney, Tullamore, Mallow, Castlebar and Monaghan. Out of forty-four towns in the south and west of Ireland only seven continued to lose population after 1901. Emigration had fallen markedly. Between 1881 and 1891 those leaving the country numbered 768,105. In the following ten years the emigrants were 430,993. Since this emigration obviously affected rural population the weight of the town in Irish national life was enormously increased relatively. In 1841 less than 20 per cent of the population lived in towns of over 1,500 inhabitants. By 1891 the proportion had reached 25 per cent, and now steadily crept forward year by year. The social consequence was the recovery of the bourgeoisie after the long years of stagnation.

According to Strauss,[1] even now "the Irish bourgeoisie existed only as a collection of minor vested interests within the framework of British capitalism". This judgment would seem too sweeping, though not without value. It must be borne in mind when considering it that

[1] Op. cit., p. 200.

British capitalism at the turn of the century was already imperialistic, but not highly monopolised. There was still much autonomy in its own provincial centres. In general its "framework" was loose enough. But Ireland was exploited not by individual capitalists, but by British capitalism as a whole. The framework in Ireland was not just an extension of the framework in England, but a very special thing, rather a system of prison bars than a framework in the economic sense, built up over the years with all the resources of the imperial State. While Irish interests were as varied as the country's chequered economy, they all conflicted with the British State.

This conflict increased with the growing prosperity. The operation of the Land Acts set free capital which was lodged in the Joint Stock banks. Some of this sought investment in Ireland. Its employment was hampered by the high level of taxation, the costliness of transport, the inefficiency of the Post Office, and the incredible tangle of government departments through which it was necessary to pilot the smallest proposal.[1] There was also the "educational chaos" and lack of technical instruction for workers. The freshly formed capital, whether of peasant or landlord origin, or arising from the improved profits of established capitalists, apart from the few favourably placed to exploit the existing regime, was confronted with an administration which blocked local enterprise at every turn.

The Parliamentary party which had played so substantial a part in securing the land reform reflected the class alignment that preceded it, when the bourgeoisie was essentially mercantile and dependent on the landlords. There was now some differentiation within it. The new conditions stimulated the establishment of a minority bourgeois party, *Cumann na nGaedheal*, founded in 1898 by William Rooney and Arthur Griffith. A few years later it adopted the name of *Sinn Fein*.

Unlike the Parliamentary party, which did not at this time insist on fiscal independence, *Sinn Fein* proposed the expanding of Irish industry behind protective tariffs against England. While the Parliamentarians hesitated before the full implications of federalism, *Sinn Fein* revived the demand for the repeal of the Union. Griffith proposed the re-establishment of the "King, Lords and Commons of Ireland" with the powers conceded by the Act of Renunciation. The origin of the revolutionary *Sinn Fein* of later years will be dealt with later. The early *Sinn Fein*, the dissident bourgeois party, was at once a goad to prick the Redmonites to action, and a wand which could be waved harmlessly by apostates from Fenianism and Socialism. But Griffith

[1] See Lord Dunraven, *The Outlook in Ireland* (1907), p. 83 et seq.

conceived the ingenious notion of capturing a majority of the new local authorities, using their limited powers to the full in support of industrial expansion, and from them welding together a National Council which would wring repeal from the Federalists at Westminster.

The Fenians had been too deeply involved with Parnell not to suffer from his downfall. They scattered in all directions, into the language movement, into the literary revival which corresponded to the strengthening of Irish economic life and its increasing urbanisation, even into the Labour movement. But above all they found an outlet in *Sinn Fein*, whose bourgeois programme was thus combined with a petit-bourgeois membership. Among the most gifted of the younger I.R.B. men who worked within *Sinn Fein* were Bulmer Hobson and Sean MacDiarmada. They were supported by the veteran Tom Clarke.

Finally reference must be made to the working class. The widespread establishment of wage labour in agriculture has been referred to. The slow revival of industry and the stemming even so incompletely of the tide of immigration increased the demand for labour in the towns. Organisation of the unskilled workers began in 1907. Titanic battles were waged. Organisation spread into the countryside. The proletariat might not yet be the most numerous exploited class in Ireland—though this time was clearly approaching—but it represented the strongest current of social discontent.

The period between 1881 and 1911 was therefore one of deep social change and deceptive calm. Agrarian reform had come, but the massive administrative apparatus of the Union stood in the way of industrial development, without which the Land Acts achieved but half the national purpose. Were the Irish people to be allowed to make the changes the situation demanded? Here was the material for the sharpest challenge of the Union in the Home Rule crisis.

It is frequently argued that the revolutionary explosions of 1916 and 1919 came about because the Tories organised armed counter-revolution to deprive the Irish people of gains they thought they had won. According to this view, if England had conceded Home Rule for all Ireland in 1912 there would have been no Rising and no *Dail Eireann*. But would there have been no revolution? Would Home Rule have sufficed when war necessitated a reversal alike of the economic trends that had emasculated Ireland since 1846 and the new conciliatory policy of British imperialism? Or would a federal Irish Parliament have found itself inevitably forced along the path of 1782 to complete separation? Was not the Ulster rebellion merely the pre-empting of its next position of retreat by an imperialism determined to yield as little and as slowly as possible, rather than the demiurge of the independence struggle?

The Irish revolution began with the Ulster crisis. This was the form taken by the first transition from politics to open violence. But then came the world crisis engulfing and transforming everything. The crisis of imperialism on a world scale made the Irish revolution an intimate part of the world revolution. The world-crisis of imperialism gathered so to speak into one sheaf all the discontents of Irish society. It renewed the unity of the most numerous and exploited classes in Ireland. It recreated a revolutionary movement in Britain. It set off a chain of revolutions throughout the world and one of them led to the first workers' State, to which the eyes of all the oppressed turned as they had turned to France in 1789. In principle at least the conditions for an Irish victory were recreated.

The Irish revolution was a national revolution. It was directed by a small people isolated by geographical position, against what was then the most powerful Empire in the world. Its objects were to secure for the Irish people control of their own destinies so that they could solve their social and economic problems themselves. Its basis was the firm ground. But its story is shot through with heroism and romance.

No one man so perfectly combines in his character the realism and the romance of the Irish struggle as Liam Mellows. He began his political life at the beginning of the revolutionary period and perished in the flames of counter-revolution at the end of 1922. A revolution cannot be understood without the examination of its base. But neither can it be understood without sharing the hopes, disappointments, fears and aspirations of its participants. This book tells the story of the revolution through the life of the man who should be its symbol. It is therefore called *Liam Mellows and the Irish Revolution*.

CHAPTER ONE

FAMILY HISTORY AND CHILDHOOD

LIAM MELLOWS was born at Hartshead military barracks, Ashton-under-Lyne, Lancashire, on 25th May 1892. His father was of Kilkenny stock, his mother from Wexford. That he was born in England, where his father was temporarily stationed, was an accident which exerted no ascertainable influence on his life or development. But his parenthood expressed two opposing traditions whose interplay must urge forward any intelligent child towards the moment he must consciously choose.

The Mellows family orginated in the county of Nottingham. The name is presumably a variant of Mellor. The first to settle in Ireland was Joseph, a bleacher, born in Bulwell in 1789. He enlisted in the 76th Regiment of Foot at Nottingham during the difficult war-time trade conditions of 1811. After service in Spain, France and Canada his regiment was embarked for Ireland in 1827, being divided between Kilkenny and Clonmel. After a complicated succession of promotions and demotions he attained the rank of sergeant, the pinnacle of success for soldiers of plebeian origin. He was part of a detachment stationed at Callan, and probably for health reasons remained there on staff duties, after the regiment had left for Dublin. In Callan he married Catherine Kelly, who bore him two children, John and Henry, in 1831 and 1834 respectively. These births are not recorded in the Catholic parish records, and if the custom of the day was followed, the boys would be educated as Protestants. Joseph was discharged in January 1835, before completing his full service, on the grounds of chronic rheumatism. He seems to have acquired a small bakery in South Bridge Street, and being brought into closer contact with the local people was received into the Catholic Church in the August of the same year. The ceremony took place in the presence of "Rev. Mr. Harney" (the Protestant incumbent) and was recorded in the Catholic register with bold flourishes as if an extremely important convert had been made.

A further child, Garrett, was born in 1839, but Catherine does not seem to have long survived. Joseph married again in 1844. His second wife was Ellen Bryan, member of a numerous local family, who bore

two girls, Frances in 1846 and Jane in 1848. The family continued to
live in Bridge Street, but it is difficult to identify the site owing to the
uncertainty of nineteenth-century numeration. The Mellows family
held the tenancy of numbers 27 and 28, which they later disposed of to
Purcell. This points to the site of Dunne's bakery.[1] At one time there
were twenty-two bakeries in the small town of Callan. These were
owned by the small farmers and army pensioners and collectively
supplied the barracks, and subsequently the Union. As late as 1965,
Joseph Mellows was still spoken of in Callan. He was a "hard-headed
but easy-going Englishman", a Catholic of convenience who shocked
his devout neighbours by "eating duck-eggs during a black fast".

Callan, nine miles south-west of Kilkenny City, is an important
settlement with a long municipal history. Intersected by the once hard-
worked Kings River with its string of defunct water-mills, it lies in the
fertile valley between the coal-bearing Slieve Ardagh and the high-
lands of Slieve na Mon. The best land was early appropriated by a
Protestant aristocracy who, in the prosperous periods when Britain
was at war, had built themselves mansions too fine for their descendants to keep up, and planted magnificent beech avenues, some remnants of which have survived the modern policy of getting tourists as
quickly as possible between the points where they spend money. In
the midst of a romantic landscape, of the type nostalgically recalled by
the ageing Yeats, the peasantry lived in a state of general starvation,
interrupted only by the annual potato harvest.

Throughout the countryside their mud cabins were dispersed. In
Callan they were concentrated. Inglis,[2] who visited the place in 1834,
had "not seen in Ireland any town as wretched . . . round a little
common that lies close to it . . . I saw the people crawling out of their
hovels . . . their cabins were mere holes with nothing within . . .
excepting a little straw and one or two broken stools." A toll for the
benefit of Lord Clifden was levied on all goods entering the town.

The surrounding district was honeycombed with secret agrarian
societies which it was the function of the Irish Constabulary ("Royal"
after 1867) to suppress, the army of occupation standing in reserve
against more general disturbances. South-west Leinster was the centre
of the Tithe War of 1831–34, several important engagements taking
place in the vicinity of Callan. The overwhelmingly Catholic tenantry
refused to pay tithes for the upkeep of the established church. The

[1] Local tradition indicates other sites, and possibly Mellows conducted his business at
different places at different times. So far documentary evidence has been found only for
the Bridge Street site.
[2] Henry D. Inglis, *A Journey throughout Ireland*, London, 1834.

people were overjoyed at the victories of Thomastown and Mullin-
ahone. The Tithes Commutation Act ended the grievance in 1837.
The landlords suffered a severe fright. Improvements could not be
delayed. In the late thirties Callan was extensively rebuilt so that when
the Halls[1] visited it in 1841, they admitted that it was "no longer a
disgrace to the noble family who are its owners".

The Tithe War was followed by the Repeal agitation, during which
Ireland was brought its closest to revolution since 1798. But the essential precondition, an alliance with the English Chartists, was refused by
O'Connell. His fear of the English democracy was excused on
"national" grounds. His equal fear of Irish democracy was shown by
his capitulation over the Clontarf meeting. The demoralisation caused
by this gifted agitator but vacillating leader left the Irish people
powerless before the economic hurricane of the "Famine". In the
disaster of 1846–48 old Ireland disappeared. The rising of 1848 claimed
the support of an exhausted nation capable for the most part only of
passive sympathy. The insurgents were fêted in Callan, and in the final
struggle at Ballingarry a few miles to the north-west, the Slieve Ardagh
miners stood firmest of all. But starvation spoke with the strongest
voice. Ireland lost over two million people by disease and emigration.
In the early fifties the "Callan Curates" tried to rally the people for
agrarian reforms which would have halted the process of depopulation.
From their initiative sprang Duffy's famous Tenant League. But political
conditions were unfavourable. The depopulation proceeded and south-
west Kilkenny lost its position as the spearhead of the radical tenantry.

Joseph Mellows lay snug in his bakery. But his two sons were
forced to emigrate. They had adopted the trade of cobblers. The
reduction in the population of small towns, consequent on the famine,
narrowed the opportunities of young tradesmen. John went to Liverpool where he enlisted in the 97th Regiment in the year 1850. Henry
followed him, not, however, into the army but to establish a shoe-
making business in Leek, in the county of Stafford. Joseph died in 1865.
His first and second families diverged. But Henry and John kept touch.
Henry married Catherine Morgan who had emigrated from Omeath
in the County Louth first to Macclesfield, then to Leek where she was
now a silk piecer. It is noteworthy that her numerous descendants for
several generations regarded themselves as Irish, but sang not the songs
of Ulster, but those of Kilkenny. For John, Liam's grandfather, and his
children Leek became the secondary home town and *pied à terre* in
Europe.

[1] Samuel and Anna M. Hall, *Ireland: its scenery, character, etc.*, Vol. 2, p. 61.

John Mellows soon transferred to the Lancashire Fusiliers. He served first in Canada, then in the Crimean War, reaching the class barrier at the rank of sergeant within five years. He fought at Balaclava, Alma, Inkerman and Sebastopol, where the aristocratic army, led by officers who had purchased their commissions, and supplied by capitalist jobbers, proved its inadequacy in every real test. A quarter of Britain's best soldiers, many of them Irish, were lost within a year. The commissioned ranks were sadly thinned. Even so, they were not replenished by those who were not "gentlemen".[1] Three generations of Mellowses served in the British Army. None passed the rank of sergeant. At Leek, as the memory of Ireland faded, the existence of anti-Catholic prejudice transformed nationalism into a species of defensive piety. In the army the class barrier prevented the "mere Irish" from joining the "establishment", but produced on the one hand Fenians, and on the other green chauvinists proud of the Irish contribution to Britain's greatness.

Sergeant John Mellows, returning to Aldershot after the war, married seventeen-year-old Catherine Larkin, probably the daughter of an Irish soldier killed in the recent campaign, and conceivably one of the numerous Larkins of Callan. The marriage took place in the register office on 20 July 1857. Almost immediately afterwards the regiment was ordered to India to suppress the Mutiny which was at the same time the first national rising of the Indian people. Catherine accompanied her husband. It is worth noting that at this time married quarters had not been established even in Britain. Sometimes couples slept in a dormitory with the single men, a curtain being hung around their bed. At other times groups of families were accommodated in one mixed dormitory. All fixed arrangements were likely to go by the board in expeditionary forces. Women would at times be sent to the rear. Prolonged separations would take place. It is not surprising therefore if the exact date and place of birth of John's son, William Joseph Mellows, father of Liam, remain uncertain. From his discharge certificate it would be concluded that he was born before 13th August 1858. But the birthplace given is Gondah, District of Oude, which the 20th Regiment did not enter until January 1859. No official record appears to have survived. It is possible that William Mellows did not know for certain the date or place of his birth.

[1] The obstinate resistance of the officer caste was illustrated in the notorious case of Lieutenant Perry, a young man of humble origin who was awarded a free commission in recognition of his father's outstanding services. He was hounded from the service by the pedigree pups, but on his experiences becoming generally known was compensated as a result of a nation-wide public subscription.

The father received the Lucknow medal and clasp before his regiment returned to Britain. Here the victors over colonial rebels were given the task of "quelling the bread riots" at Plymouth. Three more children were born in the next five years, according to family tradition, two boys, John and Frederick, and a girl, Mary. It is surprising that they seem to have escaped registration either in England or in Ireland whither the regiment was despatched next year. Sergeant Mellows was stationed at the Curragh where he completed twenty-one years of regular service in 1871. He secured the post of sergeant instructor to the Lancashire Militia, and on the day of his appointment entered his eldest son, probably as a boy musician, in the regiment he was leaving. The family moved to Lancaster where they lived in barracks until the father's sudden death from lung cancer in 1873 at the early age of 42. John was buried with full military honours. His wife, who was only thirty-three years old, must have decided to remarry as soon as possible. The boys were entered with the Royal Hibernian Military School, Phoenix Park, Dublin, while the girl seems to have gone to live at Leek. There is a tradition that Liam Mellows attended the Royal Hibernian Military School. There is no trace of his name in such records as have survived. But a Frederick Mellows was withdrawn in 1886. Another scrap of tradition is worth noting. It has been said that when W. J. Mellows married, his wife's family broke off relations with her because he was a Protestant, and that they lived at Aldershot. It seems just possible that the tradition refers to John, who may have remained Protestant until after his marriage. But it is certain that his brother Henry married a Catholic, and that W. J. Mellows was a Catholic all his life.

That John was a model soldier there is no doubt. The tradition seems to have gripped his son William even more effectively. Here was a man without a country. His country became the army. His occasional leaves he spent with his sister in Leek, where Henry's family and the Morgans kept Irish sentiment alive. William Joseph was sent to Newry in 1872, then to Canada for four years. He was promoted corporal before leaving Cyprus for Malta in 1880, and sergeant in 1882 after returning to Ireland and while stationed at Cork. His battalion was then transferred to Fermoy, where he was promoted colour sergeant and used to play in the band, gorgeously attired. There he met a young dressmaker from Wexford, Sarah Jordan, who worked in Queen's Square. The two decided to marry, but before they could do so, Sergeant Mellows was transferred to Chatham, whence he returned to Fermoy for the ceremony on 8th December 1885. The wedding took

place in the Catholic church and a dispensation from the Bishop of
Cork made it possible during the closed period.

As has been seen, the Mellows tradition was that of British and
Irish workers and farmers who were forced into military service to
make a living. The Jordan tradition was completely different, that of
privilege established by successful resistance. Sarah Jordan was born at
Monalug, Co. Wexford, in 1865, the youngest of a family of eighteen.
Her father, Patrick Jordan, was born in County Wexford in 1817,
probably of the Jordans of Enniscorthy. No revolutionary halo clings
to his name. He was a land steward by profession. But through his
marriage with Jane Carty, of Coolgreany, and long residence amid
the scenes of Wexford's most glorious episodes, he must have absorbed
the strong popular sentiment and passed it on to his children. "How
could I be anything but a Republican, being a County Wexford
woman," Sarah Jordan used to say. But the slow encroachment of the
Republican upon the Imperial tradition required social development to
set in motion. At the time of her marriage Sarah Jordan accepted her
husband's position unconditionally and thought of no more than her
good match.

That the couple visited Leek at Christmas 1885 is shown by an
insurance policy taken out with the Leek Burial Society on the 26th
December 1885. A photograph believed to be of William Joseph (but
which could conceivably be that of a brother) was taken by Wakeman's
of Plymouth and must relate to the same period. The next certain date
is that of the settlement of the family in Manchester in May 1886,
where the first child, Jane Henrietta, was born at Salford Barracks on
the 4th November.

William Joseph was promoted staff quartermaster sergeant on the
7th February 1889, being simultaneously transferred to Military Staff
Clerks and sent to Glasgow. Here the young couple established their
first civilian home and bought a piano in Edinburgh. In October of
the same year they moved to Ashton-under-Lyne where they received
the lease of a house at 26 Curzon Road, halfway between the barracks
and the town. Here was born John Henry Mellows, who did not
survive. The family moved into married quarters at Hartshead
Barracks, and it was here that the third (possibly the fourth) child was
born on the 23rd May 1892. He was named William[1] Joseph after the
father. As a matter of interest it is to be noted how scrupulously the
Mellows family maintained the tradition of naming the first son after

[1] In Irish *Liam*.

the grandfather, and the second after the father. While at Hartshead William senior was transferred to the Army Pay Corps in April 1893. Another son, Frederick Jordan, was born there in June 1894. The family saw the last of England in the following February when SQMS Mellows was transferred to Dublin and took up residence at 10 Annadale Avenue, Fairview. Here the youngest child, Herbert[1] Charles, was born in March 1896.

It is doubtful whether Liam ever resided at Fairview. His health was giving cause for anxiety, and it was decided to send him to Wexford where Patrick Jordan had recently retired from his position as land steward to the Beaumont family at Hyde Park, near Castletown. The Pennine slopes were not as disfigured and derelict as they are now. The boy may have clambered over the clay banks of the ravine below Hartshead Barracks, from which the whole of Cheshire is to be seen. But to come suddenly to the Garden of Ireland from all that bleakness, into the freedom of the countryside, from the military rigour to a place where you did as and when you pleased, from the dreary routine and shouting, must have made an impression even at the age of three.

His grandparents had been compelled to vacate the lodge at Hyde Park and now lived with Julia Jordan at Macoyle, between Castletown and Inch. She seems to have taken an enormous interest in the fair-haired youngster in her charge. Macoyle, sometimes colloquially called "Jordan's Hollow", is situated in the extreme north-east corner of County Wexford. Two miles away is a sea coast of sand-dunes and low cliffs. To the landward is a complete ring of mountains. The indented ridge of Tara Hill commands the south. The southern slopes of the Wicklow mountains on the west rise to the high peak of Croaghan Kinshella, recalling through its name the ancient tribe whose territory lay on the far side. Further north are lower coastal ridges and the gap through which the insurgent forces drove to the capture of Arklow in 1798. This area was the first and best organised in Wexford, both Protestants and Catholics being members of the United Irishmen. At Inch, Anthony Perry was given the infamous gunpowder cap. The Beaumont of the day had done his full share of the flogging and half-hanging that accompanied the counter-revolutionary terror. But all that now survived of the family was one old lady who spelled her name Beauman. They had belonged to the old "quality" who would give their tenants poultry at Christmas, un-hesitatingly call at their houses for refreshment or a chat, and with as

[1] Later nicknamed "Barney".

little compunction destroy a field of standing crops in pursuit of a hare. Now that land division was well advanced the old aristocracy was changing its character.

Grandfather Jordan had known personally hundreds who had taken part in the revolution of 1798. In Murtagh Kavanagh, the Beaumonts' gardener, Liam Mellows found a story-teller who had preserved the United Irishmen's political tradition. He communicated the Beaumonts' lurid past and told of John Kinsella the Land Leaguer murdered by "emergencymen" at Coolgreaney only ten years previously. Liam remained at Macoyle at least until his Aunt Julia married Robert Whitmore, a local farmer's son then living in Dublin. Another aunt, Mrs. Corcoran, was then recalled from Yorkshire to look after the old people. Liam may then have gone to Annadale Avenue, or have remained at Castletown until his parents moved to Cork a year or two later. The second alternative is in accord with the tradition that he spent a total of five years in County Wexford, and if that assumption is correct, he was probably taken to the laying of the foundation stone of the 1798 Centenary Memorial in Gorey at the end of October when the greatest concourse ever known in the town assembled by trap, side-car, bicycle and on foot. The cross was designed by Martin Roche of Gorey, said to be a grandson of Edward Roche, the rebel general, and many other grandchildren of the United Irishmen were present.

At Cork, Liam and Frederick went to the military school at the Wellington Barracks. The family had a small house in Ballyhooley Road at 2 St. Joseph's Terrace. Owned by the African Missions it was on permanent lease to non-commissioned staff officers of the British Army. The South African war was in progress at the time and the local boys used to play in the two quarries above and below the road. In the favourite game of "Boers versus British" Paul MacSweeney next door used to support the Boers whilst the Mellows boys were "British". But they were not "British" in contradistinction to being Irish. During a history lesson an Irish teacher, speaking of Sarsfield's campaign, permitted an inadvertent throb of pride in his voice when quoting the famous reply, "Sarsfield's the word—and Sarsfield's the man!" "Up Ireland!" shouted Liam, only to be quelled by a frigid glance and told privately to restrain his emotions in front of Englishmen.

The sojourn in Cork was short. By 1900 the family was back in Dublin living on McCaffrey's Estate, Mount Brown. There Frederick and Herbert attended St. James's Street Christian Brothers School, while Liam, whom his father hoped would finally break the class barrier and become an officer, was sent to Portobello garrison school, where he organised the Irish boys against the bullying of the English. The unifying interest and main recreation of the family was music. Liam and Frederick played the fiddle, Jane the piano, and one visitor remarked that the house was "like an orchestra". The mother's influence steadily seeped upwards. The weekly musical evenings were spent playing through O'Neill's "Irish Airs" from cover to cover, those who were not playing an instrument singing the words. The father was a benign dictator. When he was about it was, "Please may I leave the table?" In his absence Frederick addressed his mother as "Sally". Each year the children spent their holidays with their relations in Wexford. When their mother came to bring them home Liam would hide up a tree. He spent his time helping with the hay, walking the strand, gathering brambles or mushrooms, or playing wherever there were horses to be found. He is remembered as a pale, pensive little boy. "What are you thinking of?" they would ask. "Ireland," he would reply. Later he spent more of his time reading Irish history, having found a copy of O'Sullivan's *Story of Ireland* in Grandfather Whitmore's house. He had long talks with Murtagh Kavanagh who lent him histories of 1798. A contemporary said, "He was always walking round with a lot of bloody ould books under his arm." Liam Mellows was now absorbing the intellectual food which was to build up the mind of a Republican.

Liam's reserve contrasted with the heartiness of his more popular brother Herbert. Never having had to live behind an ideological wall, Herbert was the complete expression of the Dublin extrovert, with all the wit and some of the superficiality of the type. In comparison Liam was a countryman, and even years afterwards was recognised in New York by the trace of a Wexford accent. He was slower, weightier and sounder.

Home circumstances were easy in Dublin. Sergeant Mellows was allowed three extra years' service as personal assistant to Colonel Treffrey in Dublin Castle, and retired on a good pension in March 1904. He secured an appointment with the Irish Agricultural Wholesale Society. His relatives in Leek used to spend holidays in Dublin, and some even settled in the city. But the Mellows stock had not the indestructibility of the Jordans. In 1906, after the family had moved to Greenfield Place, Jane died of tuberculosis. For a time also, Herbert was extremely delicate. Liam left school in 1907, working first as a clerk in the Junior Army and Navy Stores, a large department store in D'Olier Street, and then at Messrs. Goodbodies, an associate of the Tullamore Tobacco firm, in St. James's Street. He used occasionally to make deliveries of agricultural stores by pony and trap, and is credited with securing the placing of local purchase contracts with Irish firms.

Liam's refusal of a military career was a disappointment to his father. But now that he had retired, he felt disinclined to pursue the matter. The younger generation was completely re-iricised. When a newly built house at 21 Mount Shannon Road was purchased in 1909 it was named Monalug, although the street was being filled with retired officers and successful tradesmen whose outlook was militantly Unionist. Around this time Liam bought his first bicycle and began to acquire the detailed knowledge of Irish topography which stood him in such good stead in the revolutionary days.

By now he could encompass the duality of his family traditions. On the one hand was the stern implacable machine which had ground and polished his father and grandfather, making out of common people the means of their own oppression. On the other was the rebel opposition, preserving its integrity, its optimism and its gaiety amid whatever trials and reverses. One was nominated West Britain, the other Irish Ireland.

One day in the summer of 1911, soon after the shopkeepers' Mafeking on the visit to Dublin of the King of England, he bought a copy of *Irish Freedom*. Its contents excited him beyond measure. He showed it to his brother Frederick and the two boys spent all night talking about it instead of sleeping. Succeeding issues were awaited with tense excitement. For here was Fenianism come to life again. Apart from the contemptuous dismissal of the coronation celebrations, there were revolutionary alternatives to the obsequious opportunism of the Parliamentarians, defiant answers to the truculent counter-revolutionaries in Ulster whose first assembly at Craigavon had taken place in September 1911. To these the October Editorial replied; "We stand for Ireland . . . not for Ireland a portion of any Empire, not for Ireland in swaddling clothes or leading strings, but for a self-reliant free Ireland." In the same issue the editor, Bulmer Hobson, contributed a thoughtful article on the approach of European war, tracing its origin to the economic rivalries of imperialist powers. Britain, first in the field, had seized vast territories in India, Ireland and Egypt, which she monopolised as commercial dependencies and spheres of investment, the "tribute of half the globe pouring in a continuous stream of gold". That her rising industrial competitor Germany would demand repartition of the colonies was a foregone conclusion. The policy of the Irish people should be to use the crisis "to try to snatch the independence of our country while England is engaged". But, Hobson concluded, "Ireland seeks to establish her independence, not to establish an Empire." This article written anonymously by a comparatively unknown journalist, may have inspired the more famous one by Roger Casement two years later, and indeed shows superior insight, probably from the influence of Connolly whom Hobson had met in Belfast.

After a period of hesitation, Mellows took his courage in his hands and walked nervously into a small newsagent's shop in Great Britain Street.[1] He had decided to join up.

[1] Now Parnell Street.

CHAPTER TWO

ANOTHER ROBERT EMMET

"From my earliest youth I have regarded the connection between Ireland and Great Britain as the curse of the Irish nation, and felt that whilst it lasted, this country could never be free nor happy."—Theobald Wolfe Tone

BEHIND the counter was a small, grey-haired, prematurely aged man, Thomas J. Clarke, the Fenian veteran. Like Mellows he had been "born in the service", at an English station. He also came from mixed Catholic and Protestant stock. He was taken to South Africa as a small child, and first saw Ireland when he was ten years old. His father, an excellent soldier reaching the class barrier and retiring with the rank of sergeant, secured a good civilian appointment at Dungannon, County Tyrone. Here the boy attended St. Patrick's School while the smoke from burning homesteads drifted across the town and evicted tenants wandered in search of shelter. Police and soldiers stood guard over the battering rams. In due time St. Patrick's school closed for lack of pupils. By now Tom Clarke had absorbed the tradition from which his father had escaped. The lesson was unavoidable. It was resistance.

Great Land League meetings were held. One of these was addressed by the Fenian leader John Daly of Limerick. Soon afterwards Clarke was sworn into the Irish Republican Brotherhood. It was he who returned the police fire in the famous "buckshot riot" and rallied the citizens to disarm the R.I.C. with their bare hands. As a result he emigrated to America. Here he fell in with the dissident section of *Clann na Gael* who rejected Devoy's policy of co-operating with the Parliamentarians. On their behalf he returned to England to take part in the "dynamite war" and after capture in 1883 he was sentenced to life imprisonment. Released in 1898 he married John Daly's daughter, Kathleen. Awarded the Freedom of Limerick for his struggle against imperialism, still he was compelled to emigrate again to find work. In the United States he became an engineer, held a trade union card, and helped Devoy found the *Gaelic American*, an outspoken opponent of the newly reunited Parliamentary Party, otherwise undistinguished.

He does not appear to have met Connolly while in the U.S.A. and indeed returned in 1907. Rumour indicated an upsurge of Fenianism at home. A number of younger men, notably Bulmer Hobson, Patrick MacCartan, Denis McCullough, all Ulstermen, had broken through the somnolence and complacency, not to say the taste for liquor, of their fathers, and given the I.R.B. a new vigorous direction. There was a struggle lasting several years. Clarke established a newsagent's and tobacconist's shop in Great Britain Street. He stocked provincial newspapers and his tiny room became the gathering point of the new revolutionaries from all over Ireland. He supported the younger men in the "new departure" of participation in Griffith's *Sinn Fein*. When Griffith lurched rightward in 1910 and many of the revolutionaries left his party, Clarke supported them once more in establishing a distinct I.R.B. journal. This was the origin of *Irish Freedom*, nominally the organ of the "Dublin Central Wolfe Tone Clubs Committee". The editor was Hobson, but since as the leading "progressive" he was anathema to the older men, the nominal editor was McCartan, at least until the old guard were finally vanquished.

The outstanding policy questions were scarcely resolved when in the autumn of 1911 the business manager, Sean MacDiarmada, was stricken with poliomyelitis. The work of despatching postal copies was being undertaken by volunteers under McCartan's supervision on the evening when Mellows called at the shop. Clarke heard his story. Its resemblance to his own aroused his special interest. He sent the new recruit to join the despatch party at 6 Findlater's Place, only a few yards away. There Mellows met the members of *Na Fianna*[1] *Eireann*, the Secretary, Patrick O'Riann, Con Colbert, and his life-long friend Eamon Martin. Mellows applied for membership at once, and promised to attend the next meeting at Camden Street together with his brother Frederick. Soon all three brothers had enrolled.

The name *Na Fianna Eireann* had been used by Hobson for his junior sports organisation in Belfast around 1902. The playing of traditional Irish games was combined with political education. The Dublin organisation, also founded by Hobson with the help of Countess Markiewicz, owed more to Baden Powell's conception. In some measure it was designed to counter the proselytising efforts of the Unionist body. At its inaugural meeting in August 1909, Hobson had been elected president. He retired within a few weeks through the necessity of returning to Belfast. The Countess replaced him and

[1] Plural of Fiann, an armed force in ancient Ireland, thus "armed forces of Ireland" or "soldiers of Ireland".

contributed premises, money and enthusiasm to the organisation over a number of years. The two I.R.B. men O'Riann and Colbert became respectively secretary and chief instructor. Round them rapidly gathered a group of able and dedicated youngsters. Old Fenians sent their sons to join. Colbert and O'Riann visited separatist schoolteachers looking for promising pupils. One of those approached was Patrick Pearse. Within a year the first *Ard Fheis*[1] was called. It was attended by representatives from Dublin, Belfast and Limerick. A year later, in 1911, the organisation was also established in Cork, Waterford, Dundalk, Newry, Listowel and Clonmel. Amongst its early sponsors were Dr. MacCartan, Helena Maloney and Roger Casement. Griffith declined to assist, probably from dislike of Hobson.

The Fianna was organised in *Sluaighte*,[2] the first established, *An ceud Sluagh*,[3] being that to which Mellows was now attached. It retained a species of informal seniority.

Within a matter of months Mellows had been promoted to the rank of lieutenant and become the secretary of the Dublin District Council. He had also joined the I.R.B. Eamon Martin had been deputed by the Fianna circle of the organisation to "sound" him for membership. A favourable report being received he had been approached during the holding of the camp at Ticknock at Easter 1912. Some of the older boys walked over the mountains to Glencree on a cold day punctuated by hail showers. The principal of the Reformatory at Glencree was a sympathiser and produced bread, and water for tea. At some point in the journey Mellows consented to join and was sworn in by Con Colbert. The date was 7th April.

For the majority of the Irish people these were days of high hope. The apparent certainty of "Home Rule" within a federal United Kingdom was weighed uncritically against its limitations and deficiencies. The end of the quarrel of ages was eloquently foreshadowed by Winston Churchill, then a Liberal, who made no secret of which partner was to be the main beneficiary. He spoke in Belfast of a "prosperous and loyal Ireland, lying like a great breakwater across our Atlantic flank". This would be "a boon to the British Empire, a wonderful reinforcement". The British Government was sharpening knives for the coming war with Germany. Twice had *Clann na Gael* succeeded in wrecking attempts at an Anglo-American alliance. "The Irish overseas have done us great harm," said Churchill. "They have

---

[1] Literally "high festival", i.e. congress.   [2] Plural of *Sluagh*, crowd or pack.
[3] Literally *The First Sluagh*. The usual modern spelling is *cead*. The word may have the sense of "leading".

been an adverse force in our colonies. They have on more than one occasion deflected the policy of the United States. They are now the most serious obstacle to Anglo-American friendship." Home Rule was to take its place in the general horse-trading. But in February 1912 the Senate so mutilated the draft of a third treaty of alliance that the international usefulness of Home Rule was notably reduced, along with the urgency of enacting it.

The seeming imminence of Home Rule stimulated intense political discussion in separatist circles. Was this half loaf better than no bread? From different standpoints Pearse, Connolly, Griffith and the I.R.B. all agreed that it should be accepted as an instalment. But already there were preparations for armed counter-revolution in the north-east. Would the Liberals stand firm and see their measure through? If they did, then separatists must follow the example of 1782 and form a "patriot opposition". If not, said Pearse from a Parliamentary platform in O'Connell Street on 31st March, there would be revolution. Pearse was not yet a convinced Republican. His speech indicates clearly what convinced him.

The debate proceeded as elsewhere in the columns of *Irish Freedom*. For the first time the expression "Irish revolution" was used in the sense of a change of class control. The Americans had had to suffer Alexander Hamilton awhile. Perhaps a Redmond or a Griffith must play this role until the Fenians had their day. The means of defeating the counter-revolution were argued. In a curiously contradictory article "John Brennan" hailed the Craigavon declaration which heralded the Tory counter-offensive as worthy of support because it represented a defiance by Irish people of the decision of a British Government. Yet in fact it was a declaration of secession from a Home Rule Parliament, an invitation to partition. Efforts were made by Connolly and others to counter this dangerous nonsense, but it caught on as a "leftist" argument against joining all national forces against Unionism and seeking the aid of British democracy, the essential conditions for a peaceful development.

Mellows and his young colleagues enjoyed the excitement of participating in great events, but did not yet try to understand them. They felt that whether before Home Rule or after it, at some time they would have to fight England. They continued the round of drills, camp and study. Their numbers steadily increased. Thus was illustrated how the promise of reform generates the forces which will revolt in its absence. For some reason official historians stress the importance of the northern counter-revolution in converting the greater part of the country to revolution. A British refusal to proceed with Home Rule, even if not masquerading as a concession to "Ulster", would have had the same result, though the development would have been formally different.

Sean MacDiarmada recovered, spent some time with the Daly family in Limerick and returned to activity in Dublin. He addressed the Wolfe Tone Clubs on 4th April. He was a man of strikingly handsome appearance, though now slightly lame. Born in Kilticlogher in County Leitrim he had been a schoolteacher until his separatist tendencies incurred the displeasure of the parish priest. He left for Belfast where he worked as a tram conductor. He was attracted to the I.R.B. by Hobson whom he had helped with his Dungannon Clubs. When these amalgamated with *Sinn Fein*, he became a full-time organiser for that party and covered the whole of Ireland on a bicycle, establishing branches and incidentally recruiting to the Brotherhood. Mellows was immensely impressed by MacDiarmada who became his hero. Possibly meeting MacDiarmada was the decisive factor in his joining the I.R.B.

On 11th April the third Home Rule Bill was read a first time. To the British it was a "Government of Ireland Bill" differing but slightly from its two ill-fated predecessors. Irish independence was limited by the familiar long list of "reserved powers", the Crown, peace and war, titles, treason, trade and navigation outside Ireland, lighthouses, coinage, copyright and patents. There were two small improvements. Nationalisation was no longer forbidden, and there was conceded a limited power to vary British excise rates with consent. The northern Unionists denounced as loudly as the Parliamentarians sang in coloratura of this "final settlement". From Socialists to *Sinn Fein* Irish separatists scanned the bill. Griffith subjected the financial clauses to scathing criticism. To those he spoke for, the tariff question was all-important. "The English Government proposes to change the manner, but not the extent of its control over Ireland," said the editorial of *Irish Freedom*. The young people noted the ominous words that followed, "We are still for war." They continued their drilling and prepared for the day.

A number of nationalist boy scout organisations had grown up. With a view to effecting their unification with the *Fianna*, Hobson proposed a federation and wrote his "Manifesto to the boys of Ireland". Mellows attended the *Fianna* Circle of the I.R.B. at which Hobson was the visitor.[1] He now met Hobson at least every month, and held him

[1] Representative of the Supreme Council.

in a respect that was not fully reciprocated. Hobson was at twenty-nine the virtual centre of the revolutionary movement. A man of fine intellect, strong personality, energy and personal integrity, he came from a background as emancipated as Mellows' was restricted. He was born in Belfast of one of those Quaker families who settled in the great valley that runs between the Lagan and the Erne. He no longer took religion seriously. He cast momentary glances at the theosophical dabblings of some of his fellow-Protestants, but was not committed. While they sought faith he kept the discipline of works. Hobson engaged in endless ratiocination and experiment, while bringing something intuitive to both of these. His mind constantly explored fresh facets of a situation. He was ideally suited to the first beginnings of a revolution before the movement had burned its boats. His activity was ceaseless. He edited *Irish Freedom*. He was chairman of the Dublin Centres Board of the I.R.B. and Leinster representative on its Supreme Council. He kept up a continuous journalistic activity and constantly attended meetings.

Every Saturday morning Hobson and O'Riann took their walk over the Dublin mountains chewing over questions of theory and policy. Mellows accompanied them. But the philosophical talk of his elders did not impress him. They were testing the principles of Irish nationality against universalities while he referred them only to the experience of the Irish people. Sometimes he infuriated Hobson by emitting some blundering pun that blasted the very pinnacle of his chain of reasoning. There was of course a political basis for this apathy. Mellows was content to be a "soldier of Ireland". Hobson was not. He was essentially a politician, and deserved success more than many who achieved it. But he had one crippling weakness, a subtly rationalised *amour propre* which paralysed him at moments when he should stoop to conquer. Other counsels could only lead to the devil; so he must make for heaven alone.

A third *Ard Fheis* was held on 14th July. The number of *Sluaighte* affiliated to *Na Fianna Eireann* had risen to twenty-two.

All sections of the population were adjusting themselves in advance for life under Home Rule and estimating the effect of the new environment on their special interests. The series of spectacular strikes led by Larkin had made obvious the revolutionary potential of the working class. *Irish Freedom* discussed the social policy of the new patriot opposition in the Home Rule Parliament. Was it to be based on the peasantry, who still awaited the division of 160,000 holdings spared by the Land Acts? Or should it reflect the new militancy of the proletariat? In a series of articles, obviously influenced by Connolly, "Crimal"[1] declared that Ireland was filled with "a deep and bitter unrest", expressing itself in a class struggle. "One class owns all the nation's wealth, and another class makes it." Elsewhere among the separatists working-class claims were denied. Griffith, in his articles, showed no doubt as to who constituted the Irish people. It was the bourgeoisie; he was most concerned that the Home Rule Parliament should institute compulsory arbitration and put a stop to strikes.

A facet of the debate was the question of winning the Protestant workers of Ulster. Would a social programme have this effect or would granting concessions "act as a safety valve" and postpone the advent of national consciousness? The great ferment that was bubbling in Ireland came at the end of thirty years of continual concessions. Surprisingly little attention seems to have been given to the Ulster Covenant of September 1912 and the more sinister Ulster Volunteers which arose from it. The first fascist movement of the century stalked unrecognised on to the stage of history.

Age slept confident in the British Parliament, the Liberal Party and John Redmond. Youth was full of its own dreams. Peadar Kearney's "Soldier Song" was published anonymously in the September issue of *Irish Freedom* and expressed exactly the expectant mood of the *Fianna*. Nevertheless, in Dublin at least, *Fianna* sentiment was firmly towards the political "left", towards an Ireland that would give full play to the energy and initiative of the common people.

In the autumn of 1912 Mellows founded the Dolphins Barn *Sluagh*. To it were attached outlying members from surrounding areas. He now made his name as an organiser. He was in general charge and acted as drill instructor. Alfred White was second in command. For teaching Irish history he secured the services of Mr. N. MacNamee who had taught his brother Herbert[2] at James's Street Schools. By February 1913 all members had uniforms. Despite the countrywide revulsion from the policies of physical force, which corresponded to the heightening hopes of Home Rule, the *Fianna* was progressing in Dublin.

This was largely thanks to the availability of instructors. Where these were absent educational and political work failed to hold the boys together. In Limerick John Daly opened a *Fianna* Hall and found the necessary workers. Elsewhere the *sluaighte* languished and a census of the membership held early in the New Year revealed that it did not

---

[1] Possibly Cathal O'Shannon.

[2] The name Barney will be used below. Sometimes in the early literature Herbert appears as "Brian". For some reason he detested the name Herbert, perhaps from the difficulty of iricising it.

exceed 300. The only solution was to appoint a full-time organiser who would act as travelling instructor.

The matter was discussed informally and came up for decision at the *Ard Choisde*[1] of 13th April 1913. Countess Markiewicz was in the chair and Hobson, Lonergan, Colbert and O'Riann were present together with country members. On O'Riann's proposal it was agreed to appoint a "travelling instructor and organiser" and to set up a special fund to maintain him. Members were asked to guarantee sixpence per week, but others were to be invited to help. These were of course Clarke, Daly, Countess Markiewicz, Casement and the adult members of the I.R.B. It was undertaken that while in the country the organiser would enjoy hospitality provided by members of the movement. Mellows was proposed for the position. He was described as an efficient and tactful organiser. He had visited Wexford over Easter and had established *sluaighte* at Ferns and Enniscorthy. On his part he explained that his expenses would be small since he would use his new Irish-built "Lucania" bicycle whenever possible. (Lest those unfamiliar with the history of the bicycle might imagine that he was sacrificing utility to sentiment in preferring the native product, it should be remarked that, thanks to the work of Dunlop, for a period Ireland led the world in bicycle design and production.) The appointment was made. Mellows was promoted captain and Alfie White took his place in Dolphin's Barn, becoming a lieutenant. At home that evening Mellows explained his decision to his mother. "I'm going to be another Robert Emmet."

He set out on his first journey on Sunday, 27th April. Full of a sense of high adventure he decided to keep a diary. He derived the notion from Wolfe Tone's famous autobiography. The journal was little more, however, than notes and jottings, which he sent to Patrick O'Riann with his first report. O'Riann passed it to Hobson who, to Mellows' consternation, published it in full in *Irish Freedom*. Thanks to that indiscretion we have a clear picture of Mellows' work and the state of the movement at the time. Slightly edited extracts follow:

WITH THE ORGANIZER[2]

April 27   Wexford met by bodyguard of Sluagh Fr. John Murphy. Afternoon drilling in preparation for Feis. 7–10.30 taught bayonet exercise.

April 28   Went to Killurin.

---

[1] Literally "High Committee". *Coisde* (*coiste*) is also used of a jury. Thus, council, or executive committee.
[2] *Irish Freedom*, June 1913.

April 29 Ferns, then Enniscorthy. Poor attendances. Bad weather. Rooms in Gaelic League premises.

April 30 Went to Gorey and Courtown.—Arklow back Wexford.

May 1 Rode to New Ross and Waterford. Made arrangements to start next Tuesday. Christian Brothers promised to help.

May 2 Rode to Clonmel via Carrick. Arrangement for next day.

May 3 Clonmel Sluagh *non est* owing to not being able to get rooms. They hope, however, to re-organise Sluagh Kickham very soon.

May 4 Rode to Cashel. Everybody away at hurling match in Dublin. Distributed literature and returned to Clonmel. The weather all week has been most miserably wet and so am I.

May 5 Rode to Kilkenny from Clonmel (31 miles) arrived late at night wet through. Heard body of scouts existed but not contacted.

May 6 Wet! Returned to Waterford for pre-arranged meeting 8 p.m. 30 boys present. Fixed further meeting for Wednesday 14th.

May 7 Wet! Returned to Kilkenny by 6.30 train.

May 8 Busy all day in Kilkenny. Arranged meeting for next Friday evening.

May 9 Rode out to Castlecomer (10 miles). Roads knee deep in mud. Met several local Gaelic Leaguers but could get none of them interested in Fianna. Returned to Kilkenny arranged one for following Friday (16th).

May 10 Intended riding to Wexford but still raining. Bodyguard met me at station.

May 11 Wexford Feis. Met man re Ardmore.

May 12 Wexford Feis.

May 13 Holiday in Wexford. Drilling, signalling, marches through town with band. 5 p.m. Lecture by Miss Browne on '98 at Exhibition Hall. Bull Ring at 8 p.m. L.M. spoke on "British Empire". Arranged to start Sluagh at Castlebridge, four miles from Wexford.

May 14 Rode to Waterford (34 miles) to keep appointment re meeting. Owing to some misunderstanding this did not take place. Disgusted!

May 15 Meeting 8 p.m. Twenty-six present. Spoke till 9.30. Arranged meeting for May 19th.

May 16 Rode to Kilkenny (32 miles). Held meeting of James Stephens Boy Scouts (independent of Na Fianna Eireann). Drilled and inspected and spoke about "British Empire".

May 17 Rode to Gowran, Co. Kilkenny (10 miles), then Dungarvan. Rode to Borris, County Carlow. Arrived 6.30.

Arranged to return next Tuesday. Left Borris 8.30 to ride
back to Wexford (38 miles) across Blackstairs mountains.
It *was* black and no mistake. Rode through night. Arrived
Wexford 12.10. Total miles for day 62.

May 18   Marched with Sluagh Fr. John Murphy to Castlebridge.
Found most of local people away at hurling match
Damn! Gathered together all the boys of the village we
could find. Delivered an oration. Wexford Sluagh gave a
display of skirmishing, etc., in village street. Returned
home a sadder and wiser, etc. At 8 p.m. a little history
chat with Wexford Sluagh. There was great enthusiasm
and proceedings terminated at 11 o'clock with singing of
national anthem.

In each place he made contact with the I.R.B. centre, Sean Mac-
Diarmada having furnished him with a list. His most successful work
seems to have been done in Wexford town where he stayed with Mrs.
Larkin, a Sinnott related to the founder of the *Sluagh*. Robert Brennan
in his autobiography recalled the exceptional vitality he instilled into
the Wexford boys.[1] At Courtown he met Sean Etchingham, a remarkable character who, starting as an illiterate stable boy, taught himself
letters and became a popular columnist and comic poet on the *Enniscorthy Echo*. He was a bachelor, having been rejected by some girl in
his youth, and declining to try again. He was a pillar of the Gaelic
League and supporter of local industrial development, while he
revolted against the sycophancy with which it was so often accompanied. One of his exploits concerned some oyster beds, the first
fruits of which were to be despatched to the King of England. After
the ceremonial packing and when the royal crates were on the train
he spread the rumour that he had smuggled a dead rat into one of
them, and the present had to be recalled. With his own hands he
built a tea-shop and cyclists' rest where members of the movement were
always welcome. He had a sense of humour that appealed to Mellows
and the two became fast friends.

At Waterford Mellows stayed with Liam Walsh, the I.R.B. centre.
The original *Sluagh* had run down, but a number of likely boys were
visited. A meeting was held in the Gaelic League room in William
Street. Mellows had the art of introducing just sufficient informality
to break the ice at a meeting of young people. He would stand in the
centre of the room with one foot on a chair, whence he would tell the

[1] *Allegiance*, p. 27. But Brennan's chronology appears to be in error.

story of the penal laws, or the history of 1798, and urge preparation for the final trial with England.

At Kilkenny he was the guest of the de Loughrey family. Peter de Loughrey was an ironfounder and general merchant with premises at 18 and 19 Parliament Street. A prominent member of the I.R.B. and *Sinn Fein*, he converted part of number 19 into premises for the movement.

Mellows returned to Dublin in time for the annual excursion to the grave of Wolfe Tone at Bodenstown, Co. Kildare. Following an unusual but commendable tradition it takes place not at the season of the patriot's death, but at the anniversary of his birth. In 1913 the *Fianna* provided a special guard of honour for Patrick Pearse who was speaking from a Republican platform for the first time. His superb oratorical gifts were combined with a delicate feeling for the susceptibilities of any Protestant who might be present. His words made a lasting impression on Mellows.

> When men come to a graveside [he said] they pray, and each of us prays in his heart. But we do not pray for Tone. Men who die that their people may be free have no need of prayers.

After the commemoration Mellows spent four more months on the road. He paid a brief visit to Dundalk, then returned to the south, working from Limerick, where he met John Daly and his family, through Tipperary and Laois to Athlone. Here he reported to Peadar Malinn, the I.R.B. centre. Apart from soldiers the largest part of the population worked in the woollen mills. These were closed for the annual holidays, from 18th July to the 25th. There were plenty of young people with time on their hands and Mellows was able to recruit what proved a very active *Sluagh* before he left for Roscommon.[1] After a brief and fruitless excursion to Killybegs, where an enthusiast had conceived the notion of a *Fianna* cavalry unit, he struck eastwards across the country to his relatives the McInlays who kept a Post Office, general store and forge at Flurriebridge, Co. Armagh. From here he could work with the *Fianna* in both Dundalk and Newry.

While at Flurriebridge he received a message from Eamon Martin summoning him to Belfast. In accordance with I.R.B. policy an anti-enlistment campaign had been begun. Adhesive leaflets attached to the lamp-posts in the Springfield and Crumlin Road areas on 6th July had

[1] It was probably during this period that Mellows spent the holiday with Bulmer Hobson at Patrick Pearse's cottage at Rossmuck.

brought two eighteen-year-old *Fianna* boys, James Twomey and Patrick Dempsey, into court for issuing a "seditious libel". One of the posters bore the message: "Sons of Belfast, the soldiers and police are used by the government to crush the working man when he stands for his rights. The soldiers and police are recruited from the people. Stop all recruiting and you will paralyse your enemies." They were remanded in custody after the first hearing on 28th July. Martin and one or two others from Dublin were staying with Francis Joseph Biggar, the Gaelic scholar who had spoken at the Robert Emmet commemoration the previous March. Insurrection in 1803 was one thing. Seditious libel in 1913 was another. Biggar showed the *Fianna* boys the door.

They went to stay with James Connolly, placing, it may be said, a serious burden on his wife's housekeeping. Mellows visited them there in August, but Connolly seems to have been away. Already Eamon was a professed Socialist and possibly on this occasion Mellows had his first introduction to Connolly's ideas. His stay was brief. Returning to Flurriebridge he organised the Newry *Sluagh*, prominent in which was Connellan, many years afterwards the Nationalist M.P.

He returned to a Dublin distracted by the great lock-out when 404 employers made their effort to starve a whole city out of allegiance to trade unionism. The population was ranged in two opposing camps. On the one side were the employers, the Castle authorities, the police, the Parliamentarians and Griffith's supporters in *Sinn Fein*. On the other were the trade unions, the Socialists and Labour men, and the entire radical section of the Republican movement including those like Eamonn Ceannt who were still in *Sinn Fein* and the great majority of the liberal middle class. Speaking to Connolly, Clarke expressed his enthusiastic admiration for this working class which carried society on its back and threatened to overturn it merely by squaring its shoulders. "After Ireland is free I'll be a socialist," he declared.

The *Fianna* was wholly committed from the start. Its class composition precluded any other stand. Newsboys who had marched under Colbert to Ticknock were now locked out by the *Independent*. Fathers, brothers and sisters were plunged into idleness. The members gave first aid to those injured in the baton charges. One of them received injuries from which he subsequently died. Mellows could spend little time in Dublin, but was unreservedly on Larkin's side. After spending a good part of September in Tuam organising the *Fianna* sports, he met Connolly for the first time. The Labour leader was at Countess Markiewicz's recuperating after his hunger-strike. Connolly was deeply impressed and told his daughter Nora "I have found a real man."[1]

After Tuam, Tullamore. Here he stayed with Mrs. Brennan, recruiting her son Seamus into the I.R.B. He used to cycle to Athlone, Birr and Tyrellspass where he stayed with the Malones. The hot September had given way to an exceptionally cold October. He rode through the frost on many a brilliant moonlight night. Since April he had visited over half the counties of Ireland and had left his mark throughout the country. In November he was recalled to Dublin. An open adult military organisation was to be established and his services were required in a larger arena.

---

[1] *Portrait of A Rebel Father*, p. 222. According to the chronology of the work the date would be 1915, but the earlier date is more probable.

CHAPTER THREE

SOLDIERS OF IRELAND

"A National Militia is the constitutional right of Ireland, the proper trustee of peace, and the warden of legal liberty."—Thomas Davis

THE immediate occasion for the establishment of the Irish Volunteers, the army of the revolution, was an article written by Professor Eoin MacNeill in the journal of the Gaelic League, *An Claidheamh Soluis*.[1] Thereafter began a struggle for control that reflected the class struggle within the national movement. It is necessary to examine with some care the circumstances surrounding its appearance.

The notorious "Ulster Covenant" by which the Unionists declared their policy of resisting Home Rule with force had been offered for public signature from September 1912 onwards. The counter-revolutionary private army, the "Ulster Volunteers", had emerged before the end of that year, and had been arming and drilling ever since. The Home Rule Bill received its second reading in January 1913. It was immediately rejected by the Lords. To over-rule their Lordships' veto it must be introduced twice more in separate sessions of Parliament. It was next read a second time on 9th June 1913, the intervening period being used by the Unionists to increase hysteria and strengthen their military force. The Lords' second rejection coincided with the height of Orange marches. It fell on 15th July. Next time the Bill was introduced in the Commons, the Upper House would be powerless to block it. Hence, the crescendo of illegal activity in the summer and autumn of 1913. This was encouraged by the participation, not to say active fomentation, of some of the highest personages in English public life. There was a corresponding permissiveness on the part of the government, to whom Home Rule was no more than a regrettable necessity.

It was natural enough in these conditions that the military activities of the *Fianna* should attract the younger members of the I.R.B. If armed struggle was coming, whether of a patriot opposition, a force to defend Home Rule, or of a nation determined to wrest independ-

[1] The Sword of Light.

ence from Britain, it could not be left to boys. Accordingly from July onwards, under *Fianna* instructors, members of the I.R.B. practised military exercises in secret. They drilled in the Foresters' Hall, Parnell Square. There seems to have survived no conclusive evidence of the kind of hostilities they expected to engage in. As Connolly remarked, physical force was easier agreed upon than its political object.

In September 1913 Unionist defiance reached a new pitch of impudence. On the 24th the Ulster Unionist Council declared itself the "Central Authority of the Provisional Government of Ulster". In accordance with previous decisions, in the event of the establishment of Home Rule, this government would hold nine counties "in trust for the Empire". What possible meaning this could have but partition and a local administration in Ulster until the United Kingdom was prepared to re-absorb it, it is hard to guess. Yet many observers saw only the form of violence and ignored the content of counter-revolution. Formally the action of the Unionists created a total split in the Irish bourgeoisie. But class interests remained. The success of Carson and his friends in rendering the working class impotent caused no tears among the 404 employers who were trying to smash Dublin trade unionism. Perhaps in the common antagonism of the whole bourgeoisie towards Labour lies the origin of the softness towards the Ulster Volunteers on the part of prominent nationalists. The rest derived from confusion.

MacNeill's article[1] appeared on 1st November. It began with a statement that by something near a miracle of political adroitness the remnant of feudal aristocracy in Ulster had secured the leadership of an alliance of wage-earners and rent-payers by conferring the stamp of respectability on "no-popery" sentiment. Then followed an argument designed to establish that while aristocracy remained entwined with Britain through family connections and self-interest, the Orangemen were unwittingly "home rulers in principle and essence". The loyalty of Orangemen to the Crown, Constitution, Empire and Union, wrote MacNeill, arose out of the notion that these entities secured them possession of Home Rule and a little more. When that little more was threatened their loyalty was transformed into antagonism. "The Ulster Volunteer movement", he proceeded, "is essentially and obviously a Home Rule movement. It claims, no doubt, to hold Ireland 'for the Empire' but really it is no matter whether Ireland is to be held for the Empire or for the Empyrean, against the Pope, against John Redmond, or against the Man in the Moon. What matters is, *by whom Ireland is*

[1] Reproduced in full in F. X. Martin's *The Irish Volunteers*, p. 57.

to be held." Hence followed the conclusion, "There is nothing to prevent the other twenty-eight counties from calling into existence citizen forces to hold Ireland 'for the Empire'." So doing would repair the cardinal error of disbanding the Volunteers of 1782 which also held Ireland "for the Empire".

The four counties excluded constituted what English Unionists were describing as "homogeneous Ulster", that is to say they contained the majority of the Protestants. MacNeill rightly contended that no homogeneity existed in them. The city of Derry, the town of Newry, the Glens of Antrim and South Derry and 100,000 Belfastmen were staunchly nationalist. But, the Professor reasoned, heterogeneity had produced its own unity. "It is manifest that all Irish people, Unionist as well as Nationalist, are determined to have their own way in Ireland. . . . It is not to follow, and it will not follow, that any part of Ireland, majority or minority, is to interfere with the liberty of any other part." He quoted from a speech he had made in the heart of "homogeneous Ulster". He had hoped for the day "when many of every creed and party would join in celebrating the defence of Derry and the Battle of Benburb".

Professor MacNeill was not a lawyer. He was a brilliantly gifted Celtic scholar. But he was highly political and knew the meaning of words. Indeed, he recognised the political implications of his own researches into ancient Irish history and had no enthusiasm for the Primitive Communism discerned by Connolly and the "Gaelic Socialists".

Here was no call for a revolutionary war for Irish independence. To discover that would be to read back into MacNeill's conception what the masses made of it. It did indeed represent the first tentative experiment of the bourgeoisie in playing with fire, but how tentative is not difficult to see. First in the description of the class structure of Ulster, homogeneous or otherwise, the capitalist class is not mentioned, yet the strongest bonds with England were capitalist, and those who maintained them directed their blows as much at socialism as at nationalism. Second, "no Popery" sentiment is represented as a phenomenon of the lower orders skilfully utilised by the aristocracy. But it was an artificially stimulated and carefully organised[1] diversion. MacNeill, of course, knew this and made the point elsewhere. Third, the element of defiance of the British Parliament which MacNeill ingeniously

---

[1] Hugh Sherman refers to the influence of Professor Salmon's anti-Catholic "Infallibility of the Church" which "found its way into manses and rectories all over Ulster. The arguments in it were retailed at the firesides of farmhouses, at casual gatherings of businessmen, wherever Protestant people with any capacity for discussion got together."

equated with Home Rule sentiment derived not from the masses
themselves, but from the history of this aristocratic indoctrination.
Far from resembling the Volunteers of 1782, the Ulster Volunteers
corresponded more closely to the Militia of 1793 whose purpose was
"to check the spirit of volunteering and maintain the peace of the
country". Carson's army has been described as the first fascist organisation in modern Europe.

The holding of Ireland "for the Empire", as the quotation marks
show, was not to be taken literally. What then was Ireland to be held
for? Obviously for the interests represented by the two military forces.
Though these were not defined, there is no indication that they were
fundamentally antagonistic. One part of Ireland was not to interfere
with the liberty of another. Indeed the simultaneous celebration of the
Defence of Derry and the Battle of Benburb, could only emerge from
dreamland into reality provided the celebrants inhabited different
states, one of them was politically powerless, or historical developments
had rendered the exercise meaningless. The picture of militant nationalism co-existing peacefully with militant anti-nationalism in one
national state was only attainable by spiriting away the bourgeoisie
with its half-hearted opposition to imperialism and its constant
conflict with the working class, together with imperialism itself and
the progressive movement within Britain. MacNeill sought to wish
away contradictions his class could not resolve. But within the wish was
the proposal to turn to force. The I.R.B. reacted at once. Hobson
visited O'Rahilly, Managing Editor of *An Claidheamh Soluis*. He ascertained that MacNeill's proposition was seriously intended. O'Rahilly
agreed to approach MacNeill, who consented to take the chair at a
preliminary meeting at Wynn's Hotel on 11th November. In the
meantime Pearse had followed up the suggestion in the next issue of the
paper. He showed how rapidly he had moved to the left by adumbrat-
ing for the first time the conception of an Irish national liberation
front with "multitudinous activity . . . all tending towards a common
objective, the Irish Revolution". Nationhood, he wrote, could not be
achieved otherwise than in arms, or at least when there were arms to
be used if necessary. But he modified MacNeill's argument, which had
been that the Ulster Volunteers had provided the excuse for the
establishment of National Volunteers. Pearse wrote:

I am glad the Orangemen have armed, for it is a goodly thing to see
arms in Irish hands. I should like to see the A.O.H. armed. I should
like to see the Transport Workers armed. I should like to see any

and every body of Irish citizens armed. We must accustom ourselves
to the thought of arms, to the sight of arms, to the use of arms. We
may make mistakes in the beginning and shoot the wrong people;
but bloodshed is a cleansing and a sanctifying thing, and the nation
that regards it as the final horror has lost its manhood. There are
many things more horrible than bloodshed and slavery is one of
them.

Every sensible man prefers to have his friends armed and his enemies
disarmed. Pearse's doctrine of the "blood sacrifice" had a rational and an
irrational aspect. On the one hand there is no freedom for those who
do not defend it; and an armed people is the best guarantee of a
democratic revolution. On the other, bloodshed in itself never sanctified anything; and in any case more than sanctification is required of it.
Two days after the meeting in Wynn's Hotel James Connolly launched
the Irish Citizen Army as a workers' defence force within the separatist
movement. The contradictions of imperialism were expressing themselves in open violence upon two fronts. When the European war
broke out in less than a year a third was added and the crisis was
complete.

The preliminary meeting was attended by Sean MacDiarmada,
Eamonn Ceannt, R. Page, T. A. Deakin, and Piaras Beaslai. These were
members of the I.R.B. Hobson judged it wise not to attend. It has
been said that he acted on I.R.B. instructions which he afterwards
ignored. The others comprised MacNeill, O'Rahilly, Pearse, W. J.
Ryan, Sean Fitzgibbon and Joseph Campbell, the poet. It was decided
in principle to establish the Volunteers, but first to attempt to broaden
the committee. Three members dropped out, namely Ryan, Deakin
and Campbell. On the 14th MacNeill was joined by other followers of
Redmond, notably L. J. Kettle and Colonel Maurice Moore. The
I.R.B. strength had been increased by the addition of Seamus O'Connor, and Eamon Martin of the *Fianna*. The advanced nationalists were
joined by Colm O'Lochlainn, M. J. Judge and the two university
students, P. J. Nolan and L. S. Gogan. It was publicly announced that a
Provisional Committee had been formed.

It was during the process of completing this committee and preparing
for the mass meeting of 25th November, that Mellows was brought to
Dublin to strengthen the *Fianna* representation. When the final list
was published it showed that the I.R.B. representation had been
brought to twelve through the addition of Mellows, Lonergan and
O'Riann of the *Fianna*, and Peadar Maicin. The Parliamentarians had
gained places for J. Gore and Tom Kettle, while the general term

"advanced Nationalist" might still be applied to Roger Casement, M. J. Judge, L. S. Gogan, J. Lenehan, Thomas MacDonagh, Joseph Plunkett, G. Walsh and P. White. Of the thirty members twelve belonged to the I.R.B. which was by far the strongest single group. It was shortly to recruit Pearse, Plunkett and MacDonagh and thus hold half the strength of the committee.

The public response to the inaugural meeting on 25th November surpassed all expectations. A few days before the event it was transferred to the Rotunda Rink, the largest hall available in Dublin. Even then two overflows were necessary. A Manifesto had been drafted by MacNeill. Its content resembled that of the article "The North began" but the presentation was simpler. The argument ran that since the Tory party had resolved to prevent Home Rule by force, thus threatening to deprive the Irish people of their constitutional rights, the nation should establish a volunteer force in order to defend them.

The aim of the organisation was to "maintain the rights and liberties common to all the people of Ireland". Nothing expressly stated that these rights were not subsumed under the constitutional right to enjoy Home Rule when it was decreed by the Union Parliament. On the other hand nothing expressly restricted them. Prominent Home Rulers sat on the platform. The first of them, L. J. Kettle, who had employed scabs on a farm in which he had an interest, was prevented from making himself heard by indignant protests from locked-out workers who were present. The second, the student son of Michael Davitt, with his father's forename, made a half-hearted speech which betrayed the hesitations of the Redmonite leadership. On the other hand Captain White of the Citizen Army mounted the rostrum amid cheers. Pearse outlined the picture of an Irish nation organised for freedom, but revived the confusion over the Volunteers in the north. He disclaimed hostility to the Ulster Volunteers, spoke of the possibility of fraternising with them, and asserted that whilst they might disagree "as to the degree of autonomy which was desirable for Ireland" they were all agreed that it was for "Ireland herself to determine that degree". That was precisely what was not agreed.

Hobson, who had been the moving spirit in all this work, now made himself unpopular with the I.R.B. by continuing his membership of the Provisional Committee. It was held that he was so prominent a physical force man that his presence would frighten off the moderates. He was disinclined to orphan his brain-child and perhaps suspected personal bias against him. MacDiarmada after his return from Limerick had spent much time at the Clarkes', where Mrs. Clarke looked after him like a mother. Hobson may have suspected danger to his position as Tom Clarke's chief confidant. Inevitably he found himself moving into a position of independence of the I.R.B. But he seems to have concurred in rejecting the Citizen Army's application for affiliation.

The foundation of the Volunteers aroused immense enthusiasm. Meetings were held throughout Ireland at which the horse-sense of the people forced on the thinkers and theoreticians a viable policy. The supporters of Home Rule were arming to meet Carson's threat, which was by many seen as the reconquest of the country for Toryism after Home Rule had been conceded. When MacNeill called for three cheers for the Ulster Volunteers at a meeting in Cork City a riot ensued. MacNeill blamed the Hibernians. Griffith expended caustic wit on his political ineptitude.

Physical force had now become a commonplace on the two revolutionary fronts. From measuring pick-handles against policemen's truncheons the Citizen Army was now defending the locked-out workers' pickets from armed blacklegs. On Christmas Day a tussle on one of the quays ended when a policeman named Kiernan was thrown into the Liffey. Stephen Hastings was arrested. He was rescued by the crowd who then tried to prevent others from throwing a lifebelt to the struggling officer. "Let him drown!" was the cry. "They should all be there." Hastings was brought up to the house of Countess Markiewicz. She asked Mellows, who was still working for the *Fianna* while devoting much of his time to drilling the new volunteer companies, to arrange his escape. He brought him to the home of Robert Brennan in Wexford, together with another worker who was implicated, and the two men were smuggled to England on board schooners.

The Provisional Committee was inundated with requests for assistance in establishing companies. MacNeill saw the need for a full-time secretary to the Committee, but was anxious not to have an I.R.B. man in the key position. He therefore persuaded L. S. Gogan to undertake the work while awaiting an appointment to the museum. Mellows busied himself with organising. Thus he attended the *Ard Choisde* of 8th February, at which Martin reported on the *Fianna* Hurling League. He played the fiddle with Barney at the piano at the *Fianna* Festival on 22nd February. But on 28th February he spoke at Wexford Town Hall at the inaugural meeting of the Volunteers in that town.

In what seems to be his first recorded speech he advanced a perfectly logical argument. "If anybody has any doubts as to the efficacy of having plenty of fighting material at the disposal of the nation, they should remember that two years ago, when the Home Rule Bill was introduced, the Volunteers were started in Ulster to prevent the Bill becoming law. They were a very small party at first. They proceeded to use the only means at their disposal to gain their ends, and that was force, and though these men are against us, they can excite our admiration for the example they have given to the rest of Ireland, because it is a simple lesson in logic that if 20,000 drilled men can hold back the Home Rule Bill, then the rest of Ireland can show that 300,000 drilled men can force it through." This "simple lesson in logic" was appreciated in London. On 4th December 1913, less than a fortnight after the establishment of the Volunteers, the importation of arms into Ireland became the subject of a government prohibition. Behind the scenes negotiations were set on foot for a compromise between Redmond and Carson, in which Lloyd George revived a proposal he had made in 1911 for "Home Rule within Home Rule", the temporary exclusion of four counties from the operation of the Bill. In effect a constitutional wall was to be erected around the 20,000 to protect them from the 300,000. The Unionists were to be taken under special protection. It was an ironical reversal of MacNeill's dream of Imperial forces holding four counties against the Ulstermen while the Volunteers held the rest "for the Empire". The proposals for partition were published on 9th March 1914, when the Home Rule Bill was offered a third time for its second reading.

The reaction of the Irish people was one of indignation, which was not yet directed against the Parliamentarians for their handling of affairs. Connolly denounced Redmondite complicity in the proposed deal and commented that it revealed "the depths of betrayal to which the so-called Nationalist politicians are willing to sink". He urged that the establishment of such a scheme should if necessary be resisted by armed force. P. S. O'Hegarty, an I.R.B. man, had argued just before the partition proposal was published that the way to "win" Ulster was to prove the capacity of the Nationalists for good government and to guarantee its "special interests". Ernest Blythe now wrote:

> Under no circumstances must we acquiesce in the cutting up of our country and the division of our people. The plea that the partition would only be temporary is a fool's plea. Six years of Home Rule with East Ulster out would only increase the alienation of the bulk of the Irish Protestants. . . . I can see how every sort of lie would be circulated, how every action of the Irish Government would be misrepresented, how it would be tormented and frustrated and forced into follies, how separate vested interests would arise in

Ulster, how the Ulster feeling of repulsion would come to be reciprocated, how in short, if there were to be partition at all it would be permanent partition. . . . The Irishman who consents to partition is a traitor and must be dealt with as one.

It was under these circumstances that MacNeill, Casement and Colonel Maurice Moore began approaches to the Redmonites for collaboration. No doubt the initiative was favoured by the absence of Hobson in the U.S.A.[1] The Curragh Mutiny took place on 20th March. Moore was going to London on the 23rd. It was agreed that he should meet Redmond. To his surprise he found himself at a meeting of the entire leadership. He made little headway, but remained in London several weeks trying to meet the politicians separately. It seems, therefore, that the Redmonites were afraid that the Volunteers would hamper their policy of compromise, as the Conservatives whittled away Home Rule, and that MacNeill, Moore and Casement were anxious to commit them to a more determined line.

On 8th April MacNeill wrote to Moore announcing that Professor Kettle and himself had been invited to draft a permanent constitution for the Volunteers. He remarked also that since the large Provisional Committee was unwieldy, a smaller governing body of three should be established. He suggested that Moore should return to Dublin, while Casement continued the discussions in London.

Precisely what the gentlemen of the movement were at while Hobson had his back turned and the practical men were busy organising and drilling is by no means certain. Passages in their correspondence may give a hint of it.[2] MacNeill told Moore that he wished to "talk over the question of Government" with him, and expressed the hope that "the country will one day know and recognise your good work". According to Moore the three were considering the possibility of the British Government's recognising the Volunteers by extending the Territorial Army Act to Ireland after Home Rule had been established. Casement argued that the federation implicit in Home Rule would make the Irish Government "provincial" unless there was a National army. The way to get one was to amalgamate with the Ulster Volunteers and have the combination recognised by England. MacNeill engagingly confessed that he "did not see the road before us", but he

---

[1] The dates of his departure and return are uncertain, but it was reported in the April issue of *Irish Freedom* that together with Pearse he spoke at the Robert Emmet Commemoration in New York. This would take place around 5th March. He probably arrived back in Dublin in April.

[2] See "History of Irish Volunteers" by Colonel Maurice Moore. *Irish Press*, 4th January–24th February 1938.

felt that ultimately "our position must be that of a fully recognised territorial force". That to reach this position Redmond's assistance was necessary is obvious.

Devlin invited MacNeill to meet him in Dublin on 15th April and to bring with him Moore and Kettle. Kettle was unable to attend. Casement took his place. By now Hobson had returned. Gogan had proved unequal to the task of dealing with the vast mass of correspondence, and following some strictures from the older man resigned. Mellows took his place. His salary was 30s. a week. He was able to call on the assistance of the *Fianna,* and much the same team that had despatched *Irish Freedom* while Sean MacDiarmada was sick, now worked every evening in the office of the Volunteers. During the day he had the voluntary assistance of Colonel Maurice Moore and Cotter.

It was at the meeting in Dublin that Devlin stated plainly that the party must control the Volunteers. Casement announced himself favourably impressed by the Parliamentarian's "sincerity of purpose". Casement was no politician, but like many of his class and background considered himself qualified by birth to make policy. He had held responsible office and shown determination and incorruptibility. But any trade union branch secretary could have given him a lesson in collective action. A week later he had revised his opinion and was opposing all links with the Redmondites as handing over the movement to the Hibernians.

MacNeill followed his course much as water finds its own level, making no resistance and heeding none. He crossed to London at the beginning of May. At that time Volunteer companies were springing up like mushrooms throughout Ireland and electing their own officers. Moore and Captain White, who had left the Citizen Army, were penetrating the fastnesses of Ulster. High policy was pursued in the grand manner. MacNeill proposed to the Parliamentarians that the Provisional Committee should be superseded by a small executive consisting of himself, Gore, Tom Kettle and O'Rahilly, to which should be added John Redmond, his brother and, possibly, Roger Casement. The gentlemen were thus to be in exclusive control. Not one worker, artisan or tradesman was to sit near the control panel, nor any member of the I.R.B. Redmond favoured the proposal, but later demanded the addition of two further nominees of his own, and wrote to MacNeill to this effect. MacNeill replied on 19th May.

There was a meeting of the Provisional Committee that night, but MacNeill considered it "premature and unwise" to inform it of the funeral arrangements that were being made for it. On the other hand he could scarcely give Redmond a formal acceptance without its authority. His message seems to have been inconclusive, and Redmond was shortly pressing for a definite answer.

While in London MacNeill attended a meeting of the Anglo-Irish Committee whose members consisted for the most part of discontented Liberal Home Rulers alarmed at the apparent spinelessness of the Asquith Government. Its formation had been stimulated by Roger Casement and its members included Lord Ashbourne, Sir Alexander Lawrence, Lady Alice Young, Captain George Fitz-Hardinge Berkeley and members of the Spring-Rice family. The meeting, which was held on 8th May at the house of Alice Stopford-Green the historian, decided that since the Orangemen had landed arms in Antrim, while the British Navy stood by to protect them, the Nationalists would be justified in doing the same in order to arm the Volunteers. In a short time a plan was evolved. Darrell Figgis was sent to Germany to buy Mausers. Erskine Childers, still a Home Ruler and Liberal-Imperialist, agreed to sail them to Ireland in his yacht. And a considerable sum of money was raised on loan. These proceedings were also kept from the Provisional Committee, though it is unlikely that its members would have disapproved. What is clear is that it entered nobody's head that the Liberal and Irish Parliamentary parties had not many years to live. Their members were the people who were thought to matter. It was they who were close to the buttons of power.

On 25th May MacNeill returned to London with Moore. Redmond was "gratified" to learn that his nominees would be acceptable. He suggested the inclusion of Joseph Devlin and Michael Davitt. Moore recorded that his proposal was reported to "the Committee", which was somewhat doubtful, but left the negotiations in MacNeill's hands. It is clear that this committee cannot have been the Provisional Committee. Hobson stated categorically that the Provisional Committee knew nothing of MacNeill's caballing in the heavens until Redmond made his demands public. He incidentally expressed the opinion that MacNeill was a "straightforward honourable man incapable of deliberately deceiving anybody". Nine-tenths of his class are such. But it is second nature to them to treat the lives and interests of the lower orders as their personal property. Possibly the committee referred to was that entrusted with drafting the constitution and its members interpreted generously their terms of reference.

Objections being raised to Davitt, negotiations hung fire. The Redmondites resorted to veiled threats. They proposed to repeat their performance of 1898 when they took the centenary movement out of the hands of those who initiated it and whom they had constantly abused for doing so. They swore from each well-thumped thorax that they alone were the true embodiment of the Volunteer spirit. Were not theirs the secret hands that had edged its foundation? And their reward? Upstarts were trying to use the Volunteers against Home Rule. As in the lock-out the main concern of the Redmondites was to thwart the popular movement. They had displayed their inability to carry the revolution even one step forward.

In the first week of June their members flooded into Dublin. Their formidable apparatus of publicity was set in motion to claim and capture the Volunteers. MacNeill was now political jelly. He was still shivering when on 10th June appeared Redmond's ultimatum to the "self-elected" men who had striven and sacrificed to give Ireland a national army. They must accept twenty-five of his nominees on the Provisional Committee or he would establish a new Volunteer centre and call on all existing companies to break with MacNeill and affiliate to it.

Casement and MacNeill were without resource in this crisis. They concluded that the only "honourable course" was to resign, that is, to abandon the movement whose fortunes they had played with to the dangers they had brought on it. They would retire from public life and throw the responsibility on Redmond. This was the language of parliamentarianism, not of revolution. Colonel Moore on the other hand was for a stand. His experiences in Derry had opened his eyes to the potentialities of the common people. "Nowhere was the movement so spontaneous and democratic," he wrote. "It sprang from the very hearts and souls of the people of the town." In the surrounding districts, Strabane, Raphoe, Castlederg and Buncrana, where the land was not only owned but occupied by the children of settlers, landless men flocked to the Volunteer standard. He was also aware that in many places the United Irish League, *Sinn Fein* and Hibernians had formed their own companies, so that a split that disrupted the national movement might not necessarily break up the local organisations.

Hobson, who had somewhat carelessly allowed things to come to this pass, was in a quandary. He had just learned for the first time from Casement of the projected gun-running. While Casement and MacNeill were not essential to its success, would their friends think it worth while taking risks for any section of a divided movement? He felt he must act quickly and without time-wasting explanations. Thus he failed to consult his colleagues in the I.R.B., and enmeshed himself in the tangle that MacNeill had created. He proposed that

c

Redmond's twenty-five should be accepted under duress. But the members of the original committee should ensure that arms reached no units not believed loyal to the movement's stated aims. Thus a further element of intrigue was introduced.

The organising committee was swayed by Hobson's arguments. The Provisional Committee, whose members had up to now known nothing of what had been happening behind the scenes, was hastily summoned. They were confronted simultaneously with a confession of incompetent stewardship and a proposal for weakening their position as principals. The I.R.B. members were understandably incensed against Hobson. Pearse and MacDiarmada were for indignantly rejecting Redmond's proposals. Let him do his damnedest. Ceannt, Plunkett and Mellows supported them. Hobson spoke last. He urged acceptance on the basis he had outlined to MacNeill and Casement. His logic convinced two thirds of the Committee, the dissentients being the five above mentioned, together with Colbert, Beaslai, M. J. Judge, and Fitzgibbon.

A public statement was issued accepting Redmond's demand under protest for the sake of unity. The minority likewise published a statement indicating dissent, but advising against the creation of further divisions. From this Mellows' name was omitted on account of his status as a full-time worker compelled to co-operate with the Redmondite nominees. The unity of the Volunteers was thus for the moment preserved, but at the expense of disunity in the I.R.B.

There were bitter recriminations. "How much did the Castle give you for doing that?" asked Tom Clarke. He and Hobson never spoke again. MacDiarmada was only less vehement. He would speak to Hobson, but was always cool. Pearse on the other hand, though he believed Hobson mistaken, never doubted his integrity. It would appear that since the foundation of the Volunteers had so broadened his sphere of action, Hobson can no longer have regarded the I.R.B. as the centre of the universe. He attended an emergency meeting of the Supreme Council from which he resigned, though he was under no necessity of doing so. He handed over the editorship of *Irish Freedom* to Sean Lester. He retained the position of Chairman of the Dublin Centres Board. Thus was created the basis of an "offensive" and a "defensive" faction within the I.R.B.

The disadvantages of Hobson's compromise were naturally more evident than the dangers which it avoided. Redmond's nominees, with such honourable exceptions as James Creed Meredith, were largely political rag-tag and bobtail. Their supreme ability was in composing expense accounts. But their arrival was taken as a signal. Throughout the country the "respectable classes" moved in to take up their natural position as leaders. Among those thus presenting themselves were the "moderate Unionist" Earl of Fingal, Lord Gormanstown, Lord Powerscourt and Captain Bryan Cooper. Even the Redmondites felt uneasy, though the newcomers willingly defended the Redmondites against the revolutionaries. From being an alliance of the Irish popular forces, the Volunteers were being transformed into a "unity of all classes and creeds" in which the landlords and upper bourgeoisie could hope for a commanding position.

The first arms landing was to have been made at Kilcoole on 25th July. Sean Fitzgibbon was in command on shore and Mellows was charged with supervising the disposal of the cargo. Eamon De Valera drove him out on his motorcycle combination. They were intercepted at the Scalp and told that the operation was postponed. Next day Childers brought his yacht *Asgard* into Howth where the landing was an outstanding success. Hobson was in charge. For several weeks the police had been accustomed to long route marches by Volunteers. They showed little interest when an exceptionally large force of Volunteers and *Fianna* moved off to Howth on 26th July.

A detachment under Cathal Brugha had been sent ahead to pose as tourists and protect the landing when it took place. The *Fianna* trek-cart was filled with stout staves turned down from pick-handles. Thanks to Childers's superb seamanship the yacht arrived exactly on time. Guns were distributed to Volunteers. Boxes of ammunition took the place of the staves in the trek-cart. The *Fianna*, as the only disciplined force that could be relied on, brought the ammunition back to Dublin.

On the way into the city, police and military offered resistance at Clontarf. A few rifles were seized, after being broken in the struggle. During a brief fracas during which revolver shots were fired, Mellows took some of De Valera's company to oppose the soldiers. A number of policemen mutinied and the forces of the Crown met with a total fiasco for which the Police Commissioner paid the price. That evening the Scottish Borderers fired on an unarmed crowd at Bachelors Walk, and public indignation knew no bounds. In the small hours of the night of 1st August De Valera once more drove Mellows to Kilcoole. Both Hobson and Fitzgibbon were present. The guns were loaded on to a charabanc which broke an axle at Bray at 5 a.m. A fleet of taxis was summoned from Dublin and the arms were brought in. For several days Mellows was busy distributing them. Soon the Redmondites discovered that the landing they had had nothing to do with had brought them nothing. Rumour had it that rifles had been hidden at Kimmage where the Plunkett family had property. Joseph Plunkett was subjected to a gruelling cross-examination at the enlarged committee, but kept his head and the guns.

Next day the long-expected European war broke out. Britain entered into hostilities with Germany on 4th August. To a later generation it was the day the old world ended. But of course the war was but a continuation of the politics that had given rise to it, and all component aspects developed after their own nature. In the Commons, Redmond offered the government unconditional support, and invited Britain to withdraw all her armed forces from Ireland which would be defended by Volunteers. Sir Horace Plunkett and Colonel Moore produced a plan for which they claimed official inspiration. The Volunteers would be mobilised and held in barracks on police duties. Moore had discussions with General Paget and rumours of "War Office control" flew through the ranks.

Representatives of Dublin companies lobbied the Committee room demanding assurances that there would be no fighting Britain's battles. The augmented committee was split into warring factions. Each meeting was more acrimonious than the last, and particularly trying to Mellows whose brother Frederick was in the final stages of the tuberculosis from which he died on 23rd August. A stable, earnest character, he was much closer to Liam than the vivacious Barney.

Day by day the possibility of a break increased. The British authorities decided to take no risks. On 15th August Volunteer premises throughout the nationalist areas of Ireland were raided by armed police and troops seeking Howth and Kilcoole rifles. It seems hardly likely that Redmond had no hint of what was afoot, though it is certainly possible. Lord Kitchener sent Major-General Sir Bryan Mahon on a tour of Ireland to report on the condition of the Volunteers. It is said that when the report reached him he did not trouble to open it. The Germans had crossed into northern France. He wanted soldiers, he said, not territorials.

While Redmond toyed with the notion of offering the Volunteers for continental service, but held his hand till the Home Rule Act was finally on the Statute Book, his landlord allies had less delicacy. Lord Powerscourt was with difficulty restrained from presenting a local company with a mammoth Union Jack. There were uneasy whispers of "recruiting". But there was also misplaced enthusiasm. People said, "we have gone back hundreds of years and the landlords are leading the people". Lord Dunsany, the Earl of Fingal and others were reviewing parades.

The Home Rule Act "became law" on 18th September. Passed simultaneously was a "Suspensory Act" providing that it did not "become law" at all. Nor could it do so until Parliament passed a third Act releasing it from suspension. This solemn humbug was thought good enough for Redmond, and appears to have been sufficient. On 20th September he made a speech at Woodenbridge advising Irishmen to fight "wherever the firing line extends". The loosely talked of amalgamation of Irish Volunteers and Ulster Volunteers now looked like being accomplished in the only place where it ever had the remotest possibility of being accomplished, in the British Army.

At the next meeting of the enlarged Committee it was clear from the start that the breach had come. Nugent picked on Pearse whom he repeatedly called a "contemptible cur", before working himself up to strike him. There was pandemonium in which revolvers were produced. Piaras Beaslai was challenging Nugent to a duel when his colleagues hustled him through the door. A brief emergency meeting was held. On 25th September members of the Provisional Committee seized the Volunteer offices by main force, the Citizen Army standing by in case of resistance, and control reverted to where it belonged. On the day that the landlords were driven out of the national movement the working class had been brought in. A manifesto repudiating Redmond was issued. Bulmer Hobson became General Secretary of the Volunteers and Mellows retained his position as secretary to the Committee.

In this capacity he summoned the meeting of 28th September at which a first estimate of the effect of the split was made. The Provisional Committee was strongest in Dublin, but telegrams of support had come from Belfast, Cork City, Sligo, Gorey, Mitchelstown, Birr, Magherafelt, Ballinagh, Glaslough and Liverpool. It was decided to call a convention of country delegates on 25th October. As this was being prepared other messages arrived. Three out of four Galway companies adhered to the original committee. From Athenry Eamonn Corbett forwarded a resolution proposed by Stephen Jordan and seconded by Fitzpatrick. The *Fianna* Convention took place on 11th October. Mellows and his friends had no difficulty in winning unanimous support.

The Redmondites canvassed hastily for the "National Volunteers" as they now described them, men they were leading into the holocaust.

They are said to have helped to persuade the *Enniscorthy Echo* to discontinue printing the *Irish Volunteer*, which Larry de Lacey was editing. Members of the Provisional Committee visited outlying companies exhorting, answering, reasoning, strengthening the committed. Mellows was sent to Athenry and brought back an encouraging report.

At the convention the total position was disclosed. Out of a previous membership of 168,000 Redmond had taken 156,000. But his forces were rapidly wasting, into the British Army and into the apathy of disgust. Hobson believed his policy was now justified by events. He thought Redmond would have taken an even more substantial section in the month of June. Clarke and MacDiarmada disagreed. They considered that the capitulation had given Redmond the blessing of the physical force party and enabled him to confuse its adherents.

What did the experiences of 1914 show? A precondition of the course events took was the policy of the Liberal Government. Its preoccupation with Ireland arose from Redmond's holding the balance of power in Parliament. Its deeper interest was the preparation of the imperialist war and suppression of the "great unrest" which had stirred Britain since it took office. Having been compelled to promise Home Rule as a condition of survival it permitted Carson to build up his counter-revolutionary army and dragoon Belfast into quiescence. Once this had happened the Parliamentary balance held by Redmond was replaced by an extra-Parliamentary balance held by Asquith. The Unionist leaders openly boasted of their illegalities, their conspiracy, gun-running and breaches of the peace. Nobody was prosecuted. That would restore the old balance of power. The founding of the Volunteers moved in the same direction. They must have no arms. Thus Redmond was forced back step by step while those he represented fought the workers of Dublin who alone could have given him the means to resist.

It was nevertheless remarkable that the authority that had imposed 105 Coercion Acts to protect the Union now proclaimed that no matter what illegalities the gentlemen who arrogated to themselves the title "Ulster" committed, they must not be "coerced". "Ulster" was of course illegally defending the Union which the government had unwillingly consented to relax. The coercion of those who were defying Parliament was the government's duty. Once Redmond permitted it to escape its responsibilities by consenting to discuss partition, he was powerless against the machinations of Lloyd George, a scoundrel without even the excuse of aristocracy.

Within Ireland it had been argued that the opportunity of 1782 had recurred. History can be a misleading mentor if it is imagined that the same situation ever occurs twice. The parallel depends on the fallacy, already noted, of regarding the Ulster Volunteers as an Irish National body. As well equate the Peep-o-Day boys with the Defenders, or Hitler's stormtroopers with the French *maquis*. The tragedy was that the British Labour movement was not advanced enough to compel Asquith to do his duty, to suppress the Orange bands and enforce Home Rule.

The astonishing feature of 1914 was the rapid emergence of the class character of revolution. In less than a year there took place developments whose equivalent occupied the whole decade 1782–93. "The landlords led the people" for six weeks. Their combination with the upper bourgeoisie contrived to do so for three uneasy months. The dream of Irish military independence legitimised by Britain survived for six and that of amalgamating with the Northern counter-revolutionaries for ten. The Irish revolution was to be plebeian now as ever. The gentry who supported the imperialist war went their own way. The working class who through the voices of Connolly and Larkin denounced the war and demanded Irish neutrality were recognised as one of the safeguards of the revolution.

This was further shown by the class composition of those Volunteers who remained faithful to the original committee. In Dublin county 3,300 out of 3,500 went over to Redmond. In Dublin City the men who had starved with Larkin were not going soldiering with Kitchener. The Provisional Committee held 1,103 out of 2,375, nearly half the total strength.

The Volunteer Convention was a business-like affair. Over a hundred delegates attended. An important decision was to appoint provincial instructors with the task of rebuilding the organisation as a mass movement. The first of these to be appointed was Mellows. After his election to the Executive Committee, he was asked to take responsibility for south Galway immediately. He accepted, the more readily since relations at home had become strained. Old Sergeant Mellows had hoped to see his boys with commissions in the British Army, breaking through that class barrier at which three generations had stalled. On 31st October Mellows left the Volunteer office and installed himself at Athenry.

CHAPTER FOUR

AWAKENING THE WEST

THE officer in charge in Athenry was Larry Lardener, who kept a small bar in the centre of the town. He secured accommodation for Mellows at Mrs. Broderick's boarding house where the less substantial commercial folk used to stay during fairs and other special events. At first Mellows found south Galway harsh and repelent with its damp skies and grey stone walls. After a time he yielded to the fascination of a varied and historic landscape which he came to know in intimate detail.

The region consists of low undulating country bounded by the sea on the west and the Aughty mountains in the south, while on the north and east it merges into the plains of east Galway that extend from the great lakes to the Suck. It is a country studded with ruins. Every square mile seems to have its castle, which except for the more elaborate edifice at Athenry consists simply of a rectangular keep surmounted by a look-out post. It was thus formerly a land of small potentates. But these had been replaced by large landlords alongside whom survived a mass of small holdings.

Statistics for south Galway alone are not available. The averages for the whole county will not, however, be far out. The area occupied by holdings of from fifteen to thirty acres in 1912 was 204,435 acres. Land in holdings of above 500 acres amounted to 286,839 acres. Yet the smaller holdings had fourteen times as much land in corn, fifteen times as much in roots and greens, carried twelve times as many milch cows, thirty times as many pigs, twenty times as much poultry and one-and-a-half times the number of sheep. The area of pasture land on the two types of holding was approximately equal, that on the large farms being 101,792 acres, and that on the small 93,642. The large farms carried only one-and-a-quarter times as many cattle over two years old as the small farms, and had no less than 179,679 acres which were put to no agricultural use at all. While much of this land would be barren mountain suitable only for hunting, shooting and fishing, the unutilised land on the small farms amounted to only 35,795 acres.[1]

[1] By way of contrast, in County Wexford the greatest area of land was distributed in medium holdings of 50–100 acres, only one-twentieth of their area being comprised in holdings of over 500 acres. In every product the medium farms were supreme and there was little land hunger.

Two classes of landholders were thus ranged in conflict. Land hunger was acute, and became increasingly so when emigration declined at the very time the Land Commission halted its work for the war.

Old walled Athenry, with twisting streets beneath its imposing castle and abbey, was the point where peasant struggles invaded the town. In 1907 the Lambert Estate came up for division. Patrick Hynes, a local builder and Fenian veteran, led an agitation for the inclusion of the town tenancies in the sale, as was possible under the Wyndham Act. There was dissatisfaction over the way the Act was being applied. Poor men were being given poor land, often without stock, which they were frequently forced to let as grazing to shopkeepers. Tenants whose houses were bought over their heads were given rent increases at a time when rents were already outstripping capacity to pay. The Town Tenants' League canalised discontent. At one tenants' meeting a landlord was compelled to attend in person and agree publicly to reduce a rent from 3s. to 2s. 6d. a week. The organisation assumed quasi-judicial functions.

Townsmen joined the countrymen in cattle-driving and wall-breaking. In May 1907, near Castle Ellen, William Ruhan and Stephen Jordan were arrested. In July P. J. Kelly, J.P., Chairman of Loughrea Rural District Council, was arrested for incitement to violence against Lord Ashtown at Carrabane, New Inn. As a result of the unity that was established between small farmers and town workers and artisans, town tenants were given small holdings when estates were broken up, and more favourable terms were won for all. At the same time, as the editor of the *Western News* ruefully remarked, the militancy that developed at Athenry pushed up wages in that town to 15s. and 17s. 6d. a week against the 12s. 6d. accepted in the larger centre of Ballinasloe.

In Galway the I.R.B. members were permitted to participate in illegal agrarian ("moonlighting") operations. This decision arose from disturbances near Craughwell in which a policeman named Byrne was shot. The I.R.B. in Loughrea, with the notable exceptions of the old Fenians Flynn and O'Flaherty, inclined to the Redmondite party and condemned "direct action" while not invariably practising what they preached. One of the members, Thomas Kenny, who was involved in the shooting incident, visited Dublin and persuaded Sean MacDiarmada to sanction taking part in agrarian struggles. The result was a split in the Loughrea organisation. MacDiarmada visited the town in 1910, could secure no agreement, and though Loughrea had been the great revolutionary centre in Land League days, he found it necessary to establish a new County Centre at Athenry. Here the merging of national and social struggles had created an excellent organisation having close links with the people of the district.

The County Centre, Richard Murphy, had built the Town Hall (i.e. the only hall in the town) which he let out for parish dances and political functions. The I.R.B. and the Volunteers had it free. When Mellows arrived a rifle range was set up in the yard where ·22 ammunition could be used. Apart from the routine clerical work of reporting on the strength and efficiency of established companies and setting up new ones, Mellows had to undertake periodical excursions outside the area. For example, when it was deemed advisable to move an arms dump near Athlone he was sent to supervise on behalf of Headquarters and arranged some exercises. The country boys were not too pleased at a townsman's telling them how to scale walls or to shoot bull's eyes. They had shot birds and rabbits from childhood. Nor did they relish his proposal that the guns should be moved in daylight as a military operation, in defiance of the police. They admired his determination, but persuaded him to their own proposal, and enjoyed his good humour at the *ceili* which followed. From then on he used often to break his journey to Dublin at Athlone.

The winter months were spent in intensive training at Athenry. Mellows hoped to have a cadre of instructors available for the spring. The leading men were John Cleary, who had attended the Convention, Frank Hynes, a carpenter and son of the Fenian, Stephen Jordan, Jim Barrett, Sean Broderick, and the Commanding Officer of the battalion, Larry Lardner. Each night the company would meet in Murphy's hall, if not to drill or listen to a lecture, to talk politics and speculate about the day when the English would be driven out of Ireland. On fine days Mellows would cycle to townlands ten or fifteen miles away, making contacts with old Fenians and their sons, preparing the way for the establishment of new companies and recruiting into the I.R.B. When it was too wet he would prepare his reports and discuss politics in Larry Lardner's bar, all the time humming snatches of nationalist songs.

Slowly he built up an organisation in town and country. There was the old Fenian Michael Fleming in Clarenbridge, with his six stalwart sons, and Matthew Neilan, a schoolteacher recently returned from England. In Killeeneen there were Eamonn Corbett, George Newell and the Walsh family, at Ballychalan, near Gort, the indefatigable enthusiast Padhraic Fahy who would cycle twenty miles in the heaviest rain to take a Gaelic class. Near Craughwell was Pat Callanan, nicknamed "The Hare", not from any reputation for speed, but from having been introduced in court during some agrarian litigation as "my nephew and heir", the aitch being aspirated. Here also was Tom Kenny, one of the few who slightly resented the intrusion of the young Dublinman, a Gaelic Athletic Association enthusiast, inclined to leftism and strongly anticlerical. His views did not impede his collecting a shilling from each of his players before an "away" match so that the parish priest could be induced to say an extra Mass at 6.30 in the morning. He co-operated with Mellows with fair grace, but was not his uncritical admirer.

As a city man Mellows was naturally under a handicap which only the help he received from the I.R.B. could remove. "Where there's land there's trouble," runs the saw. It was necessary to consider family connections, family histories and family antagonisms. Part of his success was due to his youth and his infectious enthusiasm. A strict disciplinarian with a contempt for "sunshine soldiers", he would spot immediately the one man in twenty whose movement was executed a fraction of a second late. But once off duty he was the *Fianna* boy again, full of laughter, bad puns and practical jokes. His attitude to religion had something of the countryman's. He could secure the co-operation of the lower clergy in a wholly natural way. These were mostly sons of small farmers and together with the schoolteachers acted as the unpaid lawyers of the poorer classes. Several priests were Volunteer officers. These included Fr. Feeney of Clarenbridge and Fr. Meehan of Kinvara. Sometimes on his travels towards Dublin Mellows would break his journey to visit Fr. Connolly of Ballinasloe.

Throughout the winter the forces of the Volunteers were rebuilt as steadily as those of Redmond dwindled. Monteith was sent to organise in County Limerick, Ernest Blythe in County Kerry. A military strategy was emerging which a section of the I.R.B. leadership must already have been planning. Arms were to be landed in Kerry and distributed by means of the north–south railway line which cuts the Dublin lines at Limerick and Athenry. The Rising in Dublin, still only in the thoughts of the few, was to be seconded by an insurrection in the west.

By spring Mellows had succeeded in training his instructors. It was now possible to drill out of doors in the fields, though discretion was becoming desirable. A great rally of County Galway Volunteers took place in Galway City on St. Patrick's Day. Soon there were companies drilling in Kinvara, Gort, Killeeneen and Clarenbridge. Consideration was being given to organising east Galway when early in May Sean MacDiarmada arrived to conduct the Divisional Elections of the I.R.B. Mellows met him at Tuam where the small group of

Fianna boys under Liam Langley had withstood the Redmondite onslaught and were trying to revive the Volunteers. In their number
were included the three brothers Connolly, all blacksmiths, the Stock-
wells, descended from tradesmen brought from England for the
building of the cathedral, Willie Cannon, Jim Malony and Brown of
the I.R.B.

It was decided to hold an anti-enlistment meeting after Mass one
Sunday in May and to seek recruits for the Volunteers. Liam Langley,
MacDiarmada and Mellows mounted a brake and MacDiarmada
left no doubt of his opposition to enlistment. Volunteer literature was
distributed and there was loud applause when he got down. This
changed to boos when Inspector Comerford stepped forward to
arrest him. He slipped his automatic to Mellows on the pretence of
shaking hands.

Mellows continued the meeting. While reading out the Volunteer
oath he turned over in his mind the possible results of MacDiarmada's
being searched. The list of I.R.B. Centres was in a notebook in his
pocket. He continued speaking awhile and to his surprise brought the
meeting to a conclusion without further interference. He then suggested to Langley that they should visit MacDiarmada at the barracks.
A policeman let them in. "He's in there," he told them. They found
him sitting between two policemen on a wooden form before a roaring
fire. Soon all four were laughing and talking. On the pretext of making
a spill to light his pipe from the fire Mellows secured the I.R.B. list
from MacDiarmada's notebook and quickly converted it to ashes.

MacDiarmada was taken to Dublin on the 3.20 train and after a
series of remands was sentenced to six months' imprisonment. He and
Clarke were in close touch with Connolly and possibly his arrest postponed the agreement between the I.R.B. and the Citizen Army by
many months. MacDiarmada was replaced by Diarmuid Lynch, a
man without social ideas. He arrived in Athenry a few days later in
order to conduct the election. Mellows reported to Dublin, returning
to Athenry unnoticed by the police by the device of mingling with the
Geraldine hurling team who were playing at Athenry on Whit
Sunday.

At the beginning of June, Mellows was satisfied that south Galway
could stand on its own feet and turned his attention to the east of the
county. He chose Mullagh, a renowned Gaelic Athletic Association
centre, as his headquarters and spent four days with the Mannion
family. After a brief interlude at Athenry, he then spent a fortnight
with the Garvies. He made contacts at Ballinasloe, Clonfert, Ahas-

cragh, and as far north as Ballygar. But on the whole the campaign was a failure, possibly from the absence of a tradition of unity of town and country in the neighbourhood of Ballinasloe.

He resolved on more intensive organisation in the South. A site for a training camp was found at Kynoch's Fort at Ballycahalan, near Gort. He and Stephen Jordan took out the parts of a large tent divided between their two bicycles. A company was established at neighbouring Derrybrien. But Mellows had further intentions. From all the companies in south Galway selected men were brought one by one into the tent and sworn into the I.R.B. Larry Garvie attended that night, and "Sonny Morrissey" whose sister Julia founded the *Cumann na mBan* in Athenry.

Since the Tuam incident the police had been paying more attention to Mellows. Many were the tricks he played on them—riding off in full regalia as if to a Volunteer meeting, and then doubling back into town by a side road, or riding ostentatiously to Frank Hynes' house, taking the bicycle inside, and dropping it over the back wall into the fields behind, while they waited at the front. It is stated that the District Inspector gave orders to his men that "that man Mellows must not be left out of their sight". One of the route marches from Ballycahalan was accompanied by forty-seven R.I.C. men.

On 10th July General Friend signed an order that Mellows must forthwith leave for England. This was served on him at Broderick's on the evening of the 11th. Francis Fahy and his wife were present, having cycled over from Loughrea where they were beginning their holiday. They agreed to look after Ballycahalan and Mellows left for Dublin as if to comply with the order. Once there he found that three other prominent Volunteer leaders had been served with similar orders, Ernest Blythe, Denis McCullogh and H. M. Pim. All these had refused to comply and had been imprisoned.

Relations with his father had reached breaking point and his mother concealed his presence in the house when she fed him late at night. After a day or two in Dublin he left for Wexford, staying at Condon's at Monalug, and then with Sean Etchingham in Courtown Harbour. Here he was arrested a week after he was due to have left Ireland, and on 30th July he was sentenced to three months' imprisonment, which he served in Mountjoy with MacDiarmada. He used to receive visits from his mother and his first cousin Rita Whitmore.

The routine of prison life at this period was described by another prisoner, Sean Milroy, in his somewhat prolix pamphlet *Memories of Mountjoy*. At this stage the category of "political prisoner" was not yet firmly established. Mellows lightened the monotony as far as was possible with his punning and play-acting. But three "politicals" in a whole prison could do little more. The effect of the sentences was simultaneously to transfer sympathy from the Redmondites to the Volunteers, and to strengthen the party of the offensive within them. It was now that Connolly began to acquire his ascendancy over Pearse and Clarke. Gradually in the minds of these men the previous conception of an insurrection conditional on conscription, an attempt by the authorities to disarm the Volunteers, or a German landing, gave way to that of an unconditional uprising which would anticipate these things. Connolly demanded openly the replacement of MacNeill and an end to the waiting policy.

In this he was almost certainly premature. There were signs of a a specious war-prosperity in the country. If rents were rising so were wages and employment. The old grievances burned as fiercely as ever, but the fuel was being redistributed. Even the rumours of conscription meant little as yet. In the first six months of 1915 only 4,061 persons emigrated as against 12,909 for the corresponding period of the previous year. The total enlistment in Ireland during the first year of the war amounted to about 75,000. Thus not a half of Redmond's Volunteers had yet enlisted for overseas service. Talk of conscription was merely a form of official encouragement. The war had dispersed the old revolutionary front without yet realigning the enemies of imperialism on its own special historical basis. The trend of the offensivist faction was a natural response to these conditions. Doubting their ability to make use of a conscription crisis if it swept suddenly upon them they began to think increasingly in terms of choosing their own time. Their great fear was that the war would end with a contented nation, and when the aftermath brought its penalties, Britain would be at peace, and everything too late.

Mellows was released in time for the Annual Convention of the Volunteers on 31st October. Once more he was elected to the Central Council. His health had suffered from the prison diet of barley chaff and black cocoa. But after a brief rest he resumed his duties in County Galway. He was now a popular hero. On 23rd November a great Volunteer rally assembled at Athenry to greet him. Joseph O'Flaherty took the chair. The main speakers were The O'Rahilly, Lawrence Ginnell, M.P., Fr. Connolly of Ballinasloe, Fr. Meehan and Fr. Feeney. At this gathering Mellows was presented with a motor-cycle which he thereafter used for his longer journeys, but soon discarded for local purposes. Motor-cycles were rare in those days and the sound of back-firing across the fields saved the police much trouble. It was now that he went to live with Frank Hynes.

When Sean MacDiarmada was released shortly before Christmas he went with Tom Clarke to recuperate at John Daly's in Limerick. It seems possible that this was when the determination crystallised to fix a date for the Rising and to form an alliance with Connolly. A meeting of the Supreme Council of the I.R.B. was called in January 1916. A Military Committee was appointed and charged with preparing and leading an insurrection at an early date within its discretion. Agreement with Connolly was reached the following week. The day decided on was Easter Sunday, 23rd April. In the belief that it would be difficult to persuade MacNeill and Hobson to agree to an unconditional insurrection the Committee decided to keep them in ignorance. They would use Pearse's position as Director of Organisation to mobilise the forces and hope that once the die was cast nobody would withdraw. Connolly assented only after much hesitation, but thereafter became the leading spirit of the enterprise.

There is evidence that Mellows was now in periodic contact with Connolly. The *Workers' Republic*, now the common organiser of revolution, was distributed in south Galway from a shop in Gort. An exercise consisting of an attack on Clarenbridge bore some resemblance to the Citizen Army's mock attack on Dublin Castle. Anti-enlistment propaganda was sharply increased, especially after the arrival from County Cavan of Ailbhe O'Monnchain as Mellows' assistant. A Belfast man, but a fluent Irish speaker, he extended the campaign into Connemara, where Mark MacDonagh of Moycullen had been jailed for three months for "prejudicing recruiting". At Oranmore on 8th February the Clarenbridge Company held up the delivery van of a publican who had been trying to recruit Volunteers into the British Army. They let loose the horses and scattered broken whiskey bottles over the road. Two weeks later, while Mellows was making a last effort to organise Redmondite Loughrea, land agitation flared up again. In a felon-setting attack the *Connaught Tribune* traced all local disturbances to one fountain-head, Mellows the "*Sinn Fein* organiser".

Police attentions increased. At this time the Scottish Socialist papers had just been suppressed and the Glasgow shop stewards put behind bars. The anti-democratic nature of the war was slowly becoming understood. Since acquiring the motor-cycle Mellows had extended the area of his command eastward as far as Daingean in Offaly, and somewhat more loosely as far as Westport in the County Mayo. He

even visited Kesh in County Sligo to confer with Alec MacCabe. On
one occasion when riding to Tullamore to meet Peadar Bracken he
recognised two R.I.C. men on the roadside halfway between New Inn
and Kilconnell. They were in plain clothes. Guessing from their
demeanour that he might be intercepted on his way back, he noticed
a boreen leading to Woodlawn Station which he could use as a
diversion. On his return he saw masked men at the same spot, and
immediately turned right down the by-road. The two men guessed his
intention and ran the half-mile along the main road to meet the other
road from the station. One of them tried to pull him from the motor-
cycle but Mellows gave him his foot in the jaw before he came off.
The other decided not to try conclusions. The machine was damaged,
Mellows was badly bruised and shaken. A meeting at Killeeneen waited
for him in vain.

On Monday, 20th March, the first shots of the coming war were
fired at Tullamore. An Englishman named Dixon had distributed small
Union Jacks to a number of "separation women" and their children.
One or two Volunteers remonstrated and the result was an at first good
humoured but increasingly ugly baiting of Volunteers. One man had a
flag thrust into his face by a child, and losing patience, seized it and
broke it. He and his comrades retired to the Volunteer Hall, followed
by an angry crowd. The road was under repair about a hundred yards
away, with piles of fresh metal heaped on the sidewalk. A three-
wheeled newsagent's trolley was pushed to this point and loaded with
large stones which were brought back and used on the Volunteer Hall
windows. Soon an upper window opened. A rifle appeared and a shot
was fired over the heads of the crowd, shattering the plate-glass
window of Melville's store. Police broke into the premises, the
Volunteers retreating upstairs. A catwalk to neighbouring premises
was constructed from a few planks, and the Volunteers escaped, but
not before two policemen had been wounded by Peadar Bracken who
was holding the stairway. He and Seamus Brennan escaped by motor-
cycle to Dublin where they joined the London and Liverpool Volunteers quartered in Plunkett's old mill at Kimmage waiting for the
Easter "manœuvres".

The next issue of the *Workers' Republic*, dated 25th March but
published on Thursday 23rd, contained a letter from Mellows addressed
to "Mr. Connolly" and signed "Liam". Since the paper was printed
on Wednesday evening, Mellows must have visited Tullamore the
day after the fracas and posted his letter to Connolly at once. Several
eye-witnesses testified to the firing of live ammunition, but Mellows

insisted that the Volunteers had fired only blanks. His object may have been to protect Brennan and Bracken. The letter also referred to the hostility of some Gaelic Athletic Association members to the Volunteers and warned of the danger that the G.A.A. might fall into imperialist hands.

Mellows returned to Athenry. He was left in peace three days. On Friday evening he was arrested in the house of Julia Morrissey, taken to Dublin by the night train and lodged in Arbour Hill. There was no charge and no trial. But he was allowed to write letters including one to Padhraic[1] Fahy asking him to take over the work in Offaly, which on Headquarters' advice he did not do. At about midday on Saturday Mellows saw Ernest Blythe, but was whisked away before he could speak to him. He was told that he was to be transported to England, and while the protest meetings filled the halls and streets of Dublin, and were made the occasion of much recruiting both to the Volunteers and the Citizen Army, he was allowed to select a place of residence. He chose Leek.

Probably through his brother, he conveyed news of his intentions to MacDiarmada who immediately consulted Connolly. Connolly sent his daughter Nora with Barney to Belfast on 1st April. At a small country cottage the Connollys rented Barney practised disguising himself as Liam and the final result deceived even Mrs. Connolly. Nora and he crossed to Glasgow on the Saturday night. At Edinburgh the night train they were taking for Manchester was delayed by the Zeppelin raids of 2nd and 3rd April,[2] and by Tuesday they were staying with I.R.B. members in Birmingham, awaiting news that the transportation had been carried out.

Taken to Holyhead under army escort, and exchanging half-frivolous half-serious chaff with the officers, Mellows was allowed to proceed to Leek on his own. His sole baggage was his fiddle and he was sitting in the small living room at 10 Rosebank Street when John Morgan returned from work. The family were delighted to see him, even when he explained that he must periodically report to the police.

He entertained them particularly by singing "Lord Waterford is dead" (a parody on the *Shan Van Vocht*) and played the old Kilkenny airs on his fiddle. Next day the Morgans took him to Rudyard Lake. On Sunday, which was Passion Sunday, there was Mass and the Stations of the Cross, after which all repaired to the Park Hotel,

[1] Padhraic (Padraig with a mark of aspiration over the d) is the Connacht form of Patrick and pronounced approximately Pawric. Padraig (with unaspirated d) pronounced Pahdric, is the form used in Ulster and Munster.
[2] The date is ascertained thanks to these raids.

kept by the church organist. In the midst of the drinking and talking a message came, "Bertie's here". Liam was up in a flash. Barney asked for the use of John Morgan's bedroom for a private talk. The brothers changed clothes and a few minutes later, after somebody had left by the front door, Barney announced he was taking Liam's place. "Till tomorrow morning," said Morgan senior.

In a taxi near the centre of the town was Nora Connolly. With her Liam drove back to Birmingham. Next day they were in Glasgow where Fr. Courtney from County Kerry provided Mellows with clerical garments a few sizes too big for him. Escape was facilitated by a strike on the cross-channel steamers from Liverpool, Fleetwood, Heysham and Stranraer. An exceptionally heavy burden fell on the Glasgow service. Police and harbour officials at Belfast were hampered by congestion. Accustomed to poorly dressed young priests from Scotland they let Mellows pass without question. He stayed at Connolly's house at Glenalina Terrace while Denis McCullough arranged transport to Dublin and Nora Connolly sought clerical garments of a better fit.

Dr. McKee, a friend of McCullough's, agreed to take Mellows to Dublin. They left on Wednesday evening, stopped overnight in Banbridge at the house of Dr. McNabb, and using McNabb's car and accompanied by Winifred Carney, James Connolly's secretary, motored to Dublin on the Thursday. Mellows was set down beside Phoenix Park. From there he walked to Frank Fahy's at Islandbridge, seeming rather crestfallen when Mrs. Fahy at once recognised him through his disguise. That evening Con Colbert and other *Fianna* boys called and there was a pillow fight.

According to Mrs. Fahy he remained at Islandbridge for about three days. She had the impression that he left for Wexford. A flying visit is conceivable, but he was at St. Enda's with Pearse on Tuesday[1] night and probably already on Monday when Eamonn Corbett came from Galway to a meeting which discussed the plans for the west. They were based on the simple strategy of keeping English garrisons occupied on the far side of the Shannon while an effort was made to gain control of the capital.

The main supplies of arms and ammunition were thus retained in Dublin. But the consignment which Casement and Monteith were accompanying from Germany, and which could hardly be brought to

---

[1] He may well have arrived at Scoil Eanna on Sunday. According to Desmond Ryan, who described the laughter when some of the pupils penetrated his disguise, he left on Thursday, 20th April. But I have given greater weight to evidence that he was in County Galway on the evening of Wednesday, 19th April.

Dublin after the insurrection had begun, was earmarked for the west. The arms were to be landed at Fenit in Co. Kerry. A train was to be seized and brought up to Limerick. While Volunteers kept the garrison busy in the city it was to be partially unloaded, and then brought round the Ballysimon loop for Ennis and Gort.

At Gort the south Galway companies were to assemble, receive their arms and begin the Rising. After destroying communications in the area east of Galway city they were to move on the Shannon, with Portumna as the main objective, and ultimately, if conditions were favourable, cross the river and proceed towards Dublin.

There were, of course, serious difficulties. Administrative control of the Volunteers rested with MacNeill and Hobson. Even though a member of the I.R.B. Hobson was kept in the dark about the plans of the Military Committee, though he was gradually led to suspect them. There was also a political difficulty. There was no policy for Ulster. When McCullough came from Belfast for orders he was instructed to muster the Belfast Volunteers at Coalisland. Thence he must march a hundred miles across country to join up with Mellows. That this was seriously intended appears from dispositions made in County Cavan. "What about the North?" asked McCullough. Not a shot was to be fired. "If we are successful we'll deal with the North later," was the reply. This raises the question of what was meant by the word "success".

On Spy Wednesday Mellows was taken west on the pillion of a motor-cyclist named Lyons. They followed a circuitous route calling first at Mrs. Malone's at Tyrrellspass, then crossing the Shannon at Banagher to come to Mannion's at Mullagh. Here Mellows found his motor-cycle. Eamonn Corbett had deposited it there after a breakdown, and had borrowed the only bicycle in the house to get back to Athenry.

Mannion found Mellows some passable layman's clothes, not an easy matter in a country of well-built men, and borrowed a neighbour's bicycle on which Mellows rode to Loughrea next night. Leaving the bicycle at Sweeney's he stayed with Joseph O'Flaherty. Good Friday being a fair day, Mannion drove his cattle into town in the morning and after selling them rode back on the neighbour's bicycle as he had undertaken to do. Mellows was thus once more without transport and though Killeeneen, his destination, was within two and a half hours walking distance, he considered it unwise to spend so much time alone on the road. During Friday O'Flaherty contrived to make contact with Corbett, who sent George Newell from Killeeneen with a bicycle party to Kilchreest. These took turns to carry Mellows on their crossbars to Rahasane whence he could cross the Dunkellin River to Killeeneen. Early on Saturday morning he was installed in Mrs. Walsh's cottage beside the schoolhouse. Here he found the uniform which had been sent by rail from Dublin on Wednesday and had been collected by Corbett and Padhraic Fahy after the Gaelic class at Athenry.

CHAPTER FIVE

THE WEST'S AWAKE

MELLOWS was not anxious to advertise his presence at Killeeneen. He issued no orders and called for no reports that did not come his way. Nevertheless reports of his arrival spread immediately. Good and bad news intermingled. Ailbhe O'Monnchain had been served with a deportation order on the day that Mellows was arrested. Fr. Feeney had found a man who superficially resembled him and dressed him in clerical garb. He had taken him to O'Monnchain's lodgings at No. 1 Francis Street, Galway. There they changed clothes and O'Monnchain walked out unrecognised. Neilan took him to stay with the O'Higgins family at Derrydonnell three miles from Athenry. Mellows' right-hand man was thus at liberty. But news of the divisions in Dublin was already causing confusion in the west.

Corbett had reported to Lardner on the St. Enda's meeting. He explained that a gun-running next Sunday was to be converted into an insurrection. Lardner's previous instructions were that the code for an insurrection would be sent from Dublin. The agreed message was "collect the premiums" and he refused to act without it. Orders issued from Hobson's office on Tuesday seemed incompatible with the St. Enda's decisions. Lardner's suspicions increased and he called a meeting of officers at Fr. Feeney's house. Corbett, Peter Howley, Padhraic Fahy and Matthew Neilan were present and it was decided that Lardner should go to Dublin on Thursday and request clear instructions from MacNeill and Pearse.

He went, but neither MacNeill nor Pearse were to be found. Hobson gave him strict instructions that no orders were to be obeyed without MacNeill's signature. This was Lardner's first intimation of divisions in the Dublin leadership, and he returned to Galway disheartened. Meanwhile Mrs. Frank Fahy had brought him a message given her by Eamonn Ceannt, and had waited all day at Athenry before giving it to Corbett. Lardner tore open the envelope and read "Collect the Premiums 7 p.m. Sunday—P. H. Pearse."

Next day came a message from MacNeill quite incompatible with Pearse's orders, and seemingly suspending the manœuvres. A meeting was held in Galway City at the house of George Nicholls, a solicitor who was a member of the I.R.B. Among those present were Fr. Feeney, Lardner, Joseph Howley of Oranmore, Padhraic Fahy, Patrick Callanan and Eamonn Corbett. There was a long discussion over the conflicting orders. MacNeill was the titular head of the Volunteers. Pearse was the leader nominated by the I.R.B. Presumably Corbett reported that Mellows was returning to Galway. He may not have known his whereabouts. Fahy urged that Pearse's orders should be adhered to. Nicholls spoke with forced bravery, "We'll go out, then, although we'll all be slaughtered." In the end it was decided to despatch a printer named Hosty to Dublin in a further effort to secure clarification. Meanwhile preparations were to be based on Pearse's orders.

Hosty was of course no more successful than Lardner. The two factions in Dublin were locked in a battle of wits. Country officers seeking explanations had alerted Hobson and J. J. O'Connell in the Volunteer office to the dangers of an army within an army. Some incautious word dropped at a meeting gave them a basis for action and they called on MacNeill late on Thursday evening. The suave professor was transformed temporarily into a man-eating tiger. Forgetting about his long lonely intrigues with the Redmondites he insisted on calling at St. Enda's where he charged Pearse with shameful duplicity and scandalous behaviour. Pearse admitted and tried to justify the deception. MacNeill and his companions departed. They wrote orders forbidding military action by the Volunteers. How many of these were despatched is not known. At 8 a.m. on Good Friday Pearse called on MacNeill bringing with him MacDiarmada and MacDonagh. They discussed the plan for an arms landing and secured his agreement to hold his hand for the present. To deprive him of his mainstay they had Hobson kidnapped that afternoon. But at night came news of the disaster in Kerry. The landing had failed and Casement was a prisoner. When this news became generally known next morning the offensivist and defensivist factions were transformed into a war party and a peace party. The war party sought to convince MacNeill that the die was cast. With no Hobson to lean on he turned to such moderates as Griffith. With their aid on Saturday he found the decision to call the whole thing off.

There was nothing for Hosty while this was going on.

MacNeill could send no couriers till Sunday morning. Some might fail to reach their destination in time. He therefore cycled into town from Dundrum and inserted an advertisement in the *Sunday Independent*, "Volunteers completely deceived. All orders for Sunday cancelled." In the castle the British authorities now debated the desirability of immediately suppressing the Volunteers. A position had been reached when a Rising could neither be prevented nor prove successful.

Desmond Ryan, who was close to Pearse throughout the last manœuvres, commented that he and Connolly were "prisoners of the formula that the lesson of Irish insurrections in the past was that 'the only failure is the failure to strike' ". Due consideration was not given to the principle that revolution is made by the masses or there is no revolution. But Connolly's great concern was lest the war should end without a blow for Irish freedom.

In Galway City the countermand was read in the morning papers. Elsewhere the Volunteers obeyed instructions to attend Communion on Sunday morning. Mellows learned what had happened on Sunday afternoon when Fr. Feeney and Eamonn Corbett arrived unexpectedly. They explained that a priest on a motor-cycle had brought a despatch from MacNeill to Athenry. This was the official countermand. Mellows ordered suspension of operations with extreme reluctance. He had come to the west in a mood to do or die. The difficulty was that it was impossible to know how far MacNeill was co-operating with the I.R.B. Things looked a little brighter in the evening when a further despatch came from Athenry to which it had been taken by a motor-cyclist named Egan. In it Pearse confirmed MacNeill's orders but instead of the word "cancelled" used "postponed". A reply was sent to the effect that Galway was always ready.

At about 1 p.m. on Easter Monday Lardner was standing by in Athenry with a group of officers. "I'm up the pole," he told Liam Langley who had arrived from Tuam for instructions. "Dublin is divided." A woman appeared. She proved to be Miss Elizabeth O'Farrell with a message which ran, "We are out from twelve o'clock today. Issue your orders without delay.—P.H.P." Three copies were to be forwarded, one to Mellows, a second to Nicholls and a third to the officer in charge of Cois Fharraige. Lardner had had his bellyful of countermands. He looked suspiciously at the new note. Instead of the usual "P. H. Pearse" it had only the initials. He guessed there was deliberate avoidance of a full signature. "It's that Liberty Hall crowd trying to stampede us," he declared and took no action. It is not even clear that he sent a copy to Mellows. The Dublin train arriving in the late afternoon brought definite information that the insurrection had begun.

Lardner despatched Neilan to Clarenbridge. He gave the despatch to one of the Flemings who hastened to Killeeneen, then alerted men at Kilcolgan and the surrounding districts. From Killeeneen came back orders for an immediate mobilisation at the schoolhouse. When Michael Fleming, the old Fenian, received the order he was eating his evening meal. He and his six sons got up with no more than a word and filed out into the rain. Soon Killeeneen schoolhouse was full of Volunteers and the newcomers were distributed in houses throughout the townland.

As the men arrived the officers conferred in Mrs. Walsh's kitchen. The original plan was in ruins, and some alternative must be found. It was easy to cut the telegraph wires at Craughwell and Athenry and to tear up rails on the Galway–Dublin line. British forces were thus immobilised at Galway. But what next? Messengers were sent to mobilise outlying districts. Patrick Callanan made for Cois Fharraige to endeavour to engage the city on the far side. Padhraic Fahy was despatched to Kinvara where Fr. Meehan had a strong company. The original intention had been to hold a big rally at Gort where the guns would be unloaded. Some recollection of this may have persisted. The Ardrahan and Ballycahalan companies were ordered to invest Gort from the other side. But around daybreak, when the officers were still discussing, Fahy's three companions returned somewhat disconsolate. Kinvara was full of strange policemen. Padhraic Fahy had been over-powered by a group of them as he left the priest's gate. The three men who were still in the car escaped with some difficulty to give the alarm.

It required this misfortune to galvanise Mellows to action. 'We must get somebody for poor Padhraic," he declared. It was expected that he would be taken by road to Galway Jail. It was proposed there-fore to occupy Clarenbridge and ambush the police as they took their prisoner through. Mellows took his men from Killeeneen along the Boherdoorogy to the cross just before Toberbracken. Turning left through the Headington Estate he emerged on the Galway road just south of Clarenbridge. Here the long overhanging boughs of a beech were lopped to make a four foot barricade to perform the double function of halting the party with the prisoner and holding off police from Kilcolgan while Clarenbridge was taken. Unfortunately, how-ever, Clare had not risen and Fahy was taken instead to Limerick.

Once the barricade was thrown up Mellows detailed men for the village. Four of them were to take the police barracks.[1] It was situated on one side of the triangle of streets beside the old Dublin road. The garrison consisted only of seven unarmed men. Mellows expected an

[1] Now disused and renamed Rose Cottage.

immediate surrender. A very old R.I.C. man answered the thunderous knocking. Told to put up his hands he obeyed with alacrity. Then in the excitement of a first engagement one of the Volunteers fumbled with his gun and fired in the air. There was a sudden wave of confusion in which the old man slammed the door and got safely upstairs. The insurgents then prepared canister bombs to blast a way into the building. But Fr. Tully, the parish priest, appeared from the church opposite and begged Mellows to avoid bloodshed in Clarenbridge. In view of assurances that the police were unarmed, he agreed. Honour had to be satisfied with the capture of four peelers from Kilcolgan who were stopped at the barricade and taken prisoner.

Realising now that Fahy was not coming, Mellows decided to make for Athenry where he could join up with Lardner. To take the direct road to Derrydonnell would be to leave the important barracks at Oranmore on his flank. A march of three miles brought him to this strategic road junction at the extreme north-east corner of Galway Bay. This time the barracks was attacked in good earnest. Explosives were being placed beneath the small bridge just north of the village when police reinforcements arrived from Galway City. In the engagement that followed several policemen were wounded and one Volunteer. Mellows himself covered the withdrawal of his men with a "Peter the Painter"—from behind a tree. He held the reinforcements off while he withdrew all his men, horses and carts down the main Dublin road, the police blazing away furiously with no more effect than to keep their spirits up. As soon as the Volunteers regrouped outside Oranmore the R.I.C. took everything of value from the barracks, locked it up and retired into the city.

Mellows met Lardner's scouts at Toberoe, halfway to Athenry. He learned that the Town Hall was being used as the insurgents headquarters. Monday night had been occupied in the making of bombs. There were normally as many as sixty policemen in Athenry on account of the prevalence of land agitation. These had been reinforced as a result of the abandonment of outlying huts and country barracks when the Rising began. All forces had been concentrated in the town. Houses adjoining the barracks had been taken over, but the police remained within. Lardner did not consider that the main purpose of holding down British forces demanded shedding the blood of these Irishmen. The Athenry police were isolated and remained supine apart from one or two minor sorties until they were relieved. This explains how Athenry remained a centre of insurgent communications throughout and that men in the field were able to visit their own houses.

Lardner had taken over the Agricultural College and Model Farm just outside the town when Mellows came up. Several bread-carts and a tea van had been commandeered. But the confiscation of groceries became unnecessary. Farmers sent their daughters with loaves specially baked in the largest bastables and supplies of milk. The people had their first glimpse of a society free from landlords, land-agents, process servers and armed peelers. The military picture now became clear. Over 500 men were assembled at the Model Farm. They had 25 rifles and 350 shot-guns together with some small arms. Some of them had never been Volunteers but had come out to fight for freedom. If the Volunteers were inadequately trained, the newcomers were not trained at all. Yet their power was greater than their numbers or their miserable equipment. The response in the countryside had warned the R.I.C. of its limitations. They concentrated in such centres as Loughrea, and Galway City, while in Athenry and Gort they were bottled up and impotent.

British troops and marines landed at the port of Galway, where a "loyal" corps of Volunteers was raised, largely for show since they were allowed no arms. Nicholls, Hardiman and several officers from Cois Fharraige were arrested and taken on board a warship. Callanan failed to get through to Iar Connacht and turned north to Claregalway where he found the local company mobilised at Carnmore. Patrick Feeney and "Sweeney" Newell cycled to Athenry for orders. They found Mellows at the Model Farm and told him that they had 150 men. "Bring them in at once," said Mellows.

It seems that as soon as Mellows had united his forces his intention was to move towards the Shannon, raising the country as he went. On Tuesday it still seemed possible that the south was up. He ordered the Gort, Ardrahan and Ballycahalan companies to remain in position for the time being. Meanwhile he despatched a message to Colivet in Limerick to find out the situation there. He was unaware that but for Dublin and Wexford only Galway had made an effective stand. These were too far away to affect his fortunes. Sean Mitchell had taken a boat-load of arms from Athlone to Banagher, but finding nobody mobilised there had returned disappointed in torrential rain. The counter-manding order had caused so much delay in Tullamore that Brennan and Bracken were unable to carry out their plan to release the Volunteers imprisoned after the incident in March. Thomas Malone was thus prevented through lack of forces from blowing up the crossing at Shannonbridge between Tullamore and Ballinasloe. His brother Seamus visited Athlone and Ballinasloe in efforts to make contact with Mellows. There was confusion at Coalisland and the long trek to the west was not attempted. The guides posted in Cavan were not required. There was a small mobilisation in Farney in County Monaghan, and a party from County Louth attacked R.I.C. men at Castlebellingham and later reported to Dublin. In Kerry, after the promising start, Casement's arrest had thrown all into confusion. In Tipperary, only the south mobilised and at that imperfectly and too late.

Even had he known the facts Mellows could scarcely have acted more wisely than he did. While he waited for news he placed himself in a position south-east of Athenry with the way open alternatively to Gort or to the Shannon. Opposite the gateway of the Model Farm a boreen ran through Rockmore to the Dublin road, by-passing the town. Traversing this and turning right across a field track he reached the back gate of Moyode House, set in a shallow depression beside the high keep of Moyode Castle. The mansion had belonged to the Persse family, but was now unoccupied as a result of land division. This was the rebel headquarters from Wednesday evening to Friday.

Though hope of assistance from the south rapidly faded, Wednesday marked the climacteric of the revolt. All day Volunteers were arriving from surrounding districts. The first, just before the evacuation of the Model Farm, were from Claregalway. These reported an engagement at Carnmore in the early morning[1] in which Constable P. Whelan was killed and an inspector wounded. He escaped capture by feigning death till the Volunteers had moved off. His men retreated towards Oranmore. One Volunteer, Michael Rafferty, was wounded by a splinter from a stone wall. Delighted at the new accessions Mellows sent Feeney and Newell to Kiltulla whence they brought the Castlegar company. Volunteers were reporting from such distant points as Tuam, Dunmore and even Mount Bellew near the Roscommon border. For the most part they were individuals, but all confirmed the imposing fact that from Oranmore to Ballinasloe, from Tuam to Kinvara, the King's writ no longer ran on 600 square miles of Irish soil.

[1] Various chronologies have been based on D.I. Ruttledge's statement at the Royal Commission that this incident took place on Thursday. I am strongly inclined to reject this evidence. It is unreliable on easily ascertainable matters as well as contradicting equally unreliable accounts published in the *Galway Express*. He provides meticulously accurate figures for the membership of so-called "Sinn Fein branches" but places Gort "nine and a half miles from Galway" instead of twenty. He has the time of Mellows' arrival in Galway five months out, the length of MacDiarmada's sentence two months out. He describes a march on Galway City on Wednesday, and its repulse thanks to bombardment by a "sloop of war" in Galway Bay of the rebel position "on a hill". I suspect the Carnmore incident had to be postponed twenty-four hours in order to accommodate this good story. The D.I. refers to the occupation of Moyode (which he calls Moyvore) although it was outside his district.

Moyode bustled with activity. Companies were drilling. Scouts were coming and going. The transport section practised the rapid harnessing of horses and the speediest loading of commandeered motor cars. Foraging parties went forth in all directions, each company being responsible for its own victuals. One seized bullocks from the estate of a noble lord. These were slaughtered as required, cut up and converted into beef stew with onions and potatoes from the farms. Cooking was done by *Cumann na mBan* girls who also provided such first aid as was required. Children in bare feet swarmed around with excited messages, news and above all rumours. Returning from an expedition which had driven back the Athenry peelers' one brave sortie from their stronghold Stephen Jordan gave voice to the general sense of adventure. There was dead silence as he sang Rooney's "Men of the West".

Throughout the spell at Moyode the insurgents heard the thud of naval artillery in Galway Bay. No better explanation has been offered than that it was intended to frighten the rebels and cheer the loyalists. Not even in the garrison town of Galway did all enter this category. On the Thursday of the Rising twenty boys of between fourteen and sixteen years of age went on strike in a woollen mill for an increase in their wage rate of 5s. to 9s. a week for a twelve hour day. The panic call for R.I.C. protection from the well-to-do denizens of Merlin Park, which probably gave rise to the myth of the march on Galway, showed uneasiness before the social forces freed by the prospect of an armed people. They must have felt highly reassured when they heard the Navy banging away.

The sound of artillery and the continuing uncertainty nevertheless told on morale. Rumours of British troop movements increased in frequency. In fact charabanc loads of police from Derry were already flooding the area round Tuam, a possible commentary on the wisdom of the policy of "not a shot in Ulster". In the evening a council of war took place, and it was agreed to allow all men without arms to disband at once, any armed man wishing to go to leave his arms for another. About 200 left, reducing Mellows' force to about 400. Among those who remained, hesitations constantly recurred. It required only that Tom Kenny the blacksmith should ride into the camp on a white pony announcing that a train of artillery and many soldiers were advancing from Ballinasloe to precipitate a crisis.

Mellows was determined to stand and make the west famous for a memorable battle even if they were all to lose their lives. "How old are you?" asked Kenny. "Twenty-four," Mellows replied, giving himself the benefit of three weeks. The blacksmith shook his head wisely. "Very young indeed! Very young, entirely!" After further discussions, in which a majority of the officers were in favour of disbandment, Mellows resigned his command which Lardner refused to accept. There was much debate after which Mellows was requested to resume it. He rallied the faint-hearts by sending out twelve motor cars in all directions seeking signs of the British forces. He himself went with Stephen Jordan in the direction of Ballinasloe, found no artillery train, but held up New Inn barracks and took prisoner an R.I.C. man who had been ordered to remain there, feign sickness and be sure to recognise any rebels that came near him. There is evidence that troops had indeed left Ballinasloe that evening, but had for some reason returned. All the scouts were back on time and reported no enemy movement.

Confidence was to some extent restored. But one question hung over all: Was Dublin still fighting? On Friday morning Fr. Thomas Fahy called at Moyode and agreed to cycle to Galway for news. The Northern police had now reached Loughrea, and some of the men disbanded on Thursday had been arrested on the way home. They were bound to discover that Athenry was undefended and march to the relief of its brave unbeleaguered garrison. It was decided therefore to retreat along Sarsfield's route towards Limerick. Camp was broken on Friday night and the Galway Brigade, now reduced to 150 men, marched southward.

Now that the Rising was entering its downward path, social issues previously submerged came to the surface. Kenny had commandeered three bullocks from a small grazier. Mellows and Neilan made him give them back. Now he objected to returning to a landlord three others that were no longer needed. The retreat was made though the front gate of Moyode, and along the boreen that runs through Bally-winna in the direction of Derryhale. This road comes within half a mile of Craughwell where the larger merchants who were members of Redmond's party had shut themselves up with the R.I.C. in the barracks. Kenny strongly objected to the detour round Craughwell. He wanted to attack the barracks and wreak vengeance on the enemies of the people. Mellows refused to agree, saying, "Our only enemy is England. These are Irishmen whose policy differs from ours, and are not our enemies." After that Kenny was seen no more. He was not a deliberately destructive character, but of the type whose egotism is expressed in bursts of ultra-leftism.

The march continued through Shanclough, Creag Castle and

Grannagh to Limepark, a large empty mansion where the party halted. Fr. Fahy now came up with them and gave his report. He understood that Dublin was in flames, and the Rising there drawing to a close. British troops were moving from Athlone and Ballinasloe and there was no effective resistance possible. He advised disbandment. Once again Mellows refused, but allowed Fr. Fahy to present his case to the officers. While he was speaking Mellows, who had had no rest for three days, fell asleep. Wakened to hear the general opinion in favour of disbandment he again dissented and warned the men that the R.I.C. prisoners would identify them and they would be arrested in their homes. O'Monnchain suggested that the handful of well-armed men should form a guerilla column and hold out as long as possible in the Aughty mountains. This was not acceptable and with great reluctance Mellows agreed that Fr. Fahy should disband the men. He could not bring himself to do so, and said that he would stay where he was till the British came and fight to the last.

When the last cart load had left there were four men at Limepark. Mellows, O'Monnchain, Frank Hynes and Peadar Howley, Captain of the Ardrahan Company, whose home was a hundred yards away. It was Hynes' decision to remain with him that turned Mellows' thoughts from a bloody self-sacrifice to the healthier alternative of escape. Hynes was a married man. The three accompanied Howley to his house where they had a hasty meal. Then they struck across scrubland now overgrown with brush to within a hundred yards of Peterswell police barracks. Turning across the fields in the direction of Dromore Hill they gained the Gort–Loughrea road, crossed it, and made for Padhraic Fahy's home at Ballycahalan. His brother took them to the house of Patsy Corless, beside a large turlough known as Lough Avalla. Here O'Monnchain hid his wallet which contained a list of addresses and a raffle ticket for a Mauser rifle. The cache was discovered during alterations to the house in 1937. They slept for fourteen hours, awakening in the late evening.

In the meantime the Corless brothers had found them a safer hiding place at Drumnaloch on the far side of the marshy turlough, which filled up after every shower of rain, and on the edge of the Aughty mountains. They moved up immediately. William Blanche and his wife welcomed them with open arms, and sat talking with them into the small hours.

Next day Blanche went to Mass at Kilbeacanty and reported that no policemen were present. They had not yet ventured from their strong points. Mellows and his companions hid in the bedroom as

Sunday callers chattered about their exploits, some of their former friends proving less than charitable after their defeat. On Monday the raids and arrests began. Blanche found them a hut on the mountainside at Cornageehy. One side was used as a cattle shelter, the other as a barn. Formerly the building was known as Cait O'Shaughnessy's cottage. The owner, William Hoode, was sympathetic but very nervous, especially when stories of the ill-treatment of prisoners began to circulate. He had no reason to fear, however. The resourceful Blanche spent all day hidden in the furze watching for peelers.

There were no beds available, but plenty of straw badly infested with mice. The roof let in rain and after a few wet days everything was sodden. It was inadvisable to light a fire since the smoke would be seen for miles. But the wet weather saved them. Lough Avalla filled up and as Blanche remarked, "Peelers are like cats. They won't get their feet wet."

They remained on the mountain until Thursday, 4th May. On the Wednesday Blanche warned them that the search parties were drawing too near for their safety. All day they spent planning a move to the south and memorising Mellows' map. The morning dawned bright and fine. The country was the radiant green of Ireland and the hills of Connemara broke the skyline. To the west the limestone domes of the Burren looked as if they had been whitewashed. They crossed some bogland near O'Shaughnessy's Bridge, and moved in the direction of Scariff where Mellows had an uncle he thought might help them. By six o'clock they were hidden in a wood alongside a demesne called Chevy Chase. There they remained all day, bathing in the river, studying the map and waiting impatiently for darkness.

After sunset they left the wood on the side away from the road. A track from Derrykeel passed through the wood making two turns to the west. To reach Derryfada and Flagmount they must make the first turn, but leave it in a southerly direction before it made the second. Presumably they left it too late and though realising they had lost their way had no choice but to walk on blindly when Mellows' pencil torch failed as they pored over the map. They struck a flagged road which led them to Gortacarnaun four miles west by south from Chevy Chase. From this position the way to Flagmount is barred by Lough Graney.

Before knocking on a door they decided on names. They were to pretend to be cattle-drovers, O'Monnchain's northern accent providing the sole element of verisimilitude. Hynes was to be called Pat Murphy, Mellows John O'Nolan, and O'Monnchain Joe MacSwiney.

For some reason Hynes, who invented the names, shook his sides laughing at the name he had planted on O'Monnchain. Presumably they believed they were at Lannaght and asked the way to Derryfada. The door was opened by a giant of a man who invited them to stay the night. O'Monnchain explained that they were in a hurry. They were anxious to reach Scariff for the fair. "Bring your friends in for tea," he said. Then he added, "You don't seem to know much about Scariff. The fair is over three days ago." He would not allow them to answer. "You're Sinn Feiners. I know what you are. 'Tis fortunate for you that you knocked at this door." The next house held an R.I.C. man home on leave. He insisted on taking them part of the way and setting them on the road that skirts the west side of Lough Graney. He told them he was William Rooney, a champion weight-lifter. They must make a right turn at Killaneena half a mile after a road comes in from the right. But unfortunately they anticipated their instructions, following a superficially similar sequence of turnings. And at Drumandoora once more they tramped away to the west.

A misty rain began to fall. They realised they were lost again. Here there was no habitation. They were on the rocky escarpment where the silurian slates pierce the old red sandstone of central Clare— a wilderness of jagged ridges, rough boulders and broken cliffs. They looked for a place to sleep. Hynes had a fleece overcoat, Mellows and O'Monnchain only trench coats and sacks on their backs for warmth. They slept from exhaustion and awakened at sunrise wet through in the midst of small caves and dry crannies in this extremely broken land-scape. Hynes retreated to a cave to finish his rest. Below was Lough Cutra which Mellows and O'Monnchain saw when they climbed a hill. Once more they had deviated four miles west and were separated from Scariff not only by Lough Graney but by a rocky plateau.

Sitting among the boulders reflecting on their bad luck they shared their only food, one potato rejected previously for its blueness. They took a south-westerly course until they reached Loughaun at the head of the Affick Valley. It was now about 6 a.m. Seeing smoke they called at a farmhouse, told their story and were provided with food without question. The woman of the house refused payment. The husband, Michael O'Hanrahan, told them how to go to Scariff round the mountain, but showed no surprise when they proposed to take a "short cut". Once up in the heather they decided to sleep out the heat of the day.

About midday Mellows was awakened by a strange voice. He saw Hynes kneeling as if praying but holding his right hand very stiffly in his overcoat pocket. A sorrowful looking Pointer dog was sniffing round O'Monnchain and a young man in smart knee-breeches was holding a handkerchief as a white flag. He was not impressed by the cattle-drover story. "You're Sinn Feiners," he said. "But they're not bad fellows at all. Indeed, I'm one myself." Already the words *Sinn Fein* had become identified with a Rising *Sinn Fein* took no part in. The young man then introduced himself as Michael Malony of Balloughtra, a captain of the Volunteers, County Clare brigade, who had come out on the mountains seeking a colt that had strayed. His knowledge of I.R.B. affairs soon satisfied the fugitives of his bona fides. He congratulated them on their wrong turnings. Scariff was "crawling with troops and peelers" and his uncle had been trying to warn Mellows off.

They were resting in a hollow of the Annagapple River. The house was little more than a mile away. Instructing them not to stir he went home for a hamper of provisions and a bundle of newspapers. Now for the first time Mellows heard the story of Dublin, the week's resistance, the ultimate surrender to superior forces and the executions now in train. Pearse, Clarke and MacDonagh had been shot during his last day at Hoode's barn. Sadness mingled with personal relief as the four went down to Balloughtra. Malony led the way to a bothan[1] almost encased by thickets of furze and hawthorn. It could scarcely be seen at ten yards distance. But its door commanded, through a gap, a magnificent view of the vale of Tulla and Slieve Bernagh beyond. Beds of dry straw had been put down, with blankets and clean sheets. Michael's father, Patrick Malony, was an old Fenian. He could hardly speak when he shook the boys' hands. All the men of the family joined them round the glowing turf as they held a cele-bratory dinner.

They inhabited the bothy together for four months. Molony took a message to Sean MacNamara, leader of the Volunteers at Crusheen. He conveyed the news of the escape to Limerick where old John Daly was expending his last days trying to help the prisoners and men on the run. Madge Daly sent Mellows £100. Malony undertook to visit Athenry to set the mind of Mrs. Hynes at rest. He chose the time of a cattle fair. He also carried a message from Mellows which Broderick was to see taken to Dublin. On this occasion he was searched so thor-oughly that his boots were taken off. While they were being examined he lit his pipe which contained the message, and so destroyed it.

Though lorry loads of police and soldiers used to pass along the

[1] Cabin or bothy.

main road scarcely a hundred yards from the bothy, there were no searches in the neighbourhood. The reason is a curious one. The District Inspector at Tulla was a Protestant. He regarded himself as one of the ruling caste and his superiors in the R.I.C. appreciated it. But to the British soldiers he was simply a "Paddy". After some mis-understanding he told his superior there was no disturbance in his district and he wanted none created. As a result the soldiers were induced to leave him alone. Mellows and his companions had blundered into the only safe place.

At first it was hard to settle down to the routine of confinement and inactivity. There were songs to while away the time. Mellows acquired a fiddle. There were stories. Mellows had a photographic memory and would take them by stages on a tour of Ireland describing the trees and houses and every turn of the road. As the hawthorn and furze faded and the orchids and clovers filled the pasture land, they would venture warily into the steep field below the bothy, snatch a trout from the stream, occasionally take a hare or snipe for the pot, help with the turf harvest and the hay.

In ones and twos the local Volunteers began to visit them. Tom Hogan whom Mellows taught the fiddle, Tom Connell who worked in Limerick, Michael O'Dea and Tom Halloran, who had fought in Dublin and suffered a short internment. Tubridy, a local newsagent, provided an occasional copy of the *Hue and Cry* containing seldom accurate and never flattering descriptions of wanted men. There were musical evenings in the bothy, later even in the Malony's house, and old Patrick always insisted on singing the fine song composed by Denis Florence McCarthy for New Year's Day 1849 when revolution's fires had failed in a countryside all but stupefied by famine,

> My countrymen, awake, arise
> Our work begins anew . . .

and to the accompaniment of loud applause he would conclude in words slightly of his own making,

> Before we quit, there's something yet
> For Irishmen to do.

Sean O'Keeffe brought a message from Limerick to the effect that around the end of August the reorganised Supreme Council wanted Mellows to go to America. His personal appearance would create a new centre for American sympathies, and help keep the country out of the war. Mellows disliked the proposal. He was too retiring to relish such a mission. He tried to have Frank Hynes sent away first, but finally agreed, and careful preparations were made.

Malony measured him for a suit and had it made by a Limerick tailor. He bought hair-dye with which Hynes dyed every hair individually, the process taking a whole day. At nightfall Malony brought a pony and trap and took Mellows to O'Brien's Castle where Sean MacNamara was waiting with two bicycles with lighted lamps. Mellows took one and MacNamara brought him through Fair Green, along a road which skirts Ennis, to Fr. Crowe's house at Doora, about two miles from the town.

Fr. Crowe had secured two novice's habits from a nun in the Convent of Mercy at Ennis. Mellows disguised himself in one of these, while the other was assumed by Miss Pauline Barry of Gort. A friend of Fr. Crowe's[1] completed the party. A strongly Unionist taxi driver named Brodie was engaged for the morrow when the four drove to Limerick and Cork, calling ostentatiously at religious houses on the way. Mellows was taken to Rochestown Priory just outside the city.

The I.R.B. sought means of getting him out of the country. There were several proposals and possibly more than one attempt. The successful plan was devised by a Dublin man, Thomas Byrne, who was in charge of the tailoring department of the Queen's Old Castle in Main Street. Aware that a former employee, Mrs. O'Regan, had seafaring connections, and that her husband was frequently with Captain Joseph Murray, Master of the *Harry Herbert*, he visited her in the Mardyke, told the whole story and asked for her assistance. Captain Murray arrived the next day and agreed to meet Byrne. A few days later Mellows left by train for Courtmacsherry where he lived at Captain Murray's house for a week, during which time the *Harry Herbert* was working round the coast and re-loading. During this period Mellows went by excursion train to Dungarvan where the finals of the Munster Hurling Championship were being played. While in Dungarvan he called on his old friends the O'Mahonys.

This event took place on 1st October. A few days later he was at sea. Captain Murray was a Unionist. He took part in the escape from a sense of compassion towards a man with a price on his head. The *Harry Herbert* was a two-masted schooner which plied between the South of Ireland and South Wales, taking oats and pit props and returning with coal. Occasionally she ran up to Liverpool for a mixed cargo. On this occasion the destination was Liverpool. It was not reached without mishap. A storm blew up over the Waterford

---

[1] Probably Fr. Tom Burke of Galway.

coast and it was decided to put in at Helvick. Here the crew betook themselves to Sylvie Murray's public house, overstayed their welcome, came to blows with the police who came to eject them, and retreated aboard the schooner. Captain Murray was in no mood to act as mediator. He hastily cast off and put out into the gale. At Liverpool port officials challenged him on the identity of the new seaman. Thanks to his well-known pro-British sympathies he was able to satisfy them.

Mellows stayed three nights with Neil Kerr. A coalman working for the Cunard Company, and an active member of the National Union of Dock Labourers, he had helped to smuggle arms into Ireland since the embargo was imposed at the end of 1913. Before he left for Mrs. O'Farrell's at Linacre, Mellows had been introduced to an official of the Seamen's Union who enlisted the help of a Captain Hoare whose duties included the selection of crews for ocean-going vessels.

A seaman's book was promised him. But an opportunity came before it arrived. On a wild night in mid-October a few friends saw him off at Lime Street. His luggage was a seaman's bag and a fiddle. He had a bottle of whiskey protruding from each pocket. He had been frequenting dockside bars to learn the required argot. He had narrowly escaped the attentions of the police who were combing all places of resort for draft-evaders, even taking this sport of theirs on to the football field. He lurched through the barrier making an attempt to simulate drunkenness.

During the train journey he contrived to gain access to the first class compartment in which the Board of Trade official in charge of the crew was travelling. As the train passed through an exceptionally long tunnel, possibly the Severn Tunnel, he seized the agent's attache case in the darkness, and threw it through the window. It contained the papers of other members of the crew. At Devonport he again pretended drunkenness and swore that he had handed the papers to the agent and that was all that he knew about them. He left the agent to talk his way out of the difficulty. Apparently he succeeded. Mellows described himself as a trimmer. But nobody had explained to him the necessity for damping ashes before drawing them up on the hoist. He nearly set the ship ablaze. "You should be in charge of horses," said the Engineer. After a spell as a stoker he was sent up as a deck hand.

The vessel was an old tramp put out of service until re-commissioned for the war. She broke down off Fastnet and was towed into Falmouth for repairs. It was from Falmouth most likely that Mellows sent a note to O'Mahony at Dungarvan. It is headed *Eit Eigin*, and is signed "L. Fireman". He urged his friend to keep working away quietly, and to take advantage of the feeling in the country which had been created since April. "As to me," he concluded, "God has spared me for another day, though a few months ago I never expected to be alive."

That the steamer's course was not rapid is certain. Mellows once recounted his sensations when a sailing vessel swept gaily past them and disappeared out of sight. The fiddle made Mellows a popular figure during the long days and nights. Finally, running short of water, the ship put in to Bermuda for replenishments. The length of the journey has been quoted as from two to four months. Its most probable duration would be of about six to eight weeks. He arrived in New York in mid-December.

He had been supplied with an address by the I.R.B. in Liverpool, that of a boarding house at 141 West 97th Street, kept by a Mrs. Murphy from Cork. Though it was late, he went there the moment he could get ashore, and found Pat Callanan, Eamonn Corbett, Hannigan, John Murphy of Dublin and Pat Brazil of Waterford there before him.

He arrived at 4 a.m. and spent the remainder of the night talking.

CHAPTER SIX

TRANSITION IN IRELAND

MELLOWS spent four years in the United States.[1] He was thus absent from Ireland during the springtime of revolution, when the mass movement against imperialism grew most rapidly and imposed unity on all currents of discontent. Unable to express itself through the traditional nationalist party it annexed Griffith's *Sinn Fein*, moulding it to the new purpose, with a new constitution and an expanded leadership. The first stage in the process can with advantage be described at this point, since Mellows' work in the U.S.A. was at all times oriented towards developments in Ireland. It will moreover be convenient to anticipate his experiences by a few months.

Official mythology makes Easter Week the demiurge of modern Ireland. A small group of heroes defied the might of British Imperialism. The national soul was re-awakened. A terrible beauty was born, and behold, the rulers of today safely installed in Leinster House, the only fly in the ointment being the parallel installation of the Unionists at Stormont. Reduced to its bare bones this interpretation of events by the bourgeoisie of today amounts to this: Actions at Westminster having failed to secure a decent bargain from the imperialists, the Rising created a position where they had to concede one. There is of course a grain of truth in it. Only the I.R.B. and Connolly's followers considered possible a successful rising against Britain. Feeling that there must at some time be a bargain, Griffith, the man above all responsible for the actual bargain struck, always denied that the Rising had done more than accelerate an inevitable process. But no formula can summarise the history of a revolution. It is necessary to see what actually happened, dealing first with British policy, and then with its impact on the classes existing in Ireland.

The Easter Rising befell at that fateful moment when the British Cabinet, summoned to discuss the crisis of its war policy, decided to fight on. So Irish food and manpower were still required. The question was how to get them. True to form, the imperialists reacted to the fright they had had with coercion. The flames of rebellion were

[1] This chapter deals with the dynamics of the revolution in Ireland. The life story of Mellows is resumed in Chapter 7.

stamped out hysterically, no matter where the sparks flew. For weeks the military were given a free hand. By 12th May they had carried out over 3,000 arrests, and 1,877 internments without trial; imposed 144 prison sentences, and performed fifteen executions, with Casement's a foregone conclusion. Liberty Hall was wrecked. Trade union records were impounded and shipped to England. A ban on all public meetings was for a time held to apply even to meetings of innocuous trade union branches.

Not unnaturally there was a strong reaction from America. While coercion was at its height Asquith charged the Minister of Munitions, David Lloyd George, with the task of devising a new policy for Ireland. This renegade Welsh nationalist and pseudo-radical demagogue, after contemplating the depths of his own bottomless ignorance, and listening to his civil servants, produced just that extension of Asquith's pre-war policy that would make it totally reactionary. Partition by consent was to be replaced by partition by compulsion. Redmond was told of proposals for introducing Home Rule with the temporary exclusion of six Ulster counties. Simultaneously Carson was assured in writing that "We must make it clear that at the end of the provisional period Ulster[1] does not, whether she wills it or not, merge with the rest of Ireland." The proposal satisfied neither. Both Carson and William O'Brien met Lloyd George on 30th May to voice their protest. The wizard explained that "something must be done to satisfy America". From then on he must handle the difficult problem of saddling the Irish with the responsibility for an arrangement they had repudiated. He was Britain's chief policy-maker in Irish affairs for the next six years. Behind all his cynical evasiveness and shameless double-dealing there was one firm principle. This was that if Britain were to be forced to concede any degree of native government in Ireland her ultimate hegemony must be insured through a new "Pale", established in the north-east.

Of all sections confronting British Imperialism the most to be feared, and the first to recover, was the organised working class. When the Irish T.U.C. met at Sligo in August, Labour was in a strong moral position. The ideal of courage would have been to condemn the Maxwell terror as part and parcel of the imperialist war, and insist at the least on a fair trial and political treatment for all prisoners taken in the Rising. From this the movement could have

[1] Since the Middle Ages, when it also included Louth, Ulster has consisted of nine counties, namely, Antrim, Down, Armagh, Monaghan, Cavan, Fermanagh, Donegal, Derry and Tyrone.

proceeded to demand the release of the prisoners and the ending of martial law. Within a matter of months, Labour would have been leading the nation. The revolution would have expressed overtly the interest of the most numerous and oppressed class, shortly to be in a position to seal an alliance with the most progressive forces abroad.

This is not what took place. Instead the delegates in effect reversed the N.E.C. decision of 1914 which condemned the war as imperialist. Eloquent tribute was paid to Connolly, but not for his part in the Rising. Indeed, in the words "he conceived his duty lay in another direction" Thomas Johnson, a man of unquestionable intellect and personal integrity, launched the erroneous theory, later expanded by Sean O'Casey, that Connolly had turned his back on the Labour Movement. Conference rose as a mark of respect for the dead "whatever their views of war or rebellion".

How is this extraordinary position to be explained? Perhaps in part by the position of support for the war taken up by some of the Belfast delegates. Perhaps by the fear some delegates felt of further reprisals against the trade union movement. But certainly the decisive influence was opposition to Lloyd George's proposals for Partition. So strong was this opposition that delegates from the south were prepared to take an indeterminate stand on every other question, rather than provide by the demonstration of disunity the slightest support for the British proposals. What would have happened if, while remaining aloof from the tactics of national insurrection, the T.U.C. had confirmed its previous opposition to the war, is difficult to say. It seems a fair guess that if disaffiliations had taken place in 1916, the following year would have seen the reverse process as part of the immense upsurge of trade unionism throughout Ireland.

For scarcely had the delegates returned to their homes when the economic consequences began to bite. Thus the 1916 harvest yielded only 1·399 starch tons per acre against 1·479 in 1915. Production of potatoes, still the staple diet of the masses, had fallen by 30 per cent. Yet there were greatly increased exports. Profiteering began. The war that had brought regular wages and separation allowances was now taking the value out of them. During the autumn workers in some areas overturned wagons to prevent the removal of potatoes from their district,[1] and the T.U.C. set its seal on this militancy with a special conference at Derry on 16th December. There it was stated that while

[1] Such a course of action had been advocated by James Connolly. It was the first new tactic employed in the revolution and it was the workers who employed it. Spontaneous local struggles to halt food exports had of course taken place in 1740 and 1847.

food prices had risen by 80 per cent, wages had risen by 10 per cent.

In this situation rising militancy expressed itself in a spectacular increase in trade union membership. The Sligo conference had 72 delegates. A year later at Derry there were 111, representing 100,000 workers, about one-fifth of the eligible labour force. But in 1918 the number of delegates had risen to 240 representing 250,000 workers. The figures thereafter remained at the high level. The decisive years were thus 1917 and 1918.

Its rapid growth in the cities was accompanied by the spread of trade unionism into the smaller towns. Trades Councils were established for example in Ballina, Ballinasloe, Carlow, Castlebar, Clonmel, Ennis, Fermoy and Tuam. Even the countryside proper was not immune. In Laois and Offaly, County Trades Councils were set up. The growth of membership was most marked in the Irish-based unions which were uninhibited by considerations of imperial defence. Such a rapid growth in membership naturally tended to change the character of Irish trade unionism. The old craft unions lost importance. At the same time both the Hibernians and the various petit-bourgeois groups were tempted to take the opportunity of fishing for support among a politically inexperienced membership. Such was inevitable in the absence of a well established socialist tradition.

The employers, against whom the edge of the wage-earners' militancy was turned, had grievances of their own. These steadily eroded their former attachments to the imperial authority. When at the outbreak of hostilities war-contracts were mentioned the leaves of their ledgers had flapped in loyal anticipation. If orders did not immediately materialise, stocks appreciated, wages depreciated and there was good excuse for dispensing with employees. But when materials fell into short supply, traditional businesses began to dwindle, and the war-contracts were still on the long finger, the grisly truth was bared. The government was quite happy that Irish industry should run down. Its manpower would become available for the armed forces.

The committee Irish businessmen established to agitate for access to war profits drew scant sympathy from the authorities. The Trench Warfare Department with millions of pounds worth of orders at its disposal told the Dublin Area Office of the Ministry of Munitions that the government had given strict instructions that no contracts should be placed in the "Southern area" of Ireland. The Chief Secretary himself, Edward Shortt, saw his attempts to utilise Irish resources vetoed by the Treasury. In exasperation he advised Dublin businessmen that to secure fair treatment from a British Government

Department they must make themselves "utterly obnoxious".[1]
From time to time a few crumbs were scattered, but the Irishmen
were never allowed a seat at the table. A number of firms offered to
make munitions. A sceptical official told them they "could as easily eat
shells as manufacture them",[2] but they might try their hands at
ammunition boxes. Their British competitors then ran a campaign to
have boxes made in Lancashire, where there was an ample supply of
Irish Labour and Irish timber.[3] A few national shell factories were
ultimately opened, but had little opportunity to show their effectiveness before the war ended. English firms were given the contracts for
building army huts in Ireland. Irish firms were not even invited to
tender. When the Castlecomer rail extension, long delayed by the
importers of Welsh anthracite, was ultimately built, the contract was
assigned to an English company. According to Arthur Griffith, who
had made himself the spokesman of industrial capital for many years,
the British Government employed every subterfuge to induce Kynoch
Explosives to leave Arklow and tolerated them only with bad grace
and from necessity.

Under emergency legislation the government controlled both railways and shipping, all materials in short supply, and the prices of
many commodities. Its powers were used consistently to the disadvantage of Irish industry. At the height of a government-sponsored
tillage campaign the Ford Company proposed to turn out tractors at
their factory in Cork. Protests from British interests induced the
government to refuse shipping space for American machinery. The
plant was not in production until 1920. The price of Irish flax was
fixed at a level below that of the inferior English product, but the
English spinner was favoured in the allocation of quantities. Sometimes
prices were so fixed as to discriminate within Ireland. The Ulster
merchant sending to the Dublin market supplies of potatoes on which
it depended six months of the year received a rate of profit four times
that permitted his southern counterpart.

The price allowed the Irish food producer was consistently lower
than that given for equivalent English produce. Most government
controls were administered by men directly interested in the British
industries concerned. In no instance did a representative of Irish
industry occupy an administrative position of any kind. The Irish
capitalists' prices were fixed by their English competitors, whether
they were buying or selling.

[1] E. J. O'Riordan, *Modern Irish Trade and Industry*, p. 285.
[2] Op. cit., p. 206.   [3] Op. cit., p. 211.

Interested trades were represented on the advisory committees which multiplied during this time. But seldom if ever was the representative of an Irish industry included. In the case of the Balfour Committee on Commercial and Industrial policy after the war a vigorous campaign was waged and representations were made to Mr. Asquith. The result was the appointment of a gentleman most governments would have found co-operative enough. He was John O'Neill, chairman of the All Ireland Munitions and Government Supplies Committee. But simultaneously there was appointed a representative of "Ulster". Despite the presence of these men not a single Irish industrial or trade organisation was invited to provide information. O'Neill declined to sign the report and submitted a minority statement.[1]

The All-Ireland Committee urged the re-establishment of the War Office testing and receiving depot which had been removed from Dublin in 1854. Irish manufacturers were at a disadvantage in dealing with Woolwich. Success crowned these efforts and the depot opened at the end of January 1918, nine months before the end of the war.

The sum extracted from Ireland by means of price manipulation could no doubt be estimated, if laboriously. That taken by other means is more easily ascertained. According to Arthur Griffith, Ireland paid excess taxation of £8,000,000 in 1916 and £15,000,000 in 1917. During the same period began the now too familiar "capital drain", the channelling abroad by the banks of the assets of their depositors. Bank deposits rose from £74,659,000 in 1916 to £121,191,000 in 1918. In part the change was inflationary, in part also it reflected the activity of agriculture and the favourable balance of trade. Thus in 1904 imports had exceeded exports by £5,560,000 (11·2 per cent), while in 1918 exports exceeded imports by £26,855,000 (21·3 per cent). But both had fallen heavily in volume, and Ireland, now compelled to be self-supporting, badly needed her own capital accumulation. Instead the banks adopted their new policy of "minimum accommodation with maximum investment". No financial barrier stood between Ireland and Britain. The attraction of wartime super-profits was irresistible. The British holdings of Irish banks, level at about £30 million since the eighties, rose from £30 million in 1913 to £60 million in 1916 and doubled again to just short of £120 million in 1918.[2]

Under these conditions, and at a time of rapid growth of monopoly within Britain, imperial capital began to make inroads. The Belfast and Ulster banks were absorbed by the Midland and Westminster

[1] Cmd. 9035 (1919).   [2] J. J. Horgan, *The Banker*, July 1948.

respectively. The Ulster and Cork Steamship companies, together with the British and Irish Steam Packet Company, passed out of Irish hands. "The commercial absorption of Ireland," wrote the *Investors' Chronicle*,[1] "which may be regarded as having commenced with the association by control or alliance of Irish railways with the English trunk lines of the west, was given a great fillip by the linking up of the banks of the two countries." It was estimated that £22 million of Irish investors' money thereby left the custody in which it had been placed. The Cork City Chamber of Commerce was the first public body to protest, and thereafter uneasiness grew. Moreover, it became clear to the bourgeoisie that "Home Rule" as understood by Redmond, even if the British were offering it, was insufficient to protect them against the new forms of national exploitation that had evolved in the midst of the crisis of imperialism. That at this very moment the government was prepared to lop off about one-half of the Irish national market showed every doubter the irreconcilable conflict of interest.

British imperialism wished to retain Ireland as an exclusive market for her manufactures while drawing on her food, manpower and accumulated capital. The economic development of the bourgeoisie ran counter to this interest which imperialism was prepared to pursue even at the risk of destroying Redmond and leaving the greater part of Ireland for the first time in centuries without a garrison class. Instead there was to be an imperial garrison in the north-east while the remainder vented its hatred upon that. This was possible because of the chasm that divided the bourgeoisie, which the government did everything possible to widen. Generally speaking Irish industry was conducted on a small scale, served local needs, and was subordinated to the main business of exporting cattle. It supplied only a proportion of the country's consumption goods and waged a constant defensive warfare against British competition. But superimposed upon such an industrial pattern was another. In the Belfast area there was industry for which the home market was not the *raison d'être*. Linen, shipbuilding, rope-making, and their ancillaries depended on foreign markets, and, except in the case of linen under wartime restrictions, on foreign raw materials. In this area traditionally Liberal manufacturers had turned Tory to preserve free trade with Britain and avoid their share of the burden of land purchase if this should be transferred to an Irish Exchequer.

The distinction had nothing to do with religion. But the fact remains

[1] Quoted J. J. Horgan, *Studies*, December 1917, p. 635.

that British policy had been to fasten on the Protestant districts an employing class dependent on an imperial trade and finance, whereas in the Catholic areas the old dependence on the semi-feudal cattle trade was permitted to continue. The opposition was by no means complete, but it was sufficient to prevent any united stand by the employers of Ireland. And as long as the working class remained under the political influence of its employers, it must remain in a similar position in all essentials. Only to the extent that the working class set itself the aim of pre-empting from the bourgeoisie the position of ruling class could it rise above bourgeois divisions and essay to lead the nation. Only through working-class internationalism could Ireland the nation be united and freed.

The British Government found no great difficulty in controlling the demands of the Irish employers for capital and labour. But appropriating the reward in terms of food and soldiers involved an irreconcilable contradiction. Compulsory tillage orders were passed involving 10 per cent of agricultural land in 1917 and 15 per cent in 1918. But little cognisance was taken of the important fact that Ireland contained three distinct types of rural economy, the western based on stock breeding, the eastern based on stock raising, and the southern based on dairying. These distinctions, which explain many an apparent unevenness of Irish political development, seemed beneath the notice of His Majesty's advisers.

In the eastern grazing counties virtually idle land could be ploughed up without disturbing a social structure based largely on wage labour. In the south, the system of combining family with wage-labour possessed considerable flexibility. Farmers used the plough for producing feed that was no longer imported, and a number of landless men enjoyed their first steady employment for years. But in the west, where land purchase was least advanced, and very small holdings providing family subsistence were clustered round virtual latifundia, matters stood differently.

The changes in land use which took place in Connacht after 1916 are summarised in the following table:

Areas under	1916	1917	1918	1925
Tillage	100	133	148	93
Hay	100	104	101	120
Pasture	100	90	88	98
Other land	100	105	104	99

The expansion of the category "other land" can probably be dismissed as attributable to reclassification of pasture as "rough grazing" by holders anxious to reduce their responsibilities under compulsory tillage orders. The most obvious change is the ploughing up of pasture, which at first sight seems very substantial. Thus the amount converted to tillage in County Mayo alone amounted to 27,356 acres in 1916–17, and a further 13,430 acres in 1917–18. Yet whereas County Cork attained 16 per cent tillage by 1917, thereafter relaxing to 15 per cent, Mayo barely achieved 10 per cent even in 1918. What were the reasons for the difference?

The two counties had a roughly similar labour force. But in Mayo out of 74,634 engaged in agriculture in 1912, only 1,882 described themselves as permanent and 3,720 as temporary labourers. Except on farms of over 500 acres the number of employees was invariably smaller than the number of farmers' relatives. In County Cork, on the other hand, out of 92,075 persons engaged in agriculture no less than 17,131 described themselves as permanent and 9,353 as temporary labourers. Thus Cork had a rural proletariat some five times as great as that of Mayo, or ten times if temporary workers were left out of account.

There was in County Cork a reserve labour force absent from Mayo. In County Mayo the expansion of tillage required the transference of land from one holder to another, from low intensity grazing ranches to high intensity mixed farms, whose holders would work it in conjunction with what they already had by the simple process of extending the hours of labour of themselves and their families. The form in which such transfer was traditionally achieved was the system of "conacre" or annual letting at agreed rent. The basis for the "Conacre War" in the west was that, though the government wanted the corn and made it profitable to grow it, the graziers had not the labour themselves and objected to handing over their land to those who had. Both in Cork and Mayo there was labour available that but for the war might have been lost by emigration. In the south, capitalist tenures made it immediately available. In 1918 tillage in County Cork even fell slightly. But in the west, feudal survivals impeded its utilisation. The transition to revolutionary forms of action therefore took place first in the west, and did not immediately spread to the south or the east.

In the confrontation that developed, workers, employers and farmers each had strong grievances against the imperial government. But none of these classes could show sufficient unity to seize the initiative. There was consequently thrown up a leadership drawn from a variety of petit-bourgeois strata, small businessmen, younger professional people, rural schoolteachers and curates, journalists and artisans. These had sufficient links with the main classes to be able to represent them. At the same time they were distinct enough to assume a unity which appeared to submerge all class conflicts in the mystical nation. Hence the euphoria of Frank Gallagher's "Four Glorious Years" and the nostalgia it turned into afterwards. The leadership was affected by imperialism in no unique way. Its members suffered the wrongs of the workers, farmers or capitalists as the case might be, often to an enlarged degree. It included many frustrated and insecure, talented and idealistic, adventurous and romantic. All felt an ardent and justifiable indignation against the power that occupied their country, controlled its international relations and monopolised its resources. But this class that was not strictly speaking a class at all, was subject to extremes of precipitancy and vacillation, such as mark the petite-bourgeoisie of all nations. Some of its members had led the Rising, like Prometheus seizing the fire. Others among them were yet to sign the "Articles of Agreement", like shop-boys dazzled by an international crook.

How a challenge to Redmond was knocked together from a multiplicity of rival groupings could form the subject of a special study. The I.R.B. played an important part, but never recovered the hegemony it enjoyed before the Rising. The process did not begin until mass discontent with the consequences of the war began to assert itself. Old policy differences, while they survived, were subject to the influence of events. The achievement of unity of action was a contradictory process, reflecting the struggles of the main classes as in a distorting mirror. Complicating factors arose with the return to Ireland of successive categories of deportees, internees, and sentenced prisoners, each possessing, according to the rough and ready classification of the military terror, its own level of culpability, which is the same thing as political determination and experience.

Within days of the last executions Mrs. Kathleen Clarke set out to reorganise the I.R.B. Her immediate aim was to afford relief to the dependents of men who had lost their living as a result of the Rising. For this purpose the National Aid Association was established. But a further purpose, for which funds and archives had been entrusted to her before the Rising, was the preparation for a further insurrection. She drew on the assistance of the women of *Cumann na mBan*, many of them members of the Irish Women Workers' Union. Most men of ability were either arrested or temporarily quiescent, but she succeeded with the aid of Seamus O'Doherty in bringing together some species of provisional Supreme Council. The organisation was at the same time, but independently, re-established in Lewes Jail and in the concentration camp of Fron Goch. There the initiative was taken by Michael Collins, a young man from County Cork who had returned from London to fight in the Post Office. Too much should not be made of the legitimacy of any of these branches. They were established in days when legitimacy was at a substantial discount. The I.R.B., and particularly its previously predominant "offensivist" wing, had suffered a severe political defeat in the failure of the Rising, and all those who sought to maintain it deserve credit.

At the other extreme was *Sinn Fein*. Griffith had been imprisoned for nothing—but the Party retained one newspaper, the monthly *Irishman*, edited with much circumspection by H. M. Pim in Belfast. In September 1916 it was transferred to Dublin and became a weekly, possibly thanks to the injection of some I.R.B. money. It plucked up courage, but continued to advocate Griffith's "Hungarian" policy, as if nothing was happening in Europe. By the irony that so often attaches to nicknames, the Rising had been dubbed by the Unionists the "Sinn Fein Rebellion". When public sympathy turned in favour of the rebels, this circumstance was of great value to *Sinn Fein*. But in the absence of Griffith's pen, little headway was made.

Between the two stools Hobson, the theoretician of "defensivism", sat disconsolately on the ground. His misfortune was that he had escaped arrest by the merest chance. A good stretch would have brought him back into the leadership, as it brought MacNeill. His hopes rested on the survival of the Volunteers, since he could move with neither *Sinn Fein* nor the I.R.B., and he busied himself with the Volunteers' Dependents Aid Committee. This was, however, amalgamated with Mrs. Clark's "National Aid" at a conference in November to which the Dublin Trades Council sent five delegates.

General Maxwell was recalled in the same month. It was not that he was thought excessively severe. Such would scarcely occur to a government engaged in the slaughter of millions. It was because the mood of sullen non-co-operation that had settled on Ireland was not conducive to enlistment. The generals still had faith in the tongues of the politicians. Macready, triumphant from the incredible reform of abolishing compulsory moustaches from the lips of British Tommies, suggested that Redmond and Carson undertake recruiting campaigns "in their respective parts of Ireland". Carson was for conscription and no nonsense. Redmond had been at intervals demanding the release of the internees. Was he to make bricks without straw? Lloyd George intrigued his way into Asquith's shoes and became premier on 6th December. With one eye on the United States he prepared the grand gesture, stating frankly that the men were a greater embarrassment locked up than free. On 22nd December those held at Fron Goch were released, on 23rd December those at Reading. They were met with bonfires and panegyrics. Among them were Arthur Griffith, from Reading, and Michael Collins.

Almost immediately there was announced a by-election in North Roscommon. Griffith, already preparing to re-issue *Nationality* with money provided by James O'Mara the Limerick bacon manufacturer, was reported to be offering Eoin MacNeill on behalf of his party. What was the I.R.B. to do about this? A candidate was found in the person of Count Plunkett, who three days before his nomination was deprived of his membership of the Royal Dublin Society for no better reason than that he was his son's father. He and his wife had suffered deportation to England for the same reason. He was adopted at a conference at Boyle, attended by Seamus O'Doherty, and presided over by Fr. Michael O'Flanagan. Griffith did not proceed with his plan. Instead he offered £150 towards the cost of Plunkett's campaign. The physical force men declined it. But they accepted workers irrespective of their brand of separatism, and the campaign brought together men who had had few previous opportunities for collaboration. Among the *Sinn Fein* men who came were Sean Milroy, Darrell Figgis and Griffith himself. Seamus O'Doherty and Kevin O'Shiel joined with Alec MacCabe and Michael Collins. Lawrence Ginnell, the only nationalist M.P. who carried on the tradition of Parnell, took part and there was a small contingent from the Irish Citizen Army.

The election was fought amid the worst snows of the century. The moving spirit was Fr. Michael O'Flanagan. Gaelic scholar, incomparable orator, and champion over many years of the small farming stock from which he sprang, he was at this time curate at Crossna and brought with him thirteen other young priests from neighbouring parishes. His speeches were suppressed by the censor. He demanded that Ireland should have freedom no less complete than that of France or Germany. But he introduced a new note, essential in the west. He demanded "the land for the people". And it was on this rather than on his somewhat vague national policy that Plunkett won the election. After his victory he announced that he would not attend at Westminster.

Within weeks the Conacre War flared in Roscommon. Estates

at Arigna, Warren, Mockmoyne and Tinnacarra were invaded by hundreds of small farmers, lightly armed with loys and an occasional pitchfork.[1] Strips were apportioned and digging was in full swing when the police arrived. They did not arrest their men without a struggle. But the farmers were overpowered, and some of them went to jail. Alec MacCabe, one of the most influential I.R.B. men in Connacht, drew the conclusion that MacDiarmada had drawn years ago in Loughrea. The land agitation could break the grip of the Redmondites.

On 23rd January 1917, President Wilson had made one of the less equivocal of his statements in favour of "Government by the consent of the governed". On 4th February Lloyd George repeated the demand like a begging echo. At the same time the Roscommon result provided unmistakable evidence of a German plot to land arms in Ireland. Seamus O'Doherty and twenty-five other prominent separatists were arrested and deported. Simultaneously the old imperial recipe—Home Rule with partition—was spiced up and placed on the mat for the dog to sniff at. Redmond showed his contempt by leading his followers from the House, thus paying dangerous tribute to his abstentionist critics.

The I.R.B. alternative to attendance at Westminster at this time owed something to *Sinn Fein*, but was not identical with it. It consisted of winning public endorsement in the next general election of the Republic established in 1916, and thereafter appealing to the Peace Conference which was expected to follow the war, over the head of the British Government. With the object of securing unity on some such policy Count Plunkett called a National Convention for 19th April. While Griffith was still urging his Hungarian policy, the physical force men could in the meantime record two victories. Michael Collins had succeeded Joseph McGrath as secretary of the National Aid. His policy was to prepare for another rising, and he began to recreate the I.R.B. cadre from his new key position. Cathal Brugha had begun the secret reorganisation of the Volunteers and in collaboration with Collins he formed a liaison committee with the Citizen Army. According to R. M. Fox this had been reorganised as the "Connolly/Mallin Social and Athletic Club" in June 1916. These joined with *Cumann na mBan* to grub up the original type from the basement of Liberty Hall and reprint facsimiles of the proclamation, which were posted throughout Dublin at Easter. A tricolour was placed by a steeplejack on the most inaccessible mast above the ruined Post Office.

[1] See O'Callaghan, *For Ireland and Freedom*, p. 29.

Over 2,000 delegates attended the Convention from national organisations, local authorities and trade unions. Count Plunkett demanded for Ireland both legislative and executive independence.[1] He called on those present to "use every means" in their power to effect "the complete liberty" of their country. On this, and on the demand for prisoner of war treatment for those in custody, there was agreement. Nobody thought of questioning the great illusion that a just peace was possible without a series of revolutions. The struggle with Griffith took place on an organisational question.

The Count wanted a new organisation to which *Sinn Fein* and others would affiliate but which would establish its own independent branches or "Liberty Clubs". But Sean Milroy, closely followed by Griffith, came forward to oppose. They suggested a federal council of existing organisations to be known as the "Executive Council of the Irish Alliance". The rather shadowy debate took substance when Fr. O'Flanagan suddenly suggested that Griffith was anxious to retain the support of Gavan Duffy's "Irish Nation League" which had only the night before taken an ambiguous decision on the subject of abstentionism. No decision being reached, Fr. O'Flanagan and Arthur Griffith were requested to meet privately and frame an acceptable compromise. This was the "Organising Committee of the National Organisation" which thereafter disputed and debated for nearly six months before being superseded. Its members consisted of Count Plunkett, Fr. O'Flanagan, Cathal Brugha, Countess Plunkett, Arthur Griffith, Stephen O'Mara, Sean Milroy, Alderman Kelly and Dr. Dillon. The two sides were closely balanced. The only immediate action decided upon was on the issue of prisoners.

At this point the masses began to impose their solution. The "National Organisation" had no name. But *Sinn Fein* had, and an undeserved reputation to boot. Throughout the country members began to flock in. The issue of *Nationality* for 19th May recorded twenty-eight applications to affiliate newly established clubs. Small farm areas were to the fore—Arigna, Gort, Castlerea and Kinvara. Members of the United Irish League and Ancient Order of Hibernians, were leaving those organisations and joining *Sinn Fein*. The process accelerated throughout the summer, and by this process *Sinn Fein* changed its character as it became a mass organisation.

Lloyd George's plan for partition could not survive the Redmondites' departure. While those soon tired of outer darkness, their action had precipitated the formation of Anti-partition Leagues throughout

[1] *Irish Opinion*, 28th April 1917, p. 2.

Ulster. Protestant churchmen joined with Catholics in a memorial of protest. Partition was British policy. But if an American expeditionary force were ever to cross the Atlantic, some way must be found of giving it at least the appearance of Irish acceptance. The election of one of the prisoners, Joseph McGuinness, in the Longford by-election of 10th May spurred the Prime Minister to action. He devised his next manœuvre, the Irish Convention. The Irish were to draw themselves into a knot already strung by the British. Then Alexander would draw his sword. And lo, partition.

On 16th May Lloyd George sent identical notes to Nationalists and Unionists offering a choice between immediate partition or an Irish Convention that would seek an agreed solution. When they chose the Convention, the powers of this body were announced. Its members were to be appointed from delegates recommended by organisations. Its powers were to be purely advisory. Its discussions were qualified by a stipulation that "Ulster must not be coerced". When Englishmen failed to agree unanimously the majority party took power. Such an arrangement was deemed too simple for Irishmen. The Organising Committee, *Sinn Fein*, William O'Brien's "All for Ireland" movement and organised Labour declined to make nominations. Sir Horace Plunkett was chairman, Lord Southborough secretary, and the government's own nominees comprised the Provost of Trinity, Dr. Mahaffy, and William Martin Murphy, the instigator of the 1913 lock-out, who had hounded Connolly to his death not two years before.

As Lloyd George matured his proposal, the campaign on behalf of the prisoners was pursued. At a great meeting at Beresford Place on 10th June, Cathal Brugha and Count Plunkett made eloquent appeals for prisoner of war treatment, or release. The prisoners themselves had brought organised resistance to a pitch that reduced governors to despair. The speakers were arrested. In the fracas that followed Inspector Mills received a blow from a hurley which proved fatal. A monster meeting in Phoenix Park protested against the latest arrests. Arrangements were begun to send up another prisoner, Eamon De Valera, in the by-election in Clare caused by the death of William Redmond, the Nationalist leader's brother.

Even Lloyd George's ingenuity quailed before representing the Irish scene as one of peace and sweet accord. President Wilson faced formidable opposition to his war policy. If the Irish Convention was to help him to get troops across the Atlantic it must be given a promising start. What more promising than that England was turning over a new leaf? The gesture decided upon was the release of the prisoners,

Brugha and Plunkett from Mountjoy, the Countess Markiewicz from Aylesbury, and the remainder from Lewes. The men from England reached Dublin on 18th June amid scenes of tumultuous enthusiasm. The reorganised Volunteers appeared in public for the first time, acting as stewards to control the crowds. Countess Markiewicz, arriving in the evening, was met by a guard of honour of the Citizen Army and was escorted in triumph to Liberty Hall. Efforts by the police to assert their authority were brushed aside in the jubilation of the people.

Dr. McCartan, a member of the I.R.B. who had been active in the transitional period, was about to sail for America with the intention of proceeding to Russia. His departure was delayed while the signatures of the released prisoners were secured to a statement addressed to the President of the United States. This was transcribed on to a handkerchief starched by Mrs. O'Doherty. It was unstarched by Mrs. Neil Kerr and sewn into McCartan's clothing. With it he left Liverpool for New York on board the *Baltic* on 20th June 1917.

CHAPTER SEVEN

LAND OF THE FREE

MELLOWS arrived in New York in time to witness the sunset of American democracy. Within months the classical scene vanished. Washington's constitution had, it is true, already sprouted grotesque parasites corresponding to the needs of monopoly capitalism. But soon there was little of the original to be seen. In January 1917 the hoardings still carried soiled and torn posters recalling the President's electoral confidence trick. "Wilson for President—He keeps you out of war" was the substance of them. His socialist opponent dropped 150,000 votes from the people's fear of splitting the peace front.

But the President was not installed a month when he raised the apparently harmless question of American mediation. This was the first step in the implementation of the secret agreement made between Sir Edward Grey and Colonel House on 22nd February 1916. America was to call a conference of belligerents. If Germany should refuse to attend, the United States would declare war on her. Should she attend and reject the American peace terms, the United States would "leave the conference on the side of the allies".[1]

This pleasant cabal was hindered first by opposition within the American administration, second by the Easter Rising, third by the indeterminate result of the Battle of the Somme, and finally by the President's need for re-election. But it was not thought possible to delay the militarisation of America. The mediation plan was accompanied by proposals for military training in High Schools. Behind the scenes measures were being prepared which ran grossly counter to the President's high promises.

After calling back to the ship to collect his pay—very much against Callanan's advice—Mellows was taken to the *Gaelic American* where his appearance excited so much interest that a pencil sketch was made.[2] He reported to the veteran Fenian, John Devoy. Seventy-four years of age, and extremely deaf, the old man retained his faculties impaired only by a certain inelasticity of mind, such as is common in even the

---

[1] Tansill, *America and the Fight for Irish Freedom*, p. 216.
[2] Original in National Museum, Kildare Street, Dublin.

most active old person. He kept general control of the policy of the paper while delegating the task of editing to assistants. But he showed he was still the man who had rescued James Stephens by the care he bestowed on the young refugees. Mellows, the first Commandant to reach the U.S.A., and arguably the senior surviving officer of the Volunteers, was particularly welcome.

To political exiles Devoy was the hearthstone of Irish America. He symbolised the cause. *Clann na Gael* was the counterpart of the I.R.B. Its membership was more varied than that of the home organisation, though its policy could be more rigid. Although it was still *par excellence* the haven of political immigrants, it had undergone evolution and differentiation in American conditions. The founding exiles had settled and become American-Irish. Their children were Irish-Americans, and as such sharply distinct from the new arrivals. Men like Joseph McGarrity, born fifty years before 1916, emigrating without a penny and building up a flourishing business as a distiller in Philadelphia, could still respond to the pulse of his native Tyrone. With others an American interest had inevitably reared itself alongside the Irish. It grew stronger with each generation, as the Irish increasingly thought of themselves as a "race" rather than as a nation.

The Friends of Irish Freedom showed those differences more markedly. Sponsored by *Clann na Gael* in the knowledge that a Rising was contemplated, they were established at the "Irish Race Convention" of 4th March 1916. The first President was a Dublin Protestant, Victor Herbert, a composer of popular operettas. The most influential member was the Irish-American jurist, Mr. Justice Cohalan, embodiment of worldly success, a man whose undoubtedly genuine Irish sympathies were already an element in purely American policy. There was also the barrister Jeremiah O'Leary, member of the 69th Regiment, in whom Irish Fenianism had become transmuted into his own attractive form of American radicalism. These men responded to similar influences in different ways.

The flood of refugees after the Rising upset the balance within both *Clann na Gael* and the Friends of Irish Freedom. Misunderstanding was inevitable. It is important to appreciate, however, that the main current of Irish emigration had been non-political, and that the main concentration would be found in the Catholic community, and in the trade unions. The Knights of Labour in particular had a strong Irish element.

At Devoy's request Mellows joined the staff of the *Gaelic American*. He did not remain long at 141 West 97th Street. War and revolution might grimace from every cloud but the stuffy middle class concentrated its gaze on its own bagatelles. The landlady refused to serve Mellows when he came down to dinner in a white Aran gansey. At a saloon in Columbus Avenue frequented by John Devoy and others a stranger fancied he detected a trace of a Wexford accent. He introduced himself as Patrick Kirwan of Gorey, and before long Mellows transferred to more homely surroundings at 73 West 96th Street. There he could collect books, entertain friends, talk half the night if he wished, and above all come and go as he pleased.

His first article in the *Gaelic American* appeared on 20th January 1917. An account of the Rising in Galway, it was signed "A Volunteer Officer". Under the same pseudonym he wrote a serial history of *Na Fianna Eireann*, which is still the best extant, though it attempts no critical assessment. The first aroused some protest from Kenny who had crossed with Callanan. The blacksmith lacked tolerance and could not forget what he fancied a wrong. He insisted on an enquiry into the incident at Craughwell, almost charging Mellows with cowardice. But upon Mellows' explanation he was compelled to withdraw. Mellows himself shrank from personal publicity. So few people knew he was in New York that towards the end of February newspapers reported his arrest in a round-up in Ireland. His further writings in the *Gaelic American* will, it is to be feared, never be firmly identified.

His first public appearance seems to have been at the *Clann na Gael* Convention of 11th February. He shared the platform with Judge Cohalan and Captain Monteith. The conference pledged $100,000 to the Victory Fund of the Friends of Irish Freedom. His instructions were to make known the facts of Easter Week to the Irish in America. He restricted himself to this task, leaving to the fearless, tireless and inspired propagandist Hannah Sheehy-Skeffington that of telling the Americans.

He became rapidly accepted as the leader of the political refugees, and was chosen by *Clann na Gael* to reply to the toast "The Men of Easter Week" at the Fenian Jubilee Dinner on 5th March. In his speech he confined himself to defending his action in helping to expel Redmond's nominees. This had "made the Rising possible" and but for the Rising "Ireland would be tamely submitting to conscription". The word "would" has of course no place in history, except for those defending a position. Mellows was defending the "offensivist" policy of forestalling conscription by means of a Rising, rather than waiting for the threat of conscription to justify and spark off a Rising.

Since the New Year the tempo of Wilson's war-policy had con-

stantly increased and many of the exiles were viewing the situation
with alarm. There were reports of a Russian collapse and rumours of
a separate peace, likely to be highly disconcerting to American big
business, as can readily be shown.

Owing to the British blockade American exporters could not
supply both sides as is the custom of neutrals. According to *The
Call*, in the year 1916 the U.S.A. invested $1,340,264,764 in foreign
loans of which four-fifths were for direct war purposes. All this
investment went to the *Entente*. By the end of the year the U.S.A.
had been transformed from a debtor into a creditor nation. By contrast Britain, whose government indebtedness at the beginning of the
war was $3,500,000,000, now owed $17,309,260,000. An *Entente*
defeat would seriously embarrass United States finance. And needless
to say, the circles among which Judge Cohalan moved were alive to
this fact.

But unlike the peoples of Europe pitched headlong into the carnage,
the Americans had time to observe its effects, and indeed upon themselves. One-fourth of all American exports were fulfilment of war
orders. The price of food rose steeply. Speculation began, and by the
end of 1916 there were demands that municipalities should sequester
supplies that were being hoarded. Early in 1917 there were food
riots in the Bronx. Starving women shouted for bread on Fifth Avenue.
Prices then fell slightly but demonstrations continued.

Wilson's mediation plan broke, as it was intended to do, on the
Entente's insistence on territorial and financial reparations. His next
move was to announce that no peace settlement was acceptable that
did not take into account the interests of the New World—that is to
say the vast U.S. loans to Britain and France. The sanctions that might
be needed to see that Britain and France paid their debts, if necessary
at the expense of Germany, underwent a strange sublimation. There
was vague lip-service to "equality of nations" and "government by
consent of the governed" to which Lloyd George chimed hypocritical
concurrence. The administration hurried through its war legislation
and began the assault on conditions of labour and civil rights.

Railwaymen threatened to strike for wage increases and against the
relaxation of safety regulations. Wilson proposed anti-strike legislation. The seventeen-year-old son of a socialist was expelled from school
for refusing military drill in peace-time. Bayonet practice was introduced and pupils who refused it were summoned and fined. Diplomatic
relations with Germany were severed on 2nd February. German shipping was impounded at Boston, Philadelphia and Panama. An attempt

to introduce an "Espionage Bill" was postponed thanks to popular opposition. The arming of merchantmen began. Seventy-three I.W.W. men were arrested in Seattle on a trumped-up charge of murder and seemed likely to follow Tom Mooney, then facing the rope for the crime of organising trade unions on the Pacific coast. Ready to hunt bigger game, General Pershing's "Punitive Expedition" was withdrawn from Mexico, and plans were made to recruit aliens of British and French nationality into the American armed forces.

The true rulers of America showed what speed and ruthlessness big business is capable of. Months before the declaration of war, an advisory commission of the Council of National Defence was secretly preparing plans. Among its seven members, all appointed by the President, was the notorious Samuel Gompers of the American Federation of Labour. In defiance of the instructions of Congress the President gave this commission executive powers, and measures subsequently approved were anticipated.

The millionaire press discovered German agents in everything its proprietors disliked. They were behind the Cuban revolt of 19th February. America altruistically offered troops to suppress it. They were plotting the return of Texas which the U.S. had annexed from Mexico. They had their eye on the Philippines. Every skeleton in the American cupboard received an airing. And if workers were short of food, was it not natural enough when German submarines were taking such a heavy toll of the ships that were taking it away? Yet it was difficult to satisfy the businessmen. "Rumours of Revolution in Germany depress the markets" ran a headline. When rumour evaporated it was, "All markets buoyant—Wheat and cotton futures soar".

All that was best in America worked for peace. The Women's Peace Party fought against the militarisation of the youth and enlisted Hannah Sheehy-Skeffington's brilliant gifts on their behalf. In the state of New York the Socialist Party of America launched a "resist war" campaign as soon as Wilson broke with Germany. Four thousand people heard Hillquit at the Carnegie Hall on 6th February. The socialist clergyman Norman Thomas filled the Cooper Union. Scott Nearing resigned his professorship rather than belie his pacifist convictions. The Labour barrister Frank P. Walsh joined with Quinlan and Elizabeth Gurley Flynn in a campaign to save Tom Mooney, which was enthusiastically taken up by the old-established *Irish World*. This newspaper, indeed, outdid all others, apart from the extreme left, in opposition to the war, declaring that the real aims of the belligerents were to further the interests of capitalists struggling for markets and spheres of influence. "Presidential dictatorship" was roundly denounced. The socialist "left" and the Irish "centre" were beginning to draw together, said the Catholic *Freeman's Journal* in a leader.

At a general meeting of the New York Socialists held on 3rd March, a resolution was adopted to the effect that in the event of war the party should "use every endeavour to hasten the return of peace, to oppose the war policies of the Government, oppose censorship of the press and the mails, the restriction of rights of free speech and free assembly, and organisation, and to fight the enactment of oppressive sedition and espionage laws". Leon Trotsky was present at this meeting, and proposed an amendment in favour of Hervé's old policy of "strikes against war". Among those who spoke were Santeri Nuorteva and Morris Hillquit. These and others were delegated to attend a special National Convention at St. Louis.

Then, on 14th March, came the collapse of Tsarism. Court circles had been angling for a separate peace. This would free the hands of the aristocracy for a struggle against the rising forces of discontent within Russia. These belonged to two categories. On the one hand the big bourgeoisie wanted a more vigorous and competent prosecution of the war that would guarantee Russia the territorial gains allocated her in the secret treaties. On the other hand the popular masses, with the industrial workers at their head, wanted an immediate peace without annexations or indemnities—just what America was going to war to prevent. As the representatives of the bourgeoisie were hesitantly steeling themselves for a Palace coup, the Petrograd garrison revolted. The bourgeoisie hastily thrust a Provisional Government into the breach. By this means they hoped to tame the revolutionaries, and divert their energies against the *Entente*. This, as was proved in the event, they lacked the power to do.

What was plain to the American socialists was that the people had made the revolution. On 20th March Madison Square Garden held its most jubilant meeting within living memory. Streets were crammed solid four blocks away. Red flags were hoisted as Cahan, Golfort and Hillquit, who had spent their youth under Tsarism, urged that the revolution should be taken up in America for the abolition of "landlords, capitalists and financiers". That same day the Spartacist Franz Mehring was returned to the Reichstag as member for Potsdam.

The State department quickly assessed the character of the changes in Petrograd, and the United States recognised the government of Milyukov on 23rd March. Petrograd was now to be "purged of traitorous Prussianism". But a section of the Socialist Party led by Spargo now disassociated itself from the New York Resolution without waiting for the Party Convention. The United States, said Spargo, should "resist international crime", by which he meant not the war but Germany's contribution to it. By a stroke of irony the *Irish World* simultaneously criticised the hesitancy of Hillquit's followers, and read the Socialists a severe lecture on consistency. The capitalist system was breaking up before their eyes and yet they did not notice it. The *Irish World*, as its subtitle "American Industrial Liberator" indicated, had a largely proletarian readership and continued some of the traditions of the Molly Maguires.

On 1st April John Devoy called a meeting of the refugees at the Shamrock Club. He informed them that America's entry into the war was now imminent. If they did not wish to risk possible extradition he advised them to take out citizenship papers at once. The suggestion took them aback and there was much indignation. They had come to the United States as belligerents against Britain. Now they might have to fight as its allies. There was talk of *Clann na Gael* being out of date and proposals were made to start another organisation. Mellows and the Citizen Army man, Frank Robbins, opposed this, and these two together with Captain Monteith made an appointment with Judge Cohalan to seek his opinion on the main point that troubled them. Would adopting American citizenship involve abjuring that of the Irish Republic? This had been proclaimed in Easter Week and they were determined to make it a reality. Unfortunately, owing to a misunderstanding the deputation arrived on a day when the judge was entertaining the celebrated Celtologist, Kuno Meyer, who had emigrated when his Chair at Liverpool grew too hot to hold him. Monteith scented a diplomatic snub and took his leave. Mellows and Robbins saw Cohalan's deputy, Kennedy, who confirmed their fears. Adopting American citizenship involved forswearing all other. The young people decided to remain as they were. Next day was Good Friday, and America entered the war.

Two days later *Clann na Gael* celebrated the first anniversary of the Rising. The main speakers were Judges Cohalan and Goff, together with Victor Herbert and R. R. Rooney. In this difficult situation Goff and Cohalan spoke with much caution. They were loyal American citizens. They supported the President and the war, for it was upon them. It was up to Wilson and Lloyd George to make good their promises and give Ireland her place among the nations. Before the meeting closed with the "Star Spangled Banner" as yet unmutilated by the excision of the anti-British stanza, Judge Cohalan took occasion to "declare publicly" that "there would not be in any quarter of the country a single man of Irish blood who would not now think of America first". A telegram was sent to the President pledging support in whatever measures he took for the maintenance of American honour and interests.

Here was the origin of a political divison which persisted after the war was over. There were two camps, those who regarded the interests of American imperialism as paramount, whatever their personal sympathies, and those who put Ireland first. And what, indeed, the well-breeched gentlemen on the *Clann na Gael* platform might ask, was a respectable citizen to do? He must either subordinate his Irish sentiments to his class interests, or subordinate his class interests and revel with Hillquit in Madison Square Garden. Jeremiah O'Leary was the odd man out. As loyal an American as Cohalan, he differed in policy, and considered the English alliance tantamount to the reconquest of America. He had long fought the "nefarious financial institution called the British Empire" which, among other things, passed laws excluding American citizens from oil and mining rights in British Guiana. He continued his satirical anti-British magazine *Bull* and protested against the war by all means open to him. He believed that the main enemy of American capitalism was England not Germany.

Cohalan and his associates now developed a complex line of policy which remained basically imperialist. A petition to the President was prepared which expressed the "earnest hope that, like Cuba, Ireland will be made free by the action of America". Congressman Mason urged that the United States should make the "complete separation of Ireland from Britain" a war aim. But it should have been clear that the aims that he already had were good enough for the President, and there is no evidence of anything being added to them. When Ireland was separate, ran the pipe dream, the Irish people might desire advice upon how to use their freedom. It was proposed that a commission of five or six people should be sent to Ireland to offer it. The Treasury should then purchase $100 million worth of Irish bonds providing they paid interest at not less than 3 per cent, and reimburse itself by selling these on the American market. For comparative purposes it is worth noting that $100 million was approximately the figure for the entire external assets of all Irish banks for the year 1913. The week Congressman Mason made his speech, Messrs. Fords announced the opening of their factory in Cork City. The Corporation agreed to forgo rates in order to encourage the investment.

The *Irish World* held to its anti-war position and assailed those who "posed as leaders of their race" for abdicating their rights as citizens. "An American", said an editorial, if he disapproves of the war, "is entitled to use all his power, individually or in co-operation . . . in compelling his servants (the officials) to bring about peace." The war was being fought for markets and investments and the aggrandisement of capitalist empires. So spoke nineteenth-century democracy, soon to be outlawed. The stand of the *Irish World* has received surprisingly little recognition.

On 23rd April an Easter Commemoration meeting was held at Boston. National figures were absent. *Clann na Gael* in that city had fallen on lean days. The younger people were anxious to revive it and on the platform were Nora Connolly, Robert Monteith, Frank Robbins and Margaret Skinnider. Mellows made his speech standing between two American soldiers, one bearing the tricolour and the other the Stars and Stripes. He conceded nothing and made a forthright assertion of Irish Nationality.

"The Irish people", he said, "stand on their inalienable right to complete national independence and nothing less will satisfy them. Ireland is one today, and recognises one enemy only, England. . . . The revolution of last year gave England the lie that she was fighting on behalf of small nationalities. . . . Constitutionalism has been on trial again and has failed miserably, as it has always failed. It has ended where it always ended, in corruption and betrayal."

Cheers rang out as he read the proclamation of Easter Week. He had replied to Cohalan. He had declared in the midst of America at war that Ireland, no less than America, had distinct national interests in no way dependent on the convenience of other countries. As a result of this meeting and a series of personal visits, three *Clann na Gael* branches were established in the Boston district.

One of Mellows's meetings was held at Westfield where Mellows met the family who were to become his closest friends in America, John and Ellen Hearn. John Hearn and his wife were both from County Waterford. Ellen had been taken to the United States as a child, but John had worked for a time as a National Teacher in Dalkey, before emigrating at the age of twenty-one. He settled in Westfield in 1889 and conducted a retail furniture business until his death in 1951.

The entry of America into the war awakened German interest in Ireland. The Rising of 1916 had been but half-heartedly supported. It was believed that England would easily break the pincer claw being thrust round her. But now a Rising might perform the more important function of delaying the American expeditionary force. Through their agents the German Government intimated to *Clann na Gael* that they would be prepared to send arms to Ireland again.

Mellows was deputed to maintain contact with them. He conceived the idea of landings in Wexford and County Down. There was to be no question next time of "not a shot in Ulster". It was tentatively agreed that if he could get to Germany he would be allowed to supervise the assembling of the arms, and to accompany them. One plan was to reach Spain by way of Montevideo. Another was through Holland. Even Turkey was considered as a country of transit. But all failed. As Mellows hung about the docks, thinly disguised as a seaman seeking a ship, but also working for the *Gaelic American*, the war crisis continued to mature.

He wrote to Mrs. Hearn on 28th May that he had been so worried that he had not the heart to write to anybody. Possibly he was referring to the danger of induction into the American Army. Or possibly he had in mind the plans for landings. There is not much doubt that around this time Volunteers were alerted to the possibility of landings of arms on the coast of Wexford, his old friend Nolan of Waterford among them. But whether Mellows was concerned with this will probably never be established. In the same letter he refers to the Espionage Bill, expressing satisfaction with the tangle of amendments and addenda that were likely to make it almost impossible to understand or apply.

At the end of April the Conscription Bill passed House and Senate. The Socialist *Call* sharply attacked it, and within weeks twenty organisations had banded together at an anti-conscription conference. On 30th May the first American conference for Peace and Democracy was held in New York. The Socialists had elected Hillquit, Berger and Lee delegates to the Stockholm Conference. The State Department refused them passports, as the British refused MacDonald and Roberts. A few days later the French followed their lead. June 6th was Registration Day in America. Mellows registered in the 8/17 Assembly District as a Citizen of the Irish Republic.

The Petrograd Soviet made its appeal for a peace without annexations or indemnities. President Wilson was embarrassed and replied evasively. There would be "no annexations or indemnities—except . . ." and the exceptions were all. He intensified the struggle against opponents of the war. On 15th June Emma Goldman and Alex Berkman were arrested at the office of the "No Conscription League". Thousands of mothers protesting against the draft were clubbed from the City Hall by the police. On 22nd June James Larkin was arrested on account of an allegedly seditious speech. Less than a week later Elizabeth Gurley Flynn was arrested at Duluth on a vagrancy charge in order to prevent her addressing a meeting. On 1st July soldiers attempted to break up the traditional Socialist meeting on Boston Common. The Socialists offered resistance and the battle raged for three hours. Congressman Mason, himself opposed to the Conscription Act, joined with Hillquit in the second American Conference for Peace and Democracy which was held at Chicago. But so far the Irish were unaffected, and the first registrations as Citizens of the Republic remained unchallenged.

On 2nd July Dr. Patrick McCartan arrived at the *Gaelic American* office and told his business to a hastily summoned meeting of the Revolutionary Directory of *Clann na Gael*. Arrangements were at once made for copying and publishing the statement of the returned prisoners. As regards Russia, Devoy was confident that it could not be reached from America. He advised McCartan to rejoin the *Baltic*. But the doctor raised the question of the Address to Wilson. A statement was drafted, discussed at a further meeting, and taken by McCartan to Cohalan's summer residence for the Judge's expert opinion. It was brought to Washington on 22nd July by a deputation consisting of McCartan, J. K. Maguire of *Clann na Gael*, and John D. Moore, secretary of the Friends of Irish Freedom. The document was signed by McCartan "on behalf of the Provisional Government of the Irish Republic". Whether Cohalan had assented to his assumption of this position would be of profound historical interest. The President declined to receive it lest he be misinterpreted as recognising a "revolutionary movement" against an allied government. But he permitted his secretary to accept it. McCartan commented that the public would not distinguish too sharply between the President and his secretary.

What was this Provisional Government and of whom did it consist? McCartan must have had in mind the reconstituted Supreme Council of the I.R.B. which in Fenian tradition was the Government of the Republic. But why the word provisional? This was to connect it with the events of 1916 and the claim that the Rising had conferred on Ireland a belligerent status that would be valid at the Peace Conference. McCartan thus took his place alongside *Clann na Gael*, neither subject to their discipline nor wholly distinct from them.

It has been suggested that this arrangement did not entirely please *Clann na Gael*, who therefore fell in with a proposal that McCartan should accompany Mellows to Germany and make such political gains as were possible while Mellows was collecting arms. He could then either return to Ireland or try to reach Russia. *Clann na Gael* undertook to facilitate the adventure.

If they achieved little success, they are scarcely to be blamed in the crescendo of war hysteria and political repression. On 27th July pickets of the Women's Peace Party were jailed for the crime of quoting President Wilson's own words. The *American Socialist* was banned from the mails, despite the efforts of a defence committee comprising Hillquit, Symon Hardman and Frank P. Walsh. A few days later *Bull* was treated similarly. In Oklahoma young men who took to the hills to avoid conscription were rounded up by armed police after bloody scenes. On 15th September there were nationwide raids on the I.W.W. and on the 29th Elizabeth Gurly Flynn was arrested again, together with Tresca Giovanitti, and lodged in the Tombs. Printed signs were posted in public places "Obey the law and keep your mouth shut", signed by Attorney-General Gregory. Gradually the average citizen became intimidated and the German contacts of *Clann na Gael* became unusable.

There were conflicting opinions on what to do next. Since April the Friends of Irish Freedom organisation had rapidly declined. J. K. Maguire and others secured the promise of an Irish Race Convention to discuss the problems raised by the war, and Murray's Hotel was booked for 25th August for a gathering to which all Irish Nationalists and Socialists were to be invited. But the leaders showed no enthusiasm. No preparations were made, and the convention did not take place.

On the other hand John D. Moore and the members in closest touch with Ireland had been greatly encouraged by developments at home. They believed that the way to revive the Friends of Irish Freedom was by a vigorous propaganda of Ireland's demand for a Republic. If this demand was incompatible with the aims of the war, then so much the worse for the war. Aided by Jeremiah O'Leary and Peter Golden of the *Gaelic American*, John D. Moore organised a meeting at Salzer's Harlem River Casino attended by 4,000 people. Instead of calling off street meetings, as the cautious advised, he multiplied them. Following one of these a speaker named Robertson was arrested and charged with seditious utterances at the corner of Broadway and 37th Street. On 25th August Jeremiah O'Leary was indicted on charges of conspiracy to violate the Espionage Act. Repression had spread to the Irish.

E

At the open-air meeting next day an American sailor who mounted the platform to support the "war aims petition" of the Friends of Irish Freedom, was arrested by the police. The crowd rescued him. He escaped. But on 29th August, the Friends found their usual stance occupied by a recruiting rally complete with bands and illuminations. They moved down to 35th Street, and in less than half an hour had the block jammed with people. Stephen Johnson denounced the occupation of 37th Street as a deliberate attempt by Mayor Mitchel to stifle free speech. He was arrested. The next speaker was removed from the platform but allowed to go free. His waving of the Stars and Stripes did not save John D. Moore. He was taken in as soon as he began to criticise Britain. Margaret Curley, niece of the Mayor of Boston, was then detained. At this point police automobiles were driven into and through the crowd, hooting, screaming, headlights glaring. Batons were drawn and the people clubbed mercilessly as they fled in panic. When friends of the prisoners came enquiring after them, they in turn were clubbed outside the men's night court at 57th Street. Thereafter street meetings became virtually impossible.

It was now that high authority seems to have decided to push Judge Cohalan off the fence on which, from the President's imperialist standpoint, he was sitting. On 16th September a statement was issued to the press with an embargo on publication till the 22nd. Cohalan received a copy almost at once.

It claimed that among the papers seized in April 1916 in the raid on the office of the German diplomat Von Igel were documents showing that Cohalan had sent through Count Bernstoff, the German Ambassador, a request to Berlin for aerial attacks on England during Easter Week and the landing of troops, arms and ammunition in Ireland from Zeppelins. As crude as most State forgeries need to be, one of the documents is said to have incriminated a man who, at the time of the alleged offence, had spent a full year mouldering in his grave.

But there is evidence that Judge Cohalan lost his nerve and was only with difficulty persuaded to issue a denial through the intervention of Dr. W. J. Maloney.[1] The result was a considerable volume

[1] Dr. W. J. Maloney, son of an Edinburgh watchmaker, left his practice in New York to join up at the outbreak of war. Seriously wounded in June 1915, during a protracted convalescence he became disillusioned after the brutalities of General Maxwell in 1916, and the shameless bargain for Italian belligerency. He resigned his commission on the 9th August 1916 after a violent quarrel with fellow-officers in a club after he had condemned the hanging of Casement. Returning to the U.S.A. to rebuild his practice he gravitated towards the Socialist Party through his friend Norman Thomas. He was introduced to the Irish movement in New York by J. C. Walsh, soon after his arrival in 1917.

of protest against the President's tactics, which were widely believed to have been a revenge for Cohalan's efforts to defeat him in the Presidential Election. Nevertheless, Judge Cohalan now dropped out of politics till the end of the war. With him a further section of the Friends of Irish Freedom sank into inactivity.

Cohalan's weakness was of course that, since he supported the war, he was hardly in a position to resist its consequences. Now that America was Britain's ally, the main support for Irish independence must come from Americans who were opposed to all imperialism, and these were to be found in the socialist movement. This explains the development of an alliance unique in American history.

Already in July it had been decided to offer Hillquit for Mayor of New York, and a committee had been formed with Alexander Trachtenberg as secretary. Hillquit took an active part in the defence of Berkman, who was attached to the Mooney case, and with Frank P. Walsh continued vigorously to demand Tom Mooney's release. While associated with all the great popular causes, he scarcely merited the title of "Liebknecht of America" that was bestowed on him by zealous admirers. Yet his very moderation may have reassured people who would hesitate to stand behind a more extreme leader.

It was natural enough that an effort should be made to enlist Irish support for him, and on 13th October the Irish Progressive League was founded for this express purpose. Those who attended the inaugural meeting included Peter Golden, J. E. C. Donnelly, who had published James Connolly's paper *The Harp*, Patrick Quinlan, Con O'Lyhane,[1] Emmet O'Reilly, and Nora Connolly, who became Treasurer. The membership grew rapidly, as the new society attracted the active members of the Friends of Irish Freedom, to which at some period affiliation appears to have been made. A series of well-attended public meetings was organised, one of which at the Terrace Garden, Third Avenue, on 25th October, was historic. Three thousand people were present and the Chairman, Charles Linehan, welcoming Hillquit "in the name of the Irish of New York", declared, "This is the first time that a gathering representative of all sections of the Irish, *Clann na Gael*, Gaelic League, Friends of Irish Freedom and Hibernians has been addressed by a Socialist." Among the speakers were Nora Connolly, Patrick Colum, and General Pierson of the Boer Army. Much play was made with the grafting shoneenism of the outgoing Mayor, the worthless grandson of the great John Mitchel.

Hillquit's candidature was supported not only by the radical *Irish*

[1] Now using the form Lehane.

World and the Republican *Gaelic American* but by the Catholic New York *Freeman's Journal*, and the effect of the alliance was felt far and wide. To some criticism from the right the *Buffalo Echo* replied:

> The Government, supported by the Liberal bloc, sought to crush the Centrists and the Socialists. The Centre party which bases its political platform on Christian principles naturally maintains an attitude of opposition to the materialistic philosophy which is the bedrock of socialism, but on this occasion, when they are threatened by a common foe, the situation called for a co-ordination of Centrist and Socialist forces.

Mellows and McCartan stood at the fringe of this movement, though Mellows was in constant touch with Nora Connolly and Frank Robbins, then a regular visitor at Kirwans. When it became clear that the *Clann na Gael* was no longer in a position to get them to Germany, the two men began to frequent the dock areas disguised as seamen. Unfortunately McCartan soon tired of the blue gansey, and to Mellows' amusement and disgust, would enter some quayside saloon bedecked with straw hat and monocle. Even this might pass muster with a double rum, but not with a small Amontillado.

Growing impatient they sought contact outside the circles normally thought reliable by *Clann na Gael*, and were finally introduced to a German-American girl who had worked for the former consulate. McCartan told her he was anxious to attend the Stockholm socialist conference. She introduced him to a former employee of the Hamburg-Amerika line, and a few nights later they met a man who promised to get them aboard ship for Holland.

All seemed well. Mellows secured a birth certificate in the name of Patrick Donnelly, McCartan borrowed that of McGarrity's nephew Francis Conlan. They obtained discharges from ships, erased the names with acid, and wrote in the names they were assuming. At the Custom House they obtained seamen's certificates without difficulty. On 3rd October McCartan signed on as messman on board the *Maumee* bound for Rotterdam. Mellows and he noted with some anxiety that the man in charge of the office had been arrested the previous night. They decided to proceed, however, and said goodbye at the Battery. Mellows was to follow on another ship in a week's time. He would have been best advised, as Devoy subsequently pointed out, to have kept well away from the German-American girl, and allowed her to communicate the plans when they were ripe. But like a gardener digging up his seeds to see how much they had grown, he called to see her once too often. Secret Service men were watching from a saloon opposite. They raided the house and on 23rd October he was arrested and driven to the office of Assistant U.S. Attorney J. C. Knox, where he was charged with conspiracy to represent himself as an American citizen with a view to procuring a false seaman's certificate. In default of $7,500 bail he was lodged in the Tombs, where Elizabeth Gurley Flynn was told of his arrival.

Built in 1838, this prison was almost as uninviting as its name. Not of course that America, with all its brutality and corruption, could ever achieve the drab inhumanity of Britain. Each cell held two cots, two stools and a shelf. The bedding was filthy and there was filth everywhere. The food was uneatable but prisoners could buy food and newspapers from a vendor. Shut up in a cell all day except for two hours in the morning and two in the afternoon, when he could walk the tiers, Mellows felt acutely the confinement and above all the lack of a bath. But after a day or two Mrs. Kirwan, with whom he communicated, sent him a change of clothes.

The newspapers next day announced the arrest of "General Leon Mellows" and Baron von Reinkelhausen by the Americans, and Dr. Patrick McCartan ("alias Francis Conlan, alias Wilson") by the British when the *Maumee* called at Halifax. Lloyd George obligingly announced a German conspiracy to stir up *Sinn Fein* feeling against the child of his heart, the Irish Convention, and thus wreck his plans for giving Ireland self-determination.

Secret Service men now introduced variety into the prison routine. They awoke Mellows in the middle of the night, dragged him from total darkness into dazzling light, asked questions repeatedly and told him that his accomplices had "squealed", and he should "confess".

They did not wait for the confession. It was published on the 26th. Mellows had "confessed" to "being acquainted with" Cohalan, Devoy and Jeremiah O'Leary. The last had been threatened with a further indictment and had disappeared. Next day Cohalan and Devoy were publicly charged with having "deserted" their agent. The press reports were transmitted to Halifax for the "softening up" of McCartan.

Imagining that Mellows was being well looked after, the refugees from Ireland had taken no immediate action. The taunt of the New York newspapers shocked them. Both Frank Robbins and Nora Connolly left their electioneering and hastened to the prison. The prisoners were in one cage, the visitors in another. Between them stalked the warders, at a leisurely pace, listening first to one conversation, then to another. The sound was of babel. Mellows was able to convey that he denied having made any confession. Then, suddenly, speaking in Irish before the warder checked him, he explained to Nora the location of documents hidden in the Kirwan's house. The police had already searched, but had missed them.

Robbins reported Mellows' position to Kenny at the *Gaelic American*, but a paralysis of policy seemed to have fallen on *Clann na Gael*. Nothing was done. Nora Connolly therefore approached Dr. Maloney who immediately offered $7,500 from his own resources. He consulted a lawyer named O'Doherty who secured Martin Conboy for the defence. Conboy felt that American real estate would prove more aceptable bail than the dollars of an alien. Through Padraic Colum, Nora Connolly made contact with Mrs. Margaret Murphy who, with the belated blessing of *Clann na Gael*, pledged two houses for Mellows' freedom. He was released on 2nd November. But his plans for returning to Ireland were shattered. He was marooned in the land of the free.

CHAPTER EIGHT

RESURGENCE

THE release of the prisoners marked the commencement of a new phase in the Irish struggle.[1] The entire surviving leadership of the national movement was now free. Throughout the country *Sinn Fein* membership grew with a fresh impetus. In the week immediately following the return eighty newly established clubs sought affiliation. But the prisoners, for all their greater prestige, were no more politically homogeneous than those outside, and differences had already revealed themselves among them.

Perhaps the leading "offensivist" was Thomas Ashe. He had early grasped the importance of political action and supported participation in by-elections while others still hesitated. A native of Castlegregory in the County Kerry and an Irish speaker, he had been for some years a school-teacher in County Dublin. He had visited the U.S.A. with Diarmuid Lynch in 1914 in order to raise funds for the Gaelic League. It was he who led the skilful actions in north County Dublin during the Rising. He was a staunch I.R.B. man.

At the other pole was Eoin MacNeill. The instinct of many of the prisoners had been to shun him. De Valera had insisted on his rehabilitation, thereby revealing that, for him at least, there would be no second Rising. Some of the I.R.B. men gravitated towards this position. They drew from defeat not the conclusion that Easter Week was ill-timed, but that the principle of national insurrection was at best "propaganda by the deed".

Before the prisoners dispersed to their homes, Michael Collins handing out the rail fares, a meeting was held. De Valera revealed his uncertainties frankly. At this point Thomas Ashe could almost certainly have taken the leadership. But the I.R.B. had not yet reorganised its forces. And Griffith was on the flank. Collins' group was pursuing the old "offensivist" policy. But the leadership established under Mrs. Clarke's auspices was following more complex designs, which were not all to her liking. Following the March revolution, which was received with general rejoicing in Ireland, came a Bolshevik declaration in

---

[1] This chapter continues the story of events in Ireland. The life-story of Mellows is resumed in Chapter 9.

favour of a British withdrawal from Ireland. It was estimated that the Soviets would soon hold power, and it was in that expectation that the I.R.B. had despatched McCartan on his way to Russia.

De Valera, leader of the prisoners, became leader of the movement. But as soon as a meeting could be convoked the three divisions of the I.R.B. were amalgamated once more under the leadership of Ashe. It is said that Cathal Brugha declined to participate. He was no less an "offensivist" than previously. But he believed that I.R.B. secrecy had wrecked the prospects of 1916 and nothing could induce him to change this opinion. Nor was De Valera present. He had given the bishops an undertaking that there would not be another Rising and had MacNeill constantly around him as an object lesson. Such a stand was the price of bourgeois neutrality at the time.

Until he contested Clare, De Valera had not made a political speech in his life. But circumstances favoured him. The Parliamentary Party had decided not to contest. But in order not to permit a *Sinn Fein* walk-over, the Crown Prosecutor for County Kerry resigned his office of profit and went forward as an independent. The Redmondites thus found themselves drawn unwillingly into battle behind an exception- ally poor candidate. On the other hand, local dissatisfaction had been exacerbated by the dismissal of a popular school-teacher, Mr. Walsh, from his post at Killaloe. Peter Clancy, the local man adopted by *Sinn Fein*, readily withdrew in favour of De Valera. The Crown Prosecutor was confronted by the Crown Prosecuted, with only one possible result, despite all the organisers the Redmondites hastily despatched into the area. As Lawrence Ginnell put it, "Mr. De Valera stands for Ireland and Mr. Lynch stands for England." De Valera's platform was the Proclamation of 1916. He declared that the only law he recognised was the law made by the Irish people. His policy for making that law effective was an appeal to the Peace Conference.

The constituency included the area where Mellows had been in hid- ing. His friends Sean MacNamara and Fr. Crowe were active in the campaign. During its course there was further significant progress in public opinion, and the first signs that the bourgeoisie were becoming vicariously revolutionary. On 19th June the Catholic hierarchy had issued a warning about "dangerous associations". They forbade the clergy to speak of "politics or kindred subjects in church". On Polling Day, 11th July, the bishops of Killaloe and Limerick made public statements in favour of *Sinn Fein*. De Valera won the seat by 5,010 to 2,035.

From now on Volunteers began to appear again in uniform. On

5th August a convention of Redmond's "National Volunteers" was held. Colonel Maurice Moore was empowered to negotiate for re-unification with the parent body. Two weeks later their hitherto inviolate arms were seized during a series of police raids, the main targets of which were *Sinn Fein* organisations. Ireland was seething with political discontent. Public meetings were held throughout the country, addressed by Griffith, De Valera, Michael Collins, Francis Fahy, Sean Milroy, H. M. Pim and Lawrence Ginnell. The latter had left Westminster when the Clare result was announced. On 11th August W. T. Cosgrave won Kilkenny for *Sinn Fein* after the *Kilkenny People* had been suppressed for supporting him. Prisoners arrested in the round up of 14th August began to refuse to recognise the courts. The following week 104 new clubs affiliated to *Sinn Fein*. Notwithstanding the renewed repression, on 19th August De Valera and Francis Fahy addressed the famous meeting at Tipperary town, where they were guarded by armed Volunteers bearing the forbidden *caman*[1] in the very shadow of the military barracks. Next week in Limerick De Valera spoke of "making British rule in Ireland impossible". In September the campaign was carried into Ulster.

During this period the I.R.B. reorganised quietly. The *Oireachtas*, which opened at Waterford on 5th August, was made the occasion for conveying the instruction that the I.R.B. must once more infiltrate and capture the Volunteers. Piaras Beaslai and Diarmuid Lynch were present. Dual control was to be re-established. The leaders felt that things would go differently another time. But some of the members doubted.

On 18th September eighty-four men detained in Mountjoy raised the old demand for prisoner of war treatment. When it was refused they systematically destroyed the fittings of their cells and declared a hunger strike. Thomas Ashe was deprived of his bed, bedding and boots and subjected to forcible feeding. He collapsed, and after a few hours died in hospital. Public opinion was shocked. The coroner brought in a critical verdict. Twenty thousand people followed the coffin to Glasnevin. Thousands more lined the streets. Ashe was accorded military honours. Three volleys were fired over the grave, after which Fr. Albert was to have delivered the oration. Suddenly Collins thrust his way forward. After a few words in Irish he declared, "That volley which we have just heard is the only speech which it is proper to make above the grave of a dead Fenian."

Collins' action has never been explained. Some might relate it to the

[1] Hurley stick.

anti-clericalism he professed while in London. His critics have seen it as
an attempt to thrust himself forward, even to become Ashe's successor.
But it is known that Ashe's position was taken by Sean McGarry who
was extremely sympathetic to Collins. It is possible that the action was
decided on by the I.R.B. The man they were burying was to them the
President of the Irish Republic. If this is so, it is a vivid reminder that
their allegiance was not to De Valera.

By the autumn of 1917 it was clear that Justices of the Peace were
becoming sympathetic to *Sinn Fein*. The authorities had experienced
difficulty in securing convictions. Like their predecessors of Repeal days
they sought to purge the magistracy. The Lord Chancellor, Ignatius
O'Brien, replaced the disaffected with stout Unionist blades. One of
those dismissed, Mr. P. Roughan of Killaloe, borrowed his reply from
Repeal days. He offered his services as an arbitrator. Under the
Arbitration Act, 1886, provided two parties agreed beforehand to sub-
mit to his decision, it became binding in law. From September onwards
an increasing volume of business was attracted to the "*Sinn Fein* Court"
at Killaloe. Cases were even transferred from the Ennis County Sessions.
The people were creating a basis for a "dual power".

As one section after another was provoked into resistance the need
for a unitary party grew more pressing. All separatist bodies were
coalescing under the title of *Sinn Fein*. External issues between them
were becoming matters of internal policy. *Sinn Fein* was no longer as
Griffith conceived it. Trade unionists in the midst of a continuous
struggle on the industrial front took their politics from *Sinn Fein*. On
25th October 2,000 delegates met in Dublin. The vital policy decisions
must at last be taken.

The people were coming to see in National Independence the escape
from land-hunger, exploitation and war. Unity was therefore essential.
But policy differences were deep. On the one hand Griffith, anxious to
assimilate the new organisation to the old, chose to regard the Convention as the tenth *Ard Fheis* of *Sinn Fein*. He refused even to con-
template another name. He was not opposed to appealing to the Peace
Conference. But possibly with more horse-sense than some of his
opponents he saw in it no more than a means of exerting pressure on
Britain, with whom the settlement must be made.

The I.R.B. likewise held to its position, but foolishly relied on caucus
manipulation instead of conducting a struggle on policy. There was
much cynical laughter when it was revealed that both Darrell Figgis,
for *Sinn Fein*, and Michael Collins, for the I.R.B., had issued lists of
recommended candidates for the new executive. The duty of defending

Republicanism fell to Cathal Brugha, Mrs. Tom Clarke, Fr. O'Flanagan and Countess Markiewicz. Unfortunately, however, the contest revolved round the issue of accepting Eoin MacNeill. There were interruptions when the Countess declared, "The Proclamation had to be reprinted at Liberty Hall on Sunday to take his name off it."[1] The fight was entered on personalities, and consequently lost. De Valera announced, "I stand or fall by MacNeill." When the votes for the twenty-four member executives came to be counted MacNeill's headed the list with 888. Cathal Brugha came second with 685, and the Countess fifth with 617. Collins barely scraped a place. With 340 votes each, he and Ernest Blythe shared the lowest qualifying poll.

There was long wrangling over the constitution to be adopted. Was the organisation aiming at a Republic or a dual Monarchy? It was De Valera, whose aptitude in the game of word-sharping may have come from constructing simultaneous equations, who drafted the winning formula. It ran:

> *Sinn Fein* aims at securing the international recognition of Ireland as an Independent Irish Republic. Having achieved that status the Irish people may by referendum freely choose their form of government.

The fallacy is, of course, that freedom to choose their own form of government by referendum required more than the status of being "recognised". It demanded actual state power in the hands of a government of the Irish people. If that were lacking the principle of choice remained inoperative.

But the formula was not intended for conceptual analysis. The delegates were not lawyers, still less mathematicians. The two simultaneous propositions could be understood differently by different people. Needless to say they were. On the one hand it was held that *Sinn Fein* would accept nothing less than a Republic, but that the Irish people might decide details of its constitution by referendum. On the other it was thought sufficient that after presenting a case to the Peace Conference, Ireland would accept what terms she could get provided these were the subject of a referendum.[2]

---

[1] This assertion could cut two ways and there is no wonder it was strongly assailed.

[2] Contemporaries agree that the formula sprang from Mr. De Valera's fertile brain. Sean O'Faolain sees in it a peace formula to please both left and right (*De Valera*, p. 69) and hints at a trace of disingenuousness. Desmond Ryan (*The Irish Struggle*, pp. 33–4) suggests that the formula was based on Lalor's letter to the second issue of the *Irish Felon* (Fogarty, pp. 79–80). There are reasons for doubting this. Lalor did not advocate "Federal Union". He referred to it in order to show that a movement which did not aim at complete independence first and foremost (that is repeal of the Union) could not possibly result in a durable or desirable association of Ireland and Britain. He did not say that association was desirable, but that unless it was voluntary it could not be. The 1917

Each side hoped to make its own interpretation prevail. Meanwhile the question of policy demanded another compromise. The result was:

This object shall be attained through the *Sinn Fein* organisation which shall, in the name of the sovereign Irish people:

a. Deny the right and oppose the will of the British Parliament or Crown or any other foreign government to legislate for Ireland.

b. Make use of any or every means available to render impotent the power of England to hold Ireland in subjection by military force or otherwise.

Griffith may have taken comfort in the limiting words "legislate" in the first clause, and "in subjection" in the second. Fr. O'Meehan objected that "any and every means" might "include anything from pitch and toss to manslaughter". On balance the politicians seemed to have successfully appropriated the ends and locked them away in the "aims and objects" clause. The military men seized on the means and, as is frequently the case in such transactions, forgot about ends until they reappeared years afterwards in a moment of terrible revelation.

One final clause declared:

And whereas no law made without the authority and consent of the Irish people is, or ever can be, binding on the Irish people, therefore in accordance with the resolution of *Sinn Fein*, adopted in Convention in 1905, a Constituent Assembly shall be convoked, comprising persons chosen by Irish constituencies, as the supreme national authority to speak and act in the name of the Irish people and to devise and formulate measures for the welfare of the whole people of Ireland.

Social programme was there none, neither for the workers nor small farmers. Countess Markiewicz made an impassioned appeal to Irish workers to resign from English and join Irish trade unions. The constituent assembly was not even pledged to perform the function inherent in its name—that of enacting a new constitution. It may be that the two facts are connected. Griffith and his followers probably felt, to varying degrees, that some connection with England, whether through a common Head of State, or the continuance of certain constitutional provisions, might prove a safeguard against social revolution.

The contest for the main executive positions reflected the political

compromise, as shown above does not necessarily involve complete separation. And Arthur Griffith who wrote the preface to Fogarty's edition of Lalor which appeared in 1918, rejected Lalor's argument and declared that "as a thinker he fails". The compromise was inspired by current need.

tussle. Griffith was determined to be President, and Plunkett who opposed him was unlikely to defeat him. A deputation waited on the former President and at political gun-point persuaded him that this position at least must be held by a 1916 man. Plunkett then also agreed to withdraw and De Valera was unanimously elected. The lesser positions were duplicated. The two secretaries were Darrell Figgis and Austin Stack. Ginnell and Cosgrave were the treasurers, while Griffith and Fr. O'Flanagan became joint vice-presidents. The executive was well larded with Griffith's supporters, but on the whole the Republicans, I.R.B. and non-I.R.B., held the balance. It was noteworthy, however, that the first I.R.B. man to be elected held only seventh place. Possibly the news of the arrest of Mellows and McCartan, which was published on the 25th, helped to injure the "offensivist" cause.

The establishment of the unitary *Sinn Fein* political party was an event of considerable importance. There was now one centre to which all who had previously hesitated could adhere. But this was no monolith. The republicans had come in hesitatingly; Fr. O'Flanagan maintained afterwards, mistakenly. Their militants were growling in the background. The workers and small farmers whose interests demanded an assault on the entire colonial system found no place in the new organisation whose leaders were to establish their constituent assembly. They supported the liberation front for what it was, and for what it was not flocked into the trade unions and Volunteers.

After the close of the public session on 27th October, the Volunteer leaders present were called together and agreed to meet again as soon as the prisoners in Mountjoy had won their release. Accordingly they reassembled on 19th November. The I.R.B. was more successful in this field. De Valera once more became President and Cathal Brugha Chief of Staff. Sean McGarry became secretary, Diarmuid Lynch Director of Communications, and Michael Collins Director of Organisation. MacNeill and Hobson presented themselves at the door. Neither of them was admitted. For Hobson it was a strange irony now that his policy seemed officially vindicated. Presumably the I.R.B. wanted no able reinforcements to the "defensivist" camp. Hobson was bitterly affronted and virtually retired from public life.

The Trade Union Congress had been held in August at Derry. The illusions regarding the war which had vitiated the Sligo discussions had to some degree dissipated. It was agreed, against the vote of "twenty-four Britishers", to send representatives to the Stockholm Conference, and to press for the recognition of the Irish Labour Party as a distinct unit in the international movement. The Executive was also mandated to support the Petrograd Soviet's demand for a peace without annexations or indemnities. The President, Thomas Mac Partlin, expressed the sense of the gathering when he declared that thousands of workers were being slaughtered every day "in the interests of greedy capitalists". But he thought that since all powers engaged in the carnage professed to be occupied on behalf of the freedom of small nations, when Ireland ultimately put forward her claim to independence "there would be no doubt that her rights would be conceded". Mac Partlin had substituted the *Sinn Fein* for the parliamentary road to independence. But the substitution was not complete. In a discussion on the franchise Bill then before the Westminster Parliament, he implicitly assumed Home Rule in the old style and remarked that "an Irish Parliament will be the real signal for the opening of the class war". In either event, the role of the Labour movement in the struggle for national independence was that of a supporter not an initiator.

It might be thought that the October revolution which brought the Bolsheviks to power on 7th November would have rapidly changed this situation. Here was the event Connolly had prophesied, "the conflagration that would not burn out till the last throne and the last capitalist bond and debenture will be shrivelled on the funeral pyre of the last war lord". But it was lighted in the East, not the West. It was by no means easy to see through the mist of censorship and misrepresentation, that here was the European crisis in which Ireland might win freedom. The Irish people gave instinctive support. As Aodh de Blacam put it, "nowhere was the Bolshevik revolution more sympathetically saluted". This showed the sound instinct of a people always quick to sense a popular cause. Understanding came more slowly as Bolshevik policy revealed itself.

The Irish Labour movement was without a periodical. But on 1st December *Irish Opinion* reappeared under the editorship of Andrew E. Malone[1] and the political control of Thomas Johnson. From the first it set out to publish the facts about events in Russia. Whereas Griffith's *Nationality* commented that the decree on nationalities which recognised the right of secession would "simplify the position of the Balts and Finns", *Irish Opinion* declared, "against that formula (of the right of secession) the greatest military victories are as nothing". The Editor began to republish the writings of James Connolly, and slowly there was resumed that process of education which Connolly had undertaken during the first years of war. But events moved quickly, and the working class was unprepared for its place in the vanguard. Hence, when for

[1] Pseudonym of L. P. Byrne.

the first time since 1789 the most revolutionary international force had become embodied not in an opposition but in a government, the strongest oppressed class in Ireland, though better organised than ever before and rapidly growing in political consciousness, was not able to imbue the national movement with its objectives.

In such conditions the Parliamentary Party was an irrelevancy. It suffered a deadly blow in the collapse of the Irish Convention. In the forlorn hope of placating the Ulster Unionists Redmond yielded to the British the bourgeois Ark of the Covenant—control of Customs and Excise. His close colleagues Joseph Devlin and the bishop of Raphoe repudiated him. He retired from the Conference a broken man and died on 9th March 1918. After conveying the Convention's report to the wastepaper basket, Lloyd George determined to press ahead with conscription.Dillon warned him that he was driving the people into the arms of *Sinn Fein*. Family sentiment and the violence of the Ballybricken mob gave Redmond's seat to his son. Lloyd George, who knew nothing of such things, professed to sense a revival of support for the Parliamentarians.

The conacre war flared more angrily than ever. The threat of conscription hung over the small farmers' sons. Here was a time when a Rising might have been planned with every prospect of success. In February estates were seized from Sligo to Clare, and this time the police were either not called in or failed to secure arrests or convictions. In some cases, as for example that of the Persse estate in south Galway, applicants for conacre announced their intention of cultivating on a co-operative basis. Cattle drives took place with increasing frequency. Diarmuid Lynch spent two months in jail for preventing the export of pigs by seizing them on the way to the quay and delivering them to the slaughterers. But this was not quite the same thing as resistance at source. The new Dublin headquarters contained no Connolly or MacDiarmada. While Volunteers were not forbidden to take part in agrarian struggles, an order of 2nd March made clear that they did so only in a strictly personal capacity. In theory at least, the national revolution was kept distinct from its social base.

The same order forbade raiding for arms. This had begun immediately after Christmas 1917, when landlords' houses were attacked at Gort, Lisbrien, Derrykeel and Chevy Chase. In January the raiders were at Kinvara, and the practice was spreading throughout the west. While it was taken for granted that the arming of Irishmen would discourage the government from imposing conscription, the means of securing arms must not discourage respect for private property.

But as fast as the more moderate leaders found scruples to the advantage of their gentleman friends, the British Government seemed determined to dispel them. On 9th April a Bill was introduced empowering the government to impose conscription in Ireland by Order in Council at any time. The reaction struck the authorities with the impact of a tank regiment. The Lord Mayor of Dublin called a conference which met on 18th April. The Parliamentarians abandoned Westminster once again and withdrew their candidate in the Offaly by-election in favour of *Sinn Fein*. It is to be noted, however, that at no point did they consider a general assault against the imperialist war or seek an alliance with revolutionary forces within England.

Nationalist, Labour and *Sinn Fein* signed the anti-conscription pledge. Perhaps so as to encourage those who feared another Rising, a deputation went to Maynooth to secure from the Catholic hierarchy permission to administer the pledge at the church gates after Mass. Two days later the Irish Trades Union Congress held a special meeting, from which there was issued a call for a one-day general strike on 24th April. This was decisive. No comparable shut-down had ever been seen in Ireland. Industries and shops closed completely, except in the Unionist districts of Belfast. The British Government had succeeded in uniting against it an array of forces not seen since the days of the United Irishmen. And, Unionist Ulster apart, the uneven development of different provinces no longer seemed to facilitate disunity. The British Government sensibly decided not to make the threatened Order in Council. But with the automatism of a conditioned reflex it adopted its time-honoured recourse—coercion.

On 25th April the clauses in the Defence of the Realm Act relating to aliens were extended to persons of Irish birth. But Englishmen in Ireland were not to be treated as aliens. There was a purge at Dublin Castle. On 1st May Shortt replaced Duke as Chief Secretary. Ignatius O'Brien who had been ridding the magistracy of *Sinn Fein* infection was rewarded with replacement by Sir James Campbell. A week later Lord French replaced Lord Wimborne as Viceroy, and General Shaw replaced Sir Bryan Mahon in the military command. It was becoming hard to find an Irishman in the central administration. The lower echelons began to feel insecure. Their loyalty, already affronted by constant policy changes, weakened steadily. In those conditions members of the detective forces began to hedge their future by warning Volunteers of actions contemplated against them.

On 15th May information of an impending wave of arrests was conveyed to Collins, who reported it to the Volunteer Executive two days later. On the one hand, the warning was not taken seriously. On the other, there were those who regarded dignified martyrdom as a political weapon. Substitute officials were decided upon, but no adequate precautions taken. In the early hours of the next morning there were eighty arrests, including De Valera, Griffith, Sean McGarry, Count Plunkett, Sean Milroy and Countess Markiewicz. The prisoners were deported to England and lodged in various prisons. The government then announced the discovery of yet another "German Plot", the evidence for which it would "not be in the public interest" to disclose. Lord Wimborne, whose temper may have been soured by the gall of dismissal, suggested that the main evidence was the "new broom" in Dublin Castle. The opinion of the Irish people was shown on 21st June when the prisoner Arthur Griffith defeated Redmond's successor, John Dillon, in the East Cavan by-election. As a result of the prominent part he played in the campaign Fr. O'Flanagan was suspended from his functions. He was alleged to have attended meetings in parishes without having received the permission of the priest-in-charge.

Although the arrests had removed from the scene members of both wings of the movement, the advantage was with the Republicans. The leadership of *Sinn Fein* passed to Fr. O'Flanagan, that of the Volunteers to Michael Collins, who showed a remarkable ability to take up the departmental burdens of others. Cathal Brugha departed for England where he remained until the war ended, preparing for the possible assassination of the British Cabinet in the event of the imposition of conscription. His place was taken by Richard Mulcahy. Sean McGarry's place in the Supreme Council seems to have been taken by Collins' friend, Harry Boland. The authorities followed up the arrests by proclaiming a number of nationalist organisations. These included *Sinn Fein*, the Volunteers, *Cumann na mBan* and the Gaelic League. The following day, 9th July, they prohibited all meetings, assemblies or processions in any part of Ireland. The government had confused the Gaelic League with the Gaelic Athletic Association, who thereupon ordered that Gaelic sports should be conducted openly at every possible venue on Sunday, 4th August. An attempt by *Sinn Fein* to defy the ban by holding meetings on 15th August led to a fresh wave of arrests, after which once again the authorities threatened to introduce conscription. Every action they took brought fresh recruits to *Sinn Fein* and to the Volunteers whose nominal strength now exceeded 100,000—that is to say the entire loss caused by the Redmondite defection had been made good. Rumour had it that conscription was to be imposed when

Parliament reassembled on 15th October. That may have been the intention. But instead it reassembled to discuss the German peace note of 6th October. The issue was never tried to conclusions. Instead Lloyd George's government decided to grab for a further term of office while the men were still in khaki and its system of war-time repression was still intact. This hasty and discreditable manœuvre sacrificed the Irish Party, and sealed the fate of the Liberals and of Lloyd George himself.

Relations between Labour and *Sinn Fein* gave rise to thorny problems. Four candidates (Unionist, United Irish League, *Sinn Fein* and Labour) were adopted in Derry. The event provoked the I.R.B. publicist P. S. O'Hegarty to urge that "where *Sinn Fein* and Labour both have claims to put forward a candidate, those claims shall be amicably settled".[1] Towards the end of the month the National Executive of the Irish T.U.C. and Labour Party issued a manifesto announcing Labour's intention of contesting the election as an independent pledge-bound party. Such action had been foreshadowed at the annual meeting in Waterford where the success of the strike against conscription was reflected in a new sense of Labour's power. The sentiment of the gathering was strongly national. Not even twenty-four Britishers could be found to challenge the current of antagonism to colonial rule in Ireland and of admiration for the Russian revolution. The manifesto now quoted the Waterford Congress and demanded that "Ireland no less than Belgium or Serbia, Poland or Finland, Bohemia or Esthonia, shall have the right to decide its own form of government, to choose its own sovereignty, to determine its own destinies without limitations, except such as are voluntarily conceded or are common to all nations."

Then followed a pledge to attempt to "win" for the workers of Ireland, collectively, the ownership and control of the whole produce of their labour. The manifesto stood for self-determination and socialism.

But what of the tactics to be employed in order to achieve these things? A section headed "Ireland and Westminster" stated that "The National Executive has therefore decided by a unanimous vote that the members of the Irish Labour Party shall not attend the House of Commons." But a sentence followed that was to have fateful consequences. "It is conceivable that altered circumstances and the interest of the workers and democracy may, however, warrant a change of policy which shall be determined by a special National Congress." Labour was

[1] *Saoghal Gaedhealach* (Irish Life), 7th September 1918.

reproducing the type of formula adopted by *Sinn Fein*, resistance to be followed by compromise. To *Sinn Fein* abstention from attendance at Westminster was the test of separatism, not Republicanism or any economic arrangement. To Labour the test of freedom was economic, and attendance at Westminster was not a matter of principle.

There was an angry reaction from O'Hegarty. Labour's decision was "unpatriotic". If Labour declined an arrangement and fought all seats the only result would be the absence of Labour representation in Parliament. *Sinn Fein* would fight all those who failed to accept abstention without reservations. The issue was debated at the *Sinn Fein* Convention on 29th October. Here it appeared that the Standing Committee had been prepared to negotiate with Labour on the basis of its manifesto. But this did not suit the I.R.B. Harry Boland read the text of the "very drastic test" that was to be applied to the nationalism of every Labour candidate. It is possible that the I.R.B. wished to control the nominations, and possibly Boland and Collins intended to make Labour representation as difficult as possible. *Sinn Fein* was to contest every seat where the full pledge was not taken. Sean T. O'Kelly protested that the Labour men were as good separatists as the members of the *Ard Fheis*. But Boland had his way.

There is reason to believe that Labour felt that the pledge demanded of them would make it impossible for the party to function independently. A special conference was called for 1st November. There it was decided to revoke the previous decision. Labour was not prepared to accept a status under the aegis of *Sinn Fein*. Nor was it prepared to fight for one without it. It was not even prepared to fight openly for an acceptable alliance, which might have been achieved on the basis of unconditional acceptance of abstention, but complete freedom on social issues. The signing of such a pledge was a small thing in comparison with the virtual exclusion of Labour from the counsels of the nation in the days that were to follow. An abdication of responsibility comparable to that of Sligo took place. Labour did not offer a single candidate.

In its dealings with the Parliamentarians of the North, *Sinn Fein* showed less purism. The suggestion was made that in constituencies where a contest between *Sinn Fein* and a Parliamentarian would lead to a Unionist victory, a plebiscite should be held in which the nationalist voters could decide who was to be their representative. The strong man Eoin MacNeill was despatched to conduct the negotiations with Dillon and Cardinal Logue. He ignored his instructions and agreed to the equal division of the eight seats. In the minds of many Socialists the contrasting treatment of Labour and Nationalist bred an incipient distrust of *Sinn Fein*. For one factor in the decision was the desire to secure a voice at Westminster through the back door.

On 11th November there was revolution in Berlin. The war ended. As if anxious to get on with the work of counter-revolution which was now before them, hundreds of British soldiers made an assault on the *Sinn Fein* premises. They were beaten off. And it was not long before their mood changed.

The khaki election was announced on 23rd November and the campaign began. Robert Brennan, the *Sinn Fein* Director of Elections, was arrested and deported to an English prison without charge or trial. He noted in his memoirs how in England war-weary soldiers and civilians sympathised with him and condemned the government. His place was taken in Dublin by James O'Mara. The censor deleted one quarter of the election manifesto that he issued. Candidates and organisers were systematically badgered and harried. Many districts were still under proclamation. Aeroplanes were used to scatter leaflets warning the people against the dangers of voting *Sinn Fein*.

The result was spectacular. Out of 105 candidates returned in Ireland, 73 were of *Sinn Fein*, 26 were Unionists, and six only were left to represent the once all powerful Parliamentarians. These were reduced from a national to a provincial party. But the party of the working class had voluntarily excluded itself. Since the party of the bourgeoisie had disappeared and that of the working class had remained in the background, the heterogeneous petit-bourgeois who had embodied the political aspect of the revolt of the masses must now show what they were made of. In any event, British Government was now devoid of moral authority in Ireland.

CHAPTER NINE

THE IRISH PROGRESSIVE LEAGUE

FOR Mellows, stranded in war-time America, his original mission completed, and no authority able or willing to suggest to him another, the sensible course was to do what lay to his hand, to strive to influence events in and from the United States. He was released from the Tombs in the last exciting days of the mayoral election contest. Although the entire Irish and Catholic press was for Hillquit, it was the Irish Progressive League that led the way. The Irish Socialists were proud of his internationalism. He had accepted the Bolshevik definition of a peace without annexations or indemnities. This was to say that not only must Germany vacate Belgium. Britain must vacate India, Egypt and Ireland.

The spirit of James Connolly was abroad. His daughter Nora, who had been Treasurer of the Irish Socialist Federation, was now Treasurer of the League. Patrick Quinlan attended from time to time. Premises were provided by J. E. C. Donnelly who had financed and printed *The Harp*. Hannah Sheehy-Skeffington provided the link with the Socialist Party of Ireland, and Con O'Lyhane, who presided over the meeting at the Imperial Hotel on 1st November, had founded the Cork branch of the Irish Socialist Republican Party. In addition there were Frank Robbins of the Citizen Army and other 1916 refugees. The core of activists included a few leading Irish-Americans, such as Peter Golden and Dr. Gertrude Kelly. As he walked home with Nora Connolly and Frank Robbins after one of the final meetings, Mellows was asked his opinion of socialism. He replied that he had read Connolly's *Labour in Irish History* and agreed with its conclusions. But he was not sure that he understood Connolly's Marxism.

A house-party was held to celebrate Mellows' release. Another of Connolly's old I.S.F. comrades was present, Elizabeth Gurley Flynn. She remarked jokingly that they had recently shared a state residence. "Indeed!" expostulated a somewhat starchy Irish-American lady, "and what were you in prison for, Miss Flynn?" Mellows interjected with something nearer scorn than was usual to him. "Don't you understand," he asked, "that there is a struggle for peace and freedom in this country too?" He never forgot his experiences in the Tombs, nor the blatancy with which American reaction fought the class war. "In the United States there is no such thing as law," he used to say. But it was in the absence of law's mystification that he first grasped the universality of the struggle to which he was devoting his life.

Hillquit came a good third, and deprived Mitchel of his mayoralty. He increased the Socialist vote from 32,000 to 140,000. The election was on 6th November. Immediately afterwards came the seizure of power by the Bolsheviks. There were no State Department plaudits this time, or boasts of purging traitorous Prussianism. Instead, Lenin was denounced as a German agent. The imperialist world held its breath before the publication of the secret treaties, that would expose the true annexationist motives of the war. The Wilson administration refused even to consider recognising the new government, and pressed on with the intensification of reaction at home.

The harassment of individual Socialists was stepped up. Several contributors to *The Masses*, including Max Eastman and John Reed (then absent in Russia), were indicted before a Federal Grand Jury on a charge of publishing articles "discouraging to loyalty". *The Call* was deprived of its second-class mailing facilities but defiantly transformed itself into an evening newspaper and fed the news-stands direct. Michael O'Callaghan, who had been out in Tipperary during Easter Week, had been arrested during the election campaign for smashing the window of a shop which displayed caricatures of the Irish leaders. Now he was committed to the Tombs and faced the possibility of deportation under charges which included murder. The United States declared war on Austria, Socialist Congressman Meyer London alone dissenting. The *New York Herald* thus acquired reinforcement for one of the most revolting press campaigns in history. On 3rd December, as Austrians queued unsuccessfully for naturalisation papers, it began the systematic publication of the names of all enemy aliens resident in New York. Untold columns of small print were crammed with names, and the process still took weeks to complete.

American policy was in ruins. But what to the ruling imperialists was a monstrous nightmare, was a ray of long-awaited dawn to the oppressed peoples. As Wolfe Tone recorded of the French Revolution, the Russian Revolution became the test of every man's political creed. And it is needless to say that Mellows, like his great predecessor, was "a Democrat from the very commencement". As Tone observed of the French Revolution, the first emotions not only of Socialists but of Radicals and Liberals were enthusiastic. Not for six months did the *Irish World* publish an antagonistic article. *The Call* demanded recog-

THE IRISH PROGRESSIVE LEAGUE

nition of the proletarian state, and maintained that position with consistency.

With the prospect of a peoples' peace, a new meaning was given to Ireland's claim for representation at the Peace Conference. Relations between the Irish refugees and the American Socialists reached an unprecedented degree of cordiality. But the Irish-Americans who supported the war found an additional reason for estrangement. Hence the Irish Progressive League, created for Hillquit's campaign, decided to maintain its organisation. It now linked the demands of the two ends of Europe—Irish representation at the Peace Conference, and recognition of the Soviet Republic. A meeting was held at the Carnegie Hall on 21st December, under the auspices of the "Friends of New Russia". The purpose was to pass a resolution for an immediate armistice and American recognition of the Soviet Government. A second resolution in the name of the Irish Progressive League was prepared by Patrick Quinlan. It called for the representation of Ireland at the Peace Conference. As Emmet Larkin remarked,[1] there was considerable joint membership of the Irish and Russian solidarity organisations. This might be anathema to Mr. Justice Cohalan, now a "voluntary prisoner" in the wilderness, but it did not prevent John Devoy from speaking frequently on Irish Progressive League platforms. The old man had been a member of the Council of the International Workingmen's Association. He was no Marxist, but he was not afraid of socialism.

Mellows' new situation was made clearer by Dr. McCartan's experience. McCartan had contrived to return to New York in December and Mellows was in court when he was remanded. Margaret Murphy's houses did service a second time. McCartan went into medical practice in Philadelphia. Mellows remained with the *Gaelic American*, devoting his leisure to cultural activities at the Carmelite school and to the politics of the exiles. He readily adopted the sole formula for fruitful work under conditions of exile, namely to combine the advancement of Ireland's independence with the protection of the immediate welfare of her children, and to make all his demands on the *American* government.

Early in January the Local Draft Board sent him a questionnaire related to possible service in the United States armed forces. He declined to complete it, and returned the following letter dated 10th January:

---

[1] *Life of James Larkin*, p. 220.

Gentlemen:

I am in receipt of your Questionnaire which I return herewith unfilled, for the following, to me, very sufficient reasons:

(1) Because I am an Irishman and have devoted all my humble efforts since I came to the use of reason to help free my country from the tyrannous domination of England. At England's hands I suffered imprisonment and deportation for my convictions and work in the Cause of Ireland, and, finally, after the collapse of the Easter Week Revolution of 1916 (in which I am proud to say I took part), was forced into exile in order to escape the fate decreed for me by the British Government—that I be shot on sight. I sought the hospitality of this country, which arrogates to itself the title of the "Land of the free", which hospitality has been denied me.

My filling up of the Questionnaire, and your placing me in any particular group or class, would not in the least alter my fixed determination that, under no circumstances could I or would I have any connection whatsoever with the armed forces of the American Government while the American Government is, by its silence on the question of the independence of Ireland, acquiescing in England's continued occupation of Ireland against the manifest wishes of the Irish people, and despite the alleged war aims of the Allies that they are fighting for the freedom of small nations and the rights of democracy; and, furthermore, while America is actively engaged in England to keep Ireland in subjection by stationing the American Fleet in Irish waters, and by persecuting Irishmen in America for their efforts on behalf of Ireland.

Were America fighting England—the greatest menace to "small nations", I would be the first man to *volunteer* for service in the United States army, and would be proud to give my life fighting against Ireland's only and America's hereditary enemy.

(2) Because, in the Questionnaire, questions are asked me, the answers to which the United States has no right to know, viz: my occupation for the last ten years.

(3) Because, under Series VII. Citizenship, of Questionnaire, questions 4 and 5, I am asked on what date and place and by what vessel I arrived in this country. This information I cannot and will not give, for to state where and by what vessel I landed in this country would be to inform the British Government of the method by which I escaped the clutches of their bloodhounds, and, consequently, as I cannot conscientiously fill out all of the Questionnaire, I see little use in filling any of it.

I am a citizen of the *Irish Republic*, proclaimed Easter, 1916, which has the allegiance of the overwhelming majority of the people of Ireland, but which this country has not yet recognised. I owe allegiance to one country only and one cause only—IRELAND, and the Cause of Irish Freedom, which is the cause of GOD.

I am forwarding a copy of this letter to President Wilson.

I am, gentlemen,

Yours respectfully,

(Signed) LIAM O'MAELIOSA

(in Beurla) Liam Mellows

CEANN CATHA, ARM POBLACHT na h-EIREANN.

(Commandant, IRISH REPUBLICAN ARMY)

On 19th January, Mrs. Sheehy-Skeffington sent President Wilson the petition which had been circulated by the Irish Women's Council. For daring to publish it both the *Irish World* and the *Gaelic American* were banned from the mails. On 28th January a convention of Irish societies met to discuss possible action. It broke up after issuing a protest. The most effective demonstration was that called by the Women's Council itself. It was held at the Carnegie Hall on 13th February and Fr. Magennis of the Carmelites considered it one of the three most important gatherings of his stay in New York. He was loud in his praises of the Socialist chairman, Edward F. Cassidy, whose support helped to rally the Irish after the unexpected blow. The platform ranged from Nora Connolly and Dr. Gertrude Kelly on the left, through Mrs. Skeffington and Mrs. Judge Rooney, to Ella and Una Ford, daughters of the editor of the *New York Freeman's Journal*. Mellows, the only male speaker apart from the chairman, denounced the attack on the Irish-American press, and accused the Wilson administration of "tying the hands of Ireland". Since the New York papers were no longer obtainable in Philadelphia, Joseph McGarrity set to work establishing the *Irish Press*. It appeared on 23rd March with McCartan as editor.

Four days after the Carnegie Hall Meeting, Dr. McCartan sent the government a note protesting against a clause in the Anglo-American War Agreement providing for the conscription of Irish nationals into the American Army. The Progressive League at once launched a campaign, and just before McCartan visited Washington to put his case before Lansing, organised a meeting at the Central Opera House. The speakers were, apart from McCartan himself, for tactical reasons chosen from Americans. They included Morris Hilquit, Joseph D. Cannon (a Socialist candidate for Congress) and Peter Golden. The work of the Irish Progressive League drew a letter of congratulation from De Valera, and was entirely successful. On 13th March it was announced that, for the present at least, Irish citizens in America were exempt from the draft. McCartan's prestige rose considerably during this campaign and he was invited to address the Second Annual Dinner of the "League of Small and Subject Nationalities" where he met Dr. W. E. Dubois, the Negro leader, and Lajput Rai, who subsequently presided at the founding of the Indian Trade Union Congress in October 1920 and was Mahatma Ghandi's immediate predecessor as India's national leader.

Meanwhile Larkin had returned to New York from what may have been an attempt to reach Russia through Mexico. In mid-February he attended a meeting to elect a delegate to the Inter-Allied Peace Council in London. J. H. Maurer, a Socialist representative in the Pennsylvania State Legislature, was chosen. Those present included Scott Nearing, Shiplacoff and Lajput Rai. Larkin was drawn from these international preoccupations by the announcement that Mrs. Skeffington was to speak to the Harlem Socialist Party on "The Economic Basis of Irish Revolution". Perhaps unaware of the wide Irish support for the Socialist Party, he gave vent from the floor of this meeting to sharp dissatisfaction with what he believed to be the Socialist Party's half heartedness in appealing to the Irish. The Chairman, Edward Cassidy, delivered an impassioned defence. The difference would seem to be that whereas the Socialist Party was winning Irish votes by supporting the struggle for independence, Larkin wanted more stress on making Irishmen into convinced socialists. Of course there should have been no dispute about either. But there was.

Four days later *The Call* published a letter from Con O'Lyhane, then issuing an ultra-revolutionary newspaper from his home in Ansonia, Connecticut. He had been for some months establishing or reviving "Connolly Clubs" in places where he had lectured. He urged others to follow suit. Larkin was already in touch with O'Lyhane. The upshot of this initiative was the establishment on St. Patrick's Day, 1918, at an "Irish Rally" at the Bryant Hall, of the New York "James Connolly Club". James Larkin was its chairman. Its purpose was the spreading of socialist education among the Irish. It is significant that Mellows agreed to speak at this rally and chose the occasion to make his first recorded statement of his general acceptance of Connolly's conclusions. According to *The Call*, all present enrolled. But if this was intended to include the speakers, and Mellows himself became a member, there is no evidence of his further participation in the work of the club. His purpose may have been to give his blessing to the project and to state his own position. This he made quite clear.

"We demand", he said. "the absolute independence of Ireland, economic as well as political. We are not fighting to free Ireland from the foreign tyrant in order to place her under the thumbs of domestic tyrants."

After describing the evolution of Irish society from the time of the "communistic clan", and contrasting this with the development of England, he declared, "Socially Ireland has never given up the ideas of her old civilisation. It is the workers of Ireland who are fighting now, it is the workers who have always fought the battle for freedom, and it is to the people that we propose to give Ireland when she is free. . . . This is the present movement in Ireland. It is not called socialism. It is called many names. Some have called it *Sinn Fein*, but call it what you will, Ireland wants to continue her old civilisation along the lines of social-ism, communism or co-operation."

Then he added the international dimension. After insisting that the Irish wanted "the whole of Ireland", he declared; "We will be rebels to England and to every form of injustice in any country the world over."

The meeting was then addressed by Agnes Bohan, Edward J. Cassidy, Frank O'Hare, and James Larkin from the chair. L. P. Lochner, on behalf of the local Socialist Party, announced the establishment of the club at 43 West 29th Street.

Mellows had, of course, reproduced the argument of Conolly's *Labour in Irish History*.[1] These sentiments were not such as to endear him to Irish-Americans to whom Russia, no longer an ally after the signing of the Treaty of Brest-Litovsk, was already being regarded as an enemy. Murmurings began, the reason for which was that Mellows and his associates were approaching all problems from the standpoint of opposition to the war. This was implicit in their demand for immunity from conscription. Progressive Irishmen were opposed to participating in a war they considered unjust. Hence their condemnation of official American policy. Hence also their contempt for Irish-Americans who lacked the decisiveness to disassociate themselves from it, and preferred to follow the mirage of an Irish revolution emerging from world reaction.

When the great anti-conscription struggle began in Ireland, the solidarity movement in the United States was led by the Irish Pro-gressive League, though the urgency of the matter drew the support of functioning branches of the Friends of Irish Freedom and *Clann na Gael*. At the outset President Wilson had urged Lloyd George to move with caution. This advice was apparently lost on him, and the release

---

[1] This work was republished by the Donnelly Press early in 1918; possibly Mellows had been re-reading it.

of Bowen-Colthurst made a very bad impression in America. This individual, the murderer of Francis Sheehy-Skeffington, had been found guilty but insane. He was now miraculously cured and was given back his commission. Mellows was deeply affected by events in Ireland. In a letter to Fr. Liam O'Donnell he spoke of his wish to be at home, "to be granted, if it were so ordained, the crowning grace of *Bas in Eireann*".[1] He quoted Davis:

> 'twere better their bayonets defying
> Than be an exile dying.

His speeches at protest meetings took on a sharper tone, more challenging than ever to pro-war Irish-Americans. He travelled considerably. With Nora Connolly he spoke at Chester, Pennsylvania. With Mrs. Skeffington, John Devoy, Dr. McCartan and Padraic Colum he addressed a meeting in Washington which was attended by so many Congressmen, Senators and Secretaries that it was said that at any time the President might be discerned scribbling at the press bench.

Lloyd George had beaten his partial retreat before the principal Irish Progressive League demonstration took place on 4th May at Madison Square Garden. The platform was a perfect expression of the unity that had been built up. On the Irish side were Fr. Magennis who took the chair, Devoy, McCartan, Colum, Golden, Mellows, Nora Connolly and Mrs. Agnes Newman, Roger Casement's sister. On the American side all were Socialists, Edward Cassidy, James Maurer, Joseph D. Cannon, Harry Weinberger, and J. D. O'Connor of the Western Miners. Seven thousand people attended, some attached to delegations from Philadelphia and Baltimore. Mellows was the first speaker after Fr. Magennis, and was to the point:

> England alone has made a knotted problem of the Irish question. It simply resolves itself into the fact that a government holds Ireland against the will of the Irish people by military force. The solution is plain. Let England get out of Ireland and leave her to work out her own destiny.

His attack on conscription provoked wild commotion. There were loud cries of "Never!" Something of the excitement of the audience conveyed itself to the speaker. Amid loud cries of assent he concluded, "America should declare where she stands! For God's sake wake up! Don't lie down like a lot of whipped curs!"

Peter Golden condemned the government of California for the

---

[1] Death in Ireland.

prosecution of Mooney and Billings. Maurer made a vigorous speech on Civil Rights. But Devoy was unexpectedly tame. He read his speech "to make sure there was no mistake". This procedure had been adopted by *Clann na Gael* and there were complaints against Mellows that he refused to conform. The old man dwelt once more on the record of the Irish as a fighting race in the service of America, and the recognition to which this entitled them. "But Ireland is not getting it," he admitted. He was like one who rebuked Satan for inconveniencing the angels in the process of promoting sin. This was the natural consequence of the line of policy *Clann na Gael* had chosen, namely to support the United States at war, and then call on the President to make good his fine phrases with respect to Ireland.

While Ireland seethed with revolt, and prepared to return Dr. McCartan for Offaly, unopposed, it was clear that an Irish Race Convention could no longer be delayed. It opened on 18th May at the Central Opera House, the day after the mass arrests and deportations of the "German Plot". There was fierce indignation and intense nervousness. The ostensible purpose of the convention was to draft a petition to the President regarding Irish representation at the Peace Conference. Attendance was sparser than last time. The platform bore the weight of some very uneasy men, anxious to get through the week-end's proceedings without a German plot in America.

A tussle between opposing tendencies appeared at the outset when after John Devoy had proposed Fr. Hurton as Chairman, Mrs. Skeffington counterposed Dr. John Kelly of Pittsfield. Larkin sprang to his feet in passionate support of the amendment, and increased the tension in the air. Devoy appealed for harmony, and Fr. Hurton was elected. Peter Golden presented the financial report. Diarmuid Lynch, who had been deported after his pig-slaughtering activities, brought greetings from Ireland. He was very much a *Clann na Gael* man. Padraic Colum followed, then T. J. Matthews, Mary McWhorter, and Justice Goff.

The key-note of the conference, said the *Irish World*, was "loyalty to the United States". As usual a question was left open, "Which United States?" The organising Committee wished for no controversy on that matter and it was decided that Mellows was not to speak. On the second day he was espied by Nora Connolly sitting obscurely in the gallery. Quietly she flitted from seat to seat whispering to the younger Irishmen and particularly those from Galway. Soon there were shouts of "We want Mellows". Mellows sat quiet. The platform looked uneasily at him. This was obviously his doing. He was beginning to know his America. When it became clear that no other business could be transacted until he had spoken, he came down from the gallery and walked up to the platform amid ceaseless and thunderous applause. Even then the platform party hesitated. But finally they gave in, and Mellows delivered impromptu the challenge he had expected to be denied.

We meet under the shadow of a terrible impending disaster in Ireland [he said]. I feel that like Nero we are fiddling while Rome is burning, to be throwing bouquets at the past deeds of the Irish race in America, or to be talking about Irish industries while our people in Ireland are going to be massacred by the British. The papers yesterday announced that five hundred Sinn Feiners in Ireland had been arrested. They gave as excuse for those arrests a German plot. That is a lie as false as hell. That "plot" has been in preparation two or three months past. We are only seeing the beginning of it, and there may be a "plot" on this side of the Atlantic as well. We find Lord French made Lord Lieutenant of Ireland, sent there to regain his military reputation which he failed to sustain in Flanders by the slaughter of defenceless Irish people.

There are times ahead that are going to try the people of Ireland as they have never been tried before. Are we going to sit here and keep our mouths shut? We all feel these things too deeply now any longer to conceal the truth. A wrong is going to be perpetrated in Ireland the like of which even the British Government never conceived before. They have stated that they have discovered a German plot, in order that they might thus alienate the sympathy of the people of America from Ireland. They could then turn round and do what they liked in Ireland, while the world looked on and laughed.

This is a question that concerns the Irish race the world over as much as it concerns the people of Ireland. And it concerns the people of America, not only the Irish, but the whole people of America, as much as it concerns the Irish race.

The American Administration, when the country entered the war, declared it was for the purpose of freeing the oppressed peoples of the world. So far that has been done with geographical reservations. If America is honest about its declaration as to why it entered the war, then those peoples should be included in these declarations.

The wrong that is going to be done in Ireland is a terrible thing. Conscription at the hands of the British Government is a crime, not alone against the Irish people but against the whole civilised world. And I say that America, by its silence on the question of Irish independence, has been and is still, until it speaks out, tacitly acquiescing in England's domination.

If there is bloodshed in Ireland, if our men and boys and women and girls are slaughtered (the fight will not alone be that of the men, the women will take part in it too) this time the fight will be for the preservation of the very life of the Irish nation. If there should be bloodshed in Ireland, the blame of that bloodshed will rest not alone on the British Government, it will rest also on America, unless America speaks out on behalf of Ireland.

The Irish people have their eyes turned to this country. They believe this country when it states the reason why it entered the war. It is not alone on behalf of all the services that the Irish have done for America, all the blood they have shed for America, it is not on behalf of this, but for the cause for which this country has declared it went to war.

They say that the Irish are pro-German. The Irish people have one enemy on this earth, and but one, and that is England. They look outside England the whole world over for aid, and if this country denies them help, it will drive them to seek help elsewhere. The Irish are no more pro-Germans than the Americans in the Revolution were pro-French.

The state of affairs at home is so desperate that you people in this country are acting like a lot of curs if you do not speak now. Blood is thicker than water, and Irish blood is thicker than any blood in the world. We Irish who still believe in Ireland, who still have the same belief in freedom, we are not going to sit down. Those who say it is disloyal to speak the truth on behalf of Ireland, those people are not Americans. They are pro-British.

Let America speak now on behalf of Ireland, or let it stop talking about the freedom of small nations. The time to do it is now, or else there may be forces over which we have no control, through which England may be swept out of Ireland.

There was wild applause. Then came cries for Peter Golden. Despite his desire to carry out his instructions, the chairman was overborne by reiterated shouts of "Golden! Golden! Golden!" Mass feeling had broken through and taken control. "Do you think I should speak now?" Judge Cohalan asked McGarrity towards the end. "Of course," McGarrity replied, and Cohalan presented the case for winning Irish freedom through American gratitude for co-operation in the war effort. But the atmosphere had changed. As well as the petition on peace aims there was a demand to Washington to halt the terror in Ireland. A deputation which was appointed consisted of Fr. Magennis, Judge Goff and Judge Rooney. Fr. Magennis became President of the Friends of Irish Freedom, but Diarmuid Lynch replaced John D. Moore as secretary. *Clann na Gael* held the key position.

The political success of the left was short-lived. The deputation to Washington was not received by the President, thanks to the advice of his secretary, Tumulty. The Friends of Irish Freedom leaders having discharged their duty, could now resume the contemplation of peace aims. The counter blows came swiftly enough. Jeremiah O'Leary had not attended the Convention. His trial for treason was due on 20th May. He created a sensation by not appearing, and it was not until 17th June that he was apprehended by Federal S.S. agents and brought from Washington under arrest. He pleaded not guilty.

A lady named Mrs. Jay had established a "Loyalty Committee", and one of her members noticing the "anti-British" oratory which issued under the Carmelite's chairmanship at Madison Square Garden had written a complaint to Cardinal Farley, Bishop of New York. On 22nd May His Eminence "informed the Father that he would not be allowed to remain in the Diocese of New York if he continued to preside at such meetings". On 25th May a Wall Street banker suggested that a suitable fate for Hannah Sheehy-Skeffington would be lynching, and the *New York Herald* followed with an "open letter" which told her that she had "better quit". On 30th May Tom Mooney was once again sentenced to hanging, and before June was halfway through Con O'Lyhane was arrested in Connecticut and joined the ever-growing band of citizens under arraignment for what the authorities called treason. When Senator Johnson learned of the Underwood resolution to limit the Senate's powers of debate, well might he comment that the administration wanted "a cowed press, a cowed people, and a cowed Congress".

And yet it is not so easy to cow Americans. The great Marx Centennial meetings at the New Star Casino and Carnegie Hall on 5th May had shown it, and the Irish Progressive League had shown it. This organisation now set about organising protests to Cardinal Farley, and Fr. Magennis received no more warnings, although it was clear that his departure from the U.S.A. would not be regretted. Mrs. Skeffington delivered a spirited reply to her critics, and the J. P. Holland branch of the Friends of Irish Freedom congratulated *The Call* on its vigorous editorial of 4th June attacking conscription in Ireland. On 11th June, 15,000 people gathered in Madison Square Garden to hear Norman Thomas, Alexander Trachtenberg, Santeri Nuorteva and Professor Lomonosoff demand the recognition of the Soviet Government. Mooney's lawyer moved for a further retrial. When on 15th June an amended agreement between Britain and America was published, it was found that Irishmen and Australians resident in the U.S.A. had been declared exempt from conscription. Mellows' part in the campaign was handsomely recognised by the Roger Casement branch of the

Friends of Irish Freedom who at their meeting of 23rd June presented him with a watch.

The Irish Progressive League announced a Mass Meeting at the Central Opera House for 28th June. Among the speakers were Nora Connolly and Mrs. Skeffington. At the last minute these were compelled to withdraw. They were sailing home on the 29th with Margaret Skinnider and were tricked into going abroad early, they believed, so that they could not attend. Mrs. Skeffington left a message urging a defence fund for Con O'Lyhane. It was too late to get substitutes. It is recorded that difficulties beset the other end of their voyage. They were arrested at Liverpool and told they would not be permitted to return to Ireland. It was some time before they succeeded in doing so.

This meeting, Mellows stated afterwards, was crucial for his relations with the *Clann na Gael*. Its purpose was to request President Wilson to intervene on behalf of the "patriotic Irishmen and women seized in Ireland recently by English autocratic authority and transported without warrant or charge to foreign jails where they now live incommunicado". The chairman was Dr. John F. Kelly. The speakers were Padraic Colum, Peter Golden, Dr. McCartan, Edward J. Cassidy and Liam Mellows. A resolution demanding the restoration of political rights to the leaders of the Irish people had been drafted by a committee consisting of Mrs. Skeffington, Peter Golden and Dr. O'Keeffe. Mellows was "ordered" by *Clann na Gael* not to attend. He did so. His speech contained no novelties. The meeting gave rise to no new sentiments, except that Edward Cassidy made the correct point that the English capitalists were the enemies of Ireland. He also made a few uncomplimentary references to the egregious Gompers who had persuaded the American Federation of Labour to turn down Irish independence in favour of Home Rule and spoke for American Labour without consulting it. There were 2,500 people present and the meeting undoubtedly carried the struggle forward.

But Mellows was at once in trouble. As he wrote to Nora Connolly a year later, an "investigation committee sat on me immediately afterwards, at which I told them what I thought of them. Result—threatened with expulsion from everything. Told them to do it. They backed down. Resigned from the office at the same time. Was begged to remain by Uncle.[1] Did so. Had the whip hand then and went to every meeting under the ban. Campaign of the most vile and vicious slander started which has lasted to the present time....[2] I am beyond redemption. Am

[1] John Devoy.
[2] It is said that the blacksmith Kenny chose this juncture to revive some of his allegations.

F

looked upon as wild, hot-headed, undisciplined—liable to get the movement into trouble—dubbed a Socialist and Anarchist. Bow-wow!"

O'Leary's jury failed to agree, but he remained in jail for another six months. On 30th June, Eugene Debs was arrested. O'Lyhane, arraigned at Hartford on 10th July, was held in prison pending the enormous bail of $15,000. The Friends of Irish Freedom collected 600,000 signatures to its petition, no mean feat in such a short time and under such conditions. It was presented on 27th August. In September Debs was sentenced to ten years' imprisonment, but released on $10,000 bail pending appeal. John Reed was tried *in absentia* at the same time. His attorney was the Irish-American barrister Dudley Field Malone who had resigned his lucrative post in charge of New York City's rate collection, in order to be free to defend victims of the witch hunt.

But now every day brought news of revolt in Europe. Vienna strikers fought the police. Anti-Austrian demonstrations shook Prague. In July there were strikes in Coventry and Birmingham, in August disaffection in both German and French armies. In India sporadic stoppages heralded the great strike wave that was to tie up industry in 1919. Everywhere there was war-weariness and unrest. The crisis the imperialists had provoked was threatening to engulf them.

Mellows' hosts, the Kirwans, did not take his part against *Clann na Gael*. They were stout admirers of Devoy. Whilst there was no question of their refusing their hospitality, Mellows felt uncomfortable, and seems to have taken his departure around the end of August.[1] Some uncertainty surrounds his movements. He undoubtedly lived for a time at the Carmelite Priory, and seems subsequently to have shared rooms with Peter MacSwiney, Terence's brother. While there were no reactionaries among the MacSwineys, Peter was the only Socialist. They lived on the East side.

Mellows now undertook the task of registering all Irish citizens, many of whom were being inducted into the forces without being told of their exemption. Registration began on 14th September in New York, and shortly afterwards in Philadelphia. An Irish Citizen's Society was founded. A spectacular case involving four young Irishmen occurred within a matter of days. They had been committed to prison for the "offence" of refusing to register as British. The Society had no funds. But Peter Golden and Clement O'Loughlin provided £4,000 bail on behalf of the Irish Progressive League. The four men, Laurence O'Neill, Stan Hehir, Paul Hynes and Patrick Fitzgerald were enter-

---

[1] Among the books he left with the Kirwans is none bearing a later date.

tained at the Central Opera House on 19th September. J. D. Cannon, J. J. Bayley, Edward Cassidy and Liam Mellows were the speakers. Next day they won their case. There is reason to suppose that Mellows pledged and over-pledged his own meagre resources in these activities.

In the final months of 1918 Mellows was "in trouble with Draft Boards almost daily". He complained that, instead of helping him, "the gang"[1] opposed and sabotaged, by threats and underhand means, but failed. But only a small minority of those eligible registered. Mellows had merely established one more Irish society, and was slowly becoming ostracised by the old one. He spent more time at the Carmelite Priory, where he introduced the teaching of Irish dancing, and won an award for singing in a Gaelic League *Feis*. The fiddle did duty once more. As the war drew to a close "everything went from bad to worse".[2] The Progressive League alone stuck to its guns, quizzed the party leaders on their attitude to Ireland and the character of the peace, and plunged into their local elections in support of the Socialist Party.

When Germany requested an armistice, New York police celebrated the event by forbidding Socialist meetings in Harlem, though Edward Cassidy contrived to outwit them and called for "a workers' peace". On 11th November came the end of the war. New York Socialists felt they would surely be allowed to celebrate that. They learned the contrary from police cudgels on 12th November. That night the Irish Progressive League held a meeting. The speakers were J. D. Cannon, Padraic Colum, Peter Golden, Francis Hackett, Leonora O'Reilly and Liam Mellows. Here was raised a new demand, the recognition of the Irish Republic. The demand for a hearing at the Peace Conference had taken on a more advanced form.

The war being over, the era of peace and rejoicing should have begun forthwith. Those who believed the purpose of the war was to destroy German militarism saw German militarism destroyed. Those who credited Wilson's fourteen points could now call for the bond. In this spirit the Executive Committee of the Friends of Irish Freedom met on 14th November and decided upon a week's propaganda in December. American policy was being refashioned, and on 8th December McCartan was to address the Senate Committee on Foreign Relations.

But though all had changed all was really the same. Revolution had not triumphed, and the peace was thus but the continuation of war by other means, but not of the simple war that had begun in 1914; it continued the complex, convoluted, part international, part civil war

---

[1] The Cohalan section within *Clann na Gael*.   [2] Letter to Nora Connolly.

into which it had evolved over four years. The aim was still to despoil
Germany, to recover the war debts, to retain conquered territories,
above all to hold back social revolution. And to those things were
added purposes deriving from bitter rivalries among the victors, only
mitigated by a common interest in the ruin of the Bolsheviks.

There were two years before the next Presidential Election, by which
time it was widely expected "normality" would be restored. For the
time being restrictions on wage-bargaining were retained, and Frank
P. Walsh resigned from the War Labour Board as a protest. There was
no amnesty of political prisoners. Dissident newspapers remained
excluded from the mails. Only a threat of an eight-hour strike on the
Pacific coast, part of a country-wide campaign for reprieve, saved
Mooney from hanging. His sentence was commuted to one of life
imprisonment. And Prince Lvov's appearance in Washington to urge
military intervention in Russia was a sharp reminder of the war-like
implications of imperialist peace.

The climax of the Friends of Irish Freedom campaign, now called
"Self-determination Week", was the great meeting in Madison Square
Garden on 10th December. It marked the triumphal re-entry into
public life of Judge Cohalan and his friends, the Judge the richer for the
$5,000 damages he had just been awarded against the *New York
Evening Mail* which had impugned his integrity as an American.

The Governor of New York, Charles S. Whitman, opened the meeting and introduced the distinguished guest of the evening, Cardinal
O'Connell no less. Judge Goff took over the chairmanship. Towards
the end of the proceedings Judge Cohalan made the main policy statement. The men and women who had held aloft the flag of Irish freedom
during the war were totally absent. And why? This was a gathering of
those who had supported the war but believed Irish freedom might
proceed from an American peace. In his statement Judge Cohalan
advocated self-determination for Ireland which would be offered
"when the Peace Conference will decree that a plebiscite of the adult
population be taken . . .". Three days later the Committee on Foreign
Relations discussed a resolution introduced by Congressman Gallagher
of Illinois. It called upon the United States representatives at the Peace
Conference to present "the right of Ireland to freedom, independence
and self-determination". At the hearing Richard Dalton, believed by
McCartan to be acting on Judge Cohalan's advice, agreed to the
deletion of the words "freedom" and "independence", leaving only
"self-determination". His argument, based on the undesirability of pre-
judging the decision of the Irish people, was theoretically unobjection-

able. But he did not define "self-determination", which is meaningless without the express right of secession.

So far so good. But on 28th December it was clear that the Irish people had decided. News came of the shattering of the Parliamentary Party by *Sinn Fein*. Mellows had been invited to none of the meetings. Feeling that he was "ostracised", he resigned from the *Gaelic American* around Christmas. Now he learned that he had been elected by two constituencies, East Galway, and Meath.

CHAPTER TEN

DAIL EIREANN

IN his book *The Aftermath* Winston Churchill revealed nostalgically his vision of the imperialist might-have-been. Thus Clemenceau, Lloyd George and Wilson agreed to establish a League of Nations which would embrace "all the dominating races of the world". They resolved upon intervention in Russia and invited Germany to assist in the task of "liberation". French fears were quieted by a guarantee from the Anglo-Saxon powers. "Having settled all vital matters" the peace-makers busied themselves with world currencies and arming the League. That is to say, all impediments and contradictions having vanished into thin air, the imperialists got their teeth into the Soviet Republic. British policy can be summarised in one word, the German war being out of the way, counter-revolution. When the epitaph of British imperialism is finally written it will be said that for this aim, pursued undeviatingly over half a century and more, it sacrificed its own existence.

In his analysis of what went wrong, Churchill only half-grasped the inevitability of the obstacles that littered the path to his mirage. The continuance of the war-time coalition, far from maintaining national unity, merely transferred the point of division to within the Liberal Party. It could not survive. Lloyd George must attempt to bestride the world with one foot slipping. The British soldiers had joined up for the war they thought was forced on them, not for another of Lloyd George's choosing. "Hang the Kaiser" and "Squeeze the Hun till the pips squeak" were the slogans of the most popular demagogues. Units of all forces mutinied for demobilisation. The town of Calais was seized and held for four days. The Town Hall at Luton was burned down.

External affairs developed no better. The "dominating races" could not agree on how much domination each was to do. The lesser breeds evinced a strong distaste for being dominated. National revolutions continued throughout the world. The German people revolted and the victors intensified the blockade while Ebert, Scheidemann and Noske watered the soil with the blood of the working class. Once secure, the German capitalists bargained for better terms until threats of re-sumption of war brought them to heel. Italy, dissatisfied with her share of the spoils, walked out of the Peace Conference and started a little plundering on the side. The United States held aloof from a League dominated by Britain and France, and in the absence of the Anglo-Saxon guarantee France sought to occupy Germany up to the Rhine.

So ran the tale of woe. But despite all this disarray in the rear, the Russian intervention was kept up. If it were to cease when could it be resumed? That was the story of the second world war. It proceeded without co-ordination. The imperialists descended like vultures. But the animal was not dead. And the sum of their individual privateering created a new possibility, the great nightmare of the twentieth century, namely that all the enemies of imperialism, the hated Bolsheviks at their head, might involve the British Empire in simultaneous disorders leading to the secession of the colonies, proletarian revolution in Western Europe, and if England escaped this, an era of dependence on the United States. All the opportunism and deviousness, the crudity, brutality and stupidity of British rule in Ireland must be related to this general perspective. In dealing with the revolt in Ireland, British imperialism's hands were tied by policies further afield.

At the end of 1918 the overwhelming majority of the Irish people wanted an independent Republic. But they were not able to establish it directly. Unlike the March and November governments in Russia, any administration arising from their constituent assembly must take shape within the British system, and endeavour by some means thereafter to shake off its fetters. That following the general election this should be attempted challenged the whole purpose of counter-revolution. But the proximity of Ireland to Britain, and the presence in Britain of millions of citizens of Irish birth and descent, fully integrated for the most part in the Labour movement, gave great significance to the social composition of its representation. And what took place was the virtual elimination of the propertied classes from the counsels of the nation.

According to Professor McCracken the *Sinn Fein* deputies comprised 31 professional men (nine of them journalists and seven teachers), 18 engaged in commerce (ten of these shop-keepers and only one in manufacturing business), 5 full-time officials of nationalist organisations, 2 local government employees, and 2 solicitor's clerks. This was a white-collar representation to be sure. But the bourgeoisie were not in it. They had become a class without a party. If they could not revive Redmondism they must capture *Sinn Fein*. Neither would be easy.

But the working class also was missing. Labour had failed to claim its rightful place. And thus was created the gap through which the bourgeoisie was finally to emerge to power.

[1] *Representative Government in Ireland*, p. 33.

For the moment, what was clear was that the workers and farmers had voted for a Republic. The bonfires and tar barrels were scarcely cold[1] when Boland and O'Kelly, the functioning secretaries of *Sinn Fein*, called a preliminary meeting of deputies for 7th January. It was decided to convene a public meeting of the Constituent Assembly for 21st January.[2]

The main policy decisions were made at a further meeting on 19th January at which Richard Mulcahy presided. Arthur Griffith, De Valera and Count Plunkett were nominated as Irish delegates to the Peace Conference. A special committee was elected to press for the release of the prisoners, among whom there were no less than thirty-four elected deputies. A document drafted by the Irish Workers' delegation to the International Conference at Berne was submitted for approval and a committee was appointed to "draw up the draft of a programme of constructive work on democratic lines in consultation with the Labour leaders". It was thus clearly accepted that the working class expected from the Republic a programme of social reform. Its existence was dependent on the support of the proletariat.

The date of the Assembly (now known as *Dail Eireann*) was made public on 17th January. Some expected the authorities to proclaim it at once. It is said that the Irish Privy Council resolved not to do so by only one vote. Twenty-seven deputies met at the Mansion House in Dublin. The public thronging the galleries was tense with curiosity and enthusiasm. Thousands gathered outside. Count Plunkett opened the proceedings by moving Cathal Brugha to the chair. The business was conducted entirely in Irish. Fr. Michael O'Flanagan, still under the ban of his bishop for *Sinn Fein* activities, recited a brief prayer. Clerks to the House were appointed. The roll was called and provisional rules adopted.

There was to be a Prime Minister to whom four departmental Ministers were to be responsible. These were to control respectively Finance, Home Affairs, Foreign Affairs and Defence. Apart from the substitution of the word "defence" for "war" (a very natural piece of diplomacy) these provisions followed the model of Westminster. There

[1] Nor indeed were the bruises healed or the windows mended in areas like east Tyrone where the celebrations of the Nationalist majority were rudely assailed by Orange mobs.

[2] The new British Cabinet had met for the first time on 10th January. Apparently they judged it wise to send Lord Haldane to Dublin on a secret mission promising a "generous measure of Home Rule" and the release of the prisoners if the Irish eschewed "violent courses". Meeting with no response he returned before the *Dail* met. Lloyd George's government resolved to "freeze" the Irish situation, maintaining military rule while they dealt with other things, but meanwhile hoping for a revival of Redmondite fortunes.

was no question of a President[1] in the American sense, though this conception was engrafted later. To Griffith the *Dail* might be the reincarnation of the co-ordinate Irish Parliament of 1782. But to others the empty chair was hypothetically filled not by the King of England but by the head-centre of the I.R.B.

The first political business was the adoption of a Declaration of Independence said to have been drafted by Gavan Duffy. A brief, dignified statement, it ratified[2] the establishment of the Irish Republic, ordained that only the representatives of the Irish people had the right to legislate in Ireland, and demanded the evacuation of the English garrison. The penultimate paragraph asked for the "recognition and support of every free nation in the world" and declared Irish independence to be a "condition precedent to international peace hereafter". As the deputies stood to pledge themselves to make this declaration good, Cathal Brugha warned them that it meant "we are now done with England". The appointment of the delegates to the Peace Conference was ratified, and they were supported by a "message to the free peoples of the world". This called for recognition of "Ireland's national status and to its vindication at the Peace Conference".

The "Democratic programme" had been drawn up by Sean T. O'Kelly on the basis of a draft by Thomas Johnson. It declared the "right of the people of Ireland to the ownership of Ireland and to the unfettered control of Irish destinies to be indefeasible". But the nation's sovereignty extended not only to all men and women but to all national possessions, "soil, natural resources, wealth and wealth-producing processes". All right to private property must be subordinated to public right and welfare. Every citizen had a right to an "adequate share of the produce of the Nation's labour". Special attenton was to be paid to the physical and mental well-being of the children. Education, health, social services, industry and trade were to be vigorously promoted. Thus, the Labour movement had had its influence on social policy,

[1] Controversy has affected this question. Newspapers reporting the *Dail* meeting referred to the election of a "provisional Prime Minister". The extant report, published some years after the event, records the election of a "President of the Ministry *pro tem*". In April he is referred to as *Priomh-Aire*, so that we must equate "President of the Ministry" with "Prime Minister". But after his resignation his successor becomes "President of the *Dail*". References to "President De Valera" in March 1918 drew comment from the British press. They assumed his valid presidency was that of *Sinn Fein*, but suspected that he was preparing the way for announcing himself president of the Irish Republic. In I.R.B. eyes this position was probably already held by Boland. De Valera assumed the title of "President of the Irish Republic" with some trepidation at a meeting in the United States early in July. He is said to have been prompted by Boland whose aim was to establish the existence of a Republic. His deputy in Ireland presumably remained President of the *Dail*.

[2] One paragraph refers to the Republic *proclaimed* in 1916, another to its *establishment* but with no date.

but was excluded from the machinery which was to carry it out.

This fact is emphasised when Johnson's draft is compared with O'Kelly's. Johnson concluded, "The Republic will aim at the elimination of the class in Society which lives upon the wealth produced by the workers of the nation but gives no useful social service in return, and in the process of accomplishment will bring freedom to all who have hitherto been caught in the toils of economic servitude." This loose paraphrase of the argument of the *Communist Manifesto*[1] was totally deleted. An earlier passage giving a syndicalist interpretation of the process of working-class power also disappeared. According to Patrick Coogan[2] O'Kelly deleted these sections following strong objections by Collins and the I.R.B., who would not agree that the programme should be put forward unless he did so.

Looking backward, in the stone-cold reaction of 1926, Beaslai, now a conservative, described the programme as "communistic". It was so radical, he thought, that *Dail Eireann* could only have accepted it from the certainty that there was no intention of implementing it. The discussions between O'Kelly and Collins show, however, that it was treated seriously. Beaslai had lost the atmosphere of the time.

Indeed, the aims of the working class had so far penetrated the national movement that the Declaration of Independence itself described one of the objects of the Republic as "equal right and equal opportunity for every citizen".[3] It should be remarked in passing that Johnson's formulation showed theoretical weaknesses, both in relation to the national question and to that of working-class power.

Next day the *Dail* met in private. Cathal Brugha was elected *Priomh Aire* and appointed his Ministers, Eoin MacNeill for Finance, Michael Collins for Home Affairs, Count Plunkett for Foreign Affairs, and Richard Mulcahy for Defence. At MacNeill's appointment only Beaslai protested. Sean T. O'Kelly was elected "Speaker of the House". This additional parallel with Westminster may have been

---

[1] See Engels's preface to the German edition of 1883.

[2] *Ireland Since the Rising*, p. 25.

[3] This declaration also was not without its retrospective critics. Figgis believed that it destroyed the Peace Conference policy by assuming what was being requested there. Frank O'Connor held that it was "an over-statement both of the intentions of the people and of their actual strength". In the context of the imperialist peace conference it suffered these deficiencies, the appeal to Peace Conference being doomed to failure in the absence of revolution in the main European countries. But in the context of the general upsurge of revolt, and the possibility of such revolutions, it was a bold but realistic move deserving a more vigorous sequel. It is significant that the *Irish Times* which dismissed the meeting of *Dail Eireann* as a "theatrical protest" feared that it would pave the way for the application in Ireland of the "principles of Lenin and Trotsky" and the "disintegration of Society" as the *Irish Times* then understood it.

intended to reassure Griffith, whose hair must surely by now be standing on end at the strange mutation of his brainchild.

Dail Eireann ushered in a period of dual power, something in a sense inherent in the *Sinn Fein* policy. It is as necessary a stage in revolution as the appearance of free radicals in a chemical reaction. But what happens next? What is the resolution? Under Griffith's scheme the two powers would come to tolerate each other under the nominal overlordship of the British Crown. But to others the logical next step was an uprising to transfer all power to *Dail Eireann*. That the I.R.B. favoured the second is implied in Collins' instructions to his scholarly young friend Esposito, whose visit to Paris in a preparatory capacity was arranged by Robert Brennan and financed by James O'Mara. Collins instructed him, in the event of his being forced to the conclusion that Ireland's case would not in fact be heard, to write to Dublin counselling an uprising. This, indeed, he did, and the clumsy manœuvre provoked the intense indignation of Cathal Brugha.

It was of course not possible to halt the mass movement while those it had brought to office harmonised their political philosophies. Ireland was still under military government. The war-time censorship continued unrelieved. Petty oppression invaded the smallest details of people's lives. Thus on 3rd January Cathal Brugha was arrested at Thurles for giving the police the Irish name by which he was generally known. Two days later a Waterford newsagent was served with a "closing order" for daring to sell the perfectly legal newspapers *Nationality* and *Young Ireland*. This kind of thing went on practically every day in every part of Ireland. Periodically there were violent incidents in which the police were not averse to using guns.

Increasingly the young men raided for arms. On 21st January at Soloheadbeg a load of gelignite was captured in a daring ambush led by Sean Treacy and Dan Breen. It was being removed from a quarry under an armed guard of R.I.C. men. These ignored the order of "hands up" and prepared to resist with their carbines. They had omitted to release the safety catches and two of their number were shot dead as a result of the delay. While in general *Sinn Fein* opinion condemned the ambush, the headquarters of the Volunteers, where the I.R.B. was strong, issued a statement (written by Beaslai and approved by Brugha) asserting the right of the "Army of Ireland"[1] to "inflict death on the enemies of the Irish State", as was done by every government at war

[1] *Oglaigh na hEireann* (the name given the Irish Volunteers). Mellows, in his reply to the American Draft Board (see above, p. 153), had used the expression *Arm Poblacht na hEireann* which corresponds to "Irish *Republican* Army". Whether any distinction is to be inferred from the variants is not clear.

with another. This statement was prepared on 23rd January and published on the 31st.

Of wider significance, however, was the revolt of the working class. On 27th January the Belfast engineers took strike action for a reduction of the working week from 54 to 44 hours. They explained clearly in their daily strike bulletin that their purpose included that of securing returning soldiers against unemployment. The strike was unofficial, being confined to London, Glasgow and Belfast. The union leaders settled for 47 hours. Militants like Gallacher and MacLean stumped Britain for the men's demands. MacLean's meetings in Cumberland were proscribed under D.O.R.A. In Glasgow, Gallacher, Kirkwood and Shinwell were arrested after the notorious baton charge in George Square carried out by hundreds of police allegedly well primed with drink.

In Belfast conditions rapidly approached those of a general strike. The engineers were joined by the transport workers, building workers, municipal workers, and even a part of the linen trade. The city was in darkness. Donegall Quay was lit by ships' generators. There was scarcely a window intact in the office of the *Belfast Telegraph*. "At last we have unity in the ranks of the workers irrespective of religion or politics," the tenth Strike Bulletin declared on 8th February. The engineers were later joined by the electricians, furnishing trades and general labourers. The Trades Council virtually governed the city.

The influence of the Belfast struggle was felt throughout Ireland. In Dublin the Trades Council called a conference to discuss the campaign for shorter hours. The Irish T.U.C. followed suit and adopted a wage target of 150 per cent above 1914 wages for a 44-hour week. Limerick building workers struck for 3d. an hour. They were followed by laundry workers, Dundalk dockers, Donegal roadworkers, Derry shipyard workers and Monaghan Asylum workers. Railway clerks met in the Gresham Hotel to discuss strike action. Congratulations were wired to Belfast from all the big cities. The workers of Ireland were stirring as a class.

That partition was not without its attraction to the bourgeoisie was shown by the comment of the *Irish Independent* which quoted one anonymous "prominent trade unionist" who had warned against "dictation from Belfast". It sourly observed that "as the Orange workers are such stout supporters of Carsonism and partition, the Southern workers should give them ample opportunity to put their partitionist and insular principles to the test in the latent revolt in which they are engaged". By contrast one of the three Carsonite Labour M.P.s declared his sympathy with the strikers.

British observers well appreciated the crucial nature of the struggle. The *Daily News* spoke of the "disruption of the Orange machine" which would have far-reaching consequences for Ireland and the world.

But what of *Dail Eireann*? Was there any appreciation that in motion at that moment was the one force that could crush Unionism and secure a united Ireland? Cathal Brugha spoke at the *Sinn Fein* Victory Concert on 31st January. He made no reference to Belfast. He declared that the housing conditions of the Dublin poor were a disgrace to civilisation. His remedy was to stop the payments of ground rents to England. While not unsympathetic to the working class he had little knowledge of its struggles, and seemingly not an inkling of the significance of the confrontation that paralysed the North. Yet if *Dail Eireann* had found a way to associate itself with the workers' demands, this was the one time when it might have had a sympathetic response, and the engineers could have contrasted its behaviour with that of their London Executive which proceeded to dissolve the Belfast District Committee for its militancy. This was the first penalty paid for Labour's absence from the *Dail*.

A *Daily News* correspondent wrote that "The political and industrial wings of the Republican movement find the moment ripe for the blow. With their banners inscribed 'Release the prisoners' and 'A forty-four hour week' the allied armies of patriots and industrialists will be able to rally three-quarters of the population. This correspondent is informed that on the *Sinn Fein* side the Fenian section has obtained almost complete control while on the Labour side power has passed entirely into the hands of the Bolsheviks. Large stocks of flour and candles are being laid up in Dublin households." The correspondent was misinformed. He echoed the fears of the Establishment. For the militants were not in sole control. The alliance was never forged. And the blow was never struck. The Belfast engineers accepted a 47-hour week, and the opportunity was lost.

While the struggle for the 44-hour week was in progress, Collins and Boland rescued De Valera and McGarry from Lincoln jail. This was on 3rd February. The remaining "German Plot" prisoners were released on 7th March. De Valera remained in hiding in Manchester a further three weeks. From the statement he issued during this time, and from conversations recorded by Robert Brennan afterwards,[1] it is clear that his guiding lights were his conceptions of statesmanship and moderation. On 24th February he published a eulogy of President Wilson. He spoke privately of proceeding at once to America, but he was dissuaded.

[1] *Allegiance.*

At his suggestion the Irish Self-determination League was established at a conference in Manchester on 30th March. The membership was confined to persons of Irish birth or descent, and its constitution debarred it from participation in British politics, a disastrous provision if the mass of the Irish in Britain had heeded it. In his St. Patrick's Day message he posed the restoration of Gaelic as the most pressing issue, trusting that at a pinch national independence might be won by a later generation.

The I.R.B. proposed a great national reception when he arrived in Dublin on 25th March. The Lord Mayor would hand him the keys to the city. Needless to say this was proclaimed. But it was proposed to defy the ban. De Valera personally urged the cancellation of the demonstration, and on 27th March he made a speech of studied moderation in which he compared the connection with Britain to a "bad joint" which had to be broken in order to be re-made. Separation was to be followed by a form of "re-association". This was the *Sinn Fein* policy which Michael Collins is said to have described as *"cac"*. If the British Government did not yet overtly associate *Dail Eireann* with world revolution, De Valera did nothing to force that opinion upon it.

Meanwhile the workers' movement went on. Ministry of Labour clerks struck for recognition on 1st March. The general strike in Boyle, Co. Roscommon, carried with it such insurrectionary implications that the British censor suppressed news of it. On 25th March at the sound of a trumpet in the Crescent, all workers laid down their tools. Their demand included a weekly wage increase from 26s. to 36s., time and a half for overtime, and 7 p.m. closing of shops except for 9.30 p.m. on Saturdays. The police and military arrested many pickets during the ensuing weeks and the Irish Transport and General Workers Union noted wryly that employers prominent in *Sinn Fein* made no objection when the "forces of the enemy" took in their recalcitrant workmen.

The pattern was to be repeated. The people were prepared to struggle for a better life. But there was no James Connolly in the Labour movement to point the way to the classical revolution he had hoped for in 1916. This would entail the merging of the separate industrial struggles into a political general strike followed by an armed insurrection. Whether this was practicable or not is, of course, sheer speculation. But the reason why Irish Labour did not discuss it would seem to have been that they had given over the leadership of the democratic struggle to *Sinn Fein*, retaining for themselves only the proletarian. Thus, if the eyes of the *Dail* were on Paris, Labour would look to the meeting of the reconstituted Second International at Berne. Here Ireland was admitted as a separate country, as of course had happened twenty years previously. Henderson and MacDonald delivered themselves of high-sounding promises, but none of these were carried out[1]. Berne was indeed the shadow cast by Paris on the international working-class movement. And as for Paris, having received no reply to his request for representation, Sean T. O'Kelly addressed to Clemenceau a second letter on 31st March.

The *Dail* met on 1st April. De Valera was elected *Priomh Aire*. That some private discussions had taken place regarding his proposed visit to America is probably indicated by the discussion of the method of selecting a President-Substitute. An enlarged Ministry was approved. Arthur Griffith controlled Home Affairs, Cathal Brugha Defence, Count Plunkett Foreign Affairs, Michael Collins Finance, while Countess Markiewicz was added as Minister for Labour, William Cosgrave as Minister for Local Government, and Eoin MacNeill for Industries. MacNeill knew nothing about industries and stated afterwards that he had joined the Cabinet for purely political reasons, presumably to keep the I.R.B. in its place. His work was performed by a Director of Trade and Commerce, Ernest Blythe, elected a few days later.

On 4th April indications of an internal policy-struggle appeared on the surface. The Minister for Defence under the rubric "Motion as to resistance to usurpation" stated that the Ministry were of the opinion that they would not be justified in calling on the country to carry out the proposals as contemplated. Clearly Griffith's plan had prevailed. The Minister for Defence (not for Finance) moved that "The Ministry be authorised to issue Republican Bonds to the value of £250,000 in sums of £1 to £1,000." A proposal from Countess Markiewicz pledging the Assembly to "a fair and full redistribution of the vacant lands and ranches of Ireland among the uneconomic holders and landless men" was withdrawn and referred to a special committee.

The public session on 10th April heard reports of increasing police violence and brutality, in particular of the kidnapping of children who were brought from Tipperary to Dublin, held incommunicado, and interrogated upon the movements of their parents. An important decision was taken. The R.I.C. were to be socially ostracised and the nation was called upon to give its support. Finally on 11th April the

[1] The Permanent Commission of the Berne International met shortly after the constituent conference and passed a resolution "that the principle of free and absolute self-determination shall be applied immediately in the case of Ireland". The resolution was reported to the British Labour Party Conference in June 1919, as the 1920 report puts it, "without objection being made".

question of social policy was raised. Alderman Kelly asked for proposals for implementing the democratic programme adopted in January. De Valera replied that "it was clear that the democratic programme, as adopted by the *Dail*, contemplated a situation somewhat different from that in which they actually found themselves. They had the occupation of the foreigner . . .". He added that he had never made any promise to Labour, because while the enemy was within their gates the immediate question was to get possession of their country. The struggles of the working class on its own behalf were not considered relevant to the task of national liberation.

De Valera concluded by a complimentary reference to Griffith as "the man who worked out schemes for meeting the exact situation in which they found themselves, and for using for the benefit of the Irish people such machinery as the British forces of occupation left at their disposal, and who had twenty years' experience of effort in that particular department". Was the tongue ever so slightly in the cheek? About the same time he told Robert Brennan that Griffith's policy gave them "nothing to go on" and that non-attendance at Westminster deprived them of a world platform. Possibly it was his intention to seek such a platform in America at once, since the arrival in Paris of three American delegates who would lobby on Ireland's behalf promised one last prospect of a hearing. On the other hand Griffith's conception was subjected to further development. The extraordinary Conference of *Sinn Fein* held on 8th April pledged support to the Irish Republic.

The movement of the workers rose to fresh heights in the series of events popularly known as the "Limerick Soviet". On 6th April Volunteers rescued Robert Byrne from the prison hospital. A policeman shot the prisoner but was himself shot dead. On 9th April the authorities proclaimed Limerick City a military area and demanded that all crossing its boundaries must carry permits. A large number of workers were accustomed to pass in and out of the city for purposes of employment. The Trades Council declared a general strike. Fourteen thousand workers downed tools. No goods were moved nor services rendered without a permit from the Trades Council. At the first sign of profiteering a schedule of permitted prices was drawn up, and posted in prominent positions throughout the city. The prices were substantially below those hitherto prevailing (for example, milk was reduced from 7d. to 3d. a pint) and were rigorously enforced by the workers representatives. The entire administration passed into their hands, the Mayor and *Sinn Fein* councillors following them in everything. The Trades Council printed tokens which were used as currency. Here was another illustration of dual power. But it contrasted with that created by *Dail Eireann* in its proletarian character. Irish T.U.C. officials hastened to Limerick. At a special meeting on 15th April the Executive endorsed the strikers' stand. After a period those workers whose movements did not require military permission were allowed to return. But the strike was kept up until the military climbed down.

The revolutionary energy of the workers seemed inexhaustible. In the midst of the Limerick events Alderman Lynch was released after six months' imprisonment for a so-called seditious speech at Bally-farnon. In defiance of the R.I.C. a group of young men raised the red flag and headed a procession to Sligo Town Hall. "The workers will not be ruled either by Dublin Castle or the Kildare Street Club," one of the speakers declared. The following day, 10th April, James Everett, Secretary of the County Wicklow Labourers' Association, was sentenced to six months' imprisonment. All business houses in the town thereupon closed and a red flag flew from the window of the Labour Hall.

A general strike was called for 1st May, though in the Belfast area it took place on 3rd May. The authorities thought to encourage law and order by prohibiting the display of red flags. The result was their appearance in places where they had never been seen before. At Kilmacthomas, in Co. Waterford, a large procession walked behind a red banner bearing the inscription "A Workers' Republic". Maynooth workers carried the red flag to Kilcock and the police dared not interfere. In Monaghan workers assembled in meeting halls, organised squads, and toured the outlying districts stopping all work. At Mary-borough[1] the stoppage was complete and red flags flew defiantly though police tried to seize one from a contingent marching in from Mellick. The police were also defied at Dunshaughlin, Mallow, Cappoquin and Drogheda.

On 4th March the Communist International was founded, and its appeal for affiliations became gradually known. The Irish Labour Party had associated itself with the left (Adler-Longuet) wing at Berne. Though some of its leaders regarded themselves as Marxists, there was no question of a change. But on 7th May a group of socialists mostly influenced by the Scottish S.L.P. founded the Irish Revolutionary Socialist Party in Belfast. Among its members were Kathleen Coyle and Jack Hedley, a naval man who had jumped ship at Cork and joined the anti-war group in Belfast. He was at that time using the name Sean O'Hagan, and had participated in the engineers' struggle. In the

[1] Portlaoise.

Socialist Party of Ireland two groups slowly emerged, that led by William O'Brien who wished to remain in the Berne International, and that of members anxious for a more revolutionary policy, led by James Connolly's son, Roderick. The vigorous Communist activities of Larkin in the U.S.A. may have been a factor in the divisions in the Transport Union which began at this time when P. T. Daly lost his position as Secretary of the T.U.C. to William O'Brien, and making full use of his loyalty to Larkin, retaliated by having O'Brien's supporters chivvied off the executive of the Dublin Trades Council. The beginning of this split, which did Irish Labour incalculable harm, was nevertheless largely based on personalities.

The Irish-American delegates reached Paris around 10th April and through Colonel House made arrangements to meet both President Wilson and Lloyd George. The appointments were later cancelled, but in compensation they received diplomatic passports on which they could visit Ireland. Accordingly Frank P. Walsh, Edward F. Dunne and Michael J. Ryan arrived in Dublin on 3rd May. They made a sensational tour of the country. Everywhere enthusiastic crowds greeted them and the tale of repression was told. They even penetrated Mountjoy where prisoners confined in cages like animals were about to be punished for shouting "Up the Republic". A special meeting of the *Dail* was held on 9th May which the delegates addressed. The police endeavoured to arrest a Volunteer officer named Kelly who pulled a revolver and escaped into the Mansion House. Large forces of police and military surrounded the building and their diplomatic passports did not save the Americans from being searched. The soldiers forming the cordon thrown across the upper end of Dawson Street were of the Wiltshires, with guns, bayonets, helmets and schoolboy faces. Women fraternised with them. "We didn't sign on for this," they replied. "We signed on for the war." The search of the Mansion House had been arranged at the Kildare Street Club. When he learned of the presence of the American delegates, Lord French intervened and the soldiers were drawn off. Neither Kelly nor other men on the run were captured.

When the delegates returned to Paris, Wilson explained to them that members of the Committee of Four, which controlled representation at the Peace Conference, had agreed on a unanimity rule. The British veto was being applied to Ireland, Egypt and other countries. On their hinting that this statement would not be well received in the United States, Wilson informed them that if they dared to attack him he would say that he had had every hope of securing Irish representation, until their indiscreet speeches in Ireland had made British consent impossible.

He added that he was afraid that his statement on self-determination had aroused hopes that could not be fulfilled. The road to international recognition through the Peace Conference was thus closed, and first Boland, and then De Valera left for the United States, partly to organise pressure on the American administration in view of the 1920 Presidential Election, and partly also to extend the sale of Republican Bonds to America. On 17th June it was announced at a meeting of the *Dail* that the President had gone abroad on national business and had nominated Arthur Griffith to fill his place. So ended the first phase in the history of *Dail Eireann*.

The Peace Conference fiasco had cleared the air. It was *Sinn Fein* again; and business-like measures, within the limitations of its policy, were adopted. Griffith dominated the proceedings with the advantage of a man who knew his own mind. He proposed the establishment of a fund for the provision of land for landless men. This is a matter to which more study needs to be given. The land question had proved the undoing of Gladstonian Home Rule. The Northern industrialists might conceivably have just stomached the revolutionary expropriation of the Southern landlords, but compensating them out of their own profits was another matter. Griffith's moderation thus tended to divide Ireland as a nation while it gave the appearance of a "unity of classes and creeds" in the South. National Arbitration Courts were decreed for every county. The employees of public bodies were encouraged to regard themselves as civil servants ultimately responsible to the *Dail*. A commission of enquiry into Ireland's industrial resources was established. Thought was given to the means of diverting income tax and customs payments into the coffers of *Dail Eireann*. It would seem to be at this point that the I.R.B. abandoned the aim of another armed uprising. It is of course needless to say that nobody contemplated the type of mass revolutionary struggle of which the working class must be the centre. The power of the Republic was to be extended, not by a direct challenge to imperialism, but by a series of encroachments.

The form of the subsequent struggle was thus set. Industrial unrest knew no remission. Later the land agitation rose to unprecedented heights. *Dail Eireann* rejected such forces as means to supreme power. But the issue of sovereignty must be joined whether with or without them. Imperialism resisted the encroachment, through intensified police and military activity. Legal advance became illegal sedition. Peaceful infiltration became a type of guerrilla warfare. The content of any war determines its form. The social policy of Griffith and the military policy of Cathal Brugha were the two faces of a coin. The conception of a democratic revolution of workers and small farmers, attracting to themselves the middle strata and neutralising the capitalists, had no place in their thinking. Enlightenment could only come from the Labour movement that was not represented in the *Dail*.

The transition to guerrilla war thus proceeded, and slowly taught Liberal circles in England that Ireland wanted freedom more substantial than that of Gladstonian Home Rule. On 13th May, Breen and Treacy rescued Sean Hogan, who had been arrested in connection with the Soloheadbeg affair, at Knocklong Station. Two R.I.C. men were killed. The Volunteers escaped to Dublin. The area around Tipperary was combed by the police. Trade union meetings were forbidden as far away as Golden, Co. Limerick. On 7th July the whole county of Tipperary was proclaimed under the 1887 "Criminal Law and Procedure Act". *Sinn Fein*, the Volunteers, *Cumann na mBan* and the Gaelic League were declared "prohibited and suppressed". Resident magistrates were given power to examine on oath any person they considered might possess useful information. Following a series of incidents in County Clare, the Act was extended to that county on 13th August. Attacks on R.I.C. posts became more frequent. As in Galway in 1916, there were moves to close outlying stations and to concentrate police in the larger centres. The evacuated posts were later burned down. Thus as the hand of repression fell more heavily on the towns, parts of the countryside became incipient "liberated areas".

During this period Michael Collins built up the Volunteers' Intelligence Service. The R.I.C. had been demoralised in its upper echelons by the political uncertainties of Home Rule. Its rank and file were increasingly feeling the effect of ostracism. Collins penetrated all levels, and before long knew the moves of the Castle immediately they were decided on. Using this information, and that provided by Post Office employees who were overwhelmingly Republican, the Volunteers were able to forestall attacks. A group of commandos called "The Squad" was organised, and the first particularly obnoxious detective to be removed by their avenging weapons was shot in Dublin on 30th July. British civil administration suffered a steady erosion. It was said that Britain could not rule Ireland, and could only prevent her ruling herself.

The first indication of second thoughts among Britain's rulers occurred when Captain Alcock touched down at Clifden after his Atlantic flight. Lord Northcliffe's message referred to the Dominion of Newfoundland, and the "future Dominion of Ireland". The idea was echoed by Asquith's Liberals and secured the approval of Southern

Unionists like Sir Horace Plunkett, whose Irish Dominion League was founded on 27th June and called for "Self-government within the Empire", the ending of representation at Westminster and the regulation of fiscal relations by treaty.

A time for talking seemed to come on 28th June when Germany finally caved in before allied bullying and accepted the peace terms. *The Times* led the way with a series of new proposals. These included "a bold plan of Home Rule" under "the aegis of the British Crown and within the framework of the British Constitution". It was insisted that "Ulster" could not be "coerced". *The Times* conducted a campaign in favour of partition. It was a semi-official newspaper and showed that imperialist aims were unchanged. The question was the means by which the Irish people could be induced to accept them. In this field there was no squeamishness. But there was shrewd calculation. The Peace Conference now being over, the passion for international recognition could be expected to cool. So *Sinn Fein* would surely decline. Emigration would ship off the discontented youngsters to America. And good sense would finally prevail, even a Redmondite revival.

The establishment of peace would, of course, bring into effect the 1912 Home Rule Act. It was already on the Statute Book, and it did not contain partition. The fact that no treaty had yet been signed with Turkey saved the British Government from the embarrassment of having to "coerce Ulster". A committee was set up which prepared three alternative Bills for cabinet consideration. They were drafted with a view to possible similar legislation for Scotland and Wales. Lord French took part in the preparatory work. He is reported to have proposed fiscal independence for Ireland. But the elected representatives of the Irish people were completely ignored.

On 7th September Volunteers under the leadership of Liam Lynch attacked a party of soldiers at Fermoy and relieved them of their arms. There was public demand that the troops be confined to barracks. It was disregarded. The soldiers ran amok and wrecked the town. Fermoy was proclaimed. The proclamation was speedily extended to the whole of County Cork, which stretches ninety miles west from Fermoy. Within three days the proclamation was extended to the whole of Ireland. On 10th September *Dail Eireann* was proclaimed. There were raids and arrests throughout the country. The offices at 6 Harcourt Street were searched from roof to cellar. And in Ulster, the land that could not be coerced, there were raids on *Sinn Fein* halls at Belfast, Derry, Enniskillen and Lurgan. The British T.U.C. protested. The answer was more raids. On 21st September six newspapers, including the *Voice of Labour*, were suppressed for the crime of publishing the prospectus of the *Dail* loan. A machine-gun post covered Liberty Hall. Industrial unrest continued.[1] Agricultural workers had been out in Meath, carters for six weeks in Newcastlewest, in Dublin printers, drapers' assistants, piano tuners, builders, and even the grave-diggers at Glasnevin. The failure of the bourgeoisie to lead a return to Redmondism is explained by the existence of a general prosperity in which labour was scarce and their own economic grievances weighed heavily on them. Government control of shipping was used to divert trade from Dublin to Belfast. When the delay in returning to the mines the labour force diverted by enlistment confronted British industry with a coal shortage, the export of Scottish coal was forbidden to the south of Ireland, including Dublin, and Irish manufacturers had to pay an extra 10s. a ton. Squeezing Ireland economically produced not emigration, but fuel for revolt.

Suppression of the *Dail* shifted the centre of national resistance to the Volunteers. At the last meeting before it was suppressed, the *Dail* had agreed on an oath of allegiance, in the American form, to be sworn by all deputies, *Dail* employees, and by the Volunteers. The proposal was made by Cathal Brugha who, like Griffith, was anxious to remove the Volunteers from the control of the I.R.B. The situation following the September proclamation was unfavourable to the summoning of a Volunteer Convention which must approve the change, but once the brigades had consented to it the oath was administered. O'Malley[2] explains that the form of organisation of the Volunteers was modified once the policy of defensive warfare was adopted by the I.R.B. Previously Volunteer companies had been based on some enemy strong-point which was to be assaulted in the event of a general uprising. Now a more fluid scheme was adopted. He emphasised, moreover, that the strength of the Volunteers lay not in the small towns containing these strong-points, but in the cities and in the open countryside, that is to say among the working class, small farmers and agricultural labourers, the classes engaged in productive labour.

With *Dail Eireann*, as he fancied, now out of the way, Lloyd George selected his preferred brand of Home Rule and made ready to impose it. The committee appointed to draft the legislation was headed by the

---

[1] At the secret October meeting of *Dail Eireann*, the last of which we have a record until the end of June 1920, there was reported the establishment of a Central Conciliation Board for Labour Disputes. Although a year later it was reported to be settling fourteen disputes a month, this cannot have had a substantial effect on industrial relations. It is noteworthy that the objections to arbitration came from the employers, among whom the large farmers were especially unco-operative.

[2] E. O'Malley, *On Another Man's Wound*, p. 106.

strongly Unionist Walter Long, and embellished with such luminaries as F. E. Smith, now enjoying the fruits of licensed rebellion under the name of Lord Birkenhead. Partition was essential to the scheme. The goal of years of treachery and tergiversation was at length in sight. Chief Secretary Ian MacPherson, the Gaelic-speaking Scot whose prejudices against all things Irish was matched by nobody in England, hastened to Dublin to "consult responsible opinion". This included the Southern Unionists, but not the elected representatives of the Irish people.

The *Sinn Fein Ard Fheis* was scheduled for 16th October. It was proclaimed. But a meeting was held in secret. Griffith naturally declined to make overtures to the self-appointed constitution-makers. He appears to have regarded the proposed Bill as window-dressing for American opinion. It would never come into effect. That he expected a long period of stalemate is shown by his speech in County Down on 17th October. He spoke of *Sinn Fein* policy in the next election, that is at the end of 1923, and promised that this time there would be no compromise with the Devlinites. Quite possibly the Bill was introduced with one eye on the United States. Certainly there was no hurry to pass it through its stages. But behind the delay was another calculation, revealed by Lord French on 23rd January 1920. There were up to 200,000 young men between 18 and 25 who but for the war would have emigrated. "Is there no hope of peace till these emigrations have taken place?" asked Jacques Marsillac of the Paris *Journal*. "No," answered the Viceroy. The bill was intended for application, as another official put it, when "law and order" had been restored.

It was introduced at Westminster on 22nd December. It is still in force in the six counties of Northern Ireland. It asserted the sovereignty of the King of England and the supremacy of the Westminster Parliament over every person and thing in Ireland. It divided the powers of state into three categories. Those most vitally affecting the lives of the people were totally withheld, such for example as control of foreign policy, including the power to make peace or war, trade with places outside the boundaries of the local administration, and the greater part of taxation. A second category was to be "transferred" to the two Home Rule Parliaments which were to be established. They included powers of local administration, including the right to introduce measures of coercion independently of the Westminster Parliament. A third category, which included the Post Office, was withheld until such time as the two administrations should establish a "Council of Ireland" to exercise them jointly. Transferred powers might be relinquished to the Council of Ireland by agreement of the administration but the powers that were withheld were to attach inviolably to Westminster. At the same time Westminster reserved to itself the right to meddle directly in Irish affairs by providing that in any conflict the legislation of Westminster took precedence over local legislation irrespective of the transference of powers.

From the effective discussion of this measure, the most emasculate of four Home Rule bills, the elected representatives of the Irish people were deliberately excluded. Lloyd George made no overtures for suspension of hostilities and attendance at Westminster. When De Valera escaped from Lincoln a special guard had been installed at the House of Commons with instructions to arrest him if he came to claim his seat. There was little need for this now. *Dail Eireann* was illegal, its members open to arrest if they were caught in any concerted action. Its work was transferred to committees. These carried the prestige of the *Dail*. Despite daily raids and arrests the sale of Republican Bonds went on. As the work was driven underground the spy, provacateur, and later the political assassin, came into his own. Free speech became a thing of the past. Thus Alec MacCabe was awarded nine months' imprisonment for advocating support of the Republican loan, Patrick O'Keeffe two years for a "seditious speech". Even the old-established Redmondite *Freeman's Journal* was suppressed on 15th December and vital parts of its machinery temporarily lodged in Dublin Castle. Once more Justices of the Peace began to resign their commissions. The R.I.C. became further demoralised and the number of those working secretly for Collins further increased.

In order to reduce the mobility of the Volunteers, the authorities decreed that no motor vehicle, a heavy lorry excepted, should be driven in Ireland without a military permit. Immediately the Irish Automobile Drivers and Mechanics Union declared a strike, which lasted from the end of November to the end of the following January. Unfortunately, there was some disunity among the trade unions whose members were affected and a compromise settlement was reached.

The elections for borough and urban district councils which took place on 15th January showed no slackening of support for *Sinn Fein*. The Republican authorities might of course have proclaimed these elections as an unwarrantable interference with their prerogative. But it was considered wisest to make further encroachments on British power within the framework of British law. The British authorities did their best to make this difficult. Waterford, Wexford and Kilkenny were placed under martial law. Candidates were arrested and deported. Election addresses were held to be "seditious literature". Yet, for the sake of appearances abroad, the elections must proceed. The single transferable vote was introduced so as to give the Unionist minority the most favourable conditions possible.

In the event eleven out of the twelve boroughs and county boroughs in Ireland were captured by *Sinn Fein*. Even in Belfast a new balance of power began to emerge: there were 37 Unionists, 5 Nationalists, 5 *Sinn Fein* and 13 Labour Councillors. In Ulster as a whole 23 urban authorities were now controlled by *Sinn Fein* and Nationalists, only 22 by Unionists. Many newly-elected authorities now transferred their allegiance to *Dail Eireann*, among them the Corporations of Dublin, Cork, Derry, Limerick and Waterford, after Belfast the five biggest cities in Ireland.

Governmental reaction was in character. There ensued a series of nocturnal raids designed to arrest "persons suspected of complicity in outrage". Those against whom there seemed a possibility of finding evidence were handed over for trial. Those against whom no evidence could be concocted were deported to England for internment.[1]

Instead of giving pause, the electoral confirmation of the people's will led the imperialist authorities to intensify repression. Apart from the harassing of individual adherents of *Dail Eireann*, attempts were made to locate the funds subscribed under the loan. In one raid on a *Sinn Fein* office the sum of £1,040 was seized. The *Dail* funds were then deposited in Dublin banks in the names of nominees. On suspecting this the Castle invoked the services of one Alan Bell, an ex-detective notorious for the employment of agents-provocateurs in the days of the Land League. He had the dubious distinction of having arrested Henry George when he visited County Galway. He was rewarded on his retirement with a resident magistracy in Lurgan, Co. Armagh. Now he was brought back into service. On 1st March 1920 he summoned the managers of Dublin banks to appear before a special commission and to provide particulars of nominees and of the deposits of suspected persons. He was shot dead in a tram on 27th March and the experiment was not repeated.

At the end of March 1920, figures were published which enable the "balance of terror" to be struck over the period since *Dail Eireann* was established. The Castle complained of a total of 1,089 "outrages" which they ascribed to *Sinn Fein*. These included 36 killings, 81 cases of shooting at persons, 54 cases of shooting into property (these would include the 30 guerrilla attacks on police barracks), 32 assaults, 426

[1] Sir Nevil Macready, *Annals of an Active Life*, Vol. 2, p. 439.

raids for arms, and 150 fires and other injuries to property. These events were never particularised and the tally may well be exaggerated. On the other hand in the same period *Sinn Fein* cited with documentary evidence no less than 6,721 outrages by Crown forces. Those included: 17 killings, one death from prison treatment, 528 armed assaults on civilians, 22,279 raids on houses, 2,332 arrests, 151 deportations, 232 courts martial, 759 sentences and 402 instances of the proclamation of meetings or the suppression of newspapers. The Crown forces were trying to beat a nation into subjection. The Irish people were defending their hearths and homes.[1]

The Government of Ireland Bill was read a second time on 29th March 1920. It was clear that the "law and order" necessary for its application was not yet restored. It completed its stages in leisurely fashion while the machinery of state was geared for a stronger effort. The R.I.C. was more demoralised than ever. Recruitment had virtually ceased. There was doubt over the reliability of the soldiers. These were boys from working-class homes, whose disillusionment with the peerage-mongering charlatan in office had produced a mood of bitterness and discontent. The class struggle in Britain was sharpening on both home and foreign issues.

At the end of March a new administration and new administrators were sent to the scene. A new phase of British operations began. Ian MacPherson was recalled and Hamar Greenwood, less prejudiced but more ruthless, was sent in his place. The Crown forces were placed under the control of Sir Nevil Macready, Commissioner of the London Metropolitan Police, whose smashing of the Police Union had earned him great admiration in government circles. A swaggering figure, fond of being photographed in imposing uniforms, he was an ideal commander to co-operate with the new auxiliary force now being recruited at Scotland Yard. He did history a service, however, in publishing memoirs which tell much of British imperial thinking at this period.

The new force, advanced representatives of which arrived in Ireland during the last week of March, was popularly known as the "Black-and-Tans" from the combination of army khaki and R.I.C. black in their uniforms. They were considered by Winston Churchill to be a most select company. In reality they consisted of ticket-of-leave men, city toughs, soldiers unable to settle down and ambitious nonentities who had failed to get on—rogues, fools, and disappointed men. As their numbers increased they became a law to themselves, and introduced an element of sordid brutality supererogatory even in the shabby

[1] E. Childers, *Daily News*, 11th May 1920.

struggle in which the British authorities were engaged. What, for example, can be said of the atrocity quoted by Lord Longford.[1]

A party of Black-and-Tans, capturing six unarmed Volunteers at Kerry Pike, near Cork, cut out the tongue of one, the nose of another, the heart of another, and battered the skull of a fourth.

The Volunteers reacted immediately to the signs of intensified terror. Over the week-end of 3rd and 4th April 1920, most of the income tax offices in Ireland were sent up in flames. From then till the establishment of the Free State there was next to no income tax collected in Ireland. On 5th April the prisoners in Mountjoy began a hunger strike. Crowds gathered each day at the gate, praying or singing rebel songs, defying the bayonets of soldiers and the guns of tanks, as aeroplanes, then a novelty, circled overhead. Tension rose steadily. On 12th April the Irish T.U.C. called a general strike. It is one of the cardinal facts of the history of these times that on every occasion when the Irish workers used their industrial strength to enforce a political decision, they were successful. The strike lasted three days, and the prisoners were then unconditionally released. Throughout Ireland bonfires were lit. Some of the celebrators were shot by the police.

The prisoners who had been deported to Wormwood Scrubs without charge or trial demanded political treatment and went on hunger strike on 21st April. Among them was the Secretary of the Irish T.U.C., Alderman William O'Brien. He had been taken from his house during a raid on 3rd March, and despite the efforts of trade unions, and questions in Parliament, the government declined either to release him or state the reason for his imprisonment. The Irish Self-Determination League demonstrated outside the jail. On occasion they were compelled to defend themselves from local hooligans. On one occasion, however, they expressed themselves antagonistically to members of the British Socialist Party, who had come to support them. At this time the great anti-Bolshevik scare was being worked up. Even in Ireland its echoes were heard, and Thomas Johnson assured Fr. Finlay that the Irish Labour Party was not Marxist and intended to remain within the Second International. Quite apart from this, the principle of non-involvement in British politics had resulted in a position where the Irish Self-Determination League did not always welcome allies even when they were available. After the Liverpool dockers had threatened to strike and the Stockport Irish offered William O'Brien as a candidate in a by-election, he was released on 6th May.

[1] Frank Pakenham, *Peace by Ordeal*, p. 51.

Despite the warnings of the Irish T.U.C. the British Government insisted on abolishing war-time price control of agricultural products. The result was a recrudescence of the land-hunger that had marked the spring of 1917. But the basis of the imperialist state had already been weakened. Instead of a demand for conacre led by the I.R.B. and seen by them as a means of defeating the Parliamentarians there took place what Kevin O'Sheil described as "a little revolution".[1] It was confined to areas where big estates had not been broken up. One of the methods of encouraging emigration adopted by the British authorities had been to paralyse the work of the Congested Districts Board. This now held no less than 60,000 acres of untenanted land in the County Roscommon alone. The small farmers and landless men availed themselves of the weakening of the state machine to carry forward the purposes for which they had supported the Republic.

The agitation began in County Galway. There were cattle drives, uprooting of fences and, after a landlord was shot, the struggle spread "with the fury of a prairie fire",[2] first throughout Galway, then over Mayo, Roscommon, beyond Connacht to west Leinster, north Munster and even parts of south Ulster. Ranches and demesnes were seized by the people, broken up and cultivated. While this was going on Lord French would never accomplish his aim of promoting emigration. But were the landlords prepared to sacrifice themselves for the preservation of the nation? They came "large and small, flocking to the Republican authorities in Dublin, beseeching them to do something".[3]

The movement of the small farmers and landless men was seen, not as a means of fulfilling the Democratic Programme of *Dail Eireann*, but as a "threat to the stability" of the national movement to which the landlords did not belong. Arbitration Courts were hastily summoned. The Republican police, selected from the Volunteers to deal with the few scape-graces and occasional interlopers who thought the liberated areas fruitful fields for adventures in larceny or poteen making, were hastily reinforced. A land bank was established to do the work which the Congested Districts Board was failing to perform. In one instance in County Mayo, where the local people were in disagreement with the decision of the Republican Court, Volunteers were brought from Clare and Donegal, and twenty-four men had been taken as hostages before the tillage operations ceased.

While the land crisis dominated the west there were challenges in

[1] Coyle, *Evidence of Conditions in Ireland*, p. 1009.
[2] *Op. cit.*, p. 1011.   [3] Op cit., p. 1007.

the south from a class too well organised to be intimidated. These culminated in what is known as the "Knocklong Soviet". In May 1920 workers at Cleeve's creameries were locked out after demanding a wage increase. The Irish Transport and General Workers Union sent three organisers, Connolly's old lieutenant John Dowling from Cobh, John McGrath from Dublin, and Jack Hedley, who had been imprisoned in Mountjoy but had been released after taking part in the hunger-strike. Together they organised the Munster Council of Action. The creamery was taken over and operated by the workers, with Hedley as manager. Passengers on the main railway line to Cork could see the red flag flying beside the tricolour and a streamer declaring "We make butter, not profits". Ninety-seven per cent of the milk usually supplied by farmers was delivered. A contract was entered into with the Belfast Co-operative Society. One of the socialists of that city was challenged by a fellow worker with the incredulous words, "Do you mean to say that that butter was made without a boss, and by those papishes?" Something of the meaning of the revolution was beginning to penetrate the Northern city. It had penetrated elsewhere too. General Sir Hubert Gough wrote an article in *Commonsense* urging the government to negotiate with *Sinn Fein*.

The "Arigna Soviet" was even more spectacular. Here, in the wild carboniferous hills above Lough Allen, the miners seized the levels when the owners refused their wage claim. Not only did they sell steam-coal to the Great Northern Railway, but they made technical improvements for which the owners agreed to pay compensation when they recovered control, as well as agreeing to honour all commercial contracts entered into by the workers.

On 10th May 1920, the London dockers prevented the loading of the *Jolly George* with arms for use against the Russian Soviet Republic. In the month that followed the famous Scottish socialist John MacLean prepared his pamphlet *The Irish Tragedy—Scotland's disgrace*, in which he called for similar action in favour of Ireland.

Should Ireland get a Republic the class war will then burst out and be fought out till Irish Labour wins and establishes Communism finally again in the "old country". The new phase in Irish life ought to be the inciting influence to British Labour, for Labour everywhere must ally against the common enemy, Capitalism, and destroy it to make way for World Communism. The victory of British and Irish Labour will pave the way for American Labour, the triumph of which will eliminate the possibility of the threatened war with America. Ireland's victory is obviously the undoubted prelude to

Labour's triumph throughout the world. . . . A General Strike then for the withdrawal of British troops from Ireland. . . .

South Wales miners decided to strike one day a month until British troops were withdrawn from Russia and Ireland. The Dublin dockers declared at once that they would not handle materials of war destined for use against their countrymen. The Irish Railwaymen followed suit. For the next six months they refused to run trains carrying war-material.[1] One man after another was dismissed. They were given no help from the British N.U.R. which was still led by the notorious J. H. Thomas who had sold Jim Larkin in 1913 and was to end his political career selling budget secrets in 1936. The involvement of the dockers nevertheless stimulated increased interest among the British workers, and the Hands Off Russia Movement was supplemented by a Hands Off Ireland Movement.

The British Labour Party met in conference at Scarborough from 22nd to 25th June. The Irish resolution represented a triumph for the left, and in particular for Ernest Cant who had worked hard for an Irish-Socialist alliance in Scotland. Thanks to his intervention the original composite resolution was materially strengthened and was proposed on behalf of the Executive by Sidney Webb. It contained the words:

The conference reaffirms the resolution passed by the Permanent Commission of the Internationale at Amsterdam in April 1919, demanding that the principle of free and absolute self-determination shall be applied immediately in the case of Ireland, confirming the right of the Irish people to political independence and demanding that this self-determination shall rest upon a democratic decision expressed by the free equal and secret vote of the people without any military, political or economic pressure from outside, or any reservation or restriction imposed by any Government. The conference accordingly demands that the Government should at once provide for an election by Proportional Representation of an effectively open Constituent Assembly for all Ireland, and the withdrawal of the British Army of occupation.

This might not have been "recognition of the Republic", but it came within an ace of it. It alarmed every reactionary in the two islands, and J. H. Thomas fought hard against it. It was nevertheless passed decisively and an enormous accretion of political strength was brought to the Irish cause.

The revolution had now reached a crucial phase. The British

[1] Irish Labour Party and T.U.C. Report (1921), p. 7.

Government was at bay in Ireland, while the British workers were challenging every aspect of its policy at home. It could well be argued that the time was ripe for what Strauss[1] called "the widening of the conflict to the social sphere through the combination of armed guerrilla warfare with the spontaneous rebellion of all the dissatisfied elements in Irish Society". The *Dail* met secretly on 29th June. But it was clear that, with the possible exception of Collins, nobody was prepared for a new departure.

In his opening statement Griffith made much of the reservation written into the Peace Treaty by the United States. One million and a half dollars were voted towards the expenses of De Valera in connection with the Presidential Election campaign and the attempt to obtain recognition of the Irish Republic from the government of the United States. It was upon this that the hopes of the *Dail* rested. Meanwhile Griffith declared that the most important home issue was the agrarian question. The establishment of the Land Bank had made possible the settlement of the land crisis in the west. The Land Arbitration Courts had "prevented the land question being used to divert the energies of the people from the national issue".

The Courts were now enjoined not to entertain any claims for the transfer of occupied land on grounds of former tenancy. It was agreed that some such claims were well-founded. Others were described as frivolous, and Austin Stack, the new Home Minister, spoke of people in Cork, Kerry and Clare who were "out to create a state of anarchy which ought to be put a stop to". Finian Lynch and Brian O'Higgins felt sure that the motion would have a beneficial effect. P. J. Ward from Donegal was not so confident. He thought the motion a mistaken one. While claims to ranches and demesne lands were not affected, it was clear that the land policy of *Dail Eireann* was in no fundamental way different from that of the British Government.

Peadar O'Donnell[2] and others have argued that the agrarian policy had fateful consequences for the whole revolution. For the first time the power of *Dail Eireann* had been directed against the masses. That Griffith had long hankered after the landlord alliance is, of course, well known. The new relation with the landlords who flocked to Dublin to save their estates implied a new relation with the Southern Unionists. Griffith had started the process which was later to produce partition and the Free State. The effect on employment was immediate. In August the *Dail* was compelled to pass a decree against emigration.

But this was not all. Stack proposed the establishment of Courts of Justice and Equity from parish to national level, together with "Courts having Criminal Jurisdiction". These became models of efficiency and incorruptibility. British justices gnashed their teeth in empty court-houses while the *Dail* Courts, meeting illegally a few yards away, were deciding the cases they had come to try. But the *Dail* had to decide the most vital thing of all. It was to administer justice. But according to what law? It was agreed to uphold "the law as recognised on 21st January 1919, until amended . . . except such portion thereof as was clearly motivated by religious or political animosity."

This was as high as the petite-bourgeoisie could rise, "the law as *recognised* on 21st January 1919". The essence of 21st January 1919 was precisely that all hitherto existing law was repudiated. "We have now done with England," said Brugha. The acceptance of the continuity of English and Republican law involved the acceptance of that most reactionary department, the English law of property.

If the small farmers and landless men were to be shown their place in the Republic, it was not possible yet to deal so unceremoniously with the workers. In the discussion of Collins' proposal that the *Dail* should attempt to collect income tax, Cathal Brugha insisted that the scheme proposed depended on the good will of Labour. In this session at any rate Collins emerged as the spokesman of the left. Not only was he prepared to trust to Labour support, he was prepared to implement a socialist programme.

He suggested that national resources should be taken over by county councils and other public bodies, so as to prevent their exploita-tion by private syndicates. Daithi Ceannt, member for East Cork, urged the public development of coal resources. But Griffith would have none of this. He was prepared to send an ambassador to the Bolsheviks. Traffic the other way was a different matter. He replied that "if the coal and other deposits of which Mr. Kent spoke existed, it was the business of the people to attract capital to work them." Capitalist dogmatism completely befogged him. The Democratic Programme of *Dail Eireann* was a scrap of paper. And Labour, alone able to defend it, was not present. The leader of *Sinn Fein* declared that the revolution had gone far enough. So ended another stage in the history of *Dail Eireann*.

Now was the time for reaction to attempt its offensive. The rural election results had still further demolished the myth of a homogeneous Ulster. The Government of Ireland Act envisaged the separation of only six counties. But these were chequered with anti-unionism. The Unionists now proposed to render the heartland of this smaller area as homogeneous as possible, by the simple expedient of driving the dissidents out, or where this was impracticable, reducing them to impotence. This was the precondition for successful partition.

Carson took the initiative. Amid complaints of the "peaceful penetration" of loyal Ulster, he declared on 12th July 1920, "I am sick of words without action." A week later action began. After a dress rehearsal in Derry, armed hoodlums descended on the Catholic areas of Belfast, setting fire to houses, looting and wrecking. In four nights of violence 19 people lost their lives and over 50 were injured. When members of the Belfast Brigade of the I.R.A. finally drove off the attackers and stood guard on the borders of the ghetto, the military, hitherto conspicuous by their absence, rediscovered the use of firearms. West Belfast became a city within a city, a haven of comradeship and humanity, constantly beleaguered, incessantly attacked, and preserved thanks only to the discipline and heroism of its inhabitants and the arms of the Volunteers.

The attack was transferred to the workshops. The Unionist gangs, some drawn from Bangor, Lisburn and the surrounding small towns where trade unionism had but restricted influence, attacked the gates of the shipyards with sledge-hammers. Meetings of Unionist extremists were held in some of the shops. One-sixth of the workers were Catholics. But to the invaders at least they were unknown. The vests and shirts of those who were at work were torn open and those who were discovered wearing Catholic emblems were forcibly driven out. Red hot rivets were held before their eyes as some were ordered to curse the Pope. One man was thrown into the dock, and while attempting to swim the Musgrave Channel was pelted with metal, emerging in streams of blood and rushing naked to the doubtful protection of a police barracks.[1] It is important to appreciate that while, to their disgrace, they took part in it, this pogrom was not initiated by the shipyard workers themselves, and that of the expelled men it was estimated that fully a quarter were Protestants, mainly staunch trade unionists and men of socialist convictions. Not a Catholic or a socialist remained in the yards.

While the dragooning of the North was under way, plans for a further repression in the South were anxiously expedited. A Bill for the "Restoration of Order in Ireland" was rushed through the Commons, and came into force on 9th August. Regulations made under the Act, appearing on the 21st, provided for presumption of guilt by association, imprisonment without charge or trial for an indefinite

---

[1] Irish Trade Union Congress Report, 1920, p. 101.

G

period, trial by secret court martial able to impose the death penalty, even in the absence of the accused's legal representative, the suppression of coroner's inquests and power to arrest witnesses and to compel them to give evidence under threat of fine or imprisonment or both. It is upon this Act that the administration in the six counties of Northern Ireland based its notorious "Special Powers Acts". From now on official outrage and legal murder were the order of the day, providing the Act could be enforced. General Macready recorded plaintively that just as the police and troops were getting into their stride, the good work was paralysed by orders to hold the battalions ready for instant despatch to England. The miners' strike was about to begin. Councils of Action against the proposed war of intervention had sprung up all over Britain, and if Sir Henry Wilson, Chief of the Imperial General Staff is to be credited, the Whitehall birds of paradise were squawking hysterically at the prospect of revolution. It was provided that every Ministry should defend its own building. On 12th August Terence MacSwiney, Lord Mayor of Cork, was arrested while presiding at a meeting in the City Hall. He went on hunger-strike immediately, and after three days was deported to London and held in Brixton Jail. Eleven others were held in Cork jail. Now police and magistrates began to resign in large numbers.

A struggle of these dimensions must of course make an international impact. Already the French and Italian socialists were conducting campaigns of solidarity with the Irish people. Developments in America will be dealt with in the next chapter. At the second congress of the Communist International, at which Ireland was represented by Roderick Connolly, Zinoviev responded to the appeal of Thompson, who with P. L. Quinlan represented the U.S.A., and made a statement favourable to Ireland. Shapurji Saklatvala, a fraternal delegate to the 1920 meeting of the Irish T.U.C., brought greetings from India, while Emmanuel Shinwell read the resolution of the British T.U.C. demanding that the administration of Ireland be handed over to the elected representatives of the Irish people. At many public meetings it was being shown that the British workers were desirous of action. The pressure of working-class opinion found expression in the resolution passed by the Labour Party Conference at Scarborough.

During September, when the danger in England had somewhat abated, General Macready introduced what he described as "official retaliation". Notices were posted to the effect that if a "loyalist's" house should be destroyed as a result of an attack, then the house of a Republican leader would be similarly dealt with. No "loyalist's" houses

were destroyed, and Macready congratulated himself. The policy of
"official retaliation" was, however, merely a cover for "unofficial
reprisals" which were encouraged by the government though no
responsibility was taken. On 20th September twenty-five houses were
destroyed in the town of Balbriggan. Its hosiery factories were wrecked.
Mills, bacon factories, co-operative creameries (including that at Knocklong) were burned down. Young Volunteers were arrested, taken away
in trucks and "shot while attempting to escape". Wanton brutality and
murder ruled unchecked. Even Sir Henry Wilson could not stomach
the indiscipline of the Black-and-Tans. He told Lloyd George that if
men ought to be murdered then the government should take responsibility for murdering them. Throughout this sombre period the Irish
people followed the daily martyrdom of Terence MacSwiney who
ultimately died after a hunger-strike of 74 days. The remains were on
the way back to Ireland via Dublin, when police swooped on the coffin,
and shipped it direct to Cork with as much ceremony as would be
afforded a box of nails. The day of the funeral was one of national
mourning.

The Volunteers fought back. Even bolder attacks on barracks and
ambushes of Black-and-Tans were attempted. Republican control
extended in areas from which the Crown forces had been compelled to
retire. A boycott of Belfast goods was instituted at the suggestion of
Sean MacEntee. It showed the Northern Republicans they were not
alone. But Ernest Blythe and Countess Markiewicz were probably on
the balance wise to oppose it. It drove in even further the wedge between Unionist Belfast and the rest of Ireland. Even in Britain far-
sighted people began to grasp the fact that British policy in Ireland had
run up a cul-de-sac. The possibility of making a deal with *Sinn Fein* was
seriously considered.

The first enquiries came from hard-headed City men concerned
about the safety of their investments. On 15th September the *Financial
Times* interviewed Griffith and MacNeill. The professor made light of
their fears. "We have no desire to harm investors in the least . . . it
would be foolish on our part to do anything to alarm them." "You
can tell your City men," said Griffith, "that they have nothing to fear
in the way of confiscation or unjust discrimination."

These replies did not pass without criticism. Cathal O'Shannon
voiced the indignation of the Labour movement. MacNeill and Griffith
had no mandate to "pledge the future of the nation". There seems to
have been no protest within *Sinn Fein* itself, though the "equal right
and equal opportunities" guaranteed to Irish citizens by the Declaration

of Independence were now being made subject to the interests of foreign financiers. The economic ground for neo-colonialism having been tested by the businessmen themselves, the political initiative was inevitable. On 6th October Brigadier-General Cockerill wrote to *The Times*, urging a truce and a conference "untrammelled by restrictive instructions and empowered by means of negotiation and mutual concession to obtain the best peace possible". This proposal was publicly welcomed by Griffith.

The acting-President of the Republic was setting the course for compromise. But the masses were unaware of it. The common people judge their leaders by themselves. Throughout Ireland workers and farmers were risking all they possessed hiding and helping men on the run. Their women were running up debts with tradespeople for food for the Volunteers. Many of these debts were not repaid for years. And those to whom the cause meant nothing but sacrifice believed the same of all who had adhered to it. Thus, as in every democratic revolution in history, the men of property had their fighting done for them.

CHAPTER ELEVEN

DE VALERA IN AMERICA

THE tremendous electoral victory of *Sinn Fein* aroused great enthusiasm in America. Mellows felt deeply the honour of his election as a representative and confessed to a sense of unworthiness. McCartan by contrast, with longer experience and less humility, behaved as if the status was something inherent in himself. In a mood of expectancy and excitement he yielded to the urge to "do something". The wisest course would have been to cable congratulations and request instructions. Instead, so far as can be ascertained, without consulting Mellows he approached McGarrity and Dr. Maloney, and these induced Judge Cohalan to invite leading figures in the Friends of Irish Freedom to a discussion at his house. Those who had borne the brunt of the struggle during the war were not even informed.

The proposition was that the Friends of Irish Freedom should organise meetings to express their congratulations to the Irish people. In the general rejoicing McCartan had worked out roles for himself and the Judge. As envoy of the Provisional Government he proposed to issue a proclamation pointing out the significance of the *Sinn Fein* victory. In addition he would inform the State Department and foreign legations in Washington that Ireland had severed all political connection with England. As for Cohalan, he wished him to cable to De Valera and Eoin MacNeill his congratulations "on the peaceful establishment of the Republic". McCartan, of course, regarded himself as the envoy of a Republic already established. Cohalan was a practical man. Not unnaturally he reacted against the doctrine that the election result established it again without any further overt action in Dublin. This was wishful thinking pushed too far.

McCartan's haste arose from elements in the American situation, and a failure to appreciate that the action taken in Dublin was now internationally decisive. On 11th December 1918, Richard Dalton, regarded as Cohalan's personal representative at Washington, had accepted the deletion from the Gallagher resolution of the words "freedom and independence" and after stating that the phrase "self-determination" was adequate, agreed that this implied that a plebiscite must be held. McCartan was anxious to commit the Judge and his associates to the acceptance of the election as a plebiscite.

Cohalan was sceptical. An election, he insisted, was not a plebiscite. The result of the discussion was indeterminate. McCartan, McGarrity and Maloney moved for a caucus meeting. They were unable to shake off Devoy. But they drew him into the drafting of McCartan's proclamation which stated that the "people of Ireland have, before the watching eyes of the world, finally achieved the independence of Ireland. In the elections that took place on December 14th last, Ireland exercised her right of self-determination." Cohalan on his part despatched the wire. It congratulated De Valera on "Ireland's overwhelming verdict in favour of President Wilson's policy of self-determination of all peoples". This might have just passed muster if President Wilson had had any such policy.

Each section arranged its own public meeting. *Clann na Gael* booked the Central Opera House for 5th January, the Irish Progressive League for the following day. Mellows was invited to speak at both meetings. At first he declined to speak for the *Clann*. But on being told that his refusal would "break the old man's heart", and no doubt in view of Devoy's collaboration with McCartan and McGarrity, he consented. The Judge expatiated on the benefits of future self-determination. McCartan developed his absurd proposition that the "principle of self-determination has been applied, and Ireland is separated from England as effectively as Norway is from Sweden". It was left to Mellows to clear up the confusion. He said:

> The Irish people have exercised, as far as lay in their power, the right of self-determination, and they have determined that Ireland should and must be free and independent . . . Ireland has won a victory, but not the great victory we want, that we all hope for, and believe in. The road to that victory that has to be travelled, is hard and thorny still.

The Irish Progressive League meeting was, by contrast, a celebration of the left, proclaiming the identity of the Irish with the world revolution. The prospect of Irish freedom was bound up with the character of the peace. Peter Golden warned that President Wilson might return from Paris the most discredited man in American history. A great betrayal was in preparation. That a peoples' peace depended on the success of the European revolution, of which Russia was the centre, was clearly indicated in the resolution:

> Whereas an army of occupation is in Ireland and in Russia, in direct violation of every principle for which the war is being fought, resolved that we American citizens, in mass meeting assembled,

demand the immediate withdrawal of both these armies so that the Irish and the Russian peoples may be left free to work out their own destiny.

Apart from Mellows and McCartan, the speakers were Rev. Norman Thomas, Dr. John Lovejoy Elliott and Alfred W. McCann. It was thus substantially a socialist platform, and proposed the correct international demand—not nebulous American recognition, but definite British evacuation.

Next evening the Irish Women's Council organised a reception for the three deputies in the U.S.A., McCartan, Mellows and Diarmuid Lynch.

It took place at the Hotel McAlpine. When the celebrations were over, Mellows had the problem of making a living at a time of rising unemployment. He thought of paying a visit to the Hearns in Westfield, then leaving for California, where he would visit Eamon Martin's friends, the Murrays. His case was still undecided. The police were possibly afraid of his disappearing like Jeremiah O'Leary, even of his leaving America by the West Coast, lighting some revolutionary tinder on the way. They paid great attention to his movements. After the Irish Citizens' Association "Annual Ball" on 18th January three state agents followed him and Thomas O'Connor home, and remained outside the apartment they were sharing all night. They followed them to Mass next morning and trailed them all day until they went to a party at the Kirwans. A number of guests were then followed home. Mellows believed that the sudden calling and postponement of his case was deliberately designed to keep him in New York.

He seems to have stayed at the Kirwans all night after the party. He recorded in his diary next day that Patrick Kirwan had been taken ill. The influenza epidemic was at its height. Early on Tuesday the doctor diagnosed pneumonia and pleurisy. Mellows stayed up at night with him, until nurses could be obtained. It would thus seem that he was not working during the day, though he used to teach Gaelic and Irish history at the Carmelite Hall in the evenings. On 24th January, though there was no class, he received a special invitation. Leaving Kirwan with some hesitation, he found an unusually large gathering, including all the Carmelite fathers and Dr. McCartan from Philadelphia. It was made clear to him that he was the guest of honour. Laudatory speeches were made and to his astonishment he was handed a cheque for $500.

At the end of the month he addressed a meeting at Syracuse, and visited Fr. McAuley of Derry in St. Joseph's hospital. That he was free to do so seems to indicate that he was still unemployed. According to a letter he wrote to Nora Connolly on 14th September 1919, he "got work along shore (docks)", when he was offered teaching. Little seems to have survived regarding this episode. Liam Pedlar recalled seeing him on the premises of "the Engineering and Fireman's Union". He speculated that work was found for him by the secretary of that Union, a Mr. Magee from Dundalk. Possibly it was clerical work in the union office. It cannot have been of long duration. Fr. Magennis offered him a post as teacher at the Carmelite School, which he accepted.

Towards the middle of February he read newspaper announcements of the third Irish Race Convention to be held in Philadelphia on 22nd and 23rd February. He was strongly resentful at not having been consulted or even notified, for the secretary of the Friends of Irish Freedom which was organising the Convention was his fellow deputy, Diarmuid Lynch. The Race Convention arose from the appointment of the *Dail Eireann* representatives to Paris, and the appeal to the free peoples of the world. It may be said that beyond this undoubted fact its chroniclers agree on very little. Mellows left for Philadelphia and took an obscure seat in the body of the hall.

The size and enthusiasm of the Convention surpassed all anticipations. But behind the scenes there was war to the knife over policy. The battle cries of the two parties were "self-determination" and "recognition". But these were mere reflections of fundamentally different lines of approach to Irish-American relations. To the recently arrived American Irish, the issue was simple enough. The people of Ireland had declared a Republic. It was up to the Irish-Americans to help them make that declaration good. Its representatives had called for recognition, in particular for representation at the peace conference. The Irish-Americans should press the desirability for such recognition on the President of the United States and endeavour to secure the hearing at Paris. This last, indeed, was agreed upon, and Frank P. Walsh, Edward F. Dunne and Michael J. Ryan were in due time sent on their way.

But to the Irish-Americans there were other questions also. They had strong and genuine sympathy with Ireland. But Ireland was not their country. This contradiction was overcome in the case of the Irish Progressive League through proletarian internationalism and adhesion to the Socialist Party which taught that the workers of the world should unite to bring peace, prosperity and democracy to all. It could not be resolved where Irish-Americans gave adherence to one or other of the established bourgeois parties. This was seen over years in the predominantly Democrat tendency of the *Irish World* whereas Republicans like

Judge Cohalan, though there was nothing Gaelic about him, gravitated to the fold of the *Gaelic American*.

It would be unjust to suggest that Cohalan was in any sense a re-actionary. Yet he accepted the written and unwritten assumptions of America's imperialist position. His sympathy for Ireland was part of his approach to American politics. He was an American first. He disliked President Wilson with excellent reason. But he gave his unconditional support during the war, and went out of his way to refer to him in his message to De Valera.

There were various possible interpretations of the expression "self-determination". It could be envisaged in conjunction with a series of national revolutions. It would then mean that any nation that wished to do so was entitled to secede from any state or states within which it found itself and to establish its own. The Irish objection to the term arose from the belief that Cohalan did not interpret it in this way.

How did he interpret it? While neither side was theoretically clear, it is a fair conclusion that he subjected it to considerations of American policy. If the United States were to recognise the rebel power within the United Kingdom, what of her relations with Britain? What was implied in relation to the Soviet power? Or Cuba? Or Mexico? A settlement in which the British Government could concur obviously had attractions for American politicians, and indeed for the American public. Self-determination as a general principle could be referred to the future. *Dail Eireann* was clamouring for recognition there and then.

On 14th January 1919, the Friends of Irish Freedom had decided to establish a Victory Fund of a million dollars. The proposal was endorsed at the Philadelphia Convention. Its prospectus illustrates fully the inter-play of Irish and American interests. The purposes were

(a) To urge that the objects for which America entered the war may be fully attained.

(b) To urge and insist upon the recognition of the Republican form of government established in Ireland.

(c) To urge that America shall not enter into any League of Nations which does not safeguard all American rights.

(d) To maintain and preserve the American ideals of government and to oppose and offset the British propaganda which is falsi-fying and misrepresenting the facts of American history.

(e) To maintain for the foregoing purposes a widespread and pro-fessional publicity campaign.

(f) To defray the expenses of the Irish American delegation to the Peace Conference.

If this document[1] had been drafted with an eye on the 1920 Presidential Election and the possible candidature of Cohalan's friend Hiram T. Johnson, it could not have been more skilfully drawn up. And it should be noted that the purposes listed gave ample room for manœuvre, which was amply availed of as events developed.

The main resolution of the Convention had been drafted on the basis of "self-determination". The reason offered was that otherwise it might not be possible to secure the participation of Cardinal Gibbons. McCartan had assented. But now he had second thoughts which Devoy and Cohalan attributed to the intervention of Dr. Maloney, who with McGarrity's approval kept the Resolutions Committee up all night fighting for an amendment. When the filibuster failed McCartan declined to sit on the platform.

Mellows did likewise, but for another reason. As soon as his presence was noticed, Cohalan sent for him, no doubt fearing a repetition of the demonstration of the previous year. He invited him to speak, but on the Saturday, the day of the small fry. Mellows declared that he would speak while Cardinal Gibbons was there or not at all. He was, of course, not a party to McCartan's agreement. In the event a compromise was compelled by Norman Thomas, who was advertised as the seconder of the Cardinal's resolution. The Socialist threatened that unless this was strengthened he would use his speech to propose an amendment. Cohalan then gave way, and it was decided to send an immediate deputation to President Wilson asking that the Irish should be heard in Paris.

Mellows returned to New York, and Cohalan led the deputation to Washington. President Wilson professed himself too busy to receive it. The Gallagher Resolution, now reduced to a request for "favourable consideration" of the Irish case at Paris, was coming before the House of Representatives. The day it passed, by 216 votes to 45, the President found time to meet the deputation, but insisted on Cohalan's withdrawing from it. When he did so, no mean feat of self-denial for an American judge, Frank P. Walsh and Judge Goff learned that the President would make no promises. The President's action helped to push Cohalan into the camp of Senator Borah whose main plank was opposition to Wilson's pet scheme for a League of Nations in which America would simultaneously co-operate with England and France and edge them out of their colonial monopoly.

It was on that day, 4th March, that Mellows began to feel unwell at school. He struggled through the day's work as pains in the head, chest

[1] Reproduced in Tansill, op. cit., p. 345.

and back grew ever sharper. At midday he met Fr. Augustine, one of
the chaplains to the rebels in 1916 who had just arrived from Ireland.
After school he set to work preparing a lecture on Emmet he was to
deliver to the Citizens' Association that evening. A message came from
John Devoy. Would he invite Dr. Maloney to testify at the trial of
Jeremiah O'Leary which was then in progress? Devoy and Maloney
were not on speaking terms after the angry scenes at Philadelphia, but
Devoy appreciated the doctor's incisive intellect when it was employed
in the right place. Mellows called on Maloney at 9 p.m. He felt weak.
He could scarcely understand what Maloney was saying, but successfully concealed his condition. He arrived at the hall for his lecture at
10 p.m. But he was unable to speak. Alf Metcalfe and Molly Murphy
undertook to see him home. They delayed at her apartment for a cup
of tea. But this failed to revive him. His head seemed on fire and he
began to show signs of delirium. On this he commented afterwards,
"They thought I was only fooling, which I often do because all I can
talk about is history." He was helped home by Dan McCarthy and
Metcalfe, who sat up all night with him.

Next day a doctor was brought. The influenza epidemic had given
New York its highest death rate since 1880. McCartan arrived. He was
due to speak at the Irish Progressive League's Robert Emmet commemoration that evening. He was alarmed and called in Dr. Maloney whose
skill narrowly saved Mellows' life. In his delirium he imagined he was
behind the barricade in Clarenbridge, and would rise in bed shouting
orders to his men. On another occasion he thought the doctor had
insulted his mother. He wanted to fight and made impotent passes at
the air.

Controversy raged in the thirties over whether Mellows' illness was
brought on by hunger and by heavy work he was unaccustomed to. As
has been seen, his unemployment can have lasted little over a month.
There is no evidence that his labours on the waterfront were specially
arduous. He received $500 on 24th January, part of which he must, of
course, have spent in going to Philadelphia. Gregg Ashe, who saw him
two years previously, said that he was short of money at this time.
Others say that all his money went promoting the objects of the
movement, so that he had no reserves. Dr. McCartan categorically
denied that his illness was brought on by malnutrition. When all the
evidence is assembled it seems best to assume merely that he fell a
victim to the influenza epidemic while financially embarrassed, but no
more than usual.

He was completely out of action for about a week. Fr. Magennis then arranged for him to spend a fortnight at St. Albert's College, Middletown, where Fr. Metcalfe, Alf's brother, was in charge. He spent the first few days in bed, got up for the first time on 18th March, and slowly entered into convalescence. On 25th March he wrote a long letter to Mrs. Hearn which demonstrated at once his revolutionary incorruptibility in political matters, and his deep personal piety in the religious field. He wrote with special sympathy of Nora Connolly. "What a sad time she is having! Her health broken, and yet working amid scenes that are daily reminders of her father." But Ireland was "still struggling valiantly", and the "Peace" conference would soon be over, "if events now portending will allow it to finish".

On returning to New York he suffered a relapse. Several more days were spent in bed. Then he learned that the Friends of Irish Freedom commissioners were leaving for Paris. McCartan and McGarrity were in New York protesting that they had not been consulted or informed until the last moment. They insisted on a meeting that would give the delegates written instructions. This was arranged at the Hotel McAlpine on 31st March. Mellows was so angry at being left in the dark that he got up, determined to be present. It had been designed as a small private gathering. But through some leakage the press learned of it and 700 people arrived. Speeches were made. McCartan and Frank P. Walsh spoke of the "rise of democracy in Germany" and expressed sympathy with the Soviet Government of Russia. But briefing the delegates was impossible.

At McGarrity's behest, a small group was ushered into one of the rooms. The question of the Republic was posed by Judge Cohalan in the role of *advocatus diaboli*. M. J. Ryan incurred McGarrity's ire by confirming that he thought Dominion Home Rule acceptable at a pinch. Frank P. Walsh was strong for the Republic. But the meeting was inconclusive. At the end Mellows collapsed. McGarrity took him to Philadelphia and sent him for a week to his summer residence in Atlantic City. Despite his illness he accompanied McCartan to Washington to protest to the Papal Delegate at Monsignor Cerretti's statement to the *New York World* that the Irish question was a matter of internal British politics.

There was a prospect that their cases would at last be heard, and the two T.D.s[1] hurried back to New York. But there was a further postponement. Despite continuing weakness Mellows resumed the daily round of teaching and lecturing. At the Citizens Association a young man called Baskerville, fresh from Ireland, spoke so passionately of the

[1] T. D. *Teachta Dala*—"Member of the *Dail*".

need for arms to defend the Republic that an Arms Committee was set up, with Mellows as chairman. Later Baskerville undertook the work himself, and was later roundly ticked off by Boland for poaching on the territory of the *Clann na Gael.*

At this point Mellows was first drawn into association with the Indian struggle. An Indian organisation, the "Friends of Indian Freedom", had been founded on the model of the F.O.I.F. Peter Golden, Norman Thomas and Dudley Field Malone had addressed it on 10th April. Lajpat Rai had attended the Philadelphia Race Convention and probably met Mellows there. On 24th April Mellows and Lajpat Rai, together with Fr. Dooley, addressed a meeting at St. John's Hall, Newark, New Jersey. Thereafter Indians contributed regularly to the *Irish Press.* The two movements grew closer together. Not only did Irish speakers support the campaign against the deportation of Indian militants, but Irish Republican seamen provided the safest line of communication between the national movement in India and the Indian exiles throughout the world.

The international aspect of the Irish struggle was becoming increasingly apparent. At the Irish Progressive League meeting on 14th April Peter Golden had "acclaimed Russia as the first government to recognise Ireland in her struggle for self-determination". At this meeting Fr. Dooley took the chair and Frank Harris and Scott Nearing were among the speakers. On the other hand anti-Sovietism was developing among Irish-Americans. On 2nd May the Irish Women's Council organised a meeting at the Hotel McAlpine to mark the third anniversary of the execution of Pearse. Miss Lola Ridge spoke of the "coming revolution" (presumably in the United States) and "Russia". Mellows' attorney, Martin Conboy, deprecated such talk, which was probably heady enough, and as Mellows put it "spoke somewhat disparagingly of Russia". Mellows contradicted him and took occasion to state that "Russia had given more encouragement to the Irish Republic than America had". This disagreement did not harm his relationship with Conboy. They had supper and walked home together.

The Irish Progressive League information bureau at Washington had now been taken over by the Friends of Irish Freedom. The young Canadian in charge of it issued a statement to the effect that the Republican government in Ireland had nothing in common with the political system of Bolshevism, since it had "fused all classes in an amity that is not known either in America or Russia". The statement was indeed a clumsy reply to the absurd allegation, originating in England, that the Bolsheviks had sent millions of dollars to the *Sinn*

Fein treasury. Martens protested to McCartan at its unfriendly tone, and McCartan assured him that the statement was not authorised by the government he had the honour to represent. He added the pointed remark, "The Republic of Ireland regards the political system adopted by the free people of Russia as the concern of the Russians."

McCartan showed courage in issuing this statement. The witch-hunt against socialists was reaching fever pitch. The allies were stripping Germany of her colonies, evolving plans for the partition of Russia and Turkey. No imperial scheme was too grandiose or too impudent. The American Socialist Party was the sole opposition and its members were swinging rapidly to the left. On 5th May, two days before McCartan issued his reply to Martens, hoodlums tried to wreck the office of *The Call*. That same day its reporter covering the strike at Lawrence was waylaid, beaten up, stripped and left with the noose round his neck when the lynchers were disturbed. Victor Berger, Connolly's old associate, had been elected to Congress. Efforts were being made to disqualify him and prevent his taking his seat.

The Irish Progressive League stuck to its guns. This was shown at the meeting of 8th May. Mellows felt ill, but attended and spoke, as he thought, "wretchedly". The other speakers with one exception were Socialists—Norman Thomas, whom Mellows thought the best, Peter Golden, Edward Cassidy, Joseph Cannon, Alfred McCann, and Patrick Quinlan. The exception was Jeremiah O'Leary, making his first public appearance after his case (he had been apprehended on a charge of treason) had been brought to a successful conclusion. He was noticed in the audience and joined the platform amid enthusiastic applause. The proposed League of Nations was well denounced. There was "thunderous acclamation" of the Russian Soviet Republic, and McCann called for "Three cheers for the Russian People. Three cheers for the Irish Republic. Three cheers for free peoples everywhere." The alliance of the Socialists and the Irish Republicans was still firm.

At long last, on 14th May, the case against Mellows on a charge of having forged seamen's papers was heard. Dr. Gertrude Kelly, who was present, recalled the incredibly dirty windows and air of gloom in the Federal Courthouse, and the one ray of sunlight which contrived to get in and lit, of all places, the dock. The District Attorney's case was that Mellows and McCartan were trying to get back to Ireland in order to take part in a revolution. The defence replied that if that were so revolution would have been put in evidence. "The time for severity in these cases is passed," said the Judge. "These obviously are political offences." They were fined $250 each. Mellows was delighted at the unexpectedly light penalty. Now he could return to Ireland. His inclination was to start at once. On 18th May he availed himself of speaking engagements in Massachusetts to pay a farewell visit to the Hearns.

On his return to New York he found that Boland had arrived. His plan of going down country to harden up had to be abandoned. Boland was described as the Special Envoy of the *Dail*. There is reason to believe, however, that he had already succeeded Sean McGarry as leader of the I.R.B. and that his object was to prepare *Clann na Gael* for a mission by De Valera. McCartan records that in the dispute between McGarrity and Devoy, Boland found for McGarrity. McCartan called a meeting of the four T.D.s and it was agreed that he also should leave the U.S.A. He felt that he was *persona non grata* with Cohalan and that Boland stood a better chance of working with *Clann na Gael*.

Mellows felt that he could relax now. He noted with satisfaction that Congressman Mason had introduced a Bill providing for "the salaries for a Minister and Consuls to the Republic of Ireland". This was good news. But his thoughts were on home. He spent a fortnight at Middletown with Fr. Feeney from Galway. There he delighted the students by constructing a boat and sailing on the lake. He was trying to accustom himself to the physical exercise necessary for the homeward journey. But on his return to New York he found his room in unexpected disorder. Boland had been there, and others too. There was a bundle of old clothes on the floor. He went out puzzled.

He was at the Priory for supper when a messenger told him that De Valera had arrived. The old clothes had been his. Rats had eaten through his seaman's bag and he had been accommodated at Mellows' while fresh attire was found. Mellows had arranged to attend a little celebration at the home of the Misses Murphy. Tom O'Connor accompanied him. John Hearn unexpectedly turned up to invite him to New Hampshire for a holiday. It was Hearn who explained what had happened. Calling that afternoon he had found De Valera, Boland, McCartan and McGarrity. De Valera had gone to Rochester to see his mother. On 14th June Mellows followed him to Philadelphia.

Mellows made no entry in his diary from 14th June to 27th June. He may possibly have accompanied Boland and McGarrity to Atlantic City on the 19th. The American Federation of Labour was in conference there, under the chairmanship of Gompers. A delegate named Rock had Devoy's approval for a motion calling for self-determination for Ireland. Much to Gompers's annoyance Boland lobbied the Irish delegates and secured the presentation and acceptance of a resolution calling for recognition. This was the sole progressive proposal adopted.

Thanks to somewhat discreditable manœuvring the platform succeeded in defeating motions in favour of ending the blockade of Russia, a strike for the release of Tom Mooney, and the establishment of an American Labour Party.

Meanwhile De Valera was in New York consulting with the *Clann na Gael* leaders. He paid a visit to Cohalan. While he recorded later that he felt the Judge was cool towards him, he must have considered it his duty to try to bring the two wings of the movement together. The left alliance could scarcely allure him at this time. During the early part of the year the Communist International had invited affiliations from the national working-class parties. Certain conditions were stipulated. The leaders of the Socialist Party, determined not to accept these, but realising that the Congress in Chicago would probably do so, resorted to large scale expulsions. By the beginning of July 1919, the membership of the party, which had stood at 110,000 at the end of the war, was reduced to some 30,000 by suspensions and expulsions.[1] The disruption of the Socialist Party encouraged the authorities to intensify the witch-hunt. The Lusk Committee began investigating "un-American" activities. On 12th June the Russian Soviet Bureau was raided. The Irish Progressive League vigorously protested and Larkin appeared at an indignation meeting in Madison Square Garden. He and his associates moved towards the formation of the Communist Labour Party. De Valera thus arrived at a time when the tide of reaction was flowing more strongly than ever and the forces of progress were in a state of confusion.

When Boland reached New York he found that De Valera had the formula which he believed would square the circle. His first public appearance was to be on 23rd June at the Waldorf Astoria. Reporters were to be handed a statement in which he described himself as the "official head of the Republic established by the will of the Irish people in accordance with the principle of self-determination". He had with him the record of the *Dail*'s first meeting, a brown covered pamphlet on to whose fly leaves were gummed the Proclamation of Easter Week, the Constitution of *Sinn Fein* and the Manifesto prepared for the 1918 election.

The day came. The ceremony opened in the Gold Room where the most distinguished guests foregathered. They included the four T.D.s, Cohalan, Gavegan, Goff, Devoy, Robert E. Ford, Fr. Magennis, Fr. Wheelwright, De Valera's half-brother, and a group of Indian nationalists. There were introductory handshakes and an Irish song. Then the

[1] Emmet Larkin, *James Larkin*, p. 231.

press conference began. Judge Cohalan stepped forward and introduced "The President of the Irish Republic". Then came a reception at which De Valera shook a thousand hands. As they drove through Central Park in an open Victoria, De Valera exclaimed light-heartedly to Mellows, McCartan and McGarrity, "I wonder what Griffith will say when he reads that I came out in the press as President of the Republic." It is clear that he anticipated no opposition from the I.R.B.

Mellows believed that Cohalan's show of co-operation was a manœuvre designed to bring De Valera under control. One of Cohalan's strongest supporters, J. J. Splain, felt that De Valera was unreasonable. He was not sufficiently impressed by the "twenty-five prominent bankers, businessmen and laywers" the Judge assembled to meet him. But he was in America to sell bonds for the *Dail*. Pillars of society and pillars of *Clann na Gael* strongly cautioned against it. Why not enlarge the Victory Fund? This could be used for campaiging in America. When De Valera insisted and won Judge Goff to his side, still no help was forthcoming. It was argued that the sale of bonds was illegal, since the U.S.A. did not recognise the government on whose behalf they were to be issued.

According to McCartan the technical difficulty was overcome by the ingenuity of Dr. Maloney who drafted the text of a bond-certificate entitling the purchaser to a bond when it became available. The Friends of Irish Freedom refused to sponsor the scheme. Accordingly the three Commissioners for Irish Independence formed an *ad hoc* committee with Frank P. Walsh as chairman. Maloney secured premises which were occupied on 23rd August, and a week later the Friends of Irish Freedom, bowing to the inevitable, closed the Victory Fund to make way for the bond drive. Thanks to McGarrity's insistence $100,000 were voted in support of De Valera's campaign.

The suite at the Waldorf Astoria was the scene of constant activity. Here came the messages from universities, Chambers of Commerce and State Legislatures inviting De Valera to address them. Mellows joined Boland and Sean Nunan in dealing with the mass of correspondence. His diary ceased on 8th July, apart from one entry in September. He had intended to be home in July. But Boland fell ill and he was asked to remain till he recovered. On 13th July he was in Chicago speaking with De Valera. The President went on to San Francisco to attend the National Convention of the Ancient Order of Hibernians. On his return on 3rd August he told Mellows that he was so impressed by the possibilities and volume of work to be done that he would like him to stay indefinitely.

Mellows remained about six weeks in New York, apart from an excursion to Kansas City probably as a substitute for De Valera. He addressed the Irish American societies of the district at their annual picnic, and the *Kansas City Star* commented on the lines of his face which they regarded as the mark of the martyr, but were more likely the result of influenza, from which even now he had not completely recovered.

Of De Valera at this time he wrote to Nora Connolly, "He has seen through them. Result, we are all thrown very much together—*An Ard*, Dr., *Seosamh, Enri* and *mise*.[1] All conceit gone from him . . . since he discovered the conditions. Never saw a sicker man. Disillusionment isn't the word." With Boland he addressed the Central Federated Union of New York on Labour Day. On 13th September the Socialist Party Convention voted for recognition of the Irish Republic. The inescapability of the alliance with the left became even plainer. Boland might attempt to seal off the young exiles from Socialist politics by appointing them consuls of the Republic. The Republic itself was compelled to appeal to the Socialists.

Their divided counsels reduced the help they could give. On the second anniversary of the Russian revolution there were three separate celebrations. Bitter class struggles convulsed the industrial scene. The Palmer raids menaced the basis of American democracy. But two days after the suppression of *Dail Eireann* Frank P. Walsh and Alfred McCann were speaking at a protest meeting. At a meeting organised by the Irish Progressive League to protest against the reign of terror in Ireland, the old stalwarts were still there, Peter Golden, Pat Quinlan the trade union leader,[2] Fr. Dooley and Lajpat Rai. Throughout the autumn the absence of Judge Cohalan from the field was as noticeable as it had been during most of the war. He and Devoy concentrated on fighting proposals for American participation in the League of Nations, and considerable sums from the Victory Fund were expended in press advertising.

On 1st October De Valera began a tour of the United States with a mass meeting at Philadelphia. The supporting speakers were McCartan, Diarmuid Fawsitt, Frank P. Walsh, Harry Boland and Sean Nunan. Liam Mellows had gone ahead to make the preliminary arrangements. He described himself as "De Valera's John the Baptist". The work was exacting, as the itinerary shows. On 3rd and 4th October De Valera was to speak at Pittsburgh. Then he was to pick up Mellows' trail and

---

[1] The Chief (De Valera), Dr. McCartan, Joseph McGarrity, Boland and self (Mellows).
[2] Not the former member of the Irish Socialist Federation.

follow through Youngstown, Akron, Cleveland, Columbus, Cincinnati, Louisville, Indianapolis, Fort Wayne, Detroit, Chicago, Milwaukee, St. Paul, Des Moines, Peoria, Springfield, St. Louis, Kansas City, Omaha, Lincoln (Nebraska), Denver, Salt Lake City, Butte, Spokane, Seattle, Portland (Oregon) and San Francisco which he was due to reach on 17th November, proceeding to Los Angeles after two days. It was intended that he should return to New York through the southern and eastern states. But in November he interrupted the tour. James O'Mara had arrived from Ireland to take charge of the bond drive which was to be launched in December.

That De Valera transformed the situation as it affected the masses is shown clearly by the amount of newspaper space devoted to the Irish question before and after his tour. For Mellows these were days of physical strain but nervous exhilaration. He delighted in action. He would arrive in a strange town, make contact with the Irish societies, which would sometimes exist in the flesh, at other times on paper only. If they were not strong or experienced enough to make arrangements he must book the hall, place the advertisements and move on to a fresh place without any means of control in the one he had left. He enjoyed the strange sensation of having enough money to do all that was needed.

The journey was packed with incidents not in themselves significant. Mellows reached Denver on 24th October while De Valera was at St. Louis, Missouri. He called a press conference, after which one reporter wrote that it had taken him ninety-one days to cross the Atlantic, and another gave him four months. He addressed a meeting of the Friends of Irish Freedom on the Sunday. While arranging a public reception for De Valera and his secretary Sean Nunan at the Brown Hotel for the Thursday, he had to keep in touch with New York regarding engagements further down the line. Whether De Valera would speak at Salt Lake City or not depended on whether he went on to Pueblo or back to Cheyenne. Mellows had already cancelled the Salt Lake City visit when a telegram from the Mayor of Pueblo intimated that a meeting had been arranged there after all. Even though De Valera needed a rest, Mellows decided to book him for the two meetings, before sending him on to Spokane. He waited till the party arrived and with them visited the grave of Buffalo Bill.

Only on the West coast were there signs of opposition. De Valera's appointment at Spokane was for 9th November. On the Sunday before, the Congregationalist Pastor Dr. Thomas H. Harper is reported to have "excoriated" De Valera as a "traitor" who had wanted a "Hun invasion". He worked his audience up to fever pitch and loud applause rang through the consecrated building. Mellows arrived next day and issued a detailed and spirited reply. When De Valera's meeting took place Mellows was already in San Francisco. The auditorium was crowded. There were a few supercilious titters when the President began to speak in Irish. Later there was rapt attention, ending with an ovation. There were objections to the display of the tricolour at Portland, Oregon, and in Los Angeles Mellows was involved in polemics in the local press.

When De Valera returned to New York, Mellows took over the remainder of the tour. The postponement of the meetings to later dates than those first advertised, and a card to his brother posted in San Francisco on 3rd December, indicate that he probably stayed about a fortnight with the Murrays. Probably about this time he wrote the article which appeared in the *Irish Press* on 6th December. Its main interest is in its reference to dual power in Ireland. "Today there are two governments in Ireland." This presentation was never made in typical *Sinn Fein* propaganda and may well derive from his acquaintance with the progress of the Russian revolution.

He wrote to Mrs. Hearn from Albuquerque, New Mexico, on 7th December:

> I'm in the best of health and spirits. Everything is going along splendidly. 'Twould take too long to tell you all about the tour, and the places I've been in . . . I'm delighted to have got the chance of seeing Arizona and New Mexico. I always wanted to see these historic spots. It is so wonderful to be down among the Indians. I'm Indian mad these days but regret time does not permit me to stay and learn all about them . . . I'm going to El Paso tonight thence to San Antonio and on to New Orleans.

He spoke at El Paso on 8th December at the Knights of Columbus Hall, and at San Antonio three days later. Up to now the weather had been exceptionally sultry for the time of the year, but now a brisk north wind struck the south-west. Despite the cold he was shown round the city by the Ladies' Auxiliary of the Ancient Order of Hibernians. He spoke at the Knights of Columbus Hall in the evening. It was announced that De Valera was absent on account of sickness but would return in the New Year. For some reason the local newspaper described Mellows as a poet.

Some of his friends afterwards spoke of a visit to Mexico where "he saw fewer guns than you'd see in Ireland". Had he paid such a visit El

Paso would have been his point of entry. But he appears to have gone to San Antonio and Houston, Texas, where he spoke on 13th December. On Christmas Eve he sent John Devoy a greetings card from Dallas. But he does not appear to have held any political meeting there. Possibly he spent Christmas there with Irish friends.

On his return to New York he found De Valera and O'Mara immersed in the bond drive, and peace patched up with the Cohalan camp. De Valera had been given a tumultuous reception as he stepped off the train from Chicago. *The Call* reporter noted, however, his new note of caution regarding the recognition of the Soviet Republic. The Palmer raids had begun in earnest on 7th November. Larkin had been arrested on 8th November. He was held on $15,000 bail, to which not only the Socialists but John Devoy contributed. The great steel stoppage had plunged the United States into the most widespread industrial struggles of their history. But the opportunism of the leaders of the Socialist Party had disarmed the political wing of the movement. Membership continued to dwindle as repression intensified. On 3rd November Los Angeles, "Allies Committee" had sent a telegram to the State Department protesting against De Valera's "revolutionary speeches", and Palmer had been invited to investigate.

After the first disagreements the Friends of Irish Freedom had co-operated in the bond drive. On 9th December De Valera attended the National Council and expressed his satisfaction. On 12th December Cohalan testified before the Foreign Relations Committee of the Senate and most ably defended the *de jure* and *de facto* status of *Dail Eireann*, adding in reply to Senator Connolly that if recognition involved war with Britain, then he would be prepared to face that prospect. At this time British and American interests were in conflict all over the world. There was open talk of the possibility of an Anglo-American war, and indeed John MacLean was to publish his pamphlet *The Coming War With America* only two months later.

While with a little stretching Friends of Irish Freedom policy could accommodate the Republic, especially at a time of Anglo-American tension, the other aspects were not forgotten. In August the *Clann na Gael* Convention at Atlantic City had resolved upon a strenuous fight to keep the United States out of the League of Nations. McGarrity regarded this campaign as a diversion. But Devoy replied that American membership of the League would be a recognition of Ireland's subjection, and that McGarrity and his friends had their priorities wrong. In the course of subsequent polemics Devoy revealed his position. It was that the "real battle [was] being fought now" in the

United States. He failed to distinguish between American imperialist and Irish national opposition to British colonialism.

But, for the nonce, all was well. De Valera held weekly conferences with the Friends of Irish Freedom leaders. Cohalan seemed convinced of the need for recognising the Republic, though the Mason Bill showed no signs of leaving the Committee stage. The bond campaign was begun in New York State. Mellows was presented to Governor Al Smith at Albany on 6th January. He was described as the President's "personal representative". De Valera followed on 21st January, by which time Mellows had opened offices in Chicago whence to work the Middle West. From time to time he returned to New York, on the 17th addressing a 3,000-strong gathering at Troy. On the 30th he accompanied Rev. Grattan Mythen, of the Protestant Friends of Ireland, to Springfield, Illinois, where they spoke in the Circuit Room of the famous old State Capital. A resolution calling for recognition of the Irish Republic was proposed by ex-Congressman Graham and carried unanimously. De Valera was to arrive on 7th February.

That day the *Westminster Review* published an interview with De Valera. In it he sought to allay fears that an independent Ireland might be used as a base from which to attack Britain. He put the matter this way:

> The United States safeguarded itself from the possible use of Cuba island as a base for attack by a foreign power by stipulating that the Cuban Government shall never enter into any treaty or other compact with any foreign Power or Powers which shall impair or tend to impair Cuban independence, nor in any manner authorise or permit any foreign Power or Powers to obtain by colonisation or for military or naval purposes or otherwise lodgment in or control over any portion of the said island.
>
> Why doesn't Britain do with Ireland as the United States did with Cuba? Why doesn't Britain declare a Monroe Doctrine for her neighbouring islands? The people of Ireland, so far from objecting, would co-operate with their whole soul.

This article provoked what Professor Tansill described as a "tempest" in Irish-American circles. Devoy denounced it in the *Gaelic American* as the admission by the President of the Republic that he would accept something less than complete sovereignty. De Valera had persuaded him against his better judgment to take an uncompromising line. Now he himself was taking a compromising one. But to Irish-Americans concerned with votes in the year of a Presidential Election, the statement was full of menace. Only one Power could conceivably desire lodgment in Ireland for operations against England. Here was Ireland offering to bargain with England and using as bait a guarantee against America. What would she do with recognition if it were given her?

De Valera was, of course, young and inexperienced. He explained that he wished to set the British talking. In Dublin, whither McCartan was despatched to explain matters, Count Plunkett, Cathal Brugha and Countess Markiewicz remained critical. Griffith and Collins approved of the interview. Up to now Brugha had steadily supported Griffith in the *Dail*. Now a new alignment began to develop.

Mellows got on with his task. On 18th February he was in Decatur. On his return to Chicago he found the *Gaelic American* with its blistering attack. The *Irish World*, by contrast, had taken De Valera's part. Here was the material for a first-class split. Dealing with Unionist objections was one thing. Handling hysterical supporters was another. From Chicago he must go to Cincinnati to start the Ohio campaign. There on 9th March he wrote of his reactions to Mrs. Hearn:

> I returned to Cincinnati from Chicago last Saturday. I had been in the latter place all during last week unwell and doing nothing. I had a slight occurrence of the after effects of the "flue" of last year and had to knock off. . . . I'm sure you must have been very worried (as the tone of your letter revealed) over the situation in N.Y. I was much worried too—so much so that it helped to make me ill; and like you I wondered whether a definite break or a tiding over was the best course. Being away in the wilds of Ohio (where they are very ignorant!) I found it hard to know what was going on . . .
>
> I was horrified beyond measure at the editorials, etc., of J. D. Now the President did not in the least lower the flag—if it were so I would be the first to protest. What he simply stated was that as England was using the argument that Ireland's freedom would mean her ruin, and she must therefore hold Ireland for her (England's) safety, he would prove that this contention was false as England's safety would be guaranteed by the following:
>
> (a) Ireland stipulating (as Cuba did in the first paragraph of the Platt amendment) that she would not allow her territory to be made a "jumping off" ground for an enemy of England.
>
> (b) By England declaring a Monroe doctrine for the two islands whereby she would regard an attack on Ireland as constituting a hostile act against herself.
>
> (c) By creating a new League of Nations that would protect the rights of every country—England included.

He accused Devoy of introducing the whole of the Platt amendment whereas De Valera had quoted only the first paragraph, and added,

"I am thoroughly disgusted with him. . . . The old man can never be the same to me. I regret it for it pains me. As for the Judge—well, the least said the soonest mended. . . . As you say, so I agree, that if it were not such a crucial hour for Ireland nothing would be more pleasant than to show up the whole hideous structure that battens on the work and sacrifices of the people at home. How dare the old man talk of the 'young men at home' in view of the treatment meted out to the young men who came over since 1916."

Mellows explained that he had written to McCartan, whom Devoy had attacked in a later editorial, urging him to keep silent. Unfortunately McCartan had been stung to a reply. Mellows went on to say that his work in Chicago and Ohio was "slow and hard and wearisome", but the differences in New York were not reproduced.

De Valera believed that the editorials in the *Gaelic American* were influenced by Judge Cohalan and the matter was developed in a series of angry exchanges. As if impelled by an inexorable law he and Boland began to explore the left alliance which had been neglected. On 23rd February the Irish Progressive League came out for the President. Negotiations were opened with Martens and Nuorteva and the Russian treaty was drafted. The authorities had blocked the drafts of the two Soviet representatives. They were accommodated out of Irish Republican funds, against which a part of the Russian crown jewels was deposited in the Bank of Ireland. De Valera attended meetings of Indians indignant at the British occupation of Constantinople and the plan to annex Turkey. The Irish societies of New York met on 28th February to discuss the special programme for St. Patrick's Day. Dr. Gertrude Kelly, delegated by the Irish Progressive League, proposed inviting representatives of other oppressed nations. The result was a large Indian contingent adding novel colour and pageantry to the traditional event. Cohalan and De Valera were at daggers drawn now. But for this occasion they shared a platform.

The Peace Treaty was ratified on the following day. De Valera sent Griffith a glowing account of the sixteenth or "Gerry reservation" which looked favourably on the desire of the Irish people for a government of their own choice. He was thankful for small mercies now. On 21st March he was to speak in Chicago, and had received an invitation to attend a banquet in his honour on the 19th. Possibly it was Mellows who informed Boland that though the tables had been booked, no guests seemed to have been invited. Boland discovered that a number of leading critics of De Valera had raranged to meet in New York while he was expected to be receiving his rebuff in Chicago. Accounts vary, but it is agreed that De Valera attended and that recriminations were followed by a very unstable reconciliation.

The murder on 20th March of Thomas MacCurtain, Lord Mayor of Cork, aroused extreme indignation. The more so since it was immediately followed by massive military preparations and the arrival in Ireland of the Black-and-Tans. At the suggestion of Dr. Maloney the Irish Women's Council sent over sixty pickets to stand outside the British Embassy in Washington denouncing the terror in Ireland. The picket began on 2nd April and a number of the women were arrested. Larkin had meanwhile organised the Free Ireland Union Labour Committee which held a meeting at the Chelsea Casino on the 3rd. On 8th April De Valera began his long postponed Southern tour, and once again Mellows went ahead to prepare the way. There was a certain rallying of the democratic forces. On 17th April the *Irish World* in an editorial attacked the Bolshevik scare. Two days later Larkin, Norman Thomas and Elizabeth Gurley Flynn appealed for unity at a meeting called to protest against the ten years' sentence imposed upon Winitsky. Next day Maloney's friend Oswald Garrison Villard published his fourteen points for the defence of American democracy.

But on 27th April Larkin was found guilty of "criminal anarchy" and was sentenced to five to ten years' imprisonment. Frank P. Walsh busied himself with the appeal. Amnesty committees were set up in New York and Boston. And the Irish Progressive League speakers' bureau began street meetings once again. On 24th May, Frank P. Walsh addressed the representatives of 500,000 New York workers in the Cooper Union. This was an Irish independence meeting such as New York had never seen, the entire audience in working clothes. The Mason Bill became an innocuous resolution. And Palmer, the raiding Attorney-General, was linked with a booze scandal.

The Friends of Irish Freedom denounced the women pickets. "Ireland will get her freedom when America has a big navy," said one of its spokesmen. Matters were coming to a head. Mellows returned to Chicago to prepare for a visit of De Valera at the time of the Republican Convention. De Valera's recognition plank was hopelessly defeated. Cohalan's self-determination plank was repudiated by De Valera. A week later J. J. O'Leary (Jeremiah's brother) launched a weekly New York *Sinn Fein* to defend the supporters of the Republic from the attacks that were a regular feature of the *Gaelic American*. Liam Mellows joined the editorial board.

On 24th June De Valera and Mellows were at San Francisco at the

Democratic Convention. Here there was more partisanship and delegates almost came to blows. But it was clear that the Democratic Party was not going to do what Wilson had declined to do. There was no Irish plank. Bourke Cockran busied himself pushing a "wet" plank. A fellow delegate asked him, "Do you put rum before the freedom of your race?"

On 14th July the Irish Progressive League held a meeting on the twin themes of "Release Larkin" and "British Troops get out of Ireland". On the 22nd it was expelled from associate society membership of the Friends of Irish Freedom. Fr. Magennis had left the United States and Bishop Gallagher was now president. De Valera moved for an Irish Race Convention. But this was refused. Preparations were then made for launching a new organisation. While still travelling frequently Mellows was again based in New York. When Terence MacSwiney, the arrested successor of Thomas MacCurtain as Lord Mayor of Cork, began his hunger-strike the women once more formed a picket line, this time at the British Consulate in New York. Later they walked the quays and called out the dockers. The spontaneous dock strike spread to Boston and all the Pacific coast. The Hindustan Gadar party joined in the protest.

In late August Mellows learned of the death of his father in Dublin and insisted that he must now return to Ireland. Writing to John Hearn on 1st September he thanked him for his condolences. Of MacSwiney he wrote:

> We, Peter MacSwiney, Pedlar and I have just finished the Rosary for Terry. It is painful to watch poor Peter feverishly watching the papers for a gleam of hope—hoping against hope, prepared to face the worst, proud of his wonderful brother, but torn with love and enduring an agony of anguish at the thought of the latter's sufferings. Oh dear! how small do we all appear in the face of this terrible tragedy. How little indeed are the ambitions that have brought the movement to such a pass here, compared with the great principle for which MacSwiney is giving up all.

On 17th September De Valera was told at a meeting of the Friends of Irish Freedom that those present had no further wish to listen to a "foreign potentate". He hastened with the plans for establishing the Association for the Recognition of the Irish Republic. John Hearn became its national organiser. Mellows assisted with some of the preparations for the Commission of Enquiry into conditions in Ireland, at which Muriel MacSwiney and Ellen Wilkinson were to give evidence. But he had lost interest in America. Through the good offices of Bill Gleeson at the Custom House he secured a seaman's passport in the name of Edward Moore, and on 2nd October sailed as a stoker on the United States vessel *Philadelphia*.

CHAPTER TWELVE

DIRECTOR OF PURCHASES

"Auferre, trucidare, rapere, falsis nominibus imperium: atque ubi solitudinem faciunt, pacem appellant."—Tacitus

THE *Philadelphia* passed the Lizard on 10th October, and tied up at Southampton next day. With a seaman who was rejoining his ship in London, Mellows made his way to Lisson Grove, Marylebone, where Sean Nunan's parents lived. The father was an old I.R.B. man, and Labour supporter. He and his wife kept open house to members of the Irish movement in London. And there were three sparkling lasses, a few years younger than Mellows, who were excited at their new romantic visitor and delighted at his combination of gravity and playfulness. Mellows needed a few days to recover from the exhausting labour of the voyage. He had never been in London before. He saw the sights, bought clothes and a few souvenirs, and familiarised himself with the situation in Ireland. After about ten days he left for Dublin, probably cutting short his stay in view of an expected rail strike.

On 9th October, Lloyd George had made his notorious speech at Caernarvon in which he flatly rejected Dominion Status for Ireland, the proposal of the Asquith Liberals. He declared vaingloriously, "We have murder by the throat." A great "Hands off Ireland" meeting filled Trafalgar Square on the 10th. The greater part of the British press was demanding changes in government policy, but reports of fresh atrocities were published every day. Mellows' old friend Dr. McNabb had been arrested for declining to provide the names of patients whose injuries might have been incurred in disturbances. On 7th October raiders had searched the houses of Dr. Kathleen Lynn, Mrs. Sheehy-Skeffington, Mrs. Tom Clarke and Mrs. Coffey hoping to find Darrell Figgis. They found instead H. W. Nevinson who was provided with blistering copy.

In the counties of Donegal, Laois and Waterford the authorities had forbidden the holding of inquests. There were thus some murders which were not to be got by the throat. Despite protests that Britain was applying to Ireland the weapon she had used on Germany, the blockade, the government prohibited the importation of cattle food. On 11th October Crown forces raided the home of Professor Carolan who was sheltering Breen and Treacy. The wanted men escaped. But the professor was put up against the wall and murdered in cold blood in his own house.

October 14th proved disastrous for the Volunteers. Following a raid on the Republican Tailor's shop in Talbot Street, Sean Treacy was recognised and shot dead after a gun battle. Joe Vize, recently withdrawn from Scotland to supervise the purchase of arms and equipment from abroad, was arrested together with Leo Henderson. Matthew Furlong blew himself up in his bomb factory. The one bright spot was that military raiding the Mater Hospital in search of Breen failed to capture him. He had escaped again. On the 16th there was a half-day general strike in Cork City for release of Terence MacSwiney. The strike was not made national and failed to achieve its object. That day there were mass floggings in County Mayo.

Mellows arrived in Dublin on 20th October and made for the home of Seamus O'Connor, one of the original Volunteers' Committee who had followed the lead of Bulmer Hobson and declined to take part in the Rising. Kevin Barry, an eighteen-year-old medical student, captured after an ambush, had just been sentenced to death. On the 25th Terence MacSwiney died in Brixton Jail. A "ring of steel" was fastened round Dublin, while the coffin was impounded and despatched to Cork. On 1st November Barry, who had been tortured, was hanged.

On 2nd November James Daly of Tyrrellspass, Co. Westmeath, was executed for his part in the mutiny of the Connaught Rangers which had been precipitated by news from Ireland. The National University was raided and 800 students were searched. On the 5th the prohibition of inquests was extended to Leitrim, Sligo, Westmeath, Meath and Wexford. Four hundred houses were searched. On the 11th, the day when the Government of Ireland Act received its third reading, Colonel L'Estrange Malone, the English Communist M.P. for Leyton, was arrested after delivering a lecture at Trinity College. He was removed to London to answer for a "seditious speech" at the Albert Hall. He had asked the rhetorical question, "What, my friends, are a few Churchills or Curzons on lamp posts[1] compared to a massacre of thousands of human beings?"

From his temporary lodgings with the O'Connors, Mellows made

[1] It depended who put them there. On 25th September 1912, referring to the likely fate of the Asquith Government if it "had the wickedness" to use "coercion" in "Ulster", Mr. F. E. Smith quoted with approval Mr. Bonar Law's threat to the Ministry that "the population of London would lynch you on the lamp-posts".

contact with Eamon Martin, whose tailor's shop was in Nassau Street, and through him with his brother and Alfie White. Soon he was visting the *Fianna* office in Westland Row and considering the possibility of resuming his old work. On the other hand the previous two months had seen attempts to establish permanent guerrilla parties, or active service units, in the rural areas. He indicated his willingness to join one of these.

He could not remain indefinitely at the O'Connors. But he dare not appear among the Unionist neighbours of Mount Shannon Road. He must have revealed something of his dilemma to Maire Comerford one evening at the house of Louise Gavan Duffy. He asked where Sean Etchingham was and she took him to Mrs. Woods at 131 Morehampton Road. The woman of the house was at first suspicious. But his good introduction, high spirits and sincerity quickly disarmed her. Soon there were gales of laughter issuing from Etchingham's room. Mrs. Woods agreed that Mellows should remain temporarily. With a few intermissions he was there for over eighteen months.

As he awaited an assignment he accustomed himself to the life of general uncertainty and violent incident. Each evening there was curfew. Citizens scurried home so as not to be found on the streets. Dawdlers were liable to be flung bodily into army wagons and carried off for interrogation, with or without ill treatment. Thereafter, their searchlights playing, military vehicles would be driven, sometimes at reckless speed, sometimes at a tantalising crawl. Every moment the ear was strained with enquiry or relaxed with uneasy relief. The British authorities were anxious to discover and put out of action Volunteer G.H.Q. Whole blocks, and areas of several blocks, would be cordoned off and subjected to house-to-house search. As the countryside continued to slip from their grasp they intensified the terror in the towns, and especially in Dublin and Cork. With mass raiding and searching went a new type of intelligence work. Special agents, drawn from the colonial services, were entrusted with the task of tracking down and if possible murdering the key men on the Republican side. By mid-November it was estimated that this "Cairo gang" had been responsible for the death of seventeen supporters of the Republic.

The application of the "Restoration of Order in Ireland Act", under which, in Churchill's words,[1] Black-and-Tans were "striking down in the darkness those who struck from the darkness", the difference being, however, that the latter were in their own country, confronted the Volunteers with grave problems. A conference which included men

---

[1] *Aftermath*, p. 289.

from the provinces was held over the week-end of 13th–14th November.[1] Important policy decisions were made. First, counter-intelligence was to deal with the "Cairo Gang". This was a matter for Collins. The war of reprisals was to be carried on to British soil. This proposal is attributed by Beaslai to Cathal Brugha, who had failed to win acceptance of his old proposal for disposing of the British Cabinet. Rory O'Connor was despatched to England for diversionary activity.

Finally there was to be a reorganisation of the supply services, with a view to increasing the quantities of war materials available, and eliminating duplication of effort. There was to be centralisation under Volunteer G.H.Q. with three interlocking directorates. James O'Donovan, a qualified chemist, became Director of Chemicals. He was to secure or manufacture from raw materials explosives for mining, bridge blowing, grenade making, etc. Sean Russell, as Director of Munitions, was to undertake the manufacture of bombs, mines, and ammunition. And Mellows, with the title of Director of Purchases, was to organise the importation of arms, ammunition, and equipment from abroad. Clearly the three responsibilities overlapped. But no difficulty seems to have arisen. O'Donovan established a factory in London, and Russell toured the English midlands for components which, combined with items of native manufacture, produced serviceable if crude weapons of offence. The three men were elevated to the Army Council and Mellows attended his first meeting on 24th November.

The work that Mellows now undertook was of a most secret and confidential nature. Few records were kept. Such as survive reveal a difficult and thankless task. It is hardly possible to set events in strict chronological order, but their overall logic can be seen. The appointment represented a stage in the simplification of a dual control of arms importation that had grown up. For many years the I.R.B. had brought in arms. It had perfected an organisation involving its members in Britain and the U.S.A. After the gun-running at Howth the Volunteers relied on this organisation for additional supplies. Since the Volunteers bought their weapons, it was of no importance that the capital used was that of the I.R.B.

[1] F. O'Donoghue (*No Other Law*, p. 153) speaks of attending a meeting "about 13th or 14th December, at which both Mellows and Vize were present". But Vize was in prison before Mellows left London. It could be that O'Donoghue's memory telescoped events and united two separate meetings in one recollection. December 13th was a Monday, an unlikely day for such a gathering. But 13th November was a Saturday. Mellows dated the opening of his departmental account from 13th November 1920. O'Donovan assigned the same date to his appointment. And the policy decisions of the conference took effect before the end of November.

When *Dail Eireann* was established the Minister of Defence exercised a general supervision over the Volunteers, but the old system was continued. The increasing demand for arms, and the demand for supplies which would not necessarily be paid for immediately by individuals or units, placed a strain on the finances of the I.R.B. It was natural enough that Collins, who was Minister of Finance to *Dail Eireann* and linked the I.R.B. arms-importing business with his work as Director of Intelligence to the Volunteers, sometimes contrived short cuts by which expenditures took place without the proper procedure. Brugha, moreover, was not a full-time worker and was not always immediately accessible.

The suppliers for their part were sometimes dedicated anti-imperialists. They wanted nothing for themselves but would stipulate that a proportion of the arms must be delivered to the Citizen Army. Others were members of the I.R.B. or of the Volunteer companies in Britain. But gun-runners cannot be choosers. Many of those with whom it was necessary to do business made light of commercial virtue, and were ready to turn a penny at anybody's expense. It was the slipping away in Scotland of some large sum upon an unfulfilled promise that led to the recall of Vize, not, of course, under the faintest stigma, but in order to establish a formal check in Dublin. The long investigation of the Scottish accounts was insisted on by Brugha because Vize was in prison. The appointment of Mellows was thus in a sense a victory for Brugha, who wished to centralise all financial responsibility under the Volunteers, over Collins, who felt that the nature of the work precluded such nice stipulations. At the same time Mellows, as an old I.R.B. man, was acceptable to "the Organisation".

The central clearing house for the traffic was in Liverpool, then Britain's largest port, and the nearest to Ireland. Seamen on the Atlantic services would bring small quantities which they handed to members of the I.R.B., first under Frank Thornton and later under Neil Kerr. Through time the continental traffic was tapped. Regular supplies were purchased from non-Irish as well as Irish seamen. The Lancashire coalfield was combed for explosives. From Birmingham came small arms, and discarded war material. Chemicals came from as far away as London. While the facts alleged by the prosecution in the trials of those who were caught may be subject to hyperbole, it is clear that many persons were involved.

The richest source of material was Scotland. In the early days material had been shipped through Glasgow. But Scottish vessels had a habit of calling at Belfast and having Orangemen in their crews. As quantities increased such Scottish traffic as was considered safe became quickly saturated. Hence arose the practice of collecting material at dumps located in Glasgow, sending it to Liverpool by road, and feeding it into the huge despatch organisation that had been built up on the Mersey. The services from Liverpool to Sligo, Cork, Waterford and Limerick were used for what they could carry, but the bulk was sent to Dublin where a receiving machinery of comparable magnitude was established on the waterfront. The dockers risked the safety of their humble homes. Many of them, like Egan and Kavanagh, belonged to the Citizen Army. They have received scant recognition of their services and some student of working-class history should rescue their fame before it is too late.

As Mellows acquainted himself with the intricacies of his new position there took place the spectacular counter coup by which on 21st November Collins' "squad" eliminated fourteen of the "Cairo Gang". The event was followed by mass arrests and the opening of the concentration camp at Ballykinlar. On the afternoon of "Bloody Sunday", as the day came to be called, Auxiliaries at the Gaelic football match at Croke Park lost their heads and fired indiscriminately into the crowd. There were fourteen deaths, and about sixty were injured. Two members of "the squad" were captured, and after being tortured were "shot while attempting to escape".

One of the agents lived at a house called "Brianna" at 117 Morehampton Road. Mellows was displeased that Collins, with whom he must have had several meetings in the past week, had not warned him of the raid. He detected the streak of vanity in Collins and told Mrs. Woods that he did not entirely trust him. For her part she protested that she considered it an honour to be working for him. Born in County Sligo of Fenian and Land League stock, she had gravitated from the Hibernians to *Cumann na mBan*. She required no political philosophy. She belonged to the democracy because there was her natural place. She would see no faults in those working for the cause. And in a sense she was right. It was never a matter of fate that the course of history which brought out Collins' virtues must later render them nugatory and destroy both him and his cause.

The difficulties of Mellows' task were sharply increased by events in Liverpool. Rory O'Connor had held a meeting of the Volunteers at which he outlined a plan for burning the docks. Accordingly on the night of 27th November, three timber yards and a number of warehouses were sent up in flames, and damage to the extent of £2,500,000 was reported. Neil Kerr, Tom Kerr, Stephen Lanigan, and many

H

others involved in the supply of arms were arrested. Strickland, though
not directly involved, was arrested in Glasgow, and brought to Liverpool where efforts were made to connect the Scottish organisation with
the incendiarism in the south. For the moment supplies from Liverpool
were cut off.

At the Army Council meeting of 3rd December there was reference
to the fact that the 3rd Tipperary Brigade had collected the sum of
£3,000 after pushing handbills through the doors of "all but avowed
enemies". The purpose was the purchase of arms. The blocking of
supplies from Liverpool led to discussion of the possibility of bringing
in large quantities from further afield, in particular Germany and
Italy. At a meeting on 11th December,[1] it was reported that following
the Treaty of Rapallo, signed on 12th November, the arms remaining
from D'Annunzio's Fiume adventure were likely to be available for
disposal.[2] It was thought feasible to load these on a Newcastle collier in
place of ballast, and bring them to Ireland *en route*. The Southern delegates were charged with finding a competent seafaring man to accompany the vessel to Ireland, and with selecting a suitable landing place
for the arms.

The German adventure was initiated by the Tipperary men. A
Volunteer called O'Mara consented to go to Germany with the £3,000.
But he had never been out of his native county and spoke no German.
By some means Seamus Robinson learned that Roderick Connolly had
returned from the second Congress of the Communist International
with a commission to take out a party of visitors anxious to see the
Soviet experiment at first hand. Among those who had agreed to go
was Eamon Martin. Robinson met Connolly at Shanahan's public
house in Foley Street, and Connolly agreed to take O'Mara as far as
Germany, provided a suitable chaperon could be secured. Possibly
through his brother Sean, a socialist lecturer in Trinity College whose
future wife was secretary of *Cumann na mBan*, Billy Beaumont was
approached and agreed to go.

He was no socialist. A former officer of the British Army, he had
become one of Collins' agents largely from a sense of adventure. He
used to play polo with the Auxiliaries and pass on their plans to Collins.
Just how Mellows was consulted is uncertain. He is said to have raised
no objection, and indeed could scarcely do so. His official channels

---

[1] This may be O'Donoghue's meeting "about 13/14 December".
[2] D'Annunzio declined to recognise the treaty. Consequently Italian troops invaded
Fiume on 24th December 1920. Resistance continued until 31st December when General
Ferrario threatened to use artillery against the town. D'Annunzio's "Arditi" were thereupon disbanded and only then did the arms become available.

were blocked. He was under pressure to supply arms. He gave his blessing to the privateers of Tipperary.

O'Mara scarcely looked the part he had to play. But in London Connolly got him to Saville Row. It was explained that he was a country boy who had come into a large fortune and was doing the grand tour. The tailor wrought a marvellous transformation. A passport was obtained through the good offices of Dr. Mark Ryan the veteran Fenian. Others of the group availed themselves of the services of Ramsay, a photographer who belonged to the British Communist Party, and whose able forgeries expedited the movements of many an itinerant revolutionary. The party travelled to Hamburg and Berlin. It is doubtful whether any success would have attended their efforts but for the good fortune of meeting Robert Briscoe who was in Berlin on business. Acting first as an interpreter he became increasingly involved in policy, and brought to the mission a commercial acumen lacking in O'Mara and Beaumont. But when he finally produced a racketeer with arms to sell O'Mara was so unnerved at his villainous appearance that he refused to do business with him. Briscoe returned to Dublin in disgust and secured Collins' agreement to alternative arrangements. Throughout the winter Collins sent out agents he thought would be useful, until they were treading on each other's toes.

Before Christmas Mellows contrived to visit Liverpool in company with Sean McGarry who knew the surviving I.R.B. men. He met Patrick Daly who had taken up the work of Neil Kerr, and made arrangements as a result of which the flow of small quantities was resumed.

Despite the curfew, Christmas passed gaily. For the first time since he left for the Rising in Galway, Mellows saw his mother. This was probably at the party given by Batt O'Connor at Brendan Road. He entertained the large gathering, which included as well as the Woods and O'Connor families, Richard Mulcahy and Gearoid O'Sullivan. He sang, played the fiddle and irreverently mimicked Dr. McCartan, John Devoy and other worthies of the cause. There was laughter and merriment such as is only possible among those sharing danger in a common enterprise.

In the South O'Donoghue and his colleagues found their man and decided their landing place. Michael Leahy arrived in Dublin on his way to Italy on 2nd January 1921. He had difficulty in finding Collins, but ultimately traced him to an upstairs room in Devlin's public house in Parnell Street. The entire headquarters staff was there, not poring over maps and plans, but holding a celebration in honour of Tom Cullen who was to be married next day. Apart from Mellows and Mulcahy, who left early, only Collins showed no sign of drink taken, and it was impossible to interrupt the party. Leahy saw two of Collins' lieutenants, Gearoid O'Sullivan and Sean O'Muirthile next day. They were of little help. Afterwards he wondered why he had not been sent to Mellows. Nevertheless he left for Genoa, inspected the ship and proposed cargo, and notified Dublin.

Throughout January Mellows busied himself with the multiplication of small orders. In January he visited Waterford and Cork. Three vessels came into Waterford, from Bristol, Liverpool and Glasgow. Sean Lane who worked for Clyde shipping used to bring small quantities of chemicals. At Cork there were possibilities of a direct traffic with the Continent. Alfie White introduced Maurice Fenlon of 51 Smithfield, who had a marine store at St. Mary's Lane and a horse repository at North King Street. White was employed by the Corporation from whom Fenelon bought scrap. He referred to having purchased damaged ammunition, sorted and resold it. He and Mellows took to each other at once. Fenelon readily agreed to seek Mellows' requirements in the course of his own business. Soon he put his own business on one side and worked exclusively for Mellows.

He scoured England for potassium chlorate from which a species of glorified gunpowder can be made. Sometimes it was imported as "white arsenic", a singularly unexplosive material not likely to invite close inspection by the uninitiated. Paraffin wax was obtained and by mixing this with chlorate at his King Street works Fenelon produced "Irish Cheddar". While this mixture had not the power of an intra-molecular explosive, its preparation was fraught with much greater danger, since it could be detonated by a flame. The primitive equipment used, with no protection against over-heating and static electricity would make any chemist's hair stand on end. There were many mishaps. The marvel is that there were not more.

Those who carried this work out were not men of iron nerves. Probably they knew little of the risks they were taking and regarded them as incidental to war. Some of the explosive was delivered to Sean Russell for incorporation in grenades. He insisted on testing the first products himself. But he was so nervous that he failed to clear the protecting wall. The men scattered and nobody was hurt. They gained experience by trial and error.

Early in the New Year the *Fianna* were forced to leave Westland Row. Mellows then established his office with Alfie White in St.

Peter's Place. Immediately opposite was the house of a prominent Irish-Irelander, Louis O'Carroll. Black-and-Tans used to sit on the steps of White's, with Mellows upstairs, while their colleagues raided O'Carrolls.

At first Mellows tried to keep records by means of a code in which items of military equipment were classified in terms of soft goods. He adopted the name of Anderson and professed to be a traveller in clothing. Following rumours that the Castle were seeking somebody of that name, he adopted the name of William Nolan. As such he visited Cork and the order book he carried survives in the National Museum. The code was soon discarded. It was inadequate for the checking of expenditure. He therefore separated the purchasing from the accounting side of the work, and later secured the services of Michael Cremin to keep his books and certify the accounts.

The Woods family gave enthusiastic assistance. Mr. Woods was a senior executive of Messrs. Nolan, the provision merchants. From time to time he used to travel the country, attending fairs and butter markets, and visiting creameries. For this business he was entitled to use a car. He would drive Mellows to the station or the boat, and sometimes undertook secret missions for him. The Nolan family, too, were convinced if not prominent nationalists. Mellows arranged to have war material consigned to them in butter boxes. On one occasion an employee seemed to be showing too much interest in some of these containers and Mr. Nolan found an excuse to dismiss him at once. He was surprised when Mellows came in person to request his reinstatement. He was a member of Mellows' staff. It was believed by many that Mellows was Nolan's nephew. When the military raided Oates' house at 108 Morehampton Road, Mellows showed himself incautiously at the gate. Mrs. Woods had to invent an identity for him.

Only one raid on 131 is recorded. The officer in charge showed obvious distaste for what he was doing. He allowed his men to sit discussing racing form with Sean Etchingham. He commented on the nationalist books on the shelves and remarked that he was a grand-nephew of Charles Stewart Parnell. Though Mrs. Woods concealed some documents on her person it was scarcely necessary. A raid without foundation was common enough. But Mrs. Woods judged it wise for Mellows to sleep elsewhere for a time. She had secured the lease of a house in Serpentine Road, so situated that there was access from its garden into the garden of 131 Morehampton Road. In it resided Peadar Ward who was working for Cathal Brugha, and his sisters. For some weeks Mellows stayed there. Then came a raid in which the military recaptured a requisitioned military bicycle that had been left in a shed. Mellows then went to the home of Mrs. Cuffe in Glenageary, only to find himself recognised by the maid, a Wexford girl called Anne Wrigley. He returned to Morehampton Road and could not be persuaded to leave again. He enjoyed the company of Sean Etchingham, Mr. and Mrs. Woods, and above all the children.

In mid-February Pax Whelan came from Dungarvan and insisted on a meeting of headquarters staff to discuss the landing of the Italian arms. Collins, Rory O'Connor, Sean MacMahon the Q.M.G. and others were present. The Southern brigades had held a conference at Glenville in Co. Cork on 12th and 13th February. The shortage of arms had been sharply complained of and some held the Director of Purchases to blame. The Cork men had made their landing arrangements at Myross a few miles east of Skibbereen. All they asked now was that the arms should be brought in quickly.

To his surprise Whelan, who commanded the Waterford Brigade, found that Collins was now opposed to the project. He raised every possible objection, and concluded by asking what would they do with a ship left on their hands. Mellows alone defended the plan and Whelan's impression was of a group of landlubbers who did not understand the sea and were determined to have nothing to do with it. The meeting ended without a decision.

In the meantime there was no news from Leahy, and Mellows decided to go to England himself, in the hope of streamlining the organisation. He found all well in Liverpool where Patrick Daly had rebuilt the organisation with commendable speed. He took Sean Russell to Birmingham where Seamus Cunningham was acquiring small arms and scrap equipment. Then he accompanied Sean Mac-Mahon to London, where he visited prominent members of the Gaelic League and Irish Self-Determination League, and renewed his acquaintance with the Nunans. In order to provide cover for this trip advertisements were published in the *Irish World* stating that he was organising in the Middle West but would address a meeting in New York at Easter. This was the origin of the myth of his second visit to America. His absence from Ireland presumably originated the story of a visit to Germany.

On his return he took up once more the question of the landing. For some reason, possibly its remoteness, but possibly also the need for a place more accessible from Germany, Mellows was dissatisfied with Myross. Pax Whelan suggested Helvick. Learning that Maire Comerford was visiting Dungarvan on 13th April, he asked her to secure an independent estimate of the depth of the water in Ring harbour. The report was favourable, and was confirmed when James O'Donovan introduced a sea-captain who brought with him complete nautical maps of the southern approaches. But on 26th April Leahy appeared. He had inspected the cargo, found the ship, and every week had sent increasingly urgent messages to Dublin. He had received no reply, and returned disgusted as he wanted to get married.

Precisely what had happened will presumably never be known. The possibility is that his messages never got beyond London. On 22nd February began the series of raids which led to the famous "Bridgman deportations". Among those arrested was Sean MacCraith, General Secretary of the Irish Self-Determination League. The organisation was thrown into chaos. No doubt one object of Mellows' trip was to ascertain what damage had been suffered by the arms organisation.

When Leahy returned Mellows was preparing to go to Scotland. Rory O'Connor's activities in England had caused fresh difficulties. In February Gilbert Barrington had come from Newcastle-on-Tyne to discuss increasing supplies from Newcastle and Durham. Mellows met him in Vaughan's Hotel. He returned with an ambitious programme for collecting arms and explosives and despatching them to Liverpool. Then Rory O'Connor arrived on the north-east coast with plans for setting fire to spirits, oil and timber at the quayside. The burnings were carried out on 28th February. Barrington recorded that the English workers showed not the slightest indignation when they met some of the incendiaries leaving the job. They seemed to have completely separated themselves from the interests of their employers.

In this case there was only one arrest and the traffic was only slightly restricted. Nevertheless Mellows began to voice serious doubts of the wisdom of the course Brugha and O'Connor were pursuing. He fought hard against its extension to Scotland where its operation would have been disastrous. He had, however, other reasons for the Scottish visit.

The investigation of the Scottish accounts had dragged on, accentuated by growing friction between Collins and Brugha. Mellows wanted to check financial statements on the spot. He was finding his work disrupted by agents of the Cork, Mayo and Sligo brigades who were operating independently in Scotland. One Glasgow Volunteer Company, consisting largely of supporters of John MacLean, seemed to be consigning too much material to the Citizen Army. And a Scottish Nationalist Volunteer force, *Fianna na hAlba*, was said to be contemplating military action for the liberation of Scotland. Mellows wondered how serious a threat to Irish supplies its arms requirements were likely to be.

He crossed at the end of April, visiting Volunteers in Edinburgh and Dundee. In Glasgow he attended a meeting at Elliot's public house, the "Bunch of Grapes", at Paisley Road toll. There he found the local men discussing a desperate adventure. Some weeks previously Frank Carty, a brigade commander in the County Sligo under sentence of death in Derry Jail, had been rescued by Charles McGuinness, who strewed chili powder to confuse the bloodhounds. McGuinness was a native of Derry City and reputed "the toughest man alive". He had run away to sea at the age of 15, and now twenty-eight years old held a master's ticket in the North German Lloyd shipping line. His father was a sea-captain and ship-owner. He smuggled Carty to Glasgow on one of his colliers. But news soon arrived that Carty, passing under the name of Summers, had been arrested in Glasgow and was to be returned. McGuinness was instructed to take six men to Glasgow, find out what vessel Carty was to travel on, and go with him. A steward would be found to put a sedative in the guards' tea, and McGuinness was confident he could get Carty over the side into a small craft.

Mellows was aware of these plans which presumably had the blessing of the Army Council. But what was being discussed at the "Bunch of Grapes" was no less than a repetition of the Manchester rescue of 1867. Seemingly the plans made had not been communicated to Glasgow as no action on their part was foreseen. The proposal was to hold up the prison van as it came from Barlinnie and to effect a rescue in the middle of the city. Mellows advised against this, explaining that head-quarters had an alternative plan, and arguing that it was foolish to jeopardise the flow of arms by rousing a public outcry in Scotland. But the plans were already in motion. Next day, an hour after McGuinness arrived in town, the van was ambushed and Assistant-Inspector Johnston was accidently shot dead. Only one man was arrested immediately. But Mellows anticipated the wave of arrests that came, and left Glasgow at once.

Those who knew Mellows during this period all testified to his tireless activity. He would work in his office all day, receive visitors until curfew, then sit up till two or three in the morning making notes of his transactions. He had little time to follow political affairs. While remaining a member of the I.R.B. he was excluded from circle meetings by the nature of his work. It is doubtful if he paid much attention to the significant changes that took place during the first six months of his appointment. But these must now be considered.

Lloyd George had delayed the progress of the "Government of Ireland Bill" out of a hope that his version of "law and order" would prevail in Ireland before it was brought into operation. The "Restoration of Order in Ireland Act", designed for this purpose, might better have been called the "Abolition of Order in Ireland Act". A succession of Liberal, radical and religious delegations visited Ireland during its operation. All returned to England to press charges of wanton destructiveness and barbarity against the servants of the Crown. Protest was constantly increasing. While the absence of Labour from the *Dail* prevented that instant recognition the British workers gave the Soviets, the left was constantly urging action on the lines of the Scarborough resolution. The government ran the risk of losing the moral authority without which any administration must be doomed.

In these circumstances imperial strategy underwent a subtle revision. It was no longer a matter of crushing Republican resistance in order to impose partition. Partition must be imposed in order to outflank that resistance and bring about an imperial peace. Henceforward, therefore, the application of the Government of Ireland Act to six counties was expedited, while *Dail Eireann* was alternatively wooed and threatened, as the terror increased and weaknesses were probed for. The aim was to deprive the Republic of a part of its territory and, having thus weakened it, bring it to terms.

As early as September 1920, the post of Under-Secretary was duplicated. Sir Ernest Clark was appointed "Ulster Under-Secretary" with the responsibility for six of the nine counties of Ulster. Alfred Cope, like Macready a former police official, was to look after the remainder. Clark busied himself with adjusting local government boundaries to give the six counties a self-contained administration, the establishment of a special constabulary, and finally with the task of Cabinet making. Those who adhered to the English Crown were a majority in little over half the area it was proposed to annex. Notwithstanding the massive Republican minority in Belfast, Lloyd George intended to add to it all that region where the King's writ could be made to run. It is remarkable that despite the constant harping on the need to safeguard the Protestant third in Ireland as a whole, scarce a whisper was heard on behalf of the Catholics who were to number one-third in an arbitrarily designated area—although experience not months old showed them to be in dire danger, and adjustment to the frontier could leave up to half of them outside it.

The third reading of the Partition Bill was taken on 11th November. Now, at last the Parliamentary Labour Party found its voice and spoke with the accents of Scarborough. William Adamson proposed:

(a) that the British Army of occupation be withdrawn;
(b) that the question of Irish government be relegated to an Irish constituent assembly elected on the basis of proportional representation by free and equal secret vote;
(c)[1] that the constitution drawn up by the assembly be accepted, provided:
  (i) it affords protection to minorities, and
  (ii) prevents Ireland becoming a military or naval menace to Britain.

Lloyd George declined to consider such proposals. Nor would he entertain that of Dominion Home Rule advanced by the Asquith Liberals. The Labour men therefore took their plan to Dublin where, on 16th November, a thousand delegates attended a special conference of the Irish Labour Party and T.U.C. After hearing the British Labour proposals outlined by Adamson, the conference unanimously endorsed them, and "for the first time since 1914, the British and Irish Labour Movement were in true alignment on the great issue of Irish self-government".[2]

The situation thus created was pregnant with danger to Lloyd George. Already he was shuttling troops across the sea as his policy provoked unrest in one country or the other. A united struggle by the two Labour movements in collaboration with *Sinn Fein* might have transformed the situation in Britain, brought down the coalition and hastened the return of the first Labour government by several years. If the forces of progress were enabled to take the offensive, the weak aspect of the Labour statement could be strengthened. If not, then it would be communicated to Irish Labour. This weak aspect was the demand for a new Constituent Assembly, rather than the recognition of the *Dail* already established. The acceptance by Irish Labour of the British view that the established Republic was negotiable arose because Labour was not in the *Dail*, and the *Dail* under Griffith's guidance was giving comfort to the enemies of Labour.

The British Labour Party sent over a commission of enquiry which left London on 30th November. On their way its members read in the newspapers the letter of Roger Sweetman, T.D. for North Wexford. His conscience had been severely shocked by the events of "Bloody Sunday". The mass arrests, the internments in Ballykinlar concentra-

---

[1] A subsequent refinement to this policy proposed embodying the restrictive clauses in a treaty between Britain and Ireland. It was furthermore explained that they were unnecessary but inserted "to meet public superstition and ignorance".
[2] *Report of Labour Commission to Ireland*, p. 58.

tion camp, nor indeed the murderous reprisals, were not what shocked him. He shrank before the logic of the war, unwilling that his side should employ the methods of the other. He proposed an immediate conference of the British Labour Party Commission, the Irish Labour Party and the Catholic hierarchy, with the object of securing a cessation of hostilities.

Adamson and Henderson consulted their Irish colleagues. It was agreed that they should explore possibilities. On 2nd December they spent the morning with the Archbishop of Dublin, and the afternoon with Arthur Griffith. He had been arrested on 26th November. The British Government had not been pleased, and Lloyd George had reminded the Castle that it was only after Cabinet decisions that O'Connell and Parnell had been imprisoned. There was talk of immediate release. But instead he was lodged in the prison hospital at Mountjoy where he lived in tolerable comfort, and was permitted what the authorities engagingly described as "privileges". Henderson seems to have believed that Sweetman's letter betokened a general weakening on the part of *Sinn Fein*. Or perhaps the imperial purple, which lies beneath the skin of many an English pink, was brought to the surface in the presence of the prisoner. Henderson told Griffith that he had come to help him get a truce. Griffith replied that he was not asking for one, but if one were offered he would not reject it out of hand. He undertook to consult Collins whom he had nominated his successor as Acting-President of the *Dail*.

The following day Cardinal Clune arrived. Lloyd George was not going to leave the initiative to Labour. He also discussed a truce with Griffith, and later saw Collins. The terms that Collins drafted on 4th December, which included freedom for the entire *Dail* to meet without interference and pursue its peaceful activities, were acceptable to Henderson who saw Lloyd George again on 7th December. In the meantime, learning of Lloyd George's professions of peaceful intent, Fr. Michael O'Flanagan, now in theory at least the Acting-President of *Sinn Fein*, telegraphed to the Prime Minister asking him to put his cards on the table. Fr. O'Flanagan was subsequently unjustly assailed for an action that was at worst hasty. He was saddled with the blame for Lloyd George's intransigent speech of 10th December. But this was no reply to Griffith or Collins, Fr. O'Flanagan or Sweetman. It was a reply to the Labour Party. It touched on matters far weightier than the terms of a truce. It was a matter of the direction an ultimate settlement must, in the Prime Minister's opinion, take.

Lloyd George reiterated his willingness to discuss terms of settlement with anybody who could claim to represent Irish opinion. But he made three clear and unambiguous reservations. The six counties he had ear-marked for annexation must be accorded separate treatment; in no circumstances would the British Government consent to the secession of any part of Ireland from the United Kingdom; nothing must detract from the security of these islands as conceived by the English Government. Negotiations for a truce continued. But the Prime Minister had made his position clear. The situation was discussed at a Special Conference of the British Labour Party on 29th December. It was decided to invite representatives of Irish Labour to take part in a campaign in the constituencies in January 1921.

Meanwhile other consequences flowed from Lloyd George's speech. His peaceful professions had been accompanied by the announcement that martial law was to be introduced in the counties of Cork, Kerry, Tipperary and Limerick. On the night of 11th December the Black-and-Tans celebrated the extended freedom this order gave them. They appeared in large numbers in Cork City at 9 p.m. and drove the citizens off the streets before curfew. Then with the aid of commandeered stores of petrol they fired the entire business quarter and left it a ruin. Two days later it was announced that after 27th December persons in martial law areas convicted of certain offences would be liable to the death penalty. All this seems to have appeared to Lloyd George a powerful encouragement to the truce his intermediaries were still discussing.

The Partition Bill received the Royal Assent on 23rd December. It was to come into effect on an "appointed day" in the fixing of which the government allowed itself ample latitude. The nominal date was 2nd August 1921.[1] But it could be advanced or retarded by up to seven months by Order in Council. If he required it Lloyd George could have it in force during the first week of January. Or he could delay it until March 1922. He could appoint different days for different provisions, could establish one administration without the other, or distribute powers and responsibilities as seemed to him best. Sir Hamar Green-wood nevertheless declared himself confident that there would be two (British) governments in Ireland within six months. *The Times* remarked, as the necessary Orders in Council were being drafted, that "Ulster" would do well to oppose moderate Labour to the "Red Flag" and a strong Catholic party to Republicanism. There was no six-county administration yet. But its policy was already worked out for it.

On Christmas Eve De Valera arrived back in Dublin. According to

[1] Section 73, Government of Ireland Act, 1920.

Dorothy Macardle the British Government suspected his presence on the *Celtic* and had the ship searched at Liverpool. Calton Younger, on the other hand, quotes a Cabinet minute of 20th December to show that it was decided to allow him to land without hindrance. One can only conclude that the search had some object other than to hinder his landing. *The Times* of 6th January reported that it was now "assumed" that De Valera was in Ireland and that his movements were "protected by a specific or implied safeguard from Dublin Castle".

The American mission had been neither an unqualified success nor a total failure. The bond drive had vastly augmented the assets of *Dail Eireann*, although the money was not yet in Ireland. To the American people Irish independence was no longer exclusively embodied in those whose pride was their stake in American prosperity. It was represented by the young President De Valera whose earnest speeches and palpable indifference to worldly possessions tallied with all that was known about *Sinn Fein*. On the other hand the United States Government had not recognised the Republic, nor was it likely to. The President-elect, Harding, had indicated that he regarded the Irish question as an internal British affair. It was likely to remain so until he had some quarrel with England.

While Tom Johnson stumped England for the Labour Party's plan of a withdrawal from Ireland, Collins called the *Dail* for 21st January. Mellows attended for the first time. But neither De Valera nor Brugha, nor indeed Collins himself, put in an appearance. The session was adjourned. On the resumption on 25th January Brugha took sole responsibility for the abortive gathering. He had been unaware that it was contemplated until shortly before it took place. He had represented to President de Valera the probable consequences of a raid. It could finish the Republic for a generation. The President agreed to cancel the meeting and Collins was notified, but apparently nobody else. There was no explanation of why what was dangerous on 21st January was safe on the 25th. Here was evidence of a growing rift between Collins and Brugha. Brugha had the courage of a lion, but was completely devoid of the imagination that gives political foresight. Isolating Collins inevitably drove him into the arms of Griffith, in whom Brugha failed to recognise the chief architect of compromise.

Possibly with no further motive than to separate antagonists De Valera proposed sending Collins to the United States to replace Boland. Collins refused. It was widely held that by now he had replaced Boland as head centre of the I.R.B. De Valera then brought before the *Dail* his proposal for "easing off" attacks on Crown forces, "as far as possible consistent with showing the country that they were in the same position as before".

There was a prolonged debate. Against any policy of seeming retreat were Beaslai, MacEntee, MacDonagh of Tipperary, who made a constructive and imaginative speech, Kevin O'Higgins, Brugha, Stack, Mulcahy, Patrick O'Keeffe, Desmond Fitzgerald, and M.P. Colivet. Mellows was present but did not speak. Only two deputies argued for a reduction in the scale of activities. They were Roger Sweetman and Liam de Roiste. Their consciences were troubling them. In vain MacEntee and Etchingham asked why British shots were war and Irish were murder. The emergence of a peace party within the *Dail* implied that social strata up to now in support of the revolution were beginning to doubt if it served their interests to continue it. Stack now proceeded to placate those interests by proposing controlled increases in rent and mortgage rates which he explained were based on British practice. But his proposal met with opposition and was withdrawn.

It would be a crude view of history that saw economic interests immediately transmuted into their corresponding political programme. But everybody who has read Dostoievsky will remember the "double thoughts" in which calculation is tacked on to principle. An army of double thoughts could march and take Rome. It is not therefore an outrage to connect the search for a basis for peace with developments in class relations.

The nature of the special grievance under which the Irish bourgeoisie laboured after 1914 has already been discussed. It was that when for the first time in over a century economic conditions tended to equalise profit-making possibilities in Britain and Ireland, the government for reasons of imperial policy intervened so as to preserve the bias. The Irish landlords and capitalists made plenty of money, of course. But they were hindered from using it to expand their activities at home. They availed themselves of an alternative that was left open, investment in Britain and the British Empire. For the smaller businessman the process was largely involuntary. He kept his reserves at the bank. There it was joined by his war profits. And the bank invested it for him abroad. The external assets of Irish banks which stood at £41 million in 1914 had risen to £126 million in 1921. The landlord and larger individual capitalist selected his own investments. These are supposed to have amounted to a similar figure, much of it involved in colonial securities. The free movement of capital between Britain and Ireland not only restricted Irish development, but introduced an element of secondary imperialism into the Irish economy, embodied in a section of the propertied classes.

This element was not substantial enough to bear the weight of a settlement along Dominion lines. Had it been so it is conceivable that phenomena of the fifties might have appeared a generation earlier, in particular the channelling abroad of accumulated capital and adult manpower, while foreign capital subjected to itself one field after another of Irish life. The relation of Ireland to England was still overwhelmingly colonial.

The average capitalist looked forward to using his war savings to expand his business as soon as government restrictions and shortage of labour and raw materials had ended. Unfortunately by this time the orders had disappeared also. The boom gave way to a slump. There were no more headlong races to El Dorado. The businessmen sulked in glum fraternity, seeking relief in reducing wages and dismissing workers. In the class war waged outside *Dail Eireann* and independently of the Volunteers, conditions changed in favour of the employers against the workers, and increasingly in favour of monopoly capital against the Irish bourgeoisie.

Meanwhile the variegated petit-bourgeois alliance of 1917 was held intact by the viciousness of the imperialist onslaught. In the first five months of 1921 the number of internees rose to 3,200. There were 1,500 prison sentences and over 1,000 in custody awaiting the form of a trial. Raids were so numerous that the newspapers no longer reported a fraction of them. The number of shops set on fire by Crown forces was 417, of farmhouses 165, of private residences 233. There were seventy-two instances of the burning of standing crops. Of all the buildings fired, 55 per cent were totally destroyed. The curfew was brought forward to 9 p.m. in Dublin. On 4th March alone eighteen persons were arrested for infringing it. On 7th March the Mayor of Limerick was murdered in the presence of his wife. On 14th March six prisoners allegedly implicated in the events of "Bloody Sunday" were hanged in pairs as they protested their innocence to the last. The Irish Transport and General Workers' Union held a four-hour protest strike, and 40,000 people gathered outside Mountjoy Jail. The resistance of the Irish people is one of the great epics of history.

Dail Eireann met again on 11th March. There were rumours of divisions in the English Cabinet. A clash of shipping interests had brought acute differences with the United States. One in nine of the British labour force was unemployed and a triple alliance of railwaymen, transport workers and miners had been established to resist the wage-cutting offensive that was in progress. To make matters worse Germany, writhing under the injustices of the Versailles Treaty, had made difficulties over reparations and the Allies had invaded once more on 8th March. There were strong motives for getting the Irish question out of the way, and talk of a general election in six counties was wide-spread, *The Times* tipping 19th April as the "appointed day" under the partition Act.[1]

The *Dail* was informed that discussions had been held with the Devlinites. There was hope of an agreement to contest the six county election on the basis of abstention from the local Parliament when it was established. It was recognised that this involved the "acceptance of a foreign law arranged by a foreign government". But what could be done? The policy of abstention apologised for the act of recognition, and a tactic suitable for an advancing revolutionary tide covered up the fact of retreat. On the other hand the proposed census was prohibited and the British Government did not dare attempt it.

The President was empowered to make a statement at his discretion in which the state of war with Britain was officially accepted and the *Dail* took responsibility for the actions of the Volunteers. There were two possible reasons apart from the desire to "regularise" the position in face of possible negotiations. On the one hand I.R.B. influence would be weakened. On the other the *Dail* would have sole discretion in the terms of a truce.

On 17th March Bonar Law resigned. He gave as his reason ill health, but it was widely believed in Ireland that he had been delaying Lloyd George's Irish proposals. On 24th March the Privy Council made the long awaited Order fixing the "appointed day" on which the general provisions of the partition Act were to come into operation. It was 3rd May.[2] But matters requiring consultations with the newly-established administration were to be deferred until after the elections. The net was thus spread in the sight of the bird. But it was going to be difficult for the bird to avoid it.

The Irish Labour Party Manifesto "The Country in Danger" was issued at the end of March. Its immediate occasion was the desperately worsened employment situation. As a result of the world slump, intensified by the imperialist terror, 100,000 Irish workers were un-employed. But its implications were vital to the future of the Republic. The Labour Party demanded that the Democratic Programme of *Dail Eireann* should be put into force at once. It was intolerable that there should be silent looms while idle weavers saw half-clothed labourers before them, that there should be land untilled while agricultural workers walked the roads. What was demanded was a programme of national emergency under which all "land and wealth-producing machinery should be loaned without charge to the nation . . . for the duration of the war".

The proposals were definite and far-reaching. They included a moratorium on rents and land annuities, limitation of capitalist profits, breaking up of grazing estates and the relinquishment by large farmers of land beyond their capacity to work. So much would demand *Dail* decree. But voluntary action should also be taken, by tradesmen to stock goods of Irish manufacture, by bank depositors to transfer their funds to institutions that used their assets to finance Irish industry, and by individuals and organizations possessing available land to offer allotments for tillage by workers.

The challenge was clear. *Dail Eireann* was the government of the Republic. Its territorial integrity was threatened from without. Its economic survival was menaced from within. Here was the programme that would rally the people and save the revolution. Was it not worthy of consideration by a meeting of the *Dail*? Or careful examination by a committee? Failing this should it occasion surprise if the working class began to trust to its traditional economic organisations and to give only half-allegiance to a Republic with only half a policy? Unfortunately the Labour proposals struck no imaginative chord in De Valera and his advisers. To Griffith, who had the experience to understand them, they were utterly repugnant. The *Sinn Fein* leaders could not understand that by accepting the social outlook of British capitalism they were inevitably drawn to accept a part of its imperial outlook on Irish independence.

In Britain the dispute with the United States had entered the phase of negotiations and Tory extremists were urging Lloyd George to "full scale war" in Ireland. There were difficulties in the way. The generals complained that British armed forces had been scattered across the globe without regard for their effectiveness. To deal with Ireland 80,000 fully trained men would be needed. From where should they be withdrawn? Moreover what needed doing in Ireland might not be tolerated by British public opinion. While this debate was in progress came an event which showed how well timed was Irish Labour's demand for economic conscription to win the war of liberation. The second great coal strike began. The troops were required in England.

Sir Henry Wilson sounded Foch who offered to replace British regiments on the continent with Frenchmen. General Macready had to supply four battalions from Ireland. "Their unexpected arrival at Liverpool did much to ease the situation in Lancashire," he wrote with the affected nonchalence of an officer not talking to his superiors. It no doubt also eased the situation in Dublin. But the state of the ruling class was not of ease but of panic which evoked the usual combination of ruthlessness and stupidity. Tanks were moved into South Wales; in the metropolis Lloyd George nervously questioned General Jeffreys on the danger of "red trench mortars on the roof of the Ritz". Though the ever-obliging J. H. Thomas was cajoled into withdrawing the support of the railwaymen from the miners, the pits remained closed throughout the summer. Such were his difficulties at home that Lloyd George could not decide whether to attempt the enforcement of the Government of Ireland Act in the twenty-six counties, or to offer further concessions at once.

Policy at the centre having reached the point of crisis, each faction in Dublin Castle followed its own inclination, with Greenwood to tyrranise, with Cope to diplomatise. While discussing with Mellows the arms requirement of the Southern divisions which were growing impatient, De Valera was informed that a raid on a house held by the same lessee had made the location of his office known to the authorities. This was on 16th April, and he and Mellows burned all papers that could be dispensed with, after which Mellows and Kathleen O'Connell took the remainder in suitcases to a a safe place. It was, however, three days before the discovery was followed up and the evacuated office was raided.

On 21st April Lord Derby appeared in Dublin and met De Valera. He is said to have offered in return for national sovereignty "Dominion Home Rule" without the right of secession. The offer was not accepted. Next day Lloyd George assured the House of Commons that no Irish settlement was possible except on the English terms. By these he presumably meant the stipulations of 10th December, in which case the "Dominion Home Rule" Lord Derby was offering applied only to twenty-six counties. Lloyd George faced a real dilemma. In order to legitimise the administration already under construction in the six counties he must bring into effect the Government of Ireland Act. But if *Sinn Fein* declined to work it in the twenty-six, what was to fill the vacuum? He seems to have decided before receiving Lord Derby's report, for on 21st April he sent instructions to the Castle to prepare for two elections.[1] He would bring the Act legally into force, and after that trust to his skill in the art of trickery and the fact that the devil

[1] Alison Phillips, p. 196.

looks after his own. Perhaps *Sinn Fein* would be prepared to work something that he could accept. And to encourage the development of good will, on 29th April forty men of the Dublin brigade of the I.R.A. were captured in a raid on Blackhall place. The reprisals continued every day.

On 2nd May Lord Fitzalan, Ireland's first and only Catholic viceroy, was installed with traditional mummery behind the barbed wire. Next day the separate elections were announced, in twenty-six counties on 19th May, in six on the 24th, then a jingo festival under the name of "Empire Day". To Cope is ascribed the sanguine notion of bringing Captain Craig, Carson's successor, to Dublin to meet De Valera. Craig was very willing. Such consultation, he remarked, was provided for in the Act which had just begun to operate. He proposed that they should discuss the establishment of the Council of Ireland. The meeting took place on 4th May. Craig was informed that *Sinn Fein* did not propose to work the Act. He reported back to the Castle, and Fitzalan then proceeded to London,[1] where at least one thing became clear.

Nomination day was 10th May and on that day *Dail Eireann* met. Apparently the decision empowering *Sinn Fein* to contest the six counties elections was taken to apply to those in the twenty-six also. But now a fateful decision must be made. What was to be the status of those elected? De Valera proposed on behalf of the Ministry that they should be recognised as the second *Dail*, irrespective of which election they were returned in. There were disadvantages here. On the one hand the number of the constituencies and the form of the election to *Dail Eireann* was being decided by the British Government on whose initiative the contest was taking place. While the Parliament of Southern Ireland would obviously never function, that of Northern Ireland would. The danger was that *Dail Eireann* might come to be identified with the Parliament of Southern Ireland. This danger would be avoided only if the first *Dail* remained in existence.

The second disadvantage was that Labour had not been informed of the proposal and had refrained from nominating candidates on the understanding that the election was to be a pure demonstration, and the first *Dail* was to continue in being. There were sharp comments on this subject when the Irish Labour Party and T.U.C. held their Annual Meeting. The Labour Manifesto had evoked no reaction from the employers but fresh demands for wage reductions. Now it seemed that *Sinn Fein*, having excluded Labour in 1919 by a test, had in 1921 achieved the same purpose by a prevarication.[2]

---

[1] *Irish Independent*, 6th May 1921.
[2] *Irish Labour Party and T.U.C. Report*, 1921, p. 19.

Mellows did not attend the May meeting of the *Dail* and it is possible that he was still in Britain. Over the Whitsun holiday he carried out one of those dangerous, frustrating and fruitless journeys he knew so well in his purchases work. His object was to discuss with officers of the Cork Volunteers the satisfaction of their seemingly insatiable appetite for arms. On Friday evening, 13th May, he set out with Mr. and Mrs. Woods. Roads had been mined and bridges blown, but the Volunteers kept open lines of communication through Wexford and Waterford. Matthew O'Brien, who knew the south-eastern route, accompanied them, together with one other. The intention was to spend one night at Mrs. Whitmore's at Castletown and proceed to Cork next day.

At Rathdrum the car broke down. No mechanic could be found. Walsh's hotel was crammed with visitors and contained a sprinkling of carousing Auxiliaries who were stationed at Aghavannagh. Anxious for other company, the party knocked at doors seeking accommodation. But people were afraid to open. When it grew dark the danger was that they would be stopped in the street and questioned. They returned to the Walsh's, where makeshift accommodation was provided. Mrs. Walsh was an old Republican. She had heard Mellows speak in the United States, and despite the disguise recognised him, but said nothing till morning.

Once the car was repaired the party drove south. Mellows insisted on stopping at Ferns where he took his friends to the "Forge of Clohogue" that inspired James Murphy's novel. They crossed the damaged bridge at New Ross, then skirted Waterford and continued through Dungarvan and Youghal, using by-roads from time to time. Their *rendezvous* was the Metropole. As they were eating a meal a warning was brought. They were advised to leave Cork without delay. Mr. Woods knew one of the warders of Clonmel Jail. There they stayed one night. While they were asleep their car was commandeered by Auxiliaries. Happily it was returned. Next night they stayed at a monastery. As they proceeded to Dublin on Monday there was further difficulty with the car. They called at De Loughrey's shop in Kilkenny, but were compelled to go at a crawl until they reached a barracks at Kilcullen. There they enlisted the help of British soldiers, who were mostly free from the viciousness of the Black-and-Tans. They reached Dublin after spending four days travelling hundreds of miles and accomplishing nothing.

The Army Council of the I.R.A. usually met on a Wednesday. The meeting in Whit week had to approve the plans of the Dublin brigade to capture and burn down the Custom House. The object of the operation was to deprive the British authorities of the records which they were using to attach payments of rates to local councils who were supporting *Dail Eireann*. Apart from this immediate object there was the matter of giving a blow to the prestige of the occupation forces and making other fields of administration difficult. Nothing is known of Mellows' contribution to the project beyond the fact that he was present when it was planned. On Thursday, 19th May, the general election in the twenty-six counties took place without incident. There was no poll. No candidates went up in opposition to *Sinn Fein*. Mellows was returned for County Galway, the new constituency created for the purpose of proportional representation. Despite the great demonstration of public opinion reprisals continued. Sean Etchingham's house was burned down on 23rd May.

The election in the six counties was a riot of intimidation and impersonation by the Unionists. The result was a foregone conclusion. The six-county area had been deliberately selected on the basis of providing the largest possible population within which a Unionist majority could be guaranteed for the foreseeable future. The predominantly nationalist people of Fermanagh, Tyrone and Derry City had been incorporated in this area against their wishes in order to create the pretence of a normal opposition. The Unionists desired above all the permanent polarisation of this factitious electorate into two camps, one of which would have a constant advantage over the other.

Six Republicans, six Devlinites and forty Unionists were returned. Of the Republicans five resided in the twenty-six counties and had seats in *Dail Eireann*. Their contesting Northern constituencies was a defiance of partition, but possessed an element of artificiality. Devlin's supporters on the other hand must face their constituents. It must be clearly understood that neither the Devlinites nor *Sinn Fein* believed the six-county administration could possibly be stable. They anticipated its early collapse. In this illusion the British Government sought to encourage them, and they are not to be criticised for accepting what then seemed obvious. Later the Devlinites decided, surely with wisdom, to enter the six-county Parliament. On 25th May the Custom House in Dublin was burned down. There was a number of casualties and about eighty Volunteers were captured. This was Mellows' birthday. He was twenty-eight.

The six-county Parliament was opened by the Viceroy on 7th June. Here was the crucial event towards which British policy had been driving, and by ignoring the social requirements of a national revolution the leaders of *Sinn Fein* had rendered themselves powerless. The six counties were lost without a blow. And once their administration was an accomplished fact, it could become the supreme weapon of blackmail, wringing concession after concession from the Republic.

The occasion was not allowed to pass without celebration. A member of Parliament suggested that now was the time to "drive *Sinn Fein* bag and baggage out of the six counties". Accordingly on 10th June the Falls Road area was invaded by armed men in uniform. They were the Special Constabulary, established by the British Government over the preceding year. With the aid of the Orange mobs, in six days they caused the deaths of seventeen citizens and drove about 150 Catholic families from their homes.

The new political balance of power was felt at once. Within a week De Valera had abandoned the demand of unfettered national independence, or the "isolated Republic", as he afterwards called it. He let it be known that he would allow the six countries local autonomy within the Irish Republic. On 14th June he wrote to Art O'Brien that the right way to a settlement was that Britain should "propose a Treaty with Ireland regarded as a separate State. Irish representatives would then be willing to consider making certain concessions to England's fears and England's interest." A day or two later he evolved the conception of "external association" of Ireland with the British Empire. The idea originated during a discussion with Brennan and Childers at the house of Mrs. O'Rahilly, and Brennan recalled the form of the geometrical chart which was drawn to illustrate it. One circle, representing the self-governing states of the Empire, enclosed five smaller circles each representing a Dominion. External to the large circle, but touching it, was another small circle representing Ireland. Throughout the subsequent discussions the idea constantly recurs that this concession was made not for England, but in the hope of winning the consent of the Unionists to a united Ireland. It was a forlorn hope.

Whispers of policy changes spread rapidly. Maire Comerford came across much uneasy talk during a visit to Limerick Junction. Some Volunteers feared that a compromise peace was being prepared. Others found peace attractive whatever its demerits. Mellows took her information very seriously. He felt that some of the younger men whose lives of intense action precluded political study had little understanding of the principles of Republicanism. The two of them cycled to Blackrock to urge on De Valera a thorough-going campaign of education. The President was preoccupied with his new difficulties and gave no more than a hearing.

On 22nd June De Valera was arrested and hastily released when the error was discovered. There is no convincing evidence that the release was made in anticipation of a peace offer. There was an "understanding" that he was not to be arrested.[1] But his momentary incarceration revealed a curious fact. He had appointed as his deputy not Collins but Stack. When the material becomes available for a definitive study of Collins it may be possible to do more than speculate on this point. It is tempting to presuppose from what happened afterwards that already he was tainted with compromise. But evidence points to the contrary. Already G.H.Q. had plans for a general attack on the "foot patrols" who were searching and questioning the citizens of Dublin. Mellows had the duty of alerting *Cumann na mBan* for first aid work in conjunction with the exercise, which would have been carried out on a substantial scale. And as late as 27th June, Collins submitted plans for a "well thought out onslaught on all the Departments which operate on behalf of the Foreign Government in Ireland". Collins advocated the offensive, but seemingly for the last time. This crisis seems to have been decisive for him.

On 22nd June also the Northern Parliament reassembled to hear a gracious speech by the King of England. Its tenor was considered moderate, but hardly justified the whoops of mystic fervour with which some have greeted it. He appealed to Irishmen "to pause, to stretch out the hand of forbearance and conciliation, to forgive and forget and to join in making for the land they love a new era of peace, contentment and goodwill". It is strange that this suggestion occurred to nobody in the British establishment until the country had been cut in two. He then appealed for the establishment of the Parliament of Southern Ireland "as a parallel to what is now passing in this hall. . . . For this the Parliament of the United Kingdom has in fullest measure provided the powers. For this the Parliament of Ulster is pointing the way." He concluded, "The future lies in the hands of my Irish people themselves. May this gathering be the prelude of the day in which the Irish people North and South, under one Parliament or two, as those Parliaments may themselves decide, shall work together in common love for Ireland upon the same foundation of mutual justice and respect."

This was self-determination within the framework of English determination, the Government of Ireland Act by sleight of tongue instead of at point of gun. Who was the author of this monumental humbug? Churchill made hasty claim for the Cabinet's collectivity. Others prefer Lord Riddell's story that after reading Lloyd George's

---

[1] See Beaslai, vol. 2, p. 242, where this is stated in a letter intercepted by Collins.

first menacing draft the King insisted on sugaring the pill so that Britain's maximum demand should be stated in its most persuasive form. It would serve equally well as a preliminary to conciliation or coercion.

The British Cabinet met. It was decided to attempt a settlement in the twenty-six counties by discussion with De Valera. Accordingly he was invited as the "chosen leader of the great majority in Southern Ireland" to "explore to the utmost the possibility of a settlement" in company with Sir James Craig. He was to bring with him such colleagues as he chose and all would be guaranteed safe conduct. It has been stated that this invitation contained no overt conditions. Implicit conditions could, however, be read at a glance. De Valera's status was delimited by British decision. The minority in Ireland was given equal status with the majority. De Valera saw yawning before him the pit into which Redmond had slipped ten years previously.

He replied that *Sinn Fein* earnestly desired peace, but saw no avenue by which it could be reached if Lloyd George denied Ireland's "essential unity" and set aside the "principle of self-determination". The phrase "essential unity" was Dominion League jargon. It did not exclude a federal Ireland in which the central government might exercise extremely tenuous power in the North. Thus the "Council of Ireland" section of the Government of Ireland Act was held to be in conformity with the principle of "essential unity" which thus meant "incomplete partition", thanks to a common subordination to the English Crown.

De Valera was anxious to avoid a position where Lloyd George could deal with himself and Craig as "two disputing subjects of the English Crown". He called a meeting of Southern Unionists to which he invited Craig. The British Government thereupon decided to brief Craig on what were described as the fundamentals of its position. Craig in his turn had no wish to represent the British Government in Dublin. He preferred to continue doing so in Belfast. He did not attend. De Valera was thus placed in a position of accommodating the Southern Unionists without getting anything in return.

Those who attended were the Earl of Midleton, a wealthy landowner, Sir Maurice Dockrell, a prosperous merchant, Mr. Andrew Jameson, whiskey-distiller and chairman of the Dublin Chamber of Commerce, and Sir Robert H. Woods, an eminent surgeon who represented Trinity College at Westminster. The conference took place on 4th July. Arthur Griffith, Eamon Duggan and Robert Barton were released from prison to attend it.

It is a remarkable fact that at this decisive point in the history of the

Republic its acknowledged leader consulted its enemies but failed to speak with its adherents. Unionism, it is true, had supporters on each side of the border. But so had the Labour movement. It was the Socialists and Labour men among the Protestants of Belfast who had been driven from their work for resisting the onrush of sectarianism. The capitalists and landlords gave their views. Labour was not invited. The *Dail* was not called, nor were the views of the army ascertained. A conference that might have been truly national became a means of consolidating the influence of the propertied classes and constituted a further stage in the rightward motion of *Sinn Fein*. Particularly sinister was the fact that the landlords, their economic power protected by *Dail* decree, were given back the place in the counsels of the nation from which they had been dislodged in 1914. The way was being prepared for the disillusionment of the working class, so poignantly illustrated in the plays of Sean O'Casey, and the imposition on the petit-bourgeois alliance of the strains under which it was to crack apart.

But for the moment all seemed well. Lloyd George had rejected a truce while negotiations were conducted. After General Smuts had visited Dublin and reported to him he conceded. At a further conference on 8th July it was agreed that De Valera should participate in a conference to explore the possibility of a conference. The military men were called in and hostilities ceased on 11th July. There were bonfires, toasts and rejoicings. The two state powers eyed each other silently like cats on a wall. But to the ordinary man everything seemed changed. The curfew ended. He could enjoy the driest summer of the century. The restriction on motor travel was abolished. The rich could drive into the mountains. Searches of ships ended. Within a few days creameries were reopening, markets and fairs were announced. There was a widespread impression that Britain had capitulated and that her troops would soon be withdrawn. Even the Volunteer leaders were caught up momentarily in the wave of relief and enthusiasm. Mellows, Brugha and Etchingham set off for Wexford like schoolboys released. At his first public appearance after two years "on the run", Etchingham was greeted with unrestrained rejoicing. "Wexford welcomes its great leader," ran the headlines of the *Enniscorthy Echo*. At last the terror was at an end.

CHAPTER THIRTEEN

NEGOTIATION AT GUNPOINT

DE VALERA left for London on 12th July. He was accompanied by Griffith, Barton, Stack and Childers. He met Lloyd George three times before he extracted from him written proposals he could put before his colleagues. The British Cabinet seems to have weighed their success in establishing Northern Ireland and found it not wanting. It enabled them to deal flexibly with the twenty-six counties. Their proposal was "Dominion" status. This involved allegiance to the English King, British retention of military and naval facilities, and free access of British goods to the Irish market. There was also a supremely objectionable provision, namely that the government of Northern Ireland was to retain all its "existing powers and privileges". By these were implied not only those meagre capabilities with which it was already endowed, but all those due to it under the constituent Act.

It was agreed that such terms were unacceptable to Ireland. De Valera made a special visit to Downing Street to convey this information. The Prime Minister, who had animated their first encounter with a *hwyl* of Pan-Celtic fraternity, now threatened full-scale war within days. The President knew a little about war and reached for his hat. The storm blew over instantly. There had been no harm meant. Perhaps Mr. De Valera would prepare a reasoned reply.

The negotiations were conducted on this basis from start to finish. The threat of war was never absent. Lloyd George knew well that a victory for the Republic in Ireland would strengthen immeasurably the independence movements in India and Egypt. On the other hand any appearance of unreasonable bellicosity would endanger the Pacific settlement which was now the main aim of British Foreign policy. The old master of bluff and duplicity found ample scope for his talents. On the Irish side, however, the negotiators were never able to make Lloyd George pay the political penalty for partition. This was because, having no internal solution to the Ulster problem, they could have no external policy either. It would be permissible to offer Ulster every legitimate economic concession within the framework of an Irish Republic. But once there was the slightest abatement of the claim to national independence for the sake of Ulster, the game was up. Britain was the arbiter.

On 24th July the *Dail* Cabinet agreed that the British terms were unacceptable. It was thought desirable to refer the matter to the *Dail*. The British authorities, by the logic of negotiation forced from their most intransigent position, consented to release members who were still in prison, though not without an effort to hold Sean MacEoin as a hostage. But already the holiday spirit had evaporated. The negotiations were going to be long and arduous. They might fail. Volunteer headquarters sent out instructions that the period of truce must be used for training and reorganisation.

On 1st August the Irish Labour Party and T.U.C. opened its Annual Meeting in the Mansion House. De Valera was on the premises on *Dail* business and was invited to say a few words. He was received with loud and prolonged cheers. He seized the opportunity of complimenting Labour on refraining from urging its own special interests while the national struggle was in progress. He promised no reward. He hinted at no collaboration. The implication was plain. The workers' business was work. Politics was for their betters. The cheers were repeated. But like the music at Don Giovanni's party, they rang with a strange foreboding, and Tom Johnson made a reply of studied uncertainty:

> The Labour movement must be acknowledged in any future Irish State . . . Whether Mr De Valera is President of the future Irish Republic, or head of any future Irish State, or whether some other person occupies that position, that Labour will assert itself I have no doubt whatever.

But how was Labour to assert itself in the circumstances which now existed?

Stewart of the Belfast Trades Council reported that maintaining the workers driven from the shipyard was costing between £5,000 and £8,000 a week. The action of the Amalgamated Society of Woodworkers who had expelled members who refused to work with Catholics was warmly approved by Congress despite some feelings in Belfast that they "ought to have consulted the local people". William O'Brien replied that if only one per cent of the joiners of Belfast supported the Executive, they were right in insisting that the only credential a man required to be allowed to work was a trade union card. He thought that if some other cross-channel executives had joined with the Woodworkers, Orange sectarianism could have been brought to heel. The English leadership had taken the easy path.

On the general question of partition the Conference was reduced to utopian generalities, namely "the adoption of a constitution for Ireland based frankly on labour and service as the condition of citizenship, and which will link the workers of Ulster with the workers of Ireland as a whole". To achieve this end Tom Johnson argued that a National Legislative Authority should be elected by voters in industrial or occupational constituencies. If this was the path forward *Dail Eireann* had little relevancy.

Of the manifesto "The Country in Danger" Johnson declared bitterly that it evoked no response but demands for reductions in wages. He continued, "Our responsibility has therefore ceased. I charge the employers of this country with thick-headedness, with carelessness of the consequence of their inactivity, and with no thought whatever of the livelihood of the people. . . . By their inactivity they have declared war. In my opinion they ought to have war . . . but let us bear in mind what it means. It means that we may have to face a definite social revolution." Under the stress of disillusionment the socialist revolution was being separated from and posed against the democratic revolution, from which alone it could develop.

The insertion of the expletive "definite" may have reassured nervous capitalists that the workers were not really threatening murder, but only "bloody murder". As Clarkson commented, "resolutions do not accomplish 'social revolution'". Yet Johnson's warning conveys one thing. If the bourgeoisie felt the existing Republic unnecessary for their future interests, the working class found it inadequate for theirs. And economic facts illustrate it. Expert enquirers estimated that the average working-class family in Dublin could not live decently on less than £4 2s. 0d.[1] a week. Some of the most skilled trades earned more than this. Painters for example had £4 6s. 6d. But carters took home only £3 5s. 0d., vanmen £3 0s. 0d., and many unskilled labourers less still. It is significant that at this time an attempt to revive the principles and practice of James Connolly was made by his son, who on 8th August reissued the *Workers' Republic*, as the official organ of the Socialist Party of Ireland. But the movement as a whole identified the national revolution with its middle-class leadership, and instead of seizing the bridge trooped off in search of another ship.

Mellows made efforts to speed up the importation of arms. He was driven to Waterford by the Woods family early in August. The object was to arrange for the concealment of guns in consignments of butter. These would be sent to the firm of MacDonald whose barrels littered the quays. On this occasion he learned for the first time of the intern-

[1] The corresponding figure for Cork City was £3 15s. 0d.

ment of his old friend Willie Walsh in Ballykinlar. He spent an evening at Gracedieu playing the fiddle with Cormac McGinley and Seamus Nolan, two former *Fianna* boys now in the Volunteers.

Briscoe returned from Germany. A meeting of headquarters staff was held to hear his report. There had been substantial purchases. One deal involved a million marks. The difficulty was transporting the material to Ireland. Billy Beaumont was talking about a submarine. Cremin, whom Mellows had sent out to control the funds, was sceptical. But Collins was attracted by the scheme. He suggested inviting Charles McGuinness to be skipper.

McGuinness had been arrested after his return from Scotland following a raid on the Ardara branch of the Belfast bank. He had escaped from jail early in July and was now in Dublin. He scornfully dismissed the notion of using a submarine. Why not a Zeppelin or a Cunarder? "What you want," he told Collins, "is a boat—one no different from a thousand others." Mellows sent him off to Germany in the wake of Briscoe.

The *Dail* met seven times between 16th and 27th August. Reports of the three public sessions are available. But accounts of what passed at the private sessions are exiguous and contradictory. In his opening statement on 16th August De Valera gave a review of events since the 1918 election in which he described the main task of the outgoing Ministry. It was to "set about making the *de jure* Republic a *de facto* Republic". But when he dealt with the mandate upon which that task was based he expressed the opinion that it was not "for a form of government so much, for we are not Republican doctrinaires, but it was for Irish freedom and Irish independence". This "could not be realised at the present time so suitably as through a Republic".[1]

His enemies repeatedly referred to this speech as proof that De Valera was abandoning Republicanism. His Republicanism may never have been completely consistent, but now he was offering what was in fact a defence. Why? A likely explanation would be that he was facing pressure for acceptance of the British terms, which Griffith had described to Stack as "pretty good".[2]

Next day he examined those terms.[3] He made it clear, without

---

[1] In these days when the belief in monarchy as a viable form of government is confined to the Nordic fringe, it is hard to take seriously proposals for a "Kingdom of Ireland". But in November 1921, Erskine Childers told an American newspaper in all seriousness that "naturally" he believed the Irish people would prefer a monarchy to a Republic, but the battle for freedom could only be fought under Republican colours.

[2] Pakenham, *Peace by Ordeal*, p. 81.

[3] Much valuable historical material is preserved thanks to this session. Sean Etchingham gave an account of his efforts to establish co-operative fishing, Art O'Connor of how he halted the "mad onrush of revolution".

specifically mentioning the Republic, that Ireland was negotiating "as a separate nation which is defending itself against the encroachment of a foreign nation". He was at pains to show that the British offer was not what it purported to be, namely one of "Dominion status". Partition destroyed any such claim. The denial of the right of secession disposed of it altogether. It was as if he was driving home to those anxious to accept "Dominion status" that they had not been offered it. The Irish counter-proposal was couched only in the vaguest terms—"An association that would be consistent with our right to see that we were the judges of what was our own interests (sic) and that we were not compelled to leave the judgment of what were our own interests or not to others—a combination of that sort would I believe commend itself to the majority of my colleagues." These are hardly words that betoken strong conviction or firm unity in the *Dail* Cabinet.

The private session of Monday, 22nd of August, was concerned with the question of negotiations,[1] and the proposed reply was read to a further session on the Tuesday.[2] It was to be delivered on the evening of the 25th and published at noon the following day. It was presumably at this Tuesday meeting that it received its "unanimous" endorsement, and that De Valera was proposed for formal re-election on the 26th. At this private session the question of the Republican oath arose and De Valera made it plain that "I do not take, as far as I am concerned, oaths as regards forms of government. I regard myself here to maintain the independence of Ireland, and to do the best for the Irish people."[3]

Much controversy has surrounded this statement. It is clear that the conception of "independence" replaces that of "the Republic", though of course the two are not mutually exclusive. In 1921 the notion of a Republic in even "external" association with a monarchy would have been looked at askance. De Valera was preparing the way for his new constitutional expedient. But the tragedy is that he did not clearly define it at once and let the world get used to it.

Why did he not do so? Perhaps he showed something of the peasant, of the man who will drop one hint and then talk of any subject on earth but the price of the cow, and indeed swear that it is not for sale. But in effect he ensured that many of his own colleagues did not know what he was aiming at. Something of his mind was revealed later in a letter to Joseph McGarrity.[4] He suspected that Ireland "would secure on paper at least the same nominal status and degree of liberty that Canada

[1] *Irish Independent*, 19th August 1921.   [2] *Irish Independent*, 24th August 1921.
[3] De Valera's own version, *Dail Debates*, 19th December 1921, p. 25.
[4] Dated 27th December 1921. Quoted O'Hegarty, *History of Ireland under the Union*, p. 766.

and Australia enjoy, except as regards Ulster and naval defence. . . .
With such an offer and no alternative before them except that of continuing the war for the maintenance of the Republic, I feel certain that
the majority of the people would be weaned from us." In other words,
all that was left of the Republic was a form of government and the
people would not fight for that. It was an unwitting condemnation of
the whole preceding line of Griffith's policy. The people could no
longer be trusted.

In passing it is perhaps as well to comment on the status of the
doctrine of "external association" in relation to the struggle for national
independence as a whole. For the revolution to go forward a single inch
it was necessary for its leaders to do what they had already refused to
do. At the same time the continued existence of a dual power had
become incompatible with the solution of their economic problems by
the main classes. Where then could the revolution go if it could not go
forward? Palpably it could retreat, the Republican power could be
allowed to wither as the British power was handed over to the leaders
of *Sinn Fein* in return for allegiance to imperial interests. Or there
might be an attempt to consolidate the ground so far won, to "externalise" the duality of government, by making all internal functions
republican while some external functions remained imperial. Obviously in this case after a temporary halt the revolution might resume its
course.

It is hard, in the circumstances, to understand the euphoria that
gripped the deputies at the public session at which the new Ministry
was elected. In response to lavish encomia from Mulcahy, De Valera
all but danced, descanted on the close unity of the Ministry and
declared gleefully, "I do feel like a boy among boys". Was this
excessive cameraderie overcompensating suppressed disagreements?
Or was there general relief that a unanimous reply had at length been
sent?

The proposal made to Lloyd George was that discussions should
begin "on the basis of the broad guiding principle of government by
the consent of the governed". But the *Dail* declined to accept conditions "that involve a surrender of our whole national position". And
on this subject a long correspondence followed. Lloyd George insisted
on allegiance to the Crown. De Valera refused to give it.

In the six counties the Unionist leaders began to fear that the process
of providing them with governmental powers was being delayed in
consequence of discussions with Dublin. The Belfast pogrom was
resumed on 22nd August and continued with but slight intermission

for six months. On 31st August there was fierce fighting. Seven were killed and forty injured. Eoin O'Duffy ordered out the I.R.A. Next day the British military took over the streets. The partitioning of the judiciary was then announced.

As the pogroms raged deputations from County Councils waited on *Dail* officials to urge action against partition, Fermanagh and Tyrone first, then Armagh City, rural councils in south Down, Derry City, the anti-partition majority in the Glens of Antrim, and finally 100,000 citizens of Belfast. In not a single county was there a homogeneous population. One-third of the people were imprisoned in an artificially delimited territory.

A strike of railwaymen was provoked by an employers' proposal to reduce wages by 9s. a week. A worker was dismissed from Cleeve's bakery at Bruree. John Dowling, John McGrath and Jack Hedley advised the workers instead of walking out to seize the factory. Bruree Workers' Soviet Mills were established. The red flag flew and a banner declared "We make bread not profits". Patrick Doherty, west Limerick organiser of the Irish Transport and General Workers Union was called by telegram to become the new manager. After about a week, roughly 26th August to 3rd September, the owners capitulated and sent up to heaven one more prayer for "strong government".

A few days later the offices of the Cork Harbour Board were seized by the workers led by Councillors Day and Kenneally. The regular officials were ejected and Day was installed in the manager's office. The dispute arose from the rejection of a demand for £3 10s. 0d. a week minimum wage. A conference was held under the auspices of the Ministry of Labour of *Dail Eireann* and a settlement was achieved that was highly satisfactory to the men. They returned to their work after singing the "Red Flag". Soon afterwards the Drogheda foundryworkers established their "Soviet". Further railway strikes were followed by a stoppage in the Kilkenny anthracite mines. All these actions involved only local workers and union officials. Those handled nationally were marked by less militancy. The Dublin and Belfast dockers tamely submitted to a wage reduction of 1s. a day.

On 7th September Lloyd George invited Irish delegates to attend a meeting at Inverness on the 20th. The purpose was "to ascertain how the association of Ireland with the community of nations known as the British Empire can best be reconciled with Irish national aspirations". In his letter he made clear that he envisaged "development within the Empire" and allegiance to the Crown of England. The *Dail* Cabinet felt that the terms of reference were broadly acceptable, but the assumptions on which they were based were not agreed. Accordingly the answer De Valera despatched entered stipulations that Ireland had declared its independence and recognised itself as a sovereign state.

A private meeting of the *Dail* was held on 14th September. The composition of the proposed delegation was reported and approved. It consisted of Griffith, Collins, Barton, E. J. Duggan and Gavan Duffy. But the mood of confidence had long evaporated. There had been difficulty in composing the delegation. Stack and Brugha had declined to participate. De Valera decided to remain "in reserve". Even Collins and Griffith had agreed to go only under protest. There were misgivings in the *Dail*, hints of which can be gleaned from the so-called Treaty debates of December and January. According to Mary Mac-Swiney, weakening at the top could be suspected when on 4th September Collins made a speech in Armagh without mentioning the Republic. An enthusiastic biographer[1] wrote of it that "responsibility had changed the whole cast of his mind". Sean Kelly, representing Louth and Meath, claimed that on 14th September he opposed to the last the sending of any delegation to Britain. And Dr. McCartan, in a presumable reference to the same debate, spoke of the "pistol of unity held at the head of every member of the *Dail*".

Lloyd George refused to proceed with the meeting unless the Irish withdrew their stipulations, though he insisted on retaining his own. Telegrams were exchanged until 20th September, when he issued an entirely fresh invitation. In this, while stating that his government's position was unchanged, he merely asserted that the discussion would take place without prejudice to it. On the 30th De Valera accepted. The proposed date was 11th October, and the venue Downing Street, London.

On 2nd October Mellows made his own position clear, in a speech at Tullamore. The occasion was that of Patrick McCartan's first appearance in his constituency after his return from Russia. Both men were aware of developing differences of opinion. Mellows was in constant touch with Brugha under whose influence it was, perhaps, that he failed to resume attendance at the I.R.B. circle meetings, a possible mistake. As for McCartan, he had been told frankly by Tchicherin that the Russians did not propose to jeopardise their relations with Britain for the sake of a Republic the Irish did not seem sure about themselves. Mellows' remarks were uncompromising:

The coming conference simply marks another milestone on the long road we have travelled, and the road we are prepared to travel,

[1] Frank O'Connor, *The Big Fellow*, p. 131.

I

be it long or short. It is not force that will tell in the end. The people's will cannot be broken so long as we stand together. It is not a question of negotiations or concessions. It is a question of our rights, and we will never give any allegiance to a British government's substitution for the people's right.

It was natural that division should spread to the I.R.B. There is evidence that in accepting his place in the delegation Collins believed that he was to be made the vehicle of a surrender. Like others he had not grasped the subtlety of De Valera's conception, because it had never received public discussion. Probably like Griffith he considered it merely a ruse to divert Stack and Brugha. Accordingly he must have considered the need to restore to the I.R.B. its former role as guardian and protector of the "Republic now virtually established". His friends warned him that if he went to London without De Valera, it would be the President, and not the I.R.B., who would emerge as custodian of the Republic. He disregarded their advice.

The Divisional Council elections were due on 15th October. Shortly before leaving for London Collins attended a meeting of members in south Munster. He caused much alarm by intimating that the "full Republican demand" was to be abated. Ernest O'Malley gate-crashed the Limerick meeting. He was disturbed both at the trend of I.R.B. policy and the pusillanimity of those who demurred at it.

To Mellows the supreme issue before the negotiators was Irish national sovereignty. He confessed later that he did not expect any agreement. He does not therefore appear to have given "external association" serious thought. He anticipated a resumption of warfare, and bent every energy to securing arms. Briscoe and McGuinness were already sending small consignments. A company had been registered at Ballinasloe under the name of Kenny, Murray, Ltd. Its legitimate trade was accompanied by the clandestine importation of arms. Mellows visited Ballinasloe from time to time to co-ordinate plans. Following some rumours of his activities the practice of searching ships entering Irish ports was resumed, but once the delegates were in London was allowed to lapse. There was a mounting campaign for the release of the prisoners, and while anxious to keep its hostages the British Government was not inclined to exacerbate public feelings.

The names of the five "plenipotentiaries"[1] were published on 2nd October. The bourgeoisie had advice instantly available for them. The Executive of the Irish Tobacco Manufacturers' and Traders' Association

---

[1] This unfortunate title was selected in the hope of compelling implicit recognition of Ireland's status as an independent State.

urged them to "insist on Ireland's right to unrestricted fiscal autonomy". The millers complained of the "dumping" of English flour. Imports were at their highest level since before the war. Dealers pointed out that cattle prices were at their lowest. There were 130,000 unemployed. These were the problems the settlement should be designed to solve.

The difficulties the delegates were likely to face were further illustrated by the issuing on 3rd October of Orders in Council constituting the separate judiciaries of Northern Ireland and Southern Ireland, in accordance with the Government of Ireland Act. A few days later came the first application to serve a writ "outside the jurisdiction", namely in Northern Ireland. Partition was pushed on regardless, under the very noses of the negotiators.

During the period of negotiations, Lloyd George had other problems too. India was on the verge of revolution. Martial law had failed to quell the upsurge of revolt. Under the treaty of alliance with Japan, Japanese troops were to be called in. But these were reported to be unreliable. A plan was evolved to seek an understanding with the moderate leader Gandhi, and in due time the Prince of Wales was despatched on a good-will tour, equipped with whisky and cigars, if the American cartoonists are to be believed.

In England the unemployed held more demonstrations and occupied public buildings in several of the big cities. Members of the Poplar Borough Council were led off to jail for paying out relief to workless men in preference to the rates which they owed to the county. Both in India and among the unemployed the resistance of the Irish was quoted as a justification of militancy.

But most of all the Irish question was linked with a Far East settlement. On 3rd October the *New York Evening Post* wrote "What happens in London after October 11th may profoundly affect the course of events in Washington." Cognoscenti were already aware of Britain's willingness to "seek a solution of the China question" with America rather than Japan. Britain was to adhere to America's "open door" policy. Japan was to be compensated for her loss of hegemony with a free hand in Eastern Siberia. In return Britain was to gain two concessions. American discrimination against British shipping, for example in the matter of Panama Canal dues, was to cease. And the United States was to disinterest herself in the Irish question.

Lloyd George intended to be present in person when the Washington Naval Conference opened on 11th November. His passage was booked on the *Aquitania*. It may be hazarded that he had long hankered for his meed of recognition on the far side of the Atlantic, and envisaged himself landing at New York with an Irish settlement in his pocket, the object of universal acclaim. And, as the *Evening Post* remarked, "eliminate Ireland from the situation and co-operation between the United States and Great Britain in the Pacific becomes an easily attainable reality". The London *Daily Chronicle* declared "the Irish question is the key to all politics".

The Downing Street Conference opened as arranged on 11th October. The five plenipotentiaries were accompanied by a staff which included Erskine Childers, who was to act as Secretary to the delegation. Presumably with the object of balancing his thorough-going Republicanism, Griffith introduced John Chartres who became a second Secretary. Chartres had served during the war in the Intelligence branch of the Ministry of Munitions, and had later become librarian of *The Times* library. He had contributed occasional articles to Griffith's newspapers. Other members of the Irish party were Desmond Fitzgerald, Minister for Publicity, Diarmuid O'Hegarty, Secretary of the *Dail* Cabinet, and Professor Smiddy to whom the delegation looked for advice on economic matters. There were no representatives of the Labour or Trade Union movement. On the British side were Sir Hamar Greenwood, Sir L. Worthington Evans, Lloyd George, Austen Chamberlain, Lord Birkenhead, Winston Churchill and Sir Gordon Hewart.

Lloyd George's aim was to gain international credit for satisfying Irish aspirations while yielding nothing that British imperialism was intent to preserve. Thus when he gave, he gave to America. When he took, he robbed Ireland. As his police clubbed unemployed demonstrators off the streets of London, he invited the delegates to name their objections to the draft offer he had made De Valera in July. The starting point was thus unchanged. If Griffith had immediately stated the Irish objections to Dominion status and proposed the alternative, the discussion might have taken another course. But, apparently in accordance with tactics agreed in Dublin, Griffith dealt with the reservations which detracted from true Dominion status. Thus from the outset negotiations were based on the British proposals.

Not that Griffith failed to win concessions. He made progress in matters of trade and finance. He secured from Lloyd George an undertaking to "stand aside" while the *Dail* made efforts to persuade the leaders of the Ulster Unionists to come into a united Ireland. This was to ask men who were already laying their hands on fame, power and opportunities for self-enrichment to place these definite prospects at the disposition of political opponents whose local representatives they had persecuted and terrified for years. The old dream of a united bourgeoisie need not be taken seriously. It need not cost Lloyd George a thought. It was on defence and allegiance, however, that the British would not move. And so matters stood on 17th October after five plenary sessions.

At the next session, 21st October, a little intrigue of Lord Beaverbrook's impinged upon the deliberations. The noble lord, becoming aware that the Bishop of Leeds was to make a pilgrimage to the Vatican, impressed upon the good prelate the value of the Pope's blessing on the conference, and suggested that it could be expressed no more appropriately than in a message to His Britannic Majesty. Accordingly His Holiness telegraphed his good wishes, and His Majesty, with or without the advice of his Prime Minister, replied in terms which asserted the principle of allegiance. De Valera at once repudiated the suggestion that the Irish regarded themselves as British subjects, and the London *Times* acting on the principle that ruling-class prejudices must not be flouted when uttered by the scion of Cerdic, cried woe to the churls who insulted the King. And all this the week-end after General Pershing, between rows of British and American soldiers, surrounded by scarlet, and glittering pomp, and in the presence of members of the Cabinet, had laid the Congressional medal on the tomb of the Unknown Soldier!

A red-faced Lloyd George demanded an explanation. And there were other complaints. One of Mellows' agents had been arrested in Cardiff. And a Captain Thompson, now in Hamburg jail, had been caught in the act of sailing out of that port a cargo of arms for Ireland. Captain Thompson was Charles McGuinness. He had reported to Cremin on 9th September. With the help of Briscoe he secured a leaky fishing vessel. Some weeks were spent caulking it. Sean Beaumont, who had followed his brother to Germany, found him a crew of German Communists prepared to sail it to Helvick. But unfortunately there was difficulty in starting the motor. While the engineers worked on it, McGuinness bought beer for the harbour workers. He made the mistake of paying in notes of high denomination. Suspicion was aroused. The Hamburg Harbour Police raided the ship as she edged her way out. "*Gott in Himmel!*" they exclaimed as they turned rifles out of bags of salt.

There was of course no danger of a breakdown. Washington was worth more than a shamrock. But Collins was compelled to agree to the discontinuation of arms imports for the duration of the truce. From the fact that Mulcahy issued no order on the subject until 31st October, it can be surmised that the undertaking was not regarded too seriously. Lloyd George availed himself of the crisis to demand clarification of the Irish attitude to allegiance. Thus came the crucial point in the negotiations, the time to present "external association" boldly and openly. There could be no war before the Washington Conference was over, and the world would see the force of the Irish arguments.

The case was put, but timidly and unclearly, as one would break the bad news to a widow by saying that her husband was not too well. Coming inside the Empire was "not quite our idea of association". The Crown would be accepted as the head of the association.[1] There would be a permanent alliance between Ireland and Britain, and what was in effect a common citizenship. Learning of the position now reached, De Valera wrote to convey the conviction of the Cabinet at home that "there can be no question of our asking the Irish people to enter into an arrangement which would make them subject to the Crown. . . . If war is the alternative we can only face it . . . the sooner the other side is made to recognise it the better." The delegates in London thereupon signed a memorial protesting against this interference with their powers. Collins is said to have been in a towering rage because he suspected he was "to be committed to a compromise and discredited".[2] Clearly he cannot have regarded "external association" seriously, even if he understood it.

Through the machinations of Cope, who had been working hard on Duggan, the plenary conference was adjourned after two weeks' negotiations. It never met again. Discussions continued in what the press called a "standing committee" of Lloyd George and Chamberlain on the English side and Griffith and Collins on the Irish. This arrangement deprived the Irish side of their two best brains, Childers and Gavan Duffy.

The first split in the delegation arose after Griffith had seen Lloyd George alone at Churchill's house. The Prime Minister told him that provided he had his personal assurance on Crown, Empire and naval facilities he would fight the Unionists to secure "essential unity". He thought he could achieve it in the form of making the six-county Parliament subordinate to Dublin instead of Westminster. Griffith undertook to give him his views and two days later he showed his fellow delegates the text of a letter he proposed to send to Lloyd George. This was on 1st November. The letter agreed to recognition of the Crown according to a formula to be arrived at later and "free partnership" in the British Commonwealth, provided he was satisfied

---

[1] A conception invented by Chartres (Pakenham, p. 178).   [2] Op. cit., p. 182.

on all the points, including "essential unity". Barton and Gavan Duffy strongly objected, and Griffith expressed himself in angry terms. On 2nd November he agreed to limit his recognition of the Crown. It was to be "as the head of the proposed Association of States". Next evening Birkenhead tricked him into accepting as an amendment "free partnership with the other States associated within the British Commonwealth". With difficulty Griffith persuaded his colleagues to agree, and the letter was despatched in this form. Lloyd George was delighted and told Griffith that if "Ulster" proved unreasonable he would resign rather than use force against *Sinn Fein*.

The ensuing period was that of Lloyd George's negotiations with Craig, who was of course, unlike *Sinn Fein*, unconditionally immune from coercion. The progress of these negotiations was daily reported in the American press. As the statesmen of the world gathered in Washington, Lloyd George was fighting his lonely battle with Ulster reaction. In the meantime he was preparing Griffith's mind for what should happen if he should lose it. Perhaps it was his duty to remain in office to save Ireland from the horrors of government by Bonar Law. On 9th November he extracted from Griffith a promise not to "queer his pitch" if as a tactical manœuvre "to deprive Ulster" of support in England, he undertook to delimit its territory by means of a boundary commission if Craig turned down "essential unity". Griffith agreed. Lloyd George was off the hook. He had been on it less than a week. Griffith did not consult his fellow delegates this time, though he reported by mail to Dublin, after he had, on the 12th, put his undertaking in writing.

The unity of the delegation had dissolved. O'Malley and Raleigh, who had ignored the instruction prohibiting Volunteer units from purchasing arms outside their area, had come to London. Raleigh was a Limerick carpenter who had offered his life savings, some £400, for the purchase of war material. Every penny counted, and the two men took their meals with the delegates at Hans Place. They pretended to be on holiday. When Collins, who was staying at Cadogan Gardens, called, O'Malley thought he was ill. Then he realised that he was drinking heavily. There was a sense of moody unease everywhere.

In the meantime Mellows had received the arms from Germany. Briscoe found a lawyer who explained to McGuinness that the export of contraband for use against England was not the gravest crime in the German calendar. He suggested that he should plead guilty and ask the indulgence of the Court. The result was a fine of about £10. Questions were asked in the Reichstag, but apparently McGuinness had no difficulty in recovering his property which he resolved to export more circumspectly next time.

He secured an option on an old tub called the *Karl Marx* which he loaded with cement for a trial run. It was to be towed out by a tug named the *Frieda*, which McGuinness purchased outright. The arms were aboard the *Frieda*, which cast off as soon as she was beyond the three mile limit, and while the *Karl Marx* sailed ostentatiously about the coast, before putting back into port, the *Frieda* swung west for Ireland. This time the crew were members of the extreme right irredentist movement, the Orgesch. Mellows was notified of the departure.

Captain McGuinness preserved the log of the voyage. He left Germany on 28th October. The distance to Helvick was little short of 800 miles, which supposing a speed of twelve knots could be covered in about three days. A watch was instituted at Helvick on 30th October. On the evening of the 29th Mellows took the train to Waterford. A rendezvous on the Cork road had been arranged with Pierce Kavanagh, who drove him to Helvick. As far as Dungarvan they carried lights, then proceeded without lights to a farm high on Helvick Head. Pax Whelan, Liam Lynch and Joe Vize, who had escaped from the Curragh on 9th September, were waiting there. They watched all night for the distress signal which was to be the sign for two fishing boats to go out to take the arms off. None came. Every night for a week Mellows got off the Dublin train at Kilmacow and was driven to Helvick. Sunday, 6th November, he spent in Dublin, but returned to the vigil next day. On the tenth he concluded with gloomy feelings that the *Frieda* had gone down.

There was great surprise and delight when McGuinness appeared in Dublin to report the safe landing of the arms on 11th November. Delayed by severe gales, he had ultimately overshot Helvick in dirty weather. By the time he burned his flares off the coast the watch had been withdrawn. In the absence of a response he made for Hook Head. Ignoring the signals of the coastguards, he sailed up Waterford Harbour and anchored behind an island off Cheekpoint, after his last shovelful of coal had been thrown into the furnace. He went ashore, covered the five miles to Waterford City as quickly as possible, and with some difficulty persuaded the Mayor, Dr. White, of the reality of his mission. Carts and wagons were assembled. The *Frieda* was warped alongside a jetty. Her 200 rifles and 10,000 rounds of ammunition were taken off. McGuinness then brought the crew to Dublin where they were distributed to Mrs. Woods, Mrs. Humphries and Mrs. Mellows, being shortly afterwards conducted to Newcastle by Eamon Martin.

Fuel was put aboard and before the eyes of the outraged harbour-master, the *Frieda* was sailed to Boatstrand, whence McGuinness took her to Cork and sold her to Captain Collins. With the proceeds, which it seems Mellows had not the heart to take off him, he bought the *City of Dortmund* from Palgrave Murphy. This vessel engaged in legitimate trade, but is said to have handled contraband in emergencies. She was the first ship to fly the Irish tricolour.

By the end of the month McGuinness was back in Germany. On Cremin's advice the Irish had decided to demand the return of sums paid to a dealer whose wares had not materialised. A confrontation was arranged in a solicitor's office. McGuinness was present. He had lived up to his reputation as a tough character. During his few weeks in Germany he had knocked out four Swedes who offended him in a bar, put his fist through the glass screen of a taxi whose driver he thought was taking him for a ride, and had tattoo marks removed from his wrist without an anaesthetic. He could be a terrifying spectacle when accompanied by a revolver. A considerable sum of money was recovered and earmarked for financing a fresh expedition.

But now all changed. On 15th November the Ulster Unionist Andrews described Lloyd George's proposal for an all-Ireland parliament as a "disgraceful betrayal". He and his colleagues resolved to yield not an inch. Lloyd George thereupon turned the pressure on to *Sinn Fein*. On the 16th Griffith spent a whole day reassuring Southern Unionists on such matters as land purchase, the second chamber, double income tax, and educational and religious safeguards. That day a new set of British proposals arrived. Simultaneously there was a decision, soon rescinded, to halt the release of prisoners from Bally-kinlar camp.

The British proposals on trade, finance, defence, the national debt and inclusion in the Empire were all there. In regard to Ulster there was a curious fiction. The six counties were theoretically to form part of the All-Ireland State, but its jurisdiction was not to be exercised until, after not more than twelve months, their Parliament had been given the opportunity to opt out and retain its position under the 1920 Act. In this case there would be a boundary commission. In the discussion that followed, attempts by the Irish to present "external association" were once more brushed aside.

Childers was now in close touch with Brugha at whose request he forwarded on 21st November a memorandum on foreign relations. It was probably in connection with this that Mellows paid his last visit to London. He did not go to Hans Place. He stayed with the Nunans, and sent one of the girls down with an envelope "to be given to Mr. Childers and nobody else".

By 1st December the Washington Agreements were already safe and dry. All that remained was to hear and disregard the objections of the lesser fry. Lloyd George then delivered what he described as Britain's final terms, which were embodied in "Articles of Agreement". These, despite minor concessions, were substantially those of 16th November, but a sinister phrase had been inserted with the object of nullifying the boundary commission. It had been conceived as drawing boundaries in accordance with the wishes of the inhabitants. Now the condition was added "insofar as is compatible with economic and geographic conditions". Finally the twenty-six countries were to be ruled by a Provisional Government to which the British would transfer power.[1] *Dail Eireann* would dissolve and the Republic come to an end.

The "plenipotentiaries" returned for a Cabinet meeting that was held on 3rd December. "On guard" messages were sent out to all units of the I.R.A. It seemed that the Truce might be ending, and all pre-cautions must be taken. Men who had lost many nights' sleep sought a decision on terms presented, as the *Daily Chronicle* admitted, with a presumption of war if they were not accepted. De Valera urged their rejection, and a further attempt to present "external association". Brugha toyed with an even stronger line, that of unrestricted national sovereignty.

These two and Stack would run the risk of war. But they did not expect it. Griffith, on the other hand, thought such risk unnecessary. The terms were the best obtainable, and were not dishonourable. Indeed, they "practically recognised" the Republic. De Valera offered to join the conference. It seems possible that he could have won a substantial adjournment followed by negotiations on a new or modified basis. But Griffith agreed to try again, and delegates, dog-tired and tetchy with frustration, rushed to the boat for no better reason than to fulfil a time schedule drawn up by Lloyd George.

There was confusion over what they had been instructed to do. They were not to accept the oath of allegiance to the English King. But neither must they risk a breakdown on the issue of the Crown. Yet no negotiator can escape the possibility of breakdown on his main stipula-tion. They drafted amendments. Despite personal tensions, inevitable where there are sharp disagreements on policy, they contrived to work together even though with increasing friction. They took back to Lloyd George external association in the clearest form yet presented.

[1] Section 17. Section 16 as finally agreed.

Unfortunately their amendments did not "read on" the precise paragraphs of the British proposals, and there was no substitute proposed for Section 17. There was no Ulster clause, but it could be argued that "essential unity" was an ever present condition from the Irish side.

Negotiations were resumed. But not for long now. Griffith sought assurances that "essential unity" was indeed part of the bargain. He wanted an undertaking from Craig. With utter unscrupulousness Lloyd George countered by producing Griffith's undertaking "not to queer his pitch" before the Unionist Conference. He accused Griffith of breaking his word. Griffith hotly repudiated the suggestion, but accepted the undertaking he had given. It was typical of his social outlook that a promise to a Prime Minister was sacred while an oath to a people was optional.

Lloyd George now made his last concessions. One was complete fiscal autonomy, the most immediate interest of the bourgeoisie. The oath of allegiance was given a less objectionable wording. There were concessions on finance and defence. Only one thing remained, the vital issue of sovereignty—Republic or Empire, which being translated is revolution or counter-revolution. It was proving no easier to externalise a dual power than to bottle a rainbow. The British would concede nothing more, said Lloyd George. Let the delegates sign the amended terms or "both sides would be free to resume whatever warfare they could wage against each other".

Griffith agreed to sign. Lloyd George insisted that every delegate must do likewise. There were hesitations which the Prime Minister strove to dispel by a histrionic evocation of the special train with steam up at Euston, the destroyer at Holyhead, all ready to take the letter to Craig that must go that night. Nobody thought of asking what Craig could do if he did not receive it. Collins gave in, then Duggan, and after a long struggle Barton. Gavan Duffy was left alone. As if under the hypnotic influence of Lloyd George he believed that his dissent was sufficient to precipitate war. A few minutes after Barton he capitulated.

CHAPTER FOURTEEN

METAMORPHOSIS

A CURIOUS little scene, of which the historical inevitability is shown by its repeated duplication, epitomises the surface politics of the ensuing period. The underlying reality was the establishment of the capitalist class in power in its two centres, while the workers stood aloof. What was immediately visible was the vacillation of the petite-bourgeoisie as its alliance faced the blow that was to wreck it.

The Dublin morning papers on 6th December carried the bare announcement that agreement had been reached in London. There had been no reference back. Hence it was widely believed in Ireland that Britain had at last relented and accepted the *Dail* terms. Mellows, Rory O'Connor, Cathal Brugha and some others were gathered after a day of rumour and speculation to talk over events and possibilities. To the general surprise Tom Johnson of the Irish Labour Party arrived and introduced the Scottish revolutionary, William Gallacher.[1] He and his colleagues in the British Communist Party had learned that things were moving towards a capitulation and he had come with a warning. The "plenipotentiaries" were going to give in.

"They'll never do that," said Cathal Brugha confidently. But almost immediately word was brought in that the British terms had been substantially accepted. The "plenipotentiaries" were on their way back. "You must intercept them and arrest them," said Gallacher. Mellows and O'Connor were immediately taken with the suggestion and leaped up ready to do it at once. Brugha demurred. "If you don't arrest them," said Gallacher, "it will not be long before they're arresting you." The Minister for Defence was unconvinced. "Irishmen won't arrest Irishmen," he replied.

The discussion continued until Brugha had to leave for the Mansion House, and the points were made so forcefully that Tom Johnson

---

[1] It is difficult to be sure of the time of this incident from Gallacher's account of it, Lloyd George's ultimatum was after 8 p.m. The last boat train left Euston at 9.30 p.m. The signing of the Articles of Agreement took place at 2.15 a.m. The day boat train left Euston at 8.30 a.m. This may have carried both E. J. Duggan and Gallacher and they would arrive at Westland Row at 6 p.m. Late editions of British papers and early editions of the *Evening Mail* contained the oath clause. The full agreement was published at 8 p.m. It would seem that Gallacher travelled on the day boat after a "tip off" early on 6th December,

became afraid of what the "gunmen" might do. "Try to understand politics," cried Gallacher. He argued that unless the revolution resumed the offensive it was doomed, and produced a social programme he suggested the Republicans might adopt. Mellows and Johnson took copies,[1] but Brugha left for the Mansion House saying, "Gallacher, you're always welcome in Ireland, but we don't want any of your Communism."

A similar scene was enacted at 71 Heytesbury Street. Those present were Liam Lynch, Count and George Plunkett, Oscar Traynor and Seamus Robinson. It was decided to arrest the plenipotentiaries, but Traynor, who must give the order, was hesitant. De Valera was consulted. "That would be the normal thing to do. But there is the wise thing also." On his return Barton asked Frank Gallagher "Why weren't we arrested when we came down the gangway this morning?" Gallagher told him that the army leaders were paralysed by division.

Vacillation followed in the political field. De Valera called together those members of the Cabinet who were in Dublin. He suggested that the signatories should be dismissed from the Cabinet and a proclamation issued at once repudiating the agreement. It was Cosgrave's turn to urge "the wise thing". Griffith was in London reassuring the Southern Unionists about their representation in the Upper Chamber of the Free State Parliament. Cosgrave persuaded his colleagues to postpone making a statement until the delegates had been heard in their own defence. A telegram was despatched, and a meeting called for 8th December.

The initiative lost was never recovered. Griffith issued a statement in favour of the settlement. There were no scruples on his side, Collins wrote in the *Manchester Guardian*. On 7th December the British Government announced the release of all internees. The *Dail* Cabinet had before it the *Irish Independent's* assurance that fifteen bishops favoured the "Treaty". What the die-hard Tory *Morning Post* described as a "finely orchestrated" paean of thanksgiving had issued from every editorial desk from the *Cork Examiner* to the *Irish News*. De Valera was defeated, for Cosgrave voted with Griffith, Collins and Barton. The President then issued his personal statement. He could not recommend the agreement. He added, "There is a definite constitutional way of

---

[1] Gallacher himself believed that this document might have been the basis of Mellows' "Notes from Mountjoy", which indeed the late Desmond Ryan once told me he thought could have been drafted by Gallacher and MacManus. This does not, however, appear to be the case. Ryan may have been thinking of the document brought to Ireland by J. V. Leckie in 1922, after the relevant part of Mellows' document had been issued.

resolving our political differences." But in counter-revolution constitutions are scraps of paper. In the United States, Cohalan attacked the "Treaty" declaring, "Lloyd George has won the greatest diplomatic triumph of his career."[1] Art O'Brien warned the Irish Self-Determination League not to rejoice too soon.

According to P. S. O'Hegarty, Mellows and Brugha "without waiting for any expression of opinion by *Dail Eireann* . . . toured Ireland in a motor car, visiting Volunteer companies and pledging them to 'maintain the existing Republic'." They had at most the five days, 9th to 13th December, for this nefarious work.[2] Meanwhile on the 10th, likewise without waiting for the *Dail*, the Supreme Council of the I.R.B. decided to throw its influence behind the "Treaty". Liam Lynch was the sole dissentient. The decisive factor was no doubt Collins' signature. On first learning the terms Mulcahy is said to have objected. Compromise had gone too far. Just what argument swayed the conclave must of course be inferred. One imagines the ghostly Republic of 1855 detaching itself from the shadows and demanding the exorcism of its living successor. There would be stooping to conquer, *reculer pour mieux sauter*, and a breathing space during which pure souls could wander with their vision in the wilderness, until ordinary mortals had made a few pounds and were once more ready for the fray.

On 14th December the *Dail* assembled. In this predominantly petit-bourgeois gathering was concentrated the power of decision of the whole nation. Outside, the Chambers of Commerce passed their resolutions. Country merchants, cattle dealers, manufacturers great and small, took up from their natural superiors, agrarian and financial, the cry for order and for the peace which alone could assure it. Also outside was the Labour movement. It gave no lead. Out of over a thousand branches and councils of trade unions, only six even passed a resolution. The *Voice of Labour* treated the issue as an irrelevancy. Only on the extreme left were warning voices heard. The Communist Party of Ireland[3] described the Treaty as a "shameful betrayal". "Thinly disguised as partners" the Irish were to become lackeys. "The so-called Free State will bring neither freedom nor peace. Instead Civil War and

---

[1] He revised his opinion after learning De Valera's position.

[2] What seems possible is that Mellows drove Brugha to meet his constituents in Waterford, breaking the journey at Courtown Harbour. An echo of the conversation with Gallacher seems to survive in the recollection of the Volunteer Francis O'Connor who was present when the two men discussed the relation between national and socialist revolutions, Brugha insisting on their complete separation, Mellows on their close connection.

[3] The Socialist Party adopted this name on applying for affiliation to the Communist International in October 1921. Simultaneously William O'Brien and Cathal O'Shannon were expelled. *Workers' Republic*, 15th October 1921.

Social hell will be loosed if it is accepted."[1] Larkin wired in similar terms from his American prison. These voices were lost in the general clamour. As the delegates took their seats both Republican police and Black-and-Tans were arresting the Wexford farmworkers on strike for trade union recognition.

The public session was concerned with two matters only, first De Valera's accusation that in failing to refer the last draft, the negotiators had ignored their instructions; and second, Dr. White's proposal that further debate should proceed *in camera*. The Speaker permitted some intermingling of these questions. Collins and Griffith were forced to rely on their plenipotentiaries' credentials to justify their precipitancy, but contradicted each other over whether these had ever been presented. The need for self-justification hardened conviction. Dr. White's motion was carried against complaints by Sean Etchingham and Daithi Ceannt that the people had been kept in the dark too long.

At the private session, which lasted several days, De Valera introduced for the purpose of discussion an alternative draft treaty, which acquired the absurd title of "Document No. 2". Among constitutional lawyers who have studied the implications of the "Treaty", it has received surprisingly little attention. Donal O'Sullivan[2] followed Beaslai in dismissing its formulations as importing no new element not implicit in the "Treaty"; Dr. Kohn[3] neglected to examine it at all. It was nevertheless a valid possible compromise between the "Draft Treaty A" for which the "plenipotentiaries" had been instructed to work, and the "Treaty" they signed.

These three documents were concerned with four major subjects, the constitutional relationship between Britain and Ireland, possible military and financial derogations from Irish sovereignty, special proposals for north-east Ulster, and transitional arrangements. The last could, of course, exercise great influence on the form and interpretation of the ultimate constitution. In the "Treaty" the acknowledgment of the Crown, oath of allegiance and Dominion Status all implied the derivation of Irish sovereignty by devolution from the imperial power. Document No. 2 asserted that all legislative, executive and judicial authority stemmed from the people. Its concessions, less substantial, and proposed for a briefer period, were such as might figure in a treaty between sovereign states. But in the matter of north-east Ulster, Document No. 2 progressed in no essential way beyond the "Treaty" position. Nor were its successional arrangements markedly superior.

---

[1] *Workers' Republic*, 17th December 1921.
[2] *The Irish Free State and its Senate*, p. 51.
[3] *The Constitution of the Irish Free State*, 1932.

In the "Treaty" *Dail Eireann* was ignored and the Provisional Government elected from the Parliament of Southern Ireland. But under Document No. 2, a "transitional government" would be elected by members of Parliament for the thirty-two counties, subject to the Ulster clauses which follow, and to this "transitional government" not only the powers held by the British Government, but those held by *Dail Eireann* would be transferred. It is possible to trace the conceptions expressed in Document No. 2 in instruments enacted throughout many subsequent years. But this fact arises neither from the inherent flexibility of the "Treaty", nor from the far-sightedness of Document No. 2, but from the continued living challenge of Republicanism in conditions of British imperial decline.

All that is certain about the debate in private session is that the deputies came out by the same door as in they went. A national division of post-Parnellian proportions was patently in the making. After the meetings Mellows would have discussions with officers from the country drawn irresistibly to Dublin by suspense and apprehension. One evening he was sitting with Liam Lynch, Rory O'Connor and Seamus Robinson in a friend's house when Earnan O'Malley arrived. O'Malley told of his meeting with J. J. O'Connell who was already mentally apportioning commands in a Free State Army of 20,000 men. How many would come from the South? "You'll have to fight in our area if you're false to your oath," said O'Malley. "It's there that you'll find immediate and terrible war." He had seen Mulcahy and was only prevented from resigning his command by the intervention of Brugha, who still hoped for a favourable vote in the *Dail*. Rory O'Connor suggested that anti-Treaty officers should break away from Headquarters. O'Malley pointed out that it was impossible to know who was on which side. At Mellows' suggestion it was decided to let the situation develop, as "the I.R.A. will never stomach the Treaty".

The public sessions were resumed on 19th December. Vastly different estimations have been published. Supporters of the "Treaty" have inclined to cynicism. Thus Beaslai spoke of the "Great Disillusionment", Frank O'Connor of the "Great Talk". One of De Valera's biographers, M. J. MacManus, more manfully speaks of the "Great Debate". The historian T. A. Jackson, who covered the proceedings for a London newspaper, said that it was impossible at the time to discern any objective class basis for the positions deputies adopted. He thought the dominant issue was the oath of allegiance, but that this was, so to speak, the phenomenal expression of the issue of partition. Examining the written record, at this distance in time, it is possible to sympathise with the dilemma of a petite-bourgeoisie, everything in whose class character made for division in face of the test, everything in whose national consciousness pressed the need for unity. Taken as a whole the debate reflected in microcosm, not only the position of Ireland in face of Britain, but the whole balance of political forces in the world.

Document No. 2 did not save the situation. The deputies were not prepared to reopen negotiations and offer it in place of the London agreement. The agreement was of course not a treaty. Document No. 2 would have been a treaty—though a very unequal treaty. The presentation of the London agreement as a treaty, concealed its fundamental difference from Document No. 2. The issue thus appeared to be one between two treaties, one very bad which could be got without fighting and a bad one that would have to be fought for.

Since there was no question that Document No. 2 would go forward, De Valera wished to withdraw it. Griffith objected. He felt that De Valera after inviting them to risk war for a bagatelle was now trying to occupy a position (known in the current lexicon of prevarication as that of "the isolated Republic") which all had long ago agreed to abandon. The weakness of the situation was, of course, that the Irish had proposed the capitulations; in the many similar negotiations of later years it was the imperialist power.

Griffith's speech to the motion of acceptance of the "Treaty" was directed against the conceptions which informed Document No. 2, though they had been his terms of reference in London. Instead of "half-recognising" the British King and Empire, he argued, the Irish should "march in with their heads up". Of course they had unfortunately never been incontestably out. The direction of his speech showed how little he understood "external association" which was to Republicans the most extreme compromise to which they would reluctantly allow themselves to be forced. It showed also how little he sympathised with Republicanism itself. Now that the bourgeoisie was poised to break out from the isolation it had endured since 1917, Griffith, its devoted ideologist of three decades, was determined to cast off all Fenian entanglements. He quoted Thomas Davis, "peace with England, alliance with England, confederation with England, an Ireland developing her own life, carrying out her own way of existence, and rebuilding the Gaelic civilisation broken down at the Battle of Kinsale". He did not touch on the subject of partition, nor did Sean MacEoin who seconded his motion.

Nor indeed did De Valera or Stack, who moved and seconded the rejection. There was confusion over whether they were advocating "external association" or "full independence and nothing short of it". But "Dominion Status" was worthily trounced. Stack denied the existence of any natural parallel between Ireland and the Dominions. With acute insight he pointed out that there the British power protected the colonists while they robbed and exterminated the aborigines. The majority of the Irish people were in the position of these aborigines.

After Count Plunkett had spoken against and Joseph MacBride in favour of the settlement, came Collins' contribution. He argued that the fact of accepting Lloyd George's invitation necessarily implied willingness to compromise and that the renunciation of the right to coerce north-east Ulster involved the acceptance of at least temporary partition. He believed that through the development of mutual understanding and goodwill, the northeast would be brought to accept an all-Ireland Parliament. His restriction of the national revolution to bourgeois purposes was exemplified in a description of the economic conquest of Ireland somewhat different from Connolly's.

> The English penetration has not merely been a military penetration.... Every day our banks become incorporated or allied to British interests, every day our steamship companies go into English hands, every day some other business concern in this city is taken over by an English concern and becomes a little oasis of English customs and manners . . . this is the opportunity of stopping it.

Erskine Childers gave an accomplished analysis of the status clauses of the "Treaty", arguing that they abrogated the whole principle of independence. Kevin O'Higgins re-emphasised Collins' argument to the horse fair. Sean MacSwiney made the most uncompromising Republican speech yet, and this possibly stung Robert Barton to confess that his sentiment was still against the "Treaty", and that he had broken his oath to the Republic only under duress. Shortly afterwards he realised that an undertaking given under such circumstances could not be regarded as binding, and participated once more in the Republican struggle. Etchingham objected to the "Treaty" on the grounds of partition and allegiance to the throne. Sean T. O'Kelly, Alderman MacDonagh, Dr. McCartan, Mary MacSwiney and Sean MacEntee all objected to partition, and Sean Moylan drew attention to the fact that for all the talk of British troops being withdrawn from Ireland, they were being reinforced in the six counties.

Richard Mulcahy made a serious well-reasoned speech eschewing cheap debating points and personalities. But he threw all his weight as

Chief of Staff behind the signatories. Belying Griffith's enthusiastic reference to Collins as "the man who won the war", he asserted, "we have suffered a defeat". It was noticeable as the debate went on that supporters of the "Treaty" confined themselves to internal Irish issues and Irish relations with Britain, that is to say to the narrow sphere inhabited by the mercantile classes. Alderman MacDonagh was the first to show that other classes had broader interests. "By the Treaty," he said, "Ireland will take part of England's debt, as well as England's oppression of every subject nationality." Here was a statement that Ireland's role within the international community was at stake.

Thanks, it is said, to I.R.B. manipulation, there was an adjournment on 22nd December. Before the *Dail* met again, the Christmas sermons had been preached. Resolutions had proliferated like groundsel. Lobbying had been in full swing. After his first Christmas at home since 1915, Mellows set off for Galway to meet his constituents. As he cycled from house to house among scenes made memorable by the Rising, he learned how deep was the fear of a resumption of war. A meeting of the *Sinn Fein* committee took place in Loughrea on 28th December. Mellows had an angry argument with Patrick Hogan outside the hall, with Frank Fahy doing his best to act the conciliator. When it was clear that the supporters of the "Treaty" were in an overwhelming majority he refused to attend the meeting, and rode off to Killeeneen where the Walsh family still stood firm. Next day he was at Ballinasloe, where the east Galway *Comhairle Ceanntair* was meeting in the Temperance Hall. Only one man spoke out against the "Treaty", namely O'Began, but nine out of the twenty-seven delegates voted against ratification.

On returning to Dublin he discovered the alarming fact that only one newspaper in the whole of Ireland, namely the *Connachtman*, of Sligo, was opposed to the "Treaty". After discussions with Sean Etchingham, Frank Gallagher and Erskine Childers, Mellows agreed to found a new weekly, *Poblacht na hEireann*, of which he was to be the nominal editor. The first number appeared on 3rd January. Revived under the abbreviated title *An Phoblacht*, this journal became one of the greatest radical newspapers in Irish history, and led mighty struggles in the nineteen-thirties. Frank Gallagher, the assistant editor, was responsible for the production. Its political tendency showed the thinking more of De Valera than of Mellows, and as Mellows' own development led him to the left, he appears to have lost interest in it. Among those who joined the editorial committee were Cathal Brugha, Sean Etchingham and Mary MacSwiney. The manager was Alderman MacDonagh.

After the resumption on 3rd January the important speeches of Constance Markiewicz and Alexander MacCabe revealed the class antagonisms which were expressed in the constitutional struggle. The Countess, who had during the recess rallied the Citizen Army almost unanimously against the Treaty, quoted a remarkable letter Griffith had written to the Southern Unionists. It contained the statement that he had agreed to a scheme that would "give them their full share of representation in the First Chamber of the Irish Parliament". As to the upper chamber, he promised to "consult them on its constitution" and that "their interests would be duly represented".

Countess Markiewicz asked by whose authority the chairman of the delegation in London made these promises. Was there to be representation by classes? If so, why single out the Southern Unionists for favourable treatment? Was it because of what they stood for? They had been the English garrison in Ireland. But they stood for something more malignant, namely, "for that class of capitalists who have been more crushing, cruel and grinding on the nation than any class of capitalists of whom I ever read in any other country. . . . They are the people who have combined together against the workers of Ireland, who have used the English soldiers, the English police and every institution in the country to ruin the farmer, and especially the small farmer, and to send the people of Ireland to drift in the emigrant ships. . . ."

When the Countess declared "I stand for James Connolly's ideal of a Workers' Republic" there were interruptions. "A Soviet Republic," shouted one deputy. She continued to protest against "this deliberate attempt to set up privileged class in this, what they call, a Free State". She turned to the colonial question. "I saw a picture the other day of India, Ireland and Egypt, fighting England, and Ireland crawling out with hands up. Do you like that? Now, if we pledge ourselves to this thing, whether you call it Empire or Commonwealth, that is treading down the people of Egypt and of India."

After referring to the subjugation of Wales by means of an imported Prince, she returned to her main theme. "The interests of England are the interests of the capitalist class. . . . It is the capitalists' interests in England and Ireland that are pushing this Treaty through to block the march of the working people in England and Ireland . . . I have seen the stars and I am not going to follow a flickering will-o'-the-wisp."

If the standpoint of the advanced workers was expressed by this child of the paternalistic landlord-entrepreneurs of Sligo, that of the merchants and manufacturers was presented by a country schoolmaster of the same county. Alexander MacCabe's speech expressed fear as eloquently as the Countess's defiance; but not fear of British imperialism, fear of those forces which Countess Markiewicz was calling on to save the nation. The "Treaty", he felt, was one that Ireland could "honourably and profitably accept". Against the sanctity of the Republican oath he posed other considerations, of a "peaceful and happy" Ireland, a "united Ireland", and the principles of Christianity. Lest it be thought that his reference to a "united Ireland" involved merely Ulster, he made the matter clear later:

> I'd prefer to see East Ulster stand out at first, so that our minorities may get a chance of having justice done to them in the making of boundaries, and for the additional reason that I would not care to see a province of the size of North Ireland as it stands come into the Irish Free State. . . . Were we to set up a Republic here in Southern Ireland, I fear the unity which we all aspire to would hardly come in this generation.

His peroration made matters clear beyond doubt:

> War against England would probably unite the country, but our enemies are far too wily to force war on us. It is not war we are faced with but disunion, internal strife, chaos, and a retreat, perhaps, to the position we held when this war began. Finally there is this aspect of the question to be considered: the moral effect of a prolonged state of war on the population. We have already seen the effect it has had on such countries as Germany and Russia, and, to a lesser extent, on England—how it has put passions of every kind in the saddle. Murder, robbery, arson, every brute instinct asserts itself when the doctrine of force alone is being preached abroad. Life will become cheap. Men will settle their quarrels with Webleys instead of their fists. The striker will abandon the peaceful method of picketing for the bomb and the torch. The landless workers will have recourse to more deadly weapons than hazel sticks in attacking the ranches . . . I stand by the goods that have already been delivered. In case this House does not stand by them I make one request to the succession Cabinet before sitting down. It is this: Give us Dominion Home Rule, give us Repeal of the Union, give us anything that will stamp us as white men and women, but for Heaven's sake don't give us a Central American Republic.

Margaret Pearse and Eoin O'Duffy followed, the latter supporting the view that it would be as well if the six counties were excluded for a while. They would learn from experience the economic pressures that would force them in, and become more amenable to terms. Then

Mellows spoke. Whereas the Countess had taken up the stand of the revolutionary workers, Mellows spoke for all revolutionary sections. He denied that at any time had he agreed to any form of compromise. He did not oppose the talks with Lloyd George. To refuse to discuss would be to lose international opinion. But the plenipotentiaries were sent to make a settlement in accordance with Irish aspirations, not to surrender. He personally did not believe an acceptable settlement could have been obtained. But that they were sent to do, or return with nothing done.

He criticised their failure to refer the last draft to Dublin. He denied their right to agree to anything inconsistent with the existence of the Republic on behalf of which they were sent. The Republic existed or it did not. The Declaration of Independence was the announcement of a Republic, not a mandate to move towards one. He was aware of public opinion. He had visited his constituency and spoken to the people at their firesides. What had gripped their minds was the fear of "immediate and terrible war". This was not the will of the people but the fear of the people. The "Treaty" was in reality a new Coercion Act, in the biggest sense possible.

"The very words 'Irish Free State'," Mellows declared, "constitute a catch-phrase. It is not a state, it is part of a state; it is not free, because England controls every vital point; it is not Irish, because the people of Ireland established a Republic. Lloyd George may well laugh up his sleeve. What must his thoughts have been, when he presented the document for signature. 'If they divide on this we can let them fight it out, and we will be able to hold the country; if they accept, our interests are so well safeguarded that we can still afford to let them have it.'"

Mellows denied that rejection was likely to invite immediate war. Rejection would put Ireland's case before the world in such manner that England dare not make war until she had some other excuse. Like Countess Markiewicz, Mellows raised the colonial question: "We are going into the British Empire now to participate in the Empire's shame, and the crucifixion of India and the degradation of Egypt. Is that what the Irish people fought for freedom for?"

He went on, "This Treaty reminds me of the Treaty of Versailles, of the miserable end up to that bloody holocaust when the nations of the earth, after fighting supposedly for ideals, parcelled out among themselves the spoils of the young soldiers. The misguided young men who fought in that conflict were left disillusioned." By contrast the people of Ireland "placed Ireland on a pedestal for the first time in the history of this country. For the first time in the history of this country we had a government established by the directly declared will of the people. . . . Ireland was put forth to the world as a headlight, as a beacon." Some thought that if they abandoned the Republic they could turn to the League of Nations to protect them from undue British interference. The League of Nations was a League of Robbers. He concluded with a warning. "You can have unity by rejecting this thing. You cannot have unity by approving of it."

Mellows' speech made a considerable impression, and he was invited to a meeting of an informal back-benchers' committee on the evening of 4th January. The aim was to find a compromise position which all deputies could support. The initiative seems to have come from Eoin O'Duffy. On the morning of the 5th it was announced that the committee was evenly divided between ratification and rejection.

That morning the *Freeman's Journal* published a scurrilous attack on De Valera and Childers which led to demands that its reporters be excluded from the *Dail*. It soon became clear that the occasion was of Griffith's making. He had handed to the press the text of Document No. 2, in its original and subsequently amended forms. These now appeared in juxtaposition, punctuated with pejorative cross-heads. As Griffith passed over to the camp of undisguised counter-revolution his scruples evaporated, and his sensitivity heightened as if his conscience was tearing at his nerves.

On 6th January, suddenly overcome with a sense of the monstrous illegality of the proceedings, De Valera resigned the Presidency. He thereby terminated the Ministry. He invited the *Dail* to re-elect him when he would appoint fresh Ministers and follow a policy based on "external association". Not unnaturally Griffith objected that his motion for approval of the "Treaty" was before the house. The ebb tide was becoming a mill race. The Speaker ruled that Standing Orders must be suspended before the President's resignation could be discussed. After increasingly bitter exchanges, De Valera withdrew his resignation on condition that the vote on the "Treaty" was taken within forty-eight hours.

The debate continued. The rift grew even deeper. Harder feelings came constantly to the surface. On the final day the British Army suddenly stirred into activity. Tanks and parties of Auxiliaries moved ostentatiously about Dublin. Griffith asserted that 98 per cent of the people wanted the "Treaty". He flatly contradicted Countess Markiewicz when she told him her constituents had supported her stand. The question was put on the evening of 7th January. Griffith's motion was adopted by 64 to 55. De Valera announced that he would resign, and invited his followers to meet him next day. The assembly closed amid emotional scenes and with a sense of the end of an epoch.

When the *Dail* reassembled on 9th January, De Valera presented his resignation. Mrs. Tom Clarke proposed and Liam Mellows seconded his re-election. His re-election would mean that the observance of the terms of the "Treaty" was largely at his discretion. From his replies to interrogation on this point it is clear that he had not given up hope. The Ministry would "not actively interfere with those who are going to complete the 'Treaty'". But ratification must wait.

Dail Eireann had accepted a proposal which involved its dissolution. But it was not yet dissolved. The new constitutional conundrum threw the proceedings into confusion. Increasingly acrimonious arguments were tossed back and forth. After Griffith had accused De Valera of a last effort to upset the "Treaty", and Collins had protested that *Dail Eireann* had no right to elect the President of the Republic but only of the Ministry, the question was put, and De Valera lost by 60 votes to 58. Expressing the position of his party De Valera said to the majority, "We will not interfere with you except when we find that you are going to do something that will definitely injure the Irish nation." He was using the word "definitely" very frequently now. It is the arch-enemy of definition. But behind all the talk lay the possibility of a metamorphosis instead of a termination of the dual power.

Collins then proposed that Arthur Griffith be elected President of the Assembly, and appoint a provisional executive. The Presidency of the Republic thus quietly lapsed, retiring into the shades of the virtually established where Collins himself was ready to accommodate it. He supported his motion with an unaccustomedly rambling speech in which Frank O'Connor seems to have read a touch of hysteria. Mulcahy, dapper and unruffled, seconded. De Valera asked whether those taking over responsibility intended to preserve the Republic until the Irish people disestablished it. Certainly, Griffith replied; after the Provisional Government was set up, a plebiscite or general election would be held on the issues of Republic or Free State. Griffith was thus in the position of a cat chased into a dairy.

Pertinent questions were asked by Mary MacSwiney, Daithi Ceannt and Austin Stack. But it was Mellows who expressed the feelings of Republicans best.

> I rise [he said], to protest with all the weight and force of my being against any attempt being made to use the name of the *Dail*, which

is the Government of the Irish Republic, and its machinery, to set up a Provisional Government, and to establish a Free State in accordance with a British Act of Parliament.

The impasse was total. If the "Treaty" party voted to dissolve *Dail Eireann* there and then, De Valera's followers would continue independently as the *Dail*. The only way to prevent the formation of an anti-Treaty Government was to have two governments, two authorities with one policy, two powers running in harness.

It was of course impossible for the Republicans to surmount the difficulty of their minority position in the *Dail*. Nobody could talk himself out of such a predicament. When the question was put, and the inevitable happened, De Valera led his supporters from the chamber, as a protest against the election as President of the Republic (he had not accepted Collins' attenuation of the office) of a man bound by his own signature to subvert it. De Valera's party returned in the afternoon, when Thomas Johnson introduced a deputation of trade unionists who were demanding action to reduce unemployment. At this time one in four of the able-bodied workers of Ireland was idle, and a further 5 per cent were on short time. Poverty had reached desperate proportions. Johnson spoke bluntly, though perhaps without realising the irony of his threat, that if nothing was done the people would "sweep *Dail Eireann* out of existence". Griffith, whose policy was responsible for this alienation of sympathy, assured the deputation that he understood perfectly the question of unemployment. The best plan was to set up a committee to consider it. De Valera's party displayed no interest. There was neither debate nor suggestion of debate. They were occupied with their frustrations, and there were more acid exchanges, some of them revealing.

De Valera informed Griffith that he could not sincerely congratulate him on his election. He foresaw the difficulty that he would be compelled to act in a dual capacity, as President of the Republic and as Minister of the Provisional Government. He asked for some statement of policy. This was given. "The *Dail* is going to remain in existence—the Republic of Ireland is going to remain in existence—until the Free State is prepared to have an election. . . . If the Irish people turn down the Free State for the Republic, I will follow in the ranks. I will back the Free State." He asked that this policy be given a fair trial.

Its dangers were at once apparent to Childers. The people were being offered the opportunity of voting for the Republic only after the machinery of the Free State had been established. He asked, "Will the

Provisional Government function under the statutory powers conferred by the Partition Act?" There was an immediate storm of protest. Griffith lost control of himself and pounded the table. "I will not reply to any Englishman in this *Dail*." He repeated himself as the clamour rose to fresh heights. "I will not reply to any damned Englishman in this Assembly." Childers had sworn an oath of allegiance to the Irish Republic. He was thus one of its citizens. When the Republic was disestablished he became an Englishman again. But was the Republic yet disestablished? In the frenzy of his guilty conscience Griffith had blurted out his secret conviction.

The Countess enquired once more about Griffith's discussions with Southern Unionists on the composition of the proposed upper legislative chamber. Griffith explained that he had met them informally "as an Irishman might meet Irishmen". It was clear that he had accepted the credentials of land and wealth. Those he had met included such fervent Gaels as Lord Midleton, who had been British War Minister during the South African conflict; Dr. Bernard, Protestant Archbishop of Dublin and Provost of Trinity College; and Andrew Jameson, member of the Irish Privy Council and former governor of the Bank of Ireland. They differed from Childers in that they were a reinforcement to the class of exploiters.

Shortly before Countess Markiewicz posed what Griffith called her "trap question" Eoin MacNeill left the chair in order to propose a resolution aimed at legitimising the course of action agreed upon by the Treaty party. It read

> That Dail Eireann affirms that Ireland is a Sovereign Nation,[1] drawing its sovereignty in all respects from the will of the people of Ireland, that all the international relations of Ireland are governed on the part of Ireland by this sovereign status, and that all facilities and accommodations accorded by Ireland to another state or country are subject to the right of the Irish government to take care that the liberty and wellbeing of the people are not endangered.

Notwithstanding the obvious concessions to the schematology of Document No. 2, De Valera was not impressed. He explained that he was accepting but one step at a time. His party regarded the motion to approve the "Treaty" merely as a "license to the Executive that they might promote the setting up of a Provisional Government in accordance with the terms". He proposed as an "amendment" the excision of the entirety of the text, and the substitution of a reaffirmation of the

---

[1] Majuscules in the official record. Perhaps the last abode of the mystical nation of the petite-bourgeoisie: for minuscules follow.

Declaration of Independence of 1919. Not unnaturally Eoin MacNeill hesitated before the gulf, and withdrew his motion. He resumed the chair to preside over the last acerbities.

There remained one issue of importance, that of the status of the Volunteers. De Valera sought a statement from Mulcahy who replied evasively at first. De Valera then added to his question a warning. "What I am anxious about is that orders given to the army will be given in the name of the Government of the Republic; otherwise I fear that there might be some trouble." Mulcahy appears to have done some quick thinking, not complete, however, until the vote of thanks to the owners of the hall had been passed and the house was about to rise. He declared to the sound of applause that "if any assurance is required, the Army will remain the Army of the Irish Republic". He might have added "until it is supplanted by the Army of the Free State". So began the process he afterwards confessed amounted to "finessing with honour". De Valera had forced Griffith into a position where the *Dail* was to be used to supplant the *Dail*; now the machinery of the Volunteers was to disestablish the Volunteers. The House then rose. The "Treaty debate" was over. So in effect was the revolutionary *Dail*. Metamorphosis had begun—into a monstrosity.

CHAPTER FIFTEEN

THE LONG-LIVED PHOENIX

"If you remove the English army tomorrow and hoist the green flag over Dublin Castle, unless you set about the organisation of the Socialist Republic, your efforts would be in vain. England would still rule you. She would rule you through her capitalists, through her landlords, through the whole array of commercial and individualist institutions she has planted in this country."

—James Connolly

FROM the close of the *Dail* debate the "Treaty" party held the initiative. Its policy was to press ahead with establishing the provisional government, hold a general election as soon as possible and set up the Free State. That Northern Ireland's part in this was no more than a legal fiction was clear from the fact that the election was to be confined to twenty-six counties. Griffith seems to have been in little doubt that the institution of bourgeois class power in twenty-six counties took precedence over the reunification of the country. Hence the brief period of willing co-operation with imperialism, in which Ministers flitted to England and back like butterflies in a field of thistles. The business classes applauded. For the first time since the collapse of Redmondism there was a policy they could make their own. At last they hoped for freedom from their humiliating dependence on the lower orders. Goodbody's took a full page advertisement in the *Freeman's Journal* of 9th January. "What is Ireland clamouring for?" they asked the nation. The answer was "Peace".

Beyond this the pro-Treaty leaders found a complex situation in which flexible manœuvring was required. The petit-bourgeois alliance of 1917 was now in process of disintegration. But the dissident fragment that could not be fitted into the new class alignment was too weighty for compulsion. It must be coaxed into conformity with bourgeois development. For attaining this end Griffith and Mulcahy were able to rely on the fact that they were not recognisably bourgeois themselves. They strove to create the illusion that the counter-revolution continued the revolution. By this means they pinned their former colleagues to the past, when their sole hope lay in making a complete break from it, making common cause with the workers, small farmers, unemployed and landless men, in taking their faction as resolutely to the left as the others had moved to the right. In these conditions the Labour movement, lacking the inspiration of a Connolly, gave voice to impeccable principles and prepared to strike a bargain with the new boss.

The I.R.B.[1] held a special consultative conference on the evening of the adjournment. Two days later the Supreme Council issued a statement reaffirming support for the Treaty and upholding the undertakings given by Griffith and Mulcahy in the *Dail*. Members of the I.R.B. were to continue to recognise the *Dail* as the Government of the Republic. Those who were Volunteers were to "continue to receive routine orders through their authorised military officers".[2] Finally it was proposed to defer further discussion of policy until the Free State constitution had been published. The notion was thenceforth sedulously encouraged that this constitution would be "republican in character", and the division rapidly widened within the I.R.B. between those who believed this and those who did not. A number of circles, like that of the *Fianna* which ejected the visitor,[3] broke away from the Supreme Council and ceased to function.

Late on the evening of 10th January, De Valera presided over a meeting of the officers of Headquarters Staff and those commanding divisions and independent brigades. An ominous sign was the absence of Mellows, O'Connor and O'Malley. Mulcahy, who had presumably delayed after the I.R.B. meeting, arrived late. De Valera appealed to him to back up his call for maintenance of unity in the Army. In particular he asked that there would be no repetition of an incident in County Clare where much uneasiness had been caused by the removal of arms from one unit to another. The commandant of the 1st Western Division, Michael Brennan, a strong "Treaty" supporter, assured the meeting that the transfer took place so as to prevent the use of the Volunteers in a land dispute. Liam Lynch, discharging emotional tensions built up at the previous meeting, excitedly denounced the "Treaty", and amid some scepticism threatened to accept no further orders from G.H.Q. Mulcahy, with customary aplomb, repeated his assurances, and invited the doubters to a quiet talk.

Next day the unemployed demonstrated in Beresford Place, and the

---

[1] F. O'Donoghue, op. cit., pp. 193 and 232.

[2] It is not clear whether the word "routine" was significant. Conceivably other, non-routine, orders may have been envisaged, emanating for example from organs of the Provisional Government.

[3] The representatives of the higher committees of the I.R.B. were called "visitors" when attending meetings of the lower. It was the custom for a "visitor" to be present at every meeting.

Irish Labour Party issued a demand for a Workers' Republic, un-accompanied, let it be said, by any policy for achieving one. In the evening the dissident officers held their own meeting and established the military Action Committee, later renamed the Military Council. Mellows did not attend, but his signature appeared on the letter which was drafted for despatch to Mulcahy. The other signatories were the G.H.Q. officers Rory O'Connor, Sean Russell and James O'Donovan, the Divisional Commandants Liam Lynch (1st Southern), Ernest O'Malley (2nd Southern), Joseph McKelvey (3rd Northern), Thomas Maguire (2nd Western), Liam Pilkington (3rd Western) and Michael Kilroy (4th Western). The Dublin and South Dublin brigades were theoretically part of the 2nd Eastern Division. Oscar Traynor signed for the city men, and for the county Andrew MacDonnell, who had spent the last two years poised rebelliously above Dublin like the O'Byrnes and O'Tooles of old.

The Military Council demanded the convocation of an Army Convention and the reconstitution of the Army Executive which, under a programme of converting the Volunteers into a regular army, had dissolved itself by a majority vote in November. They demanded a reaffirmation of allegiance to the Republic, now not quite the same thing as allegiance to *Dail Eireann*. The army should be under the supreme control of its own executive which would draft a constitution for submission to a further convention. It was proposed that the preparation of the convention should be entrusted to a committee composed of equal numbers chosen by the Minister for Defence and the Military Council.

The letter seems to have been sent on 12th January, the day when by Royal Proclamation the jail gates were opened and the prisoners sent out on to workless streets and broken down farms. Now to its sup-porters the benefits of the "Treaty" beamed their brightest. Mulcahy must have felt he could rely on a majority to support the policy he had outlined in the *Dail*. All that was necessary was to placate the cranks and purists. On the 13th he sent a reply asserting that the control of the army was vested in the *Dail* as government of the Republic. Any pro-posal to change its status was a matter for the *Dail*. But he offered to meet the signatories and discuss their proposals on 18th January.

On 14th January the Southern Parliament, complete with the four members for Trinity College, but without the member for Fermanagh who sat in the *Dail*, met at the invitation of Arthur Griffith. Even a Philadelphia lawyer could scarcely contrive a legal basis for this initiative by the President of *Dail Eireann*. His ostensible capacity was that of Chairman of the Irish delegation to London. As such his rights derived from the Irish Republic. But this the British Government had refused to recognise. The "Treaty" had not yet been given the force of British law. So that Griffith could not even claim the authority of the King's Most Excellent Majesty. That the situation was anomalous Winston Churchill admitted at Westminster. But he was equal to it. He urged the Commons to press ahead with the Irish Free State Agreement Bill which, he held, against other authorities, would regularise matters.

The Southern Parliament elected the Provisional Government. Collins was chairman; Griffith and Mulcahy confined themselves to the *Dail*. Four Ministers of *Dail Eireann* accepted parallel posts in the Provisional Government. Theoretically, perhaps, they became answerable to the Southern Parliament. But they were never called upon to answer. The Southern Parliament met no more. What would have happened if instead of boycotting the assembly the opponents of the "Treaty" had attended determined that where decisions were taken discussion would be raised, has been the subject of surprisingly little speculation. It might have revealed the British intention of leaving the twenty-six counties without representative government. The extraordinary fact is that this Provisional Government was to draft a constitution for an "Irish Free State" that nominally covered thirty-two counties, but there was no provision for any representation from the six counties, not even from the areas the boundary commission might be expected to transfer. It seems an inescapable conclusion that the British government never seriously questioned the inevitability of partition.

There was hasty burning of papers in Dublin Castle. The old nest of rapine and oppression was handed over to Collins on 16th January in the absence of the press. Then the power into which the British power was being transformed began to look about for appliances. Evacuation of the Black-and-Tan and Auxiliaries began at once. Barracks were scheduled for transfer in such order as would safeguard Britain's ability to return in case of emergency. The Provisional Government, having for the moment no armed forces but the Volunteers, who had sworn allegiance to the *Dail*, prepared to established a new police force, the *Garda Siochana*,[1] and a professional army. It decreed the continuance of British laws and services, and made arrangements for conducting the affairs of fifty-nine departments of state when they had been handed

[1] Civic Guard. An order disbanding the Company police of the Volunteers was issued by G.H.Q. on 20th January.

over. The old apparatus thus continued under new management. But now businessmen could make their mercenary representations to the Board of Trade without attracting the smallest unpatriotic stigma. The mountain had indeed come to Mohamet.

It is not certain that Mellows attended Mulcahy's meeting on the 18th. He was called out of Dublin in connection with a mission that had now become politically irrelevant. An Irish Race Convention had been called for 21st January in Paris. De Valera, the invited chairman, was anxious to prevent the "Treaty" party from substituting Eoin MacNeill. He decided to anticipate the Professor and present him with an accomplished fact. But he had no passport, and to apply for one from the Provisional Government would be distasteful on the one hand, indiscreet on the other. It was decided that Eamon Martin would cross to London, make the necessary arrangements with the Communists, and have Ramsay, the photographer, ready when De Valera arrived. As it happened, Ramsay was working Bournemouth beach, and the photograph had to be taken at a small shop in the Strand. To avoid attracting attention the Rosslare route had been selected, and Mellows and Andrew Woods motored over the ground a few miles behind De Valera. Mellows lost his way in a dense coastal fog, narrowly missed driving over a cliff, and reached Dublin late on the 18th after sleeping at Enniscorthy asylum.

At the conference, which was held at the Banba Hall, Mulcahy faced the fact that the Military Council was already preparing for a Convention on 5th February. He had no choice but to make the plan his own but with a time limit extended to two months. The meeting was acrimonious. To Mulcahy's assurance that the army would remain the army of the Republic, Rory O'Connor shouted "A name will not make it so". O'Malley denounced the members of the *Dail* Cabinet and Headquarters Staff as imperialists, marking time till the Free State could be defended with arms supplied by the British. At one point James O'Donovan rounded on Collins, told him he was a traitor and declared that he should have been court martialled long ago. Collins jumped to his feet. Apologies were demanded and refused. Mulcahy, for the moment under the necessity of relying on the Volunteers, offered to allow two "watchers" at every meeting of the Headquarters staff, to see for themselves that nothing was being done to subvert the Republic. The implication of this offer must surely be that Mellows, O'Connor and Russell had already been squeezed out of the main deliberative gatherings.

On the day of the conference Dublin tramwaymen accepted a wage reduction of 4*s.* a day which was to come into effect in two stages. Postal workers were threatened with a reduction of 10*s.* a week. Unemployed workers led by Liam O'Flaherty seized the Rotunda and ran up the red flag. They held out for four days. Tired of the constant flow of propaganda in favour of the "Treaty" Seamus Robinson's men seized the offices of the *Clonmel Nationalist.* And William O'Brien made his modest contribution to the cause of unity, by inviting dissatisfied members of anti-Treaty Volunteer units to enlist in a new "workers army". As. R. M. Fox's history shows,[1] his aim was to neutralise the Republican tendencies of the Citizen Army by submerging it in a wider organisation whose views were more acceptable to the "Treaty" party.

The Provisional Government had its own plans for the discontented and the unemployed. Recruitment for a regular army was begun at once. Pro-Treaty officers were gathered in Dublin. On 1st February Michael Collins as Commander-in-Chief took their salute as they passed the ceremonially guarded headquarters of the Provisional Government at the City Hall, and to the accompaniment of solemn speeches and much rich sentiment they were installed at Beggars Bush barracks. Nobody has ever established a legal basis for this action. The prudential basis was nevertheless clear. The "Treaty" party were anxious to extricate themselves from dependence on the Volunteers.

The Bank of Ireland lent the Provisional Government, now described by Lord Dunraven as the sole bastion against chaos in Ireland, the sum of a million pounds. The British Army was deployed in a protective circle round north Dublin and the House of Commons was prevailed upon to risk £500,000, with the stipulation that it should not be spent all at once. A Committee under the effective chairmanship of Darrell Figgis[2] was established to draft the Free State Constitution. Among its members was Dr. Maloney's protégé, C. J. France. Dr. Maloney appears to have been taken in by the "Treaty" and while France may have successfully communicated elements of American Republicanism, his efforts to facilitate American economic co-operation came to grief as if upon some hidden codicil to the Washington Agreement. Apart from the non-effective chairman he was the sole apology for a Republican on the committee. And no representative of the great unwashed vulgarised its genteel sessions.

As the Provisional Government illegally equipped itself with the tushes of power, the struggle for the control of *Sinn Fein* began. This proceeded under conditions that were becoming more favourable to the Republicans. The fog surrounding the London agreement had

---

[1] *History of the Citizen Army,* p. 216.   [2] The nominal Chairman was Michael Collins.

K

thinned slightly thanks to the series of self-explanatory events. On 21st January Collins met Craig in London and succumbed once more to the monstrous apparatus of political blackmail that had been created by Lloyd George. It was the apparatus that had imposed the "Treaty", and the apparatus that was to enforce it. Six Irish counties were held as hostages in the hands of British imperialism. Half a million Catholics were in the hands of Craig. In return for dubious assurances regarding their physical and economic safety, Collins agreed to abandon the Belfast boycott and, in effect, to recognise the legitimacy of the six-county regime within Ireland. "Ulster is daily drawing closer to the motherland", mouthed the *Freeman's Journal*. That newspaper now found the impertinence to denounce the Republicans for delaying the foundation of the "Gaelic State".

Disillusionment came speedily, except for those with their heads in the sand. Craig claimed Lloyd George's authority for an interpretation of the "boundary clause" of the "Treaty" that ruled out all but the most trifling revision of the line of the border. The alarmed citizens of Derry sent Collins a deputation consisting of seven Nationalists and five Unionists. They demanded that he insist that Derry form part of the Free State. Cut off from its Donegal hinterland it must face economic ruin. Three days later came a similar deputation from south Down. Newry's prosperity within the six counties depended on the continuance of the Belfast boycott. Now that this had ended there must be inclusion in the Free State. A further conference between Collins and Craig, this time in Dublin, was a total failure. The pogroms intensified and were accompanied by clashes on the border, which culminated in a desperate affray at Clones on February 8th.

The *Sinn Fein Ard Fheis* had been scheduled for 7th February. On 19th January Sean T. O'Kelly issued from the office of *Poblacht na hEireann* a confidential circular urging "reliable persons" to do all that was possible to secure the election of delegates opposed to the "Treaty". On 21st January Mellows telegraphed to Padhraic Fahy inviting him to meet him next day at Athenry. Driving a Benz motor car left in Ireland by Briscoe he called at Dr. Brian Cusack's surgery in Oldtown. He found his colleague struggling with a minor operation in defective light, and held a hand torch for him until the task was finished. It was late when they left for the west. They spent the night at Tyrrellspass with the Malone family, who insisted on leaving their beds to welcome the visitors.

Mellows and Cusack spent the next three days in intensive canvassing. Old friends at Athenry, Gort, Kinvara and Ballinasloe were visited one after another. Special attention was paid to influential priests. Finally when the south Galway *Comhairle Ceanntair* of *Sinn Fein* met at Loughrea on Thursday, 26th January, by a majority of one, Padhraic Fahy was elected to attend the Dublin *Ard Fheis* with a mandate to vote against the "Treaty". In Wexford Sean Etchingham secured a similar decision by his own casting vote.

Mellows returned to Dublin and plunged into a variety of activities. The *City of Dortmund* arrived in Dublin from Germany with a cargo of musical instruments. Mellows sought to recruit a sound Citizen Army crew who would know how to secrete arms if need be, and would be proof against the blandishments of the "Treaty" party. He approached the docker Andrew Egan and other key men of the Liverpool arms chain. He bought guns and chemicals, to O'Donovan's delight laying his hands on a quantity of dinitrotoluene, which while not of the potency of T.N.T. could be used to enliven the paraffin wax and chlorate mixtures which were up to then available. He urged one backslider after another to return to the support of the Republic.

Industrial unrest meanwhile reached a pitch described by the *Freeman's Journal* as "insurgency". On 25th January the workers seized Mallow Mills which they held until Liam Lynch, on Mulcahy's orders, dispossessed them on 10th February. On the 27th lightning strikes paralysed the Cork-Bandon and Great Southern and Western railways. Within a week railway communications had ceased. Both the *Ard Fheis* and the proposed last meeting of *Dail Eireann* were postponed by two weeks. On 30th January dockers ceased to work at the North Wall. They were protesting against a reduction of 6d. a day. Seven hundred canal workers went on strike. The Provisional Government held a special meeting to consider the crisis. Cobh railwaymen seized the terminus and appointed their own stationmaster. On 10th February the G.S.W.R. men announced their intention of running the line themselves. All Cork termini had been taken over before the settlement was announced on the same day. Farm-workers had been on strike at Bulgaden, Co. Limerick, since 2nd November. On 30th January Sean Moylan found against them at a *Sinn Fein* arbitration court. There was wall-breaking and hay-burning at Bruree and Kilmallock, and land was seized in Limerick and Mayo which local Volunteers were ordered to seize back.

The disturbances on the border became so widespread and serious that on 13th February the British Government suspended evacuation and Collins left for London, swearing to heaven that the opponents of the "Treaty" had been discovered preparing a *coup d'état*. From all "quiet" parts of the six counties police were moved into the border areas. In London an agreement was reached by which representatives of the two sides would co-operate to maintain peace on the border. Evacuation was resumed on the 15th. Next day a number of Unionists in I.R.A. custody were released.

The first national organisation to declare against the "Treaty" had been *Cumann na mBan* whose executive committee made its position clear early in January. At a special conference on 5th February Mary MacSwiney's motion reaffirming allegiance to the Republic and denouncing the London Agreement was carried by 419 votes to 63. Mrs. Wyse Power thereafter organised a Free State Women's organisation prominent among whose leaders were the wives of the "Treaty" party Ministers. As fresh contingents of "Treaty" supporters arrived from the country at Beggars Bush barracks, and recruiting for the new police force proceeded apace, the growing volume of opposition was shown when, on 12th February, the opponents of the "Treaty" held a monster meeting with three platforms in O'Connell Street. This meeting seemed to foreshadow a possible alliance between *Sinn Fein* and the radical left. De Valera, Stack and Alderman MacDonagh were joined by the Countess Markiewicz, Mellows and Nora Connolly. Next week the process was repeated at Cork. De Valera, Cathal Brugha, Mellows and Countess Markiewicz were met at the station by the Lord Mayor and cheering crowds. Volunteers led by bands marched to the Courthouse where De Valera said a few words from the steps. Mellows hastened to the Wallace sisters to arrange accommodation for the Countess. He was in high spirits and teased them by saying their visitor was going to read them a great lecture. There were enthusiastic audiences at platforms on Grand Parade, Mellows speaking with Cathal Brugha, Mary MacSwiney and the Countess. He remained in Cork several days, discussing with Michael Leahy and other officers the possibility of capturing the arms and ammunition which the British were proposing to evacuate from Cork Harbour. Later he spoke in Limerick, Ennis, Athenry, Tuam and Claremorris.

When the postponed *Ard Fheis* met on 21st February 3,000 delegates assembled in Dublin. After De Valera and Stack had denounced and Griffith and Collins had defended the "Treaty", the sense of the meeting became apparent. There was a majority against it. This was an important result. It might have provided consistent Republicans with an opportunity to extricate themselves from entanglements which had hampered their freedom since 1917, to rally the forces of opposition to the "Treaty" and swing public opinion behind the demand for a revision before relationships had congealed. What happened showed the full beauty of the petite-bourgeoisie in action.

Mulcahy, whose virtue was at least that he knew his own mind, proposed an adjournment until 11 a.m. next day. The leaders met behind the scenes. When the delegates took their places next morning they were still in conference. Somebody started the singing of patriotic songs. Soon the hall resounded. Political differences were forgotten. When De Valera and Griffith returned the stage was set for the announcement that "unity" had been preserved. It had been agreed that the *Ard Fheis* should be invited to adjourn for three months. In the meantime the Standing Committee with its pro-Treaty majority should be replaced by a board of officers. *Dail Eireann* should continue to meet as before the London agreement, but from now on no adverse vote should require the resignation of the President or Cabinet. The general election should be deferred until the constitution of the Free State should be available to the electorate. The benefits claimed for this remarkable "package deal" were first that *Sinn Fein* should not divide, second that the signatories of the London Agreement would have time to draft a constitution and third that the publication of the Constitution would help the electors to decide between the Free State and the Republic.

The balance of advantage must surely have favoured the "Treaty" party. While it is true that Griffith and Duggan were summoned to London immediately to explain themselves, they seem to have had little difficulty in satisfying Churchill. The imperialist historian Professor Allison Phillips,[1] the possessor of a strong nose for nationalist outrage, commented that the "Treaty" party had appreciated "the necessity for a temporising policy". They had won three months' unchallengeable control of *Dail Eireann*. During this three months they also controlled the Provisional Government and administered the affairs of the twenty-six counties in all respects but a part of the military. It would be strange if they could not improve their position during this time. And the six-county administration could do likewise. At the same time the *Dail*, for what it was becoming worth, was given a temporary respite.

Dorothy Macardle[2] considered the *Ard Fheis* agreement a rebuff to British policy, but in one important respect it accorded with it. The statement spoke of an election in which the people would "decide between the Republic and the *Saorstat*".[3] Under whose auspices were the elections to be held? The implication was clear.

[1] *Revolution in Ireland*, p. 259.　　[2] *Irish Republic*, p. 693.　　[3] *Saor Stat*, Free State.

It may well be that the opponents of the "Treaty" felt that splitting *Sinn Fein* would increase the danger of civil war. They were to learn that it is not only possible to plunge into it. One can vacillate into it. For having avoided a vote in order to preserve unity De Valera must immediately resume his controversial speeches, the sole logic of which was the split he was afraid to make. Once more he had indulged his fatal predilection for offering verbal solutions to real problems. It may even be decided, when historians make a fuller examination of the period of the Provisional Government, that a franker division in the political field might have averted that which appeared in the military. But once again such a policy led in the direction of the "men of no property".

None of these considerations affected the delegates to the slightest degree. Questions were invited. Those who asked them were shouted down. When the motion to approve the leaders' agreement was put none opposed it. If their contact with affairs of state was giving the "Treaty" party some of the devious ruthlessness of government, their opponents shivered more indecisively the further they were driven into the wilderness. When the *Ard Fheis* closed it was clear that the canvassing and propaganda work had gone for nothing. A mood of exasperation with *Sinn Fein* and its leaders began to spread among the Volunteers.

On 21st February also, the Irish Labour Party and T.U.C. held a Special Congress in the Abbey Theatre to discuss electoral policy. Presumably the date had been decided before the postponement of the *Ard Fheis*. The workers' assembly betrayed no cognisance of what was proceeding in another place. Cathal O'Shannon took the chair, and Thomas Johnson read a memorandum prepared by the National Executive. It emphasised that Labour had stood for the complete withdrawal of all British armed forces from Ireland, self-determination and territorial integrity. "Those whom we trusted, and who were best able to weigh the forces material and moral on either side . . . decided that the terms of peace were the best that could be obtained in the circumstances." A new situation now existed, in which a constitution was to be drafted for twenty-six counties. Labour could not afford to stand aside. It was not acceptable that a general election should be no more than a plebiscite on the "Treaty". Labour insisted that its voice be heard on such matters as unemployment, the cost of living, housing, compulsory tillage, education, pensions, banking and credit, and the management of the railways. He moved that Labour should offer candidates in the coming election.

Helena Maloney proposed an amendment which was as near as permissible to a direct negative. The discussion proceeded on the amendment. Its content was less ethereal but more parochial than that of the *Dail* debates. International affairs intruded not at all. Imperialism was not mentioned. The delegates ransacked the ideologies of syndicalism, pacifism and social democracy for some semblance of a firm standpoint. There was for the most part a revulsion from nationalism. This was the form in which the breach with the petite-bourgeoisie expressed itself. There was no suggestion that Labour should take up the national struggle where "those they trusted" had laid it down. The seizures of land and factories were not subjected to the slightest scrutiny. The delegates were there to accept history, not to make it. The working class had a consultative assembly when conditions cried out for a general staff.

If Labour lacked inspiration, the small Communist Party possessed little else, and was constantly tempted into pronouncements which while losing no support gained little either. The principles of internationalism and anti-imperialism shone brightly above. All that was necessary was to "apply" them. The party supported the anti-Treaty wing of *Sinn Fein*, but warned them that the three months' false unity would tell against them. It supported Labour's decision to participate in the coming election, while passing scathing comments on the pusillanimity of its leaders. It tried its own hand at solving the conundrum set when the irresistible force of Irish Republicanism met the immovable object of British imperialism. The result was unhappy and mercifully not developed. The *Workers' Republic* spoke of a "Bolshevik Republic an integral part of the British Empire", and added that those unable to grasp this conception had "minds that cannot reach beyond the presently obtaining order of things". Behind this understatement one can discern a purpose of transcending national antagonisms through the unity of the working class.

Some of the *Ard Fheis* delegates remained in Dublin for a conference of the G.H.Q. staff and Divisional Commandants held on 24th February. Despite multiplying challenges to his authority Mulcahy seemingly felt that he could make an *Ard Fheis* of an Army Convention. This he proposed for Sunday, 26th March, and went so far as to accept as its basis O'Connor's proposals of 12th January. The *Dail* Cabinet sanctioned the proposal on 27th February, but it was not brought before the *Dail*. From the day of its reassembly on 28th February, it was plain that authority had passed from it. Mellows did not attend. He arranged to pair with Eoin O'Duffy so as to be free for military

business. At the same time he handed over the nominal editorship of
Poblacht na hEireann to Erskine Childers. Yet, like birds homing to a
tree from which their nest has been blown, Republican deputies
constantly invoked the prerogatives of the *Dail* as the sovereign
assembly of the nation. They asked questions relating to services controlled and financed by the Provisional Government and were surprised and aggrieved when nothing was forthcoming. While public
attention was focussed on the *Dail*, the Provisional Government did as
it pleased, under the chairmanship of Collins and with the advice of the
civil servants.

As the British forces withdrew and fine Irish uniforms appeared at
Beggars Bush, barracks and depots were taken over by local Volunteers. Already units were becoming classified as supporters or opponents of the "Treaty". Transfers from one to another established
homogeneity and laid the basis for conflicts on a geographical basis.

The first such befell the strategic city of Limerick. On 18th February,
Liam Forde of the mid-Limerick brigade had issued a statement denouncing the Chief of Staff, Eoin O'Duffy, as a traitor, and declaring
his command independent. Four days later three other brigades issued
a similar statement from O'Malley's headquarters at Tipperary.
O'Malley was then in Dublin. On his return to Tipperary he threw in
his lot with the seceders. Eoin O'Duffy's reply was to send members of
Collins' "squad" from Dublin and invite "Treaty" supporters into the
city. Some of these being arrested, he transferred Limerick City from
the command of the 2nd Southern to that of the 1st Western Division,
and ordered Michael O'Brennan to take over strong points evacuated
by the British. O'Malley retorted by bringing his myrmidons from
Tipperary, and installing himself at the Glentworth Hotel. He was
shortly joined by Tom Barry of Cork, Michael Kilroy from Castlebar
and O'Gorman of Castlerea. There was growing danger of civil war
as the contending parties brushed aside the interventions of municipal
and clerical dignitories. On 10th March Liam Forde and Seamus
Robinson were in Dublin where there were negotiations with Mulcahy.
At his suggestion Liam Lynch was sent as peacemaker. He effected a
settlement said to have been tolerable to the Republicans.

There was no move against Tipperary except an invitation to
O'Malley to report to Dublin for court martial. It is illustrative of the
extreme weakness of the state machinery that he disregarded this
order with complete impunity. Tipperary was not of the strategic
importance of Limerick. Moreover it bordered on east Limerick where
a pro-Treaty Brigade was wrestling on the side of "law and order" with

labour and agrarian disputes which were sweeping the area. Martial law and a curfew had been imposed. John McGrath and John Dowling had been arrested and only the threat of a general strike throughout the area brought the military men to their senses and secured their release. By contrast, in Tipperary Town, where the workers seized the gasworks on 4th March, they were unimpeded by the local I.R.A.

The apparent deadlock in the twenty-six counties gave the secessionist administration in the north-east what its leaders considered a golden opportunity. They conceived the notion of establishing undisputed control over every townland allocated to them under the Government of Ireland Act. The pogroms against the Catholics of Belfast were intensified. As before, their sole protectors were the Volunteers, who, it must be recorded, also protected Protestants in Catholic areas who were under attack by citizens who had been deranged by persecution and terror. On 15th March Dawson Bates told the Northern Parliament that the Government was at war with the I.R.A. and that it was proposed to operate on that basis throughout the entire six counties. He then introduced the notorious "Civil Authorities (Special Powers) Act", which was in essence a refinement of the British "Restoration of Order in Ireland Act" of 1920, the refinement which attracted most attention being the introduction of flogging for political offences.

At this time there were 13,000 British toops, 2,000 R.I.C. men,[1] 5,000 A Special Constables and 20,000 B Specials. Asked to define the the status of the last, Lloyd George replied that they most closely resembled the Italian *Fascisti*. Sir Henry Wilson issued from retirement to advise on the organisation of these forces for the "defence of Ulster". On 22nd March no less than 500 Catholic houses in Rathfriland were subject to search. It was asked why the Protestant houses were not searched. "It was unnecessary," came the explanation. "Every Protestant house in the district had a man in the search party." In the early hours of the 24th occurred one of the most infamous massacres in Irish history, when uniformed men broke into the house of the Mac-Mahon's in Hunter Street, Belfast, and slaughtered the entire family but for the youngest child who had succeeded in hiding. On the same day the bodies of three young Catholic men were found lying on roadsides in County Tyrone. Inevitably the I.R.A. defended itself and its supporters, and reports of actions taken were reported to headquarters in Dublin. Refugees carrying their pathetic bundles became a common sight in the capital. On 25th March armed men of the Dublin brigade[2]

---

[1] Shortly to be reinforced from south of the border and renamed the Royal Ulster Constabulary.　　　　　　　　　[2] *Freeman's Journal*, 27th March 1922.

seized the Fowler Memorial Hall, headquarters of the Orange Order, to house expelled families. Soon they were supplying them with food seized from firms trading with Belfast.

On 8th March, while the Limerick dispute was still unresolved, Eoin O'Duffy had uttered to Rory O'Connor the first threat that the Army Convention might be prohibited. He was told that the Military Council were determined to have it and would if necessary call it themselves. Mulcahy did not wish to lose Lynch's co-operation. The election of delegates from brigades proceeded and was completed by the 14th. It was then apparent that four-fifths of the Volunteers were opposed to the "Treaty". The *Dail* Cabinet met on the 15th. Collins had that morning heard from Winston Churchill that an adverse decision at the Convention would be "a very grave event at this juncture". Mulcahy was compelled to confess that he could not guarantee the contrary. It was agreed that the Convention should be declared illegal and proclaimed. The decision was made public in a curious way. Griffith sent Mulcahy instructions that the Convention was not to be held. He is said to have described them as surprising.

The Military Council met at once. A Shadow General Staff was elected, headed by Liam Lynch, and with Mellows as Quartermaster General. Rory O'Connor, James O'Donovan and Sean Russell held their existing positions. Traynor found them temporary headquarters in Parnell Square. Ernan O'Malley confirmed the invitations to as many units as possible, and inserted a statement in the newspapers. The signatories of the invitation, according to the calculation of Florence O'Donoghue, represented 63 per cent of the total strength of the Volunteers. Mulcahy's threat to suspend the "mutineers" was ignored and he was compelled to warn O'Duffy to avoid precipitate action. On 17th March Mellows and Seamus Robinson drove to Helvick to arrange the landing of arms which Charles McGuinness was already loading at Bremerhaven. These would go to the Republicans.

It is possible that soon after the *Ard Fheis* agreement De Valera and his closest associates regretted it. That they returned with renewed vigour to the castigation of the "Treaty" party in the constituencies is certain. Their refusal to make *Sinn Fein* the vehicle of the struggle against the "Treaty" placed them under the necessity of establishing a new organisation. This was founded on 1st March and called *Cumann na Poblachta*. On St. Patrick's Day De Valera spoke at Thurles. The proclamation of the Army Convention was then known. But the tenor of his remarks implied no discouragement of the breach that appeared to be imminent. If the "Treaty" should be ratified, he said, "they would have to wade through Irish blood, through the blood of the soldiers of the Irish Government, and through perhaps the blood of some of the members of the Government, in order to get Irish Freedom". In Waterford he declared that once the "Treaty" was ratified "full freedom was only obtainable by civil war". He continued in this bellicose vein for some weeks. The explanation that suggests itself is that he was trying to use the army situation to frighten the "Treaty" party into a compromise. Later, when it was clear that this had not happened, he dismissed his own speeches as harmless, and blamed the army officers for their precipitancy, professing regret that he had not opposed them from the start.

On 22nd March Rory O'Connor gave his famous press conference at Suffolk Street.[1] It showed "much feeling but little art". A sympathetic listener would at once recognise the sound kernel of his case. The loyalty Griffith claimed from the army was not that which they had sworn. They had sworn loyalty to the Republic, not to the process by which Griffith was engaged in pulling it down. Mulcahy demanded obedience because the army was still the army of the Republic, but he himself acted on an entirely different principle. He was allowing officers and men to transfer to the paid forces of the Provisional Government. The Volunteers must now resume their independence, since they could give allegiance to none of the four governments now operating in Ireland. Did this betoken an attempt to establish a military dictatorship? "You can take it that way if you like," said O'Connor. His incautious remark was used by Mulcahy as a retrospective excuse for proclaiming the Convention.

The "banned convention", as it came to be known, opened at the Mansion House with 211 delegates present, representing about four-fifths of the total strength of the Volunteers. Liam Mellows took the chair and explained the purpose of the gathering.

While accounts of the proceedings do not agree in all particulars it is possible to obtain a fair picture of what took place. After the introductory statement Mellows invited nominations for the post of Convention chairman. The First Southern division favoured Liam Lynch, the second Sean Moylan. The First Southern mustered 54 out of the 211 delegates. Lynch was elected.[2] The first motion on the agenda legitimised the admission of representatives of *Na Fianna Eireann* and the Republican police. After a statement by Liam Lynch, Mellows

---

[1] D. Macardle, p. 205, says in the office of the *Cumann na Poblachta*. While this may be correct, it should be noted that the Military Council used an office in the same building.

[2] O'Donoghue gives the impression that Mellows presided throughout.

proposed, and Rory O'Connor seconded, the motion to reaffirm the resolution of 11th January. The vote was unanimous. The Volunteers were now pledged directly to the Republic, under an executive shortly to be elected. It was agreed that a new constitution should be submitted to a further convention on 9th April. The election of the executive was carried out in accordance with motions from the floor, subject to provisions for ensuring its all-Ireland composition. Mellows received 184 out of the possible 211 votes.

The official business completed, the proceedings were thrown open to delegates' resolutions. The first of these, proposed by Tom Barry, was subjected to somewhat one-sided examination in Beaslai's *Life of Collins*.[1] It urged the *declaration*[2] of a dictatorship with a view to *ordering*[2] the dissolution of all pretended governments in Ireland by *prohibition*[2] of Parliamentary elections until such time as they could be held without threat of war from Britain and on adult suffrage. The dictatorship *would*[2] overthrow the four governments in Ireland opposed to the Republic.

Beaslai's conclusion was that the Republican Volunteers wished to "inflict upon the people a military tyranny more drastic and more irresponsible than any inflicted by the British". But in support of his argument he broke the rules of chronology and cited disturbances which took place before the Convention. The drafting of Barry's resolution was crude. Its politics were inchoate. He was then a shock-headed youth bursting with the arrogance of physical well-being. But he expressed the will for survival of the power the "Treaty" party was subverting. Declaring, ordering, prohibiting are fine words if people can be got to obey. But how overthrow four governments? Only by erecting a fifth, a government of will and idea that would smite all rebels against the Republic.

But where was the Republic? In the *Dail*? Hibernating in the voluntary sedation of *Sinn Fein* unity? Or simply in the minds and feelings of those who had risked their lives for it and to whom it was still the overmastering political fact of Irish history? It was clearly undergoing a transference from the realm of actuality into the realm of sentiment. The Republic now virtually disestablished had relieved its armed citizens of the obligation not to defend it. The dual power had thus reappeared like a Phoenix from its own ashes, but this time somewhat the worse for the flames.

The difficulties facing the Volunteers were formidable, indeed insuperable. Connolly's warning had gone unheeded. The green flag

---

[1] Vol. II, p. 378.   [2] Author's italics.

had been raised above Dublin Castle by those to whom the Workers' Republic was anathema. So British imperialism still ruled. The capitalist class was in process of installation as the new garrison. But the petit-bourgeois politicians who were facilitating the process had disillusioned the working class with republicanism. The division between Treatyite and anti-Treatyite was the reflection of a more fundamental cleavage. Such was the substance, and so many saw it from abroad. Those nearest the point of decision were overwhelmed by the difficulty of formulating policy and securing agreement on it. While De Valera and his immediate associates explored the possibilities of making intermediate stands against the full operation of the London agreement, and Roderick Connolly and his colleagues worked on a programme for a further revolution, the men of the army executive seemed to have little left but their own sincerity. They were for the most part young and unaccustomed to policy making. Now that immanent reality seemed to have lost all intrinsic consistency, they adopted a temporising strategy, contradicted by acts of tactical offence. Their plight epitomised that of the Irish nation.

CHAPTER SIXTEEN

NO KING IN ISRAEL

"Man can do as he wills. But can he will as he wills?"—Artur Schopenhauer

"Tausch wollt ich, wollte keinen Raub."—Goethe

THE three months beginning with the banned Convention and ending with the outbreak of civil war present the historian with a spectacle of extraordinary complexity. Some have discovered in it the quality of a Shakespearean tragedy where the chief characters move steadily to doom as necessity reveals itself in the clash of wills. To understand the period it is essential to know what that necessity was. It was the superior strength of imperialism confronting a national revolution that had cut itself off from its mass base. In all that happened the prime mover of reaction in Ireland was the British Government. The reiterated determination not to tolerate a Republic in Ireland was the fundamental cause of the division amongst Irishmen. These were being urged unwillingly towards civil war, when quite modest concessions from Britain would have restored a working harmony. British imperialism was bent on stamping out the last spark of revolt. Its policy can only be explained as part of its world and particularly its European strategy.

The map printed opposite shows which divisions of the I.R.A. supported or opposed the "Treaty". When all necessary qualifications have been made the pattern revealed seems logical enough. In Ulster, divisions in the occupied area inclined to the Republic, in the evacuated area to the Provisional Government. In Southern and Western areas, with their land-hungry small farmers or large agricultural proletariat based on dairying, the tendency was Republican; in the midland ranching districts where, it is said, 500 acres can be managed by a man with a stick and a dog, it was towards the Provisional Government.

Dublin City presented a more complex picture. Oscar Traynor, the Commandant, and his assistant Sean Mooney were strongly for the Republic. About three-quarters of the Brigade staff followed them. Of the four territorial battalions, three, namely the first based on the

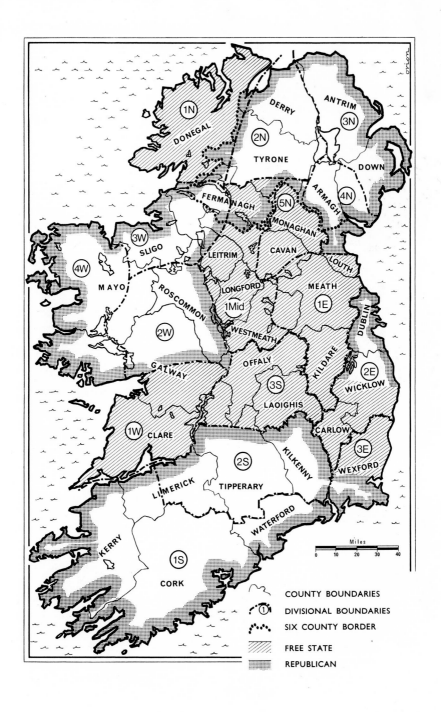

COUNTY BOUNDARIES
DIVISIONAL BOUNDARIES
SIX COUNTY BORDER

FREE STATE
REPUBLICAN

North-west quadrant, the third on the South-east and the fourth on the
South-west, were Republican. But the second, based on the North-east,
and including much strong working-class and Larkinite territory, was
for the Provisional Government. One reason was no doubt the attitude
of the Labour Party which failed to spring to the defence of the
Republic. Another was the popularity of its leader, Tom Ennis. Esti-
mates of rank and file opinion vary widely. To assume an equal
division would probably not be far out. But it is to be noted that no
strongpoint yielded by the imperial government was allowed into the
hands of the Dublin Volunteers. As the Provisional Government's
army was built up at Beggars Bush, pro-Treaty Volunteers transferred
to it. Consequently the Dublin Brigade later came to have an overwhelmingly Republican character.

The general pattern of distribution appears on the face of it to sub-
stantiate T. A. Jackson's thesis that the fundamental issue was partition,
the crucial point upon which Griffith had bungled the negotiations. It
may be observed that in 1921 Irish trade was in approximate balance.
The social element which could view with most equanimity the
severance of the industrial North from the agricultural South of Ireland,
was precisely that of the owners of large landed property and the
associated cattle trade.

It might appear superficially that the Republicans were well placed to
win an election. The largest town whose Volunteers were unmistakenly
pro-Treaty was Carlow. But of course the I.R.A. was one thing; the
mass of the people was another. The political campaign of the opponents of the "Treaty" had provided them with no convincing reason
for risking a fresh struggle with Britain. They saw the British go and
were thankful for that. The fact of external coercion ran through every
aspect of Irish life from the tenement to the big house, from Dublin
Castle to Fair Head or Caherciveen.

It is not always appreciated how constantly the British Colonial
Office intervened. An important example will serve as an introduction
to the examination of events as they unfolded themselves. By the end
of March it was clear that the attempt to operate Lloyd George's
scheme had led to inevitable crisis on the border. Churchill summoned representatives from both sides to a tripartite conference in
London. The Free State Agreement Bill was to go for the Royal Assent
on 31st March, and at midnight of that date the Provisional Government was to receive the unction of legitimacy and become responsible
for its own finances. Collins crossed on the 27th, Griffith, Duggan and
Kevin O'Higgins on the following day.

It was a week dizzy with events. The Volunteer Executive met several times, and established an Army Council of which Mellows became secretary. The new constitution was drafted and sent out with a circular to all units repudiating the control of Mulcahy and O'Duffy. The Belfast boycott was reimposed. O'Duffy over the same period suspended the "mutineers", replaced Mellows with Vize as Director of Purchases, released all Volunteers from the duty of obeying officers who supported the Executive, disclaimed responsibility for debts incurred by Republican units, and occupied some of Russell's munition shops in Dublin. There were clashes in the country and MacEoin with difficulty held the important town of Athlone. On 29th March, the *Upnor*, loaded with Haulbowline arms, was captured at sea and taken in to Ballycotton. And on the day the two General Staffs excommunicated each other the anti-Treaty deputies met, seemingly without Mellows, and offered to suspend their political campaign if the "Treaty" party would do likewise, in order to focus public attention on the six counties.

While Ireland was in an uproar the interchanges proceeded in London. After three days there issued the remarkable document which is sometimes given the inaccurate title of the "Craig-Collins agreement".[1] Its designation was "Heads of agreement between The Provisional Government and Government of Northern Ireland". "Peace is today declared," ran its first paragraph. So there had been war! But what kind of a peace is not clear. From Churchill's correspondence it is easy to see what he at least was working towards. It was a position where the regime in the twenty-six counties would actively encourage the Nationalists of the North to accept their station in life and co-operate with the Northern Ireland Government.

Nobody with knowledge of Ireland would have believed that such an agreement would or could be kept. Either it was inspired by Churchill or it was devised to deceive Churchill. In it the two governments undertook to co-operate from that day forward in restoring order in the "unsettled areas". Craig, Lord Londonderry and E. M. Archdale committed the Unionists to stricter control of police methods, and to the recruitment of Catholic Specials in "mixed" areas. Those whose houses were searched for arms would now be guaranteed a proportion of their co-religionists in the search-parties. A Special Court would be established for trial without jury, to which a person charged with a serious offence could be referred by the Attorney-General or (equity of equities!) at his own request. A committee

---

[1] This term is better applied to the agreement of 21st January.

composed of equal numbers of Catholics and Protestants would be established to investigate complaints of sectarian violence.

In return for these weighty assurances the four signatories of the Provisional Government undertook that I.R.A. activity would cease in the six counties. The two administrations undertook to facilitate the return to their homes of expelled persons. All three promised to release from custody prisoners who had committed political offences before 31st March, and there were appeals against inflammatory speeches.

Two important paragraphs specially involved the British Government on whose behalf the agreement was countersigned by Churchill and Worthington Evans. The first promised that the Westminster Parliament would be asked to vote £500,000 for relief work in the six counties. This must be expended on behalf of Catholics and Protestants in agreed proportions. The other has been offered as evidence that neither the British Government nor the six-county authorities really desired the partition they had worked so hard to effect. It provided that in the month immediately following the passage of the Act confirming the Constitution of the Free State, but before the Northern Ireland Parliament exercised its option of withdrawing from it, there would be a further tripartite conference with a view to ascertaining whether means could be devised to secure the unity of Ireland, and failing this, whether agreement on the boundary question could be reached without setting up the commission envisaged in Article XII of the London Agreement.

What had the Provisional Government gained? First there was the long-term principle that the Dublin administration still had a legitimate interest in the internal affairs of the six counties. This principle had a bearing on subsequent military developments. Second there was the precedent that the British Government might stipulate that any subsidies paid to Belfast should be distributed on a non-sectarian basis. The remainder was a series of promises, prospects and uncertainties. The cessation of I.R.A. activities in the North might have assisted the consolidation of the six-county regime, but it is doubtful if either side expected much from it. What then did the Provisional Government yield? It yielded the "most favourable interpretation" of the Treaty which Griffith had advertised when he returned from signing it.

The tripartite agreement was not signed two days when Specials, breaking into houses in Stanhope and Arnon Streets in Belfast, murdered an old man, a soldier home on leave, and a father and his two children aged thirteen and seven. The authorities flatly refused to hold an enquiry. Even if the Provisional Government had controlled the six county divisions, and had worked to muzzle the I.R.A. in the face of such provocation, it is plain that they would have been unable to do so. Inevitably there came the demand to send arms, even officers experienced in guerrilla warfare. A loose compliance with such requests became essential to Mulcahy if he was to retain his influence with the I.R.A.[1] Resistance in the North was linked to the Provisional Government through the 4th Northern Division which, though anti-Treaty in sentiment, preserved its connections with Beggars Bush. Its Commandant Frank Aiken instituted himself a kind of unofficial generalissimo for the six counties.

According to his notebook Mellows had agreed to speak in Galway on each of the first two Sundays in April. He remained in Dublin and indeed took no further part in the campaigns of *Cumann na Poblachta*. On 2nd April 3,200 out of the 3,600 members of the Dublin Brigade marched behind five bands to a demonstration at Smithfield. Three hundred *Fianna* boys joined them. The oath of allegiance to the Republic was administered afresh, by Mellows to the men of the Third battalion, by Traynor to those of the First.

On 4th April readers of the *Westminster Gazette* could study the Order in Council by which the British Crown had transferred eight major departments of State to the Provisional Government. Among other revealing items were the conditions under which the Irish people were to "decide freely" between the Free State and the Republic. The Free State Agreement Act stipulated that the general election should take place before 31st July. It also stipulated that the members then elected should constitute only a "Provisional Parliament" which was to have no power to elect or dismiss a Ministry until fresh British legislation conferred that power upon it. This it was proposed to do when the Free State Constitution was given legal effect. By these provisions the British Government had evolved safeguards not contained in Article XVII of the "Treaty" and Collins and Griffith could have repudiated them. During the course of the day of publication there was repudiation of its own kind in the South. Charles McGuinness sailed in the *Hannah* and landed his arms cargo at Ballynagowal, Helvick. Local Volunteers under Pax Whelan spirited away the rifles, some of which were held in places as far away as Birr, Co. Offaly.

[1] There are difficulties in nomenclature. But armies are best classified by their ultimate political control. Thus the "Free State Army", the "Staters", "*Dail* forces", etc., of the literature are here called "Provisional Government forces" until the Free State is established in December 1922. The words "Irish Republican Army" are now restricted to forces upholding the Republic. But the word "Volunteers" may occasionally be used for the diminishing number of unpaid soldiers on the Treaty side. Expressions like "irregulars" are merely contemporary insults not worthy of perpetuation.

The Second Army Convention met on 9th April in militant mood. There were further reports of minor clashes with Provisional Government troops throughout the country. Volunteers were transferring their allegiance to the Executive, while the Provisional Government was making good its losses by recruiting disbanded British soldiers from Irish regiments and former R.I.C. men. Among those to return to the I.R.A. between the conventions were some who did trojan service later, for example Joseph MacHenry and William Gannon.

The Constitution was voted on paragraph by paragraph and adopted with minor amendments. The names of the members of the new Executive that was elected were listed by Florence O'Donoghue in order of votes received.[1] They were: Liam Lynch, Liam Mellows, Rory O'Connor, Joseph McKelvey, Florence O'Donoghue, Sean Moylan, Sean O'Hegarty, Liam Deasy, Seamus Robinson, Ernest O'Malley, Peadar O'Donnell, Joseph O'Connor, Frank Barrett, Thomas Maguire, P. J. Rutledge, and Thomas Hales. As has been explained, the two Southern Divisions cast the most substantial body of votes, and it is significant that Mellows, O'Connor and McKelvey should precede eight of their nine representatives.

A resolution instructing the Executive to proclaim the forthcoming general election was passed by a small majority.[2] It was discussed at a meeting of the Executive on 11th April and a proclamation was drafted. The majority held the view that a general election on the issue of the "Treaty" was intolerable while the threat of war by British imperialism still hung over the country. But a minority of three, namely Sean O'Hegarty, Florence O'Donoghue and Thomas Hales, objected and offered their resignations from the Executive. To Mellows' great indignation they made a counter-proposal that the Executive should negotiate with the Provisional Government's forces with a view to army reunification on the assumption, as Sean O'Hegarty put it, that the Free State was inevitable. Mellows pointed out that they had been elected to the Executive with a mandate to uphold the Republic. But their resignations were not accepted. It was hoped that they would change their minds, and that further disunion would be avoided. They were able to prevent the issuing of the proclamation, however, by announcing that they would not obey it.

---

[1] *No Other Law*, p. 224.

[2] Dorothy Macardle (*Irish Republic*, p. 722) says it was rejected on the advice of Cathal Brugha, O'Donoghue that it was "referred to the Executive", O'Malley that it was passed at the Convention and discussed by the Executive, Mellows that it was discussed and adopted at the Executive. Whether Cathal Brugha was present is doubtful. He was that day addressing a meeting in Navan.

That day the Belfast shipyard workers reaped the reward of loyalty in the form of a wage reduction of 10s. 6d. a week with a further 6s. in prospect.

The appearance of a party of compromise within the Executive so soon after its establishment led some to think the three Cork men were little better than agents of the Provisional Government. But it would probably be wiser to trace their attitude to contemporary pressures. On the morning the Executive met, the newspapers carried the "anti-militarist" manifesto of the Labour Party. Labour was opposed to the consequences of the London agreement without possessing any understanding of their cause. Thus policy ran like quicksilver in all directions at once. The rural Trades Council of Laois was concerned at the drift to civil war and passed a resolution of alarm at De Valera's speech at Thurles. Possibly the feeling reflected in this resolution influenced the Third Southern Division which from being predominantly anti-Treaty passed over to support of the Provisional Government. In Waterford, on the other hand, the Trades Council demanded more militant action to halt the pogrom in the North, and protested against the ending of the Belfast boycott. The National Executive statement demanded that all armed forces should be responsible to the civil authority. But "there was no king in Israel, and every man did as he thought best". Which authority was the "civil" authority? The Irish people had not been consulted on the subject. Appeals for peace from the bourgeois side were fraught with the same uncertainty. The Archbishop of Dublin invited both wings of *Sinn Fein* to confer with him with a view to settling this vexed question. It was announced on 12th April that De Valera, Brugha, Collins, Griffith and Stephen O'Mara would meet him next day.

The Army Council did not wait for the result of these negotiations. At a meeting on the morning of 13th April it decided to order the seizure of buildings in Dublin for use as Volunteer headquarters. The main place selected was the Four Courts. This huge rambling building on the Liffey cannot have been chosen on military grounds. It is more likely that, since it was still a centre of British legal activity, to attack it was in accordance with the policy of challenging British imperialism but not the *Dail*.

Men were summoned hastily from Tipperary and arrived just before midnight on 13th April. On the stroke of twelve members of the Dublin brigade rounded up the police and sent them home. The Tipperary men were installed as a temporary garrison. They busied themselves piling sandbags and law reports in the window recesses.

Mellows and O'Malley strolled round the premises allocating offices to members of the staff. A few days later the Dublin brigade under Patrick O'Brien provided the garrison.

On the other hand the Army Council could not ignore the widespread demand for peace negotiations. It was felt that the precondition was a united army. The Executive therefore judged it wise to make plain the conditions on which this would be acceptable to them. A statement was drafted which Mellows addressed to the Secretary of *Dail Eireann* on 14th April, the conciliation conference having then been adjourned. There were six conditions:

1. To maintain the existing Republic.
2. That *Dail Eireann*, as the Government of the Republic, is the only government of the country.
3. To maintain the army[1] as the Irish Republican Army under the control of an elected independent Executive.
4. Disbanding of the Civic Guard, the policing of the country to be carried out by the Irish Republican Army, as decided by the Executive of that army.
5. All financial liabilities of the army to be discharged, and future requirements met by *An Dail*.
6. No elections on the issue at present before the country to be held while the threat of war with England exists.

How real that threat was had received further illustration two days previously when Churchill had declared, apropos of the "Republican coup", that an "independent Irish Republic the Government could neither agree to nor tolerate".

Mellows received no more than a formal acknowledgment from *Dail Eireann*, and at once a marked deterioration of relations between the two armies set in. In some cases the "Treaty" forces interfered with Volunteers enforcing the Belfast boycott. It became financially difficult to maintain the Republicans in barracks. Already in February, when the expenditure on the Volunteer section of the army had been sharply curtailed, officers had had recourse to raiding for funds. In certain areas dog license fees had been collected by the local Commandant. Now the practice was resumed on a wider scale in Galway and elsewhere. The result was opposition from "Treaty" forces under the slogan of "law and order". When on 14th April, without asking Headquarters' advice, Liam Pilkington proclaimed the meeting Griffith was to address in Sligo, he chose to raise the same cry. The meeting was likely to produce

[1] The army in this sense means the totality of military forces under the control of pro-Treaty and Republican authorities.

disorder. While Rory O'Connor, who looked after publicity for the Executive, professed agreement with this stand, in reality the Army Council were perturbed. They feared the setting of a precedent they could not maintain. Griffith went to Sligo. There was an ostentatious show of resistance, some harmless swashbuckling by General MacEoin, and a patched up peace. There was no deep bitterness on either side.

On 19th April, as British troops occupied the positions on Lough Swilly assigned them by the "Treaty", three separate meetings took place in Dublin. The first was the adjourned Archbishop's conference, which remained in deadlock and was further adjourned till the 26th. The only new factor was the appearance of a Labour deputation which urged that representatives of the Executive should be invited to the conference. The deputation visited the Four Courts and seems to have won a favourable response. Griffith and Collins, however, declined to sit in the same room as Mellows and O'Connor. Thomas Johnson recalled that relations between the "Treaty" and anti-Treaty parties were now characterised by "absolute distrust". The main issue of difference was the date of the election and "neither side had any faith in the honour or honesty of its opponents".

The second meeting was the last conference of the I.R.B. According to O'Donoghue,[1] it was attended not only by Lynch but by McKelvey. Collins argued that it might be possible to secure unity on the basis of the Constitution then being drafted. It would be available in four weeks' time. Lynch demanded, but did not receive, an assurance that the constitution would be a Republican one. A committee was elected which met at intervals over the next ten days but without result. Lynch and McKelvey presented arguments in favour of the Army Council's six points. They were rejected. Thus ended the last constructive effort of the I.R.B., which now for most practical purposes ceased to exist.

The third meeting was a conference of unpurchased tenants held at the Catholic Commercial Club at which it was decided to establish a Land League to press for the resumption of land purchase. Larkin's old lieutenant, O'Brien Hishon, was one of the leading figures, and Joseph Johnston delivered a lecture on agricultural co-operation. The under-privileged classes were beginning to organise themselves, in the absence of action by their former leaders. It may have been as a result of this conference that the Army Executive began to discuss an agrarian policy. Apart from this, Army Council meetings were dull frustrated gatherings, from which no useful line of action seemed ever to emerge.

On Sunday, 23rd April, *Na Fianna Eireann* held its convention. There

[1] *No Other Law*, p. 133.

were 187 delegates. Countess Markiewicz was re-elected President, and an *Aeriocht* followed at St. Enda's in the evening. Rory O'Connor and Mellows were guests of honour and Mellows made a brief speech in which he told of the early days of the organisation that seemed by now to have been founded in another world. There was a touch of nostalgia. He recalled that the *Fianna* knew nothing of politics or political methods. "They loved their country whole-heartedly and in Easter Week acted with sacrifice and heroism."

On 20th April the Labour Party Executive had issued its call for a general strike "against militarism". This was widely understood to mean against the Army Council. The date chosen was 24th April, sixth anniversary of the Rising of 1916. Cynics commented that the N.E.C. was absolving itself from commemorating Connolly or celebrating May Day. The Manifesto issued for the occasion was one of worthy sentiments in stumbling confusion. It demanded that the *Dail* should assert its sovereignty "over all other Councils or Governments in Ireland". This would be to reject the "Treaty" had the words been taken at their face value. But the legal fiction was being popularised that the Provisional Government was in some mysterious way acting not as the agent of the British Government but as the agent of the *Dail*. The great service Labour could have performed would have been to appeal to the British workers to insist on the withdrawal of Churchill's threats, so that the Irish people could compose any differences that had grown up among them without having to consider whether their agreement had foreign approval or not.[1] This they failed to do. Their reprobations were hurled at no definite target. The strike was thus a complete success that proved a complete failure, except perhaps in strengthening the public desire to avoid civil war. The Citizen Army, which had been called out over the heads of its own committee by O'Brien's "Workers' Army", withdrew from that organisation which ceased to exist.

[1] In January 1922, the *Labour Monthly* commented editorially, "The Lloyd George–Griffith Treaty, if it is ratified and put into effect, means the coalition of British and Irish capitalism against Labour. It does not mean the freeing of the nationalist stage for the Labour struggle. It means that the nationalist opposition will continue in the form of the irreconcilable republican followers of de Valera, the Government will be carried on by the Griffith-Collins group in friendly co-operation with British Imperialism, and the labour movement will be effectively paralysed between the two . . . the British workers will be blind indeed if they do not recognise it for the danger that it is to their own movement as much as to the working-class movement of Ireland." Such was the position taken up by the most advanced representatives of the British working class. There seems to have been lacking the means of translating this analysis into policy. The Irish Self-determination League divided on the "Treaty", and though the London organisation remained sound, it was hard for the mass of the British workers to evaluate the babel that ensued.

When the *Dail* met on 26th April Mellows had seen to it that every member had a copy of the Army Council's statement. Griffith opened the session with a bitter attack on the "lawless minority" and ventured the optimistic opinion that but for their activities the country would be enjoying full employment, and the Belfast pogrom, which had continued throughout April, would have been ended. De Valera made a reply which drew attention to the fact of British coercion, described the Provisional Government as a usurpation and accused the "Treaty" party of preparing a Free State army to enforce British policy in Ireland. He quoted the Labour manifesto against militarism with effect, though scarcely in the sense intended by its authors.

The resulting debate was the most acrimonious yet, and Griffith began to show a mental degeneration that may have had a pathological cause. When Sean MacSwiney ventured to raise a point of order he interjected that it was not a point of order, before he had heard it, and called the deputy a gunman. In his interchange with Erskine Childers he sank to the level of the gutter, describing him as "an Englishman who has spent his life in the Military Secret Service of England", something he knew to be untrue. When Childers objected, he accused him of incitement to murder and insolently addressed him as "Childers". The Speaker made no effort to afford protection.

It was a bizarre scene. The Dublin worker faced the Anglo-Irish aristocrat. But this Dublin worker had spent his life as the political ideologist of the capitalists. When their interests demanded the lowering of the national flag, he had lowered it on their behalf. He had gained nothing for himself and to that extent felt righteous within. But like Faust when Mephistopheles reduced to ashes the humble peasant's cottage he had coveted for his grandiose plan, he had come face to face with the real meaning of his actions. And the accusing voices of Philemon and Baucis were embodied in the suave protests of a man who had abandoned his career of privilege because he had learned some of the principles that Griffith had set aside. Thus imperialism makes swines of all who embrace it. Griffith knew in his heart that he had been cheated. He turned the venom of his remorse against the "damned Englishman". England had oppressed his country and persecuted his religion for hundreds of years. England had destroyed his own integrity as an Irishman. And now an Englishman, even if a hybrid Englishman, dared to stand before him as the custodian of what he had been robbed of. His outbursts were testimony to the fact of imperialist coercion which he sought to preserve his self-respect by denying.

The *Dail* discussed defence on 28th April. Most of the members would have read the indiscreet interchanges between O'Duffy and Lynch which had appeared in the press. In *An tOglach* of 22nd April, an article had been published over the name of Eoin O'Duffy, in which the 1st Southern Division was accused of inefficiency in the supply of men and arms to the Northern divisions. These must have been well aware that under the tripartite agreement the "Treaty" party had agreed to discontinue I.R.A. activity in the North. Why then try to blame the 1st Southern? Possibly the purpose was to divert blame for the failure to assist when the pogrom resumed. The *Irish Independent* reproduced O'Duffy's letter on 26th April. On the 27th Lynch replied. He gave particulars of arms, ammunition and men sent to Beggars Bush, and alleged that none of the material had been forwarded. The men had been accommodated for a week and then sent home. This may well have occurred as a direct result of the signing of the tripartite agreement.

Since then, of course, the agreement had been broken by the six county authorities and the question of action in the North seemed likely to arise again. It was not, however, discussed by the *Dail*, but remained beneath the surface of army relations. To the I.R.A. help for the North was an issue on which it might be possible to win unity for a joint struggle against British imperialism. To the "Treaty" forces it was on the one hand a legitimate reply to Craig's treachery, on the other a means of diverting the Republicans against another enemy.

Mellows' speech in the *Dail* reflected this interchange. He described Mulcahy's report as "characterised by sleight of hand". He objected to the building up of a mercenary army which was being superimposed on the Volunteers, thus destroying the "Volunteer spirit" of the people's army. He denied that it was as a result of the Convention that the Belfast pogrom had risen to fresh heights, pointing out correctly that it did so before the January agreement was signed. He confirmed that arms had been sent from the South of Ireland. He suspected that they were being held in Dublin to strengthen the "Treaty" forces against the Republicans.

Meanwhile the Army Council had worked out its agrarian policy, and on 1st May P. J. Ruttledge, "Director of Civil Administration", issued an order to divisions recognising the Executive. It instructed local commandants to seize certain lands and properties and hold them in trust for the Irish people. These included all lands in possession of the Congested Districts Board, all properties of absentee landlords and those who spent the greater part of their time abroad, and all but 100–200 acres and the mansion houses of landlords residing permanently in

Ireland. Exception was to be made in cases of landlords having favourable national records. In general, stock and implements should be taken over with the land. Every effort should be made to increase the number of workers employed pending sub-division. Divisional Land Courts were to be established, and cases of unjust seizure which were proved to the satisfaction of the Court, were to be followed by restitution. Two points should be noted. The I.R.A. was prepared to assume some of the features of a revolutionary government. And its land policy differed from that of the *Dail* in the following important respect. Under Griffith's plan the landlords kept the land until the Republic was consolidated, after which it might dispossess them. Under Ruttledge's the land went to the people now, and compensation awaited the victory of the revolution.

The publication of the revolutionary land policy was not, of course, followed by immediate action. It may well have encouraged the land seizures and cattle drives then proceeding in districts where there was land hunger. It would certainly have had electoral significance if adopted by *Cumann na Poblachta* in a campaign against the "Treaty" party. There was no reaction from P. J. Hogan's department of the Provisional Government and no desire on the part of the press to give it publicity.

On 1st May also the I.R.A. raided the branches of the Bank of Ireland and commandeered sums amounting to £44,073 to meet the needs of the Volunteers. This was used in part to pay debts to traders that had been repudiated by Mulcahy, for maintaining the headquarters, and possibly in part for arms purchases. Mellows had retained some thousands of pounds he had held in his capacity of Director of Purchases. It is perhaps to be doubted that these would have sufficed to pay Briscoe the £10,000 he received in May for the completion of what it was hoped would be the biggest German arms deal of all. The total purchase budget for 1922, apart from this item, does not seem to have exceeded £2,600. As will be seen, however, it would be mistaken to assume that such purchases were made with a view to civil war.

It was late on May Day night that the Army Council learned what some of the members of the Executive had been up to. On the preceding Friday Sean O'Hegarty, an exceptionally staunch I.R.B. man, had met Collins to discuss his conviction that the people were going to accept the "Treaty" whatever happened. The two men decided upon efforts to secure army unification on that basis, making use of the very natural reluctance of the Republicans to be led into civil war. The two men met again on Saturday, 29th April, this time with Mulcahy, and it was agreed to call a larger meeting composed of six officers from each camp. At no point was the Army Council consulted.

Apart from those named, the "Treaty" side comprised Eoin O'Duffy, Gearoid O'Sullivan and Sean Boylan, Commandant of the 1st Eastern Division. Those added on the Republican side were Florence O'Donoghue, Humphrey Murphy, Tom Hales and Dan Breen. The unequally matched teams met together on 1st May. The previous understanding was enlarged to include the holding of an agreed election which would retain the two wings of *Sinn Fein* in their existing proportionate strength, and elect a coalition government. At this point Collins discovered a sudden compunction for Labour. They must on no account be kept out. O'Hegarty agreed. A manifesto was drafted and sent to the press. It was from the evening papers that the Army Council first learned of it. They issued a reply which appeared alongside it next morning. The plan was described as a "political dodge". The three Cork men thereupon resigned from the Executive.

The *Dail* met again on 3rd May. It was Griffith who made the announcement that some officers who had recently been in conference wished to be heard as a deputation. The five "Republicans" entered accompanied by Sean Boylan, and the anti-Treaty O'Hegarty led the way in proposing peace on the basis of accepting the "Treaty". Dr. Hayes was enthusiastic and suggested that the *Dail* should set up a comparable committee which might be expected to arrive at a comparable result. Mellows denounced the proposal as a manœuvre. Only on the basis of acceptance of the Republic could unity be regained. He was supported by Daithi Ceannt and Sean Moylan who disclosed that he too had attended the meeting and was the only officer present who declined to sign the manifesto. Mellows later referred to these events as the "Mulcahy affair". It is clear that he had formed his own judgment of the origin of the intrigue.

The *Dail* decided to appoint its committee and adjourned for forty minutes while the parties elected their representatives. The "Treaty" party appointed Sean Hales, Patrick O'Malley, James O'Dwyer, Joseph McGuinness and Sean MacEoin. The opponents of the "Treaty" appointed Mrs. Tom Clarke, P. J. Ruttledge, Harry Boland, Sean Moylan and Liam Mellows. This time the Republicans had the stronger team.

There was some discussion of the possibility of securing a truce in the sporadic hostilities which were taking place between the two armies. There had been shootings in the midlands and some less sanguinary ructions at Kilkenny arising from interference with the Belfast boycott.

Seamus Robinson at Ballycullen was proposing to increase their scale, and threatened to cut off Kilkenny from Dublin, when Prout of the pro-Treaty forces occupied the city. Mulcahy protested to the *Dail* that all that he could do had been done. He had failed to influence the Republican side. Mellows replied that Mulcahy had declined to provide a basis on which a truce could endure. He favoured a truce. But he could not accept one on the terms of the officers' manifesto. It was Griffith who proposed that the Committee of Ten should be empowered to seek a truce along lines to be explored by themselves. So began the involved discussions which lasted until 20th May.

The Committee of Ten had its first meeting immediately after the adjournment. The question of the truce was taken first, and the principle of an immediate unconditional cessation of hostilities being found acceptable, Mellows and MacEoin were despatched to their respective garrisons to effect it. They brought together the Chiefs of Staff and after about three hours it was agreed to desist from all warlike acts until Monday, 8th May. Further discussions resulted in an indefinite armistice denunciable at forty-eight hours' notice on either side. Lynch's instructions were issued from the Four Courts on 6th May and provided for the general release of military prisoners, cessation of raids, including boycott raids for investigatory purposes, and the seizing of revenues. By 9th May, however, it was clear that the "Treaty" forces were using the truce for the purpose of suborning Republicans from their allegiance. Instructions were issued that those caught red-handed should be court martialled, but some sentence other than imprisonment should be imposed. At the same time the raiding of banks and the commandeering of motor cars, which had been forbidden to the Republicans, was taken up by criminal elements and *agents provocateurs*.[1]

The British were still evacuating. Installations in Cork had been handed to the 1st Southern Division of the I.R.A. The Curragh was taken over by the Provisional Government's troops. The "Treaty" party manœuvred desperately for an agreement on the basis of the "Treaty". But in London, Churchill was growing impatient. The Irish, he said, had hardly given due thought to the importance of holding an election on the issue of the "Treaty". On May 10th he uttered the piteous complaint that they showed a "general disinclination to kill one another".

While the Committee of Ten was meeting the Chiefs of Staff were once more discussing military action in the six counties. It would seem

---

[1] It may be added that sometimes students fired shots while passing Beggars Bush out of sheer high spirits. Much "provocation" had little more in it than this.

likely that contact was resumed following the recriminations at the end of April. The plan agreed upon was to launch retaliatory attacks on Crown forces throughout occupied Ulster. All five Northern Divisions and the first Midland were to participate. The signal for action was to be the capture of Musgrave Street police barracks in Belfast. The attack on the barracks was prepared with great care and took place on 17th May. Unfortunately some of the defenders were alerted, shots were fired and the attacking party was compelled to withdraw.

It was agreed that whether the barracks was captured or not an offensive in the country districts was to follow two days later. The 3rd Northern moved on the 19th. Among those who participated were Sean Murray and his unit in the Glens of Antrim. Raids across the border from Donegal took place. But the pro-Treaty forces had no heart for the affair and the offensive was allowed to peter out. It was sufficiently alarming, however, to render the six county authorities a little less confident in the pursuit of their religious war.

It is possible, of course, that Collins, Mulcahy and O'Duffy promised to support the Northern campaign only in order to ensnare a section of the Executive forces. But this would not be the inevitable conclusion. There was no doubt that Collins was genuinely concerned at the fate of his co-religionists in the North. It is more likely that the fear of social revolution on the Dublin side of the border paralysed pro-Treaty operations in the North.

Agrarian war flared up in Leitrim and Roscommon. On 12th May the South Leitrim Brigade of the 1st Midland Division issued a proclamation threatening severe penalties for those taking over lands without lawful authority. Pro-Treaty troops were reported to be protecting large grazing ranches near Boyle and Castlerea. In Gowal, Co. Leitrim, a branch of the Citizen Army had been established by Patrick Gralton. He had been arrested for participating in agrarian struggles and taken to Athlone. Following demonstrations of protest in the neighbourhood of Carrick-on-Shannon on 6th May he was released. But two others were arrested, including his chief lieutenant Gilroy. It was understandable that the 1st Midland Division could not send many men across the border.

In the south the most extensive factory seizures of the whole period took place on 13th May, once again led by Dowling, McGrath and Hedley. Messrs. Cleaves had threatened to close all their creameries unless the workers accepted a wage reduction of $33\frac{1}{3}$ per cent. Red flags were hoisted as the Soviets were declared at Carrick-on-Suir, Bansha, Clonmel, Kilmallock, Mallow, Knocklong, Bruree, Dromen,

Athlacca, Tankardstown, Ballingaddy and Aherlow. In 1920 the workers had enjoyed the support of the farmers. Now there were refusals to supply milk and resolutions were passed demanding that the Provisional Government should "govern or get out". There were thus strong reasons why the right and centre of the *Sinn Fein* alliance should seek some position of accommodation.

Prospects and difficulties were revealed when on 17th May the final conclusions of the Committee of Ten were laid before the *Dail*. There had been a failure to agree. Seamus O'Dwyer read the report of the pro-Treaty delegates, Harry Boland that of the Republicans. It was common ground that there should be an agreed election in the sense that *Sinn Fein* would contest as one unit though now admittedly composed of two parties. It was agreed that all other interests were free to offer candidates, but it was taken for granted that the result would be an overwhelming *Sinn Fein* majority. Following its election a coalition government was to be installed, which would call a further general election in the event of a breakdown in the alliance.

There was disagreement on the proportion in which the supporters and opponents of the "Treaty" were to be selected for the joint panel. The pro-Treaty delegates demanded 60 per cent of both candidates and ministerial posts. Their opponents made it a matter of principle that the existing proportions must be maintained. Their reason was explained by Mellows. Any change in proportions might be interpreted as showing approval of the "Treaty" whereas Clause One of Boland's draft agreement[1] ran "no issue is being determined by the election". The purpose was to conform under duress with the Free State Agreement Act, but to interpret this election in an Irish way, as had been done in 1918 and 1921. As Mellows put it in the debate that followed, "We are prepared to enter into a coalition, a coalition in which without detriment to principles we hold, we might be able to work side by side for the good of the country and—it is true—take everything that we could get and give England nothing. That was our position. To evade the Treaty. You are all anxious to evade the Treaty if you can and when you can. We are anxious to evade the Treaty and we will acknowledge it to the world."

As the debate proceeded the mood of conciliation that had been present in earlier sessions began to change. General MacEoin claimed that the terms of reference of the Committee of Ten included acceptance of the "Treaty". Mellows interrupted to remind him that both sides had agreed to confer without prejudice to their respective positions. If

[1] *Dail* Report, p. 412.

it was agreed that the "Treaty" should be evaded, there still remained for decision the basis of the evasion. Was the "Treaty" to be accepted and then evaded in the operation, or was there some way of evading the acceptance? Later in the bitterness of civil war Mellows seems to have looked back on the *Dail* negotiations as no more than a device of the "Treaty" party to disarm the Republicans in face of the critical issues of election and constitution. It may possibly have been so with Mulcahy, who admitted a little "finesse", but was not necessarily so with the "Treaty" negotiators. Indeed, the continuing strength of Republican sentiment was compelling members of the "Treaty" party to modify their strict stand on the letter of its terms. Consequently the *Dail* was given a new lease of life. The prospect was no longer its supersession by the Provisional Parliament, but its fusion or identification with that assembly.

De Valera repeated that his party would never "definitely" commit themselves to the "Treaty". Mary MacSwiney declared that the "Treaty" was already broken by the British action in the six counties. Cathal Brugha, whose intellectual resources had been taxed beyond their limit by the involuted sophistries in which he now thought he saw even Mellows ensnared, suggested that they cut the Gordian knot by declaring war on the North. Better to die by an Orange bullet than in fratricidal conflict with his old colleagues. He wanted nothing more to do with politics. Gavan Duffy argued that it was impossible to avoid an election fought on the issue of the "Treaty". Collins repeated the old argument that the "Treaty" only regularised an accomplished fact. There was applause when De Valera declared that the representatives of the Irish people were entitled to use any machinery set up by a pretended authority in the cause of stable government.

So for a time it became conciliation once more. By 18th May it was clear that the "Treaty" party, like the Republicans, had begun to differentiate. Griffith moved the holding of a general election on 16th June in a speech of unexampled acerbity. He spoke of an "insolent denial" to the Irish people of the right to accept or reject the "Treaty", apparently quite forgetting that he was a party to that denial. "I see no difference", he said, "between English Government in Ireland and the attempt of a minority to deny the Irish people the right of expressing their opinions." These, he suggested, were gentlemen "largely coming by birth and descent from the adjoining country". Many of them had spent their lives against the Irish people. He spoke of brigandage and robbery and the "destruction of our commercial life", and suggested that his opponents would bear the brand of Dermot MacMurrough through generations of Irish history. This extraordinary tirade justly attracted reproof from the Speaker.

The next contribution came from Kevin O'Higgins. He was anxious for a general election on the issue of the "Treaty". He thought that should civil war break out, it would not involve that issue at all. It would be for the sacred right of the Irish people to decide any issue small or great that arose in the politics of the country. A man who killed without a constitutional mandate from his people was a murderer. Hearing the quondam revolutionary mouth the demagogy of authority was too much for Mellows. He jumped to his feet and shouted "Easter Week". But O'Higgins continued in the same vein and publicly thanked the fate that had spared him the "oil and water" or "wolf and lamb" coalition.

Cathal Brugha reminded deputies that an election on a "Treaty" affecting thirty-two Irish counties was taking place in twenty-six only. It was illustrative of the ostrich-like powers of self-deception developed at the time that Patrick Hogan asserted that the thirty-two county Free State already existed, that the Provisional Government held administrative powers in the six counties and that the Council of Ireland clause of the 1920 Act would go into effect. Boland appealed to the *Dail* not to decree an election for twenty-six counties. But again the anti-Treaty party failed to present to the *Dail* an alternative line of action.

Mulcahy sought to mitigate the sharpness of Griffith's attack, and to Griffith's embarrassment it was decided to discuss the two alternative drafts presented by the Committee of Ten. It was then revealed that De Valera and Collins had been discussing their possible reconciliation. Presumably it was in the hope of forestalling this development that Griffith had made his bitter attack. It was suggested that a report be drawn up to show what points of disagreement still remained, and Collins and De Valera undertook to turn their attention to this matter.

A comparison of the drafts will show what was at stake. The pro-Treaty draft provided for

(a) An agreed election.
(b) Parties to be nominated in proportion five to three.
(c) Elections held on the one day throughout Ireland.
(d) Other interests free to contest.
(e) Government to consist of President and ten Ministers, six from the government side and four from the opposition.
(f) In the event of a dissolution a new election as soon as possible.

The anti-Treaty draft provided for

1. No issue determined by the election.
2. A National coalition panel to go forward.
3. Parties to be nominated in proportion to existing strength.
4. Parties to nominate candidates through executives at present established
5. Other interests free to contest.
6. Constituencies where no election held represented by present deputies.
7. Government to consist of President, Minister of Defence and nine others, five from the majority, four from the minority, each to choose its own nominees.
8. In the event of dissolution another election to be held.

The main differences were therefore on the following questions:

The issue to be determined by the election.
The proportion of each party to be nominated.
The proportion of each in Ministerial positions.
Provision for representation from constituencies in occupied Ulster.

Less than twenty-four hours later the *Dail* assembled once more. The Speaker read the terms of a "National Coalition Joint Statement". Agreement had been reached. Griffith then moved his resolution on the election "subject to the agreement".

It provided for

(I) A National coalition.
(II) Parties to be nominated according to existing strength.
(III) Candidates to be nominated through existing executives.
(IV) Other interests free to contest.
(V) Constituencies where no election held represented by existing deputies.
(VI) Government to consist of President, Minister of Defence and nine others, five from majority, four from minority and each to choose own nominees.
(VII) In the event of dissolution a new election as soon as possible.

Clearly the anti-Treaty party had given up its first stipulation, that no issue was determined by the election. But on the other hand it was not stated what issue, if any, was to be determined. In return the anti-Treaty party secured the remainder of its draft virtually unaltered, and the provision for constituencies in occupied Ulster clearly breached the Free State Agreement Act and the provision in the "Treaty" by which the power of the Irish Free State was not exercisable in the six

L

counties until they had been given an opportunity to withdraw from it.

What then had happened behind the scenes? More than has ever been disclosed, beyond a doubt. Newspaper reporters noted that Collins and De Valera were joined by Mulcahy, Boland and Sean T. O'Kelly. From 3 p.m., when the deputies began to arrive, the anti-Treaty party sat in the chamber while Griffith and the Cabinet deliberated among themselves. It is a reasonable speculation that Collins convinced De Valera that the Constitution that was to be submitted to Westminster within a few days was as near Republican as was possible in the "Treaty" framework. The pact could then be drawn up on Boland's draft. The first paragraph became unnecessary, as the election was to be based not on the "Treaty" but on the new constitution. The question now was whether the British Government would accept the constitution and allow Irishmen to live together in peace.

The *Dail* rose before 6 p.m. A few hours later Mellows took part in a curious episode which it is natural to connect with developments in Ulster, but which may have been for him merely a holiday. Into the Woods family's touring car with its specially fitted engine eight people were packed for a journey to County Sligo. Mellows was at the wheel. With him were Mrs. Woods, Rory O'Connor, Sean Russell, George Plunkett and his brother, and Captain Charles McGuinness. A cousin of Mrs. Woods, a Sergeant Flannery of the R.I.C., was invited at the last moment, and was crammed into the boot. He had retained his rank and safety in County Tipperary by acting on the principle that while God is undoubtedly good the devil is not so bad either. It was to his mother's house in Clooncunny that the party was going. The sergeant was in plain clothes in anticipation of early retirement.

They left Dublin at dusk. Mellows drove fast. But it was 2 a.m. before they reached their destination. The townland of Clooncunny straddles a steep-sided isthmus between what are really two wings of Lough Gara. O'Connor, who was slightly asthmatic, remarked on the proximity of water though he could not see it. The family expected them and the whole party sat up talking and listening to Mrs. Woods' ghost stories. The Flannery family spoke of an old fort on their land known locally as the *Caltra*.[1] It was reputed to be haunted. Nobody would willingly pass it at night, and those who had done so unwittingly had remarked a curious phosphorescence. Mrs. Woods was for paying a visit at once. The others demurred. When she said she was determined to go Mellows got up to go with her and Sean Russell then accompanied them. They found a circular rampart about thirty yards in

[1] Pre-Christian burial ground, Modern Irish uses a Latin word.

diameter and some three feet high. Within it the grass reflected the early morning light with unusual greenness.

The landscape stirred the imagination. Miles of dark red bogland broken only by the scattered hills of the Curlew range stretched into the distance. Below on each side was a large sheet of water tongued by innumerable promontories, that to the north silver grey, that to the south dark as the bogs beyond it. The earthwork seemed to be the remains of a substantial fortification which commanded the one strip of passable terrain between east and west. The mind was driven back to the semi-mythical battle of Mag Tuired, fought on a larger isthmus less than ten miles to the north-east, after which the *Fir Bolg* retreated into Connacht and the fate of the most ancient Ireland was sealed. Mellows was deeply impressed and made a note that he must find out more about the *Caltra*.

Scarcely had they returned to the cottage when a car arrived from Sligo, and took away McGuinness, Russell and the two Plunketts. There was little sleep for the others, however. Mellows was pre-occupied, tightlipped and tense. O'Connor was edgy and unwell. When Patrick Flannery disturbed him while seeking a collar to wear at Mass, he awoke with a start and reached for his revolver. The day was spent by the lake. Mellows set up a target and lent Sergeant Flannery his Webley to display his uncanny prowess as a shot. The sergeant also contrived a brief visit to Boyle barracks, assuring those present that nothing unusual was happening—just Tom Flannery home for a holiday. Once again the car from Sligo arrived in the small hours, and Mrs. Woods plied Mellows with caffeine tablets as they drove back to Dublin.

CHAPTER SEVENTEEN

LAST HOPE OF FREEDOM

URING the final month of the revolutionary power all the contradictions besetting it appeared magnified to grotesque proportions. The components of the disintegrating petit-bourgeois alliance showed a last brief burst of energy like flies in St. Martin's Summer. There were short-lived motions of renegotiating the "Treaty" in London. The joint election campaign brought estranged friends together. But their efforts rapidly took the form of a joint struggle against Labour. Army reunification was attempted in the midst of preparations for a crusade in Ulster. But scarcely was it under way when its driving force seemed suddenly withdrawn from it. At the same time every discontent reached the boiling point of violence. The inescapable choice showed plainer every day. Either the Irish nation united in defiance of imperialist dictation, in which case the war on the common people must be called off, or one part of the nation must borrow England's power to crush the remainder. Either alternative had its dangers. It is a fierce indictment of Lloyd George and his Tory friends that such a dilemma should have been presented.

On 22nd May Churchill invited the signatories of the London Agreement to Westminster. His object was to question the compatibility of the pact with the "Treaty". Next day the Irish Labour Party announced its intention of opposing panel candidates. It had not been consulted upon either pact or constitution, nor the possibility of defending them against British aggression. The *Sinn Fein Ard Fheis*, recalled on 23rd May, approved the pact with only one dissentient and complete unconcern for the sensitivities of Labour. The Communist Party of Ireland denounced the pact, claiming that it tied De Valera to Collins as Collins was tied to the Empire. At the other extreme Darrell Figgis, forgetting his *Sinn Fein* discipline, issued a public appeal to businessmen to offer their own candidates. On 25th May, a Farmers Party was founded, its main plank law and order. Clearly only some spectacular success across the water could save the proposed coalition.

Griffith and Duggan left for London on the night of the 25th.

Collins followed next day. They took with them an account of the new pitch of terror reached in Belfast, and a constitution which applied literally the agreed principle that Ireland's national rights were equal to those of Canada. On 23rd May the six-county administration had declared illegal the I.R.A., the I.R.B., *Na Fianna Eireann* and *Cumann na mBan*. A Bill was announced under which troops and special constabulary would be indemnified against the consequences of illegal acts performed in the course of their duties. In a series of lightning raids 202 arrests were made in one night. Collins no doubt hoped that under persuasion to alleviate the pressure of reaction in the North, Lloyd George would make concessions which would secure him at least the benevolent neutrality of all but the most irreconcilable Republicans.

The meeting of "Treaty" signatories took place on 28th May. The British pressed the issues of pact and constitution which they alleged broke the letter of the agreement. The Irish assured them that there was no intention to do any such thing. Collins was able to point to the proclamation issued in that morning's *Dublin Gazette* in which he had summoned the "Provisional Parliament pursuant to the Free State (Agreement) Act" and the Governor General's calling of the Provisional Parliament in accordance with Section II of the Government of Ireland Act 1920. The British delegates were visibly mollified. Griffith then pressed for the declaration of martial law in the six counties and a public enquiry into Orange atrocities.

Meanwhile in Dublin a joint Army Council had been set up, consisting of Mulcahy, O'Duffy, O'Sullivan and MacMahon on the "Treaty" side, and Lynch, O'Connor, Moylan and Mellows on the other. The Council nominally controlled the entire armed forces of the country. But the separate commands at Beggars Bush and the Four Courts were maintained. The inaugural meeting probably took place on 25th May, for on the morrow Lynch sent out orders showing marked changes of policy. There was an instruction for dealing with persons charged with "unsoldierly conduct" in "either section of the army". There was an instruction to "help and facilitate" the government in its land policy by providing lists of ranches that might be acquired for division among landless men. Meanwhile land, stock and property seized from loyalists in reprisal for Belfast atrocities must be returned. Every effort should be made to prevent "agrarian crime". Volunteers must not take part in the land agitation, and the functioning of "British" Courts was not to be interfered with. Here was a complete programme of collaboration with the Provisional Government.

It may be wondered whether these concessions attracted any *quid pro quo*. Both Mellows and O'Malley recorded exasperation at Lynch's propensity for compromise with the "Treaty" party. Mellows noted his willingness to bring the former Executive member O'Donoghue back into prominence. O'Malley criticised his refusal to permit the establishment of an operations department that would plan the defence of the Four Courts. At the same time it is clear that Mellows also believed in the possibility of reconciliation. In his notebook is the record of his conversation with a deaf-mute injured in a road accident whom he visited in hospital. "Republicans and Free State now one" appears in Mellows' hand.

It is tempting to seek the explanation in the columns of the newspapers of 28th May, which reported the massing of Republican forces on the border, 500 at Ballyconnel, 200 at Blacklion, near Cavan, with a substantial reserve at Dromahaire, Co. Leitrim. Incidents were reported at Jonesborough on the border of Louth and Armagh, and between Donegal and Tyrone. The invasion of Derry was stated to be imminent. So seriously was the situation taken that Churchill announced that naval vessels including a destroyer had been despatched to Irish waters, and these duly arrived at Lough Foyle to repel the expected attack.

All this had to be faced by Griffith and Collins when they met Churchill on the morning of the Commons debate on Ireland on 31st May. They assured the Colonial Secretary that no Provisional Government forces were involved. Churchill insisted on further discussions, and the meeting of the *Dail* was postponed from 2nd June to 8th June. There seems to be no evidence that "Treaty" forces were sent north, although "Treaty" Volunteers within the six counties were undoubtedly involved. There was substantial recruitment of Volunteers for a projected northern campaign, no less than 166 men from the Limerick City Battalion handing in their names for such duty. There were also recruits from the 4th Western Division. On Whit Saturday, 3rd June, the joint Army Council held a special meeting attended by pro-Treaty officers from the six counties. Of this meeting Mellows wrote that he disagreed with Mulcahy's Ulster policy, while Lynch supported it. From this it may be guessed that the decision was to employ only Republican forces on the border,[1] thus allowing the Provisional Government to extricate itself at any time.

---

[1] Mr. Calton Younger offers the evidence on hearsay that "local inhabitants" in the vicinity of Belleek stated that they had seen "no Free State men" among the 200 Republicans gathered in the area. They would, however, not necessarily recognise possible Volunteers from distant pro-Treaty units.

Similar considerations applied to the question of arms. Those supplied to the Provisional Government by the British authorities were identifiable and likely to cause embarrassment if captured. Arms captured from the *Upnor* and from other sources were brought to Dublin and taken to Beggars Bush for exchange. Both 1st and 2nd Southern Divisions were involved, the reception accorded the anti-Treaty men depending largely on what was believed to be the state of the negotiations at the time. Thus when Seamus Robinson and Michael Sheehan took 200 rifles from Tipperary to Beggars Bush there were objections to issuing weapons in exchange. Robinson told Sean MacMahon that he would not leave the premises without them. MacMahon, a kindly man, not of strident personality, ordered that they should be issued. The Tipperary men then examined every gun for defects, though what they handed in had been far from perfect. Robinson afterwards held that the whole exercise was an elaborate pretence designed to conceal the true intentions of the "Treaty" party. It could equally be regarded as part of a policy aimed at compelling British intervention against Unionist excesses without resuming the national struggle.

Of the meeting of 3rd June Mellows recorded his impression that Mulcahy was trying to push decisions on army reunification in the absence of Rory O'Connor and the presence of pro-Treaty officers not directly involved. It was also the beginning of the rift between Lynch and Moylan on the one side and Mellows and O'Connor on the other. It appears that the meeting discussed and approved Moylan's "preliminary memorandum", the eleventh paragraph of which dealt with the army in Ulster. This paragraph provided for efforts to recruit Volunteers in "disturbed districts" where there was no organisation, and to bring them into barracks in the twenty-six counties for training. "These elements that make for disorder," the memorandum concluded, "might if properly trained and handled develop into first class Volunteers." The preoccupation was not with revolution but with order.

While the army reunification talks were proceeding Mellows had other trouble: his arms organisation in England had been thrown into confusion by arrests following an unsuccessful raid on a factory at Hay Mills in Birmingham. Among those arrested were twelve Irishmen and one English Communist prominent at open-air meetings in the Bull Ring, a forum where from time to time the police sought to encourage industry by breaking the heads of the unemployed. There were arrests in widely separated parts of England. The arrests took place on 29th April, the only man to escape being Patrick Daly who returned to his lodging in Liverpool after the police had left it. The charges involved conspiracy to subvert the Provisional Government. The defence made much of the circumstance that the person allegedly conspired with, Liam Mellows, was prominent in public life within the jurisdiction of the said Provisional Government. Eleven men were charged, including Seamus Cunningham of Donegal, and the case continued till 26th May. At that point it was adjourned. Nine men thereupon returned to Ireland, on bail of £100 each. Their appearance was the signal for a military enquiry at the Four Courts. A leading republican solicitor Sean O'hUadhaigh took the chair. Efforts were made to discover how the British authorities had uncovered so much of the republican secret organisation. Efforts were made to blame Mellows who had entrusted a message to a holiday-making schoolmaster who, while honest enough, was no adept at conspiracy. He explained that the forces available to him consisted at all times of "a miscellaneous collection of individuals—members of Volunteer companies, I.R.B. and others. The Director of Purchases had no direct authority over them. Consequently there was always trouble through conflicting orders." The raids and other operations in England had seriously hampered his efforts to obtain arms.

On Sunday, 4th June, while Griffith and Collins were busy making the alterations which the British Government had insisted upon in the draft Free State Constitution, the war on the border reached its pinnacle. A fierce battle was fought near Pettigo. British troops were brought into action, and reinforcements brought to Derry. There was intense firing between Strabane and Lifford, and the Commandant of the Derry Specials declared a blockade of County Donegal. Clones in County Monaghan was packed with people unable to cross the border to their homes in County Fermanagh. The British captured Belleek on 7th June, and proposed a three mile neutral zone which their officers were given to understand that they were to occupy.

Griffith and Kevin O'Higgins took back the revised constitution on 6th June, and army reunification talks were in fresh difficulties on the 7th. There had been an understanding that, since Griffith was likely to be President, the Minister for Defence would belong to the anti-Treaty party. It was agreed unanimously to put forward the name of De Valera. This proposal was rejected by Collins. The anti-Treaty party therefore sought the post of Chief of Staff and proposed Lynch. Mulcahy objected that Lynch would be unacceptable to the British and suggested Eoin O'Duffy. It was on the 9th that the final proposals were presented. The six principal staff appointments were to be held by O'Duffy, Lynch (deputy Chief of Staff for reorganisation), Liam Deasy (deputy Chief of Staff in charge of training), Florence O'Donoghue (Adjutant-General), Sean MacMahon (Quartermaster-General) and Gearoid O'Sullivan (Director of Intelligence). The Army Council was to consist of Mulcahy, Eoin O'Duffy, O'Sullivan, Lynch, Moylan, O'Connor, Mellows and O'Donoghue. This arrangement was recommended by Lynch and half-heartedly supported by Moylan. The great majority of the Executive found it unacceptable and O'Malley communicated this fact to Mulcahy on the 10th.

The direction in which other matters were tending was revealed at the election meeting in the Mansion House on the 9th. Griffith was at the Colonial Office being squeezed for fresh concessions. The *Dail* had met and to Cathal Brugha's gallant defence of Erskine Childers, Collins had replied with sulky obstinacy while De Valera had urged that Griffith's slanders could now well be forgotten. The meeting was addressed by De Valera, Mulcahy, Boland, Stack, Mrs. Tom Clarke and Collins. Collins' contribution was an undertaking that the new coalition government would "put down brigandage, protect life and property, and enforce payment of taxes". He defined brigandage as "seizures of factories and the red flag". Next evening De Valera spoke at Mallow in the same vein. The purpose of the pact, he said, was to restore power to a central authority, and the two sides had come together on the basis of "law and public order". On the very next day when members of the Transport Union put pickets on shops in Clonmel that refused to sell butter manufactured at the Soviet creameries, anti-Treaty Volunteers arrived 200 strong and threatened to fire if the pickets did not disperse. They declined to disperse. Blank shots were fired, without effect, and having thus disgraced themselves the troops returned to barracks.

Next day Michael Collins left for London for the last stage of the negotiations. It was now clear that Lloyd George was insisting on a constitution that would make the pact meaningless. Mulcahy sent O'Malley a note which retreated from the proposals of the 9th, claiming that the appointments already agreed upon were merely illustrative speculations upon what might be decided by the coalition government to which the whole question must now be referred. His communication arrived on 13th June. On that day unemployed workers seized Greenmount Mills, then in liquidation in Dublin, and announced the formation of a co-operative society to continue the business.

Counsels of desperation now came from the North where the pogrom continued unabated. On 12th June a proposal was submitted that 1,000 men should be drafted into Belfast for the purpose of burning the city to the ground. It is unlikely that this suggestion ever reached the Four Courts. But undoubtedly plans were made, and were communicated to the Belfast brigade through an officer of the 4th Northern Division. The folly was averted through the intervention of ecclesiastical authority which by good fortune became aware of the danger. Those with a nose for origins might care to note how terrorism was adopted when the action of the masses was rejected, and wonder how far Collins was implicated in the proposed incendiarism.

In the last days of the election campaign the basis of the pact had already been undermined in London. Collins met Churchill at the Colonial Office on 13th June. The conference was attended by representatives of the Southern Unionists. The meeting over, he left at once for Cork. There without warning he repudiated the pact and invited the electorate to vote for the "Treaty" candidates. Mellows had left for Galway when deadlock was reached. He undertook a little canvassing and addressed one meeting, at Ballinasloe. He did not appear intensely interested in the campaign. It had been noticed that he appeared to be brooding. Late at night he used to drive out to Bray and lean over the railings of the deserted promenade watching the waves. He would take friends with him but say little to them.

He made his speech at Ballinasloe at a pact meeting on the eve of poll. He spoke in favour of breaking up the ranches and compensating the owners, but condemned any seizure of land as a religious reprisal. There had been instances of this in the neighbourhood.[1] Mellows showed characteristic courage, if not of the vote-catching kind, in making his statement at this time. He told the meeting that he preferred a Protestant who believed in the Freedom of Ireland to a Catholic who did not. The fight would go on until complete independence was achieved.

One of the few Republican candidates who had learned at last the need for a social policy was Harry Boland. In Roscommon he spoke of solving the pressing problems of land settlement, housing and unemployment. Unlike Mellows, he was enthusiastic about the pact. He undertook on behalf of his colleagues to help the "Treaty" party "make

[1] Younger refers to a letter addressed to Mellows by Colonel Maurice Moore around 9th May, complaining of such actions in Mayo. Moore informed Mulcahy that Mellows had not replied. There is, however, reference to the incident involving a Mayo family named Brown in Mellows' notebook. The incident was outside his constituency, but there is no reason to believe that he failed to pass the complaint on.

every ounce they could out of the 'Treaty' position". But the "Treaty" itself must not come before the people for judgment until a later date. It must first pass the Lords; its financial terms must be settled; the boundary commission must have reported and the six counties have finally decided whether to "remain" part of the Free State. In the meantime the Third *Dail* would devise some means by which the "Treaty" would not come up for decision at all. All this was, of course, sheer fantasy. What was to happen at the end of it all if the people decided to reject the "Treaty?" Its basic terms would have been put into effect. Not only a general election was to be "deemed" other than it in effect was, but a whole chain of constitutional developments. The people would awake in handcuffs.

The Labour Party eagerly seized on Boland's references to social policy and advertised prominently in the newspapers its claim to have the answer to what Boland had posed as questions. Its programme was that the people should be allowed to decide the form of government under which they should live, and should exercise sovereignty not only over persons, but over property. The army should be the servant of the civil power. All willing to work should be guaranteed employment at a living wage. There were to be reductions of taxation on food and tobacco. Compulsory tillage should be enforced to the extent of 20 per cent of agricultural land. A national housing authority should be established and maintained by state funds. The railways and canals were to be nationalised, a national banking system set up to assist Irish industry. And all widows and orphans of the Anglo-Irish war were to be supported by the state. The Republicans could not compete with this. The working class looked for social reform. The bourgeoisie busied itself with affairs of state. The petit-bourgeois Republicans were left with nothing but the tissue of illusion in which they had wrapped everything when they faced the electors on 15th June.

The Constitution was not published until the morning of the poll, and many electors voted without having seen it. It struck anger and consternation into the spirits of the Republicans. Lloyd George had succeeded in imposing the harshest possible interpretation of the London Agreement. He set the Irishmen the task of liquidating their revolution. In vain Griffith and Collins had repeated the manoeuvres of last year. The ground had been worked over before. They failed to bring about a break on partition. They feared to break on the question of sovereignty. They feared imperialism, and they feared the people. But they had decided that they feared imperialism less.

The Constitution was made subordinate to the "Treaty" and

inoperative in any respect in which it contravened it. An obligatory oath of allegiance to the English crown was imposed on every member of the legislature as a condition of taking his seat. The representative of the Crown had the power to summon and dissolve parliaments, appoint all judges, and impose a veto on legislation of which he disapproved. Citizens of the Free State could appeal from its highest judicial authority to the English Privy Council. The *Sunday Times* commented, "the English victory is complete".

Republicans rightly complained of the obsolete electoral register and of the late publication of the Constitution. But whether the latter contributed much to their discomfiture is doubtful. It is argued that few electors had the opportunity for more than a glance at the document on which their democracy was in future to be based. While that is true, what is questionable is that careful study would have led them to place their trust in the anti-Treaty party which had manifestly lost the day and appeared to have been led by the nose into a bad bargain. The fact that the Constitution was in conformity with the "Treaty" must have been generally known. The Republicans had placed themselves in the classical position of a centrist party that gives hostages to its reactionary opponents.

The election was held on the basis of the single transferable vote. Eight days elapsed before the full results were available. They were days of disillusionment, sadness and menace. On 14th June the Executive met to discuss Mulcahy's note. With Lynch, Deasy and Moylan in resolute disagreement a resolution was passed to the effect that unification negotiations must cease at once. Tom Barry had successfully urged that the issue should be discussed by a convention. Accordingly the "extraordinary convention", summoned in great haste, met at the Mansion House on 18th June.

The Army Council had sat up half the night in wearisome quest of a policy. Only two possibilities presented themselves; the first to attack the British forces remaining in Dublin and thus provoke a struggle in which the national forces would be reunited; and the second to launch a further attack across the border with the same object. In the morning the documents for the convention could not be found, and not until shortly before it opened at 11 o'clock were they discovered as a result of frantic searches.

There was difficulty in finding a chairman. One after another those who were invited declined. Finally Joe O'Connor of Cork City consented to serve. Liam Mellows opened the discussion. In somewhat dispirited fashion he described the genesis of the split in the Executive, which threatened the I.R.A. with the secession of its largest division. It was felt that the proposals of Lynch would hand over the control of the army to the Free State and reduce the Volunteers to the status of territorials. The midnight council had decided that before Lynch could move the acceptance of Mulcahy's proposal, Tom Barry should put the proposition that the I.R.A. issue an ultimatum to British troops to evacuate Ireland within 72 hours or face immediate attack. He offered no argument in favour of this course, which was discussed until eight in the evening.

The British troops were, of course, confined to Dublin, Lough Swilly and the six counties. They were shortly to be established at Berehaven. There was an air of unreality in these proposals which was very apparent to the countrymen. More fundamental, however, was the social division now appearing between proletarian Dublin and the agrarian South. A further stage had been reached in the disintegration of the alliance of 1917. The stage was being set for the bourgeoisie to assert a supremacy it need share with nobody.

Barry's resolution was carried by a tiny majority. The voting rights of some delegates were then challenged. The challenge being upheld, a second vote produced a similar indecisive majority against. The next item on the agenda was Lynch's proposal to work the now uncertain agreement with Mulcahy. Rory O'Connor declared that if such a proposition was even discussed at the conference he would leave it at once. When after further wrangling it was agreed to deal with it, the supporters of Barry's resolution rose from their seats and walked out.

In the excitement Mellows left his hat behind. He stopped at the door, suddenly struck by the folly and sterility of what was happening. After a brief consultation with O'Connor and McKelvey he sent a young officer into the room to recover the hat and take the opportunity to announce a second convention next morning at the Four Courts. Brugha was speaking. He was opposed to both resolutions and urged reconciliation on the basis of the unity of all forces in support of the Republic. There was dead silence when the announcement was made, but a few more left. Those like Ernest O'Malley who remained to the end had difficulty in getting back into the Four Courts. Lynch and his supporters were firmly excluded. There was great satisfaction in the ranks of the "Treaty" party. What Lloyd George had done to them, they had done to their opponents. At the conference at the Four Courts, Joseph McKelvey was elected Chief of Staff in place of Liam Lynch.

During the next days of agrarian struggles and election results, the

Republicans were disorganised and powerless. Neither Lynch's nor Barry's resolution could be put into effect. The men in the Four Courts turned to the only alternative left open—the attack on the British in the six counties. Reinforcements were despatched to Donegal. Tuesday, 20th June, was the anniversary of the birth of Wolfe Tone, and on this occasion, instead of awaiting the traditional ceremony on the Sunday following, the Four Courts garrison went out to Bodenstown in military transport vehicles. There was something symbolic in this deliberate isolation of the revolutionary army.

Mellows delivered the oration. It was on this occasion that the famous photograph was taken, showing an expression of grimness and pain. In his speech he replied to the talk then current that the Republican movement was now dead. Certain people had taken the road of expediency and had descended to hypocrisy to achieve their object, but the Republicans would not deviate from the straight road. It was regrettable that their people had yielded to the threat of England, but Republicanism would go on in spite of what had happened. . . . So long as the Declaration of Independence stood, the Republic existed, and they would allow nobody to subvert it. It could not be made too clear that their only enemy was England. Let it not be thought that they were out to fight any other enemy. Though the outlook was black and the odds against them heavy, they would continue the struggle, believing that their cause was just.

That evening there was a sad little concert in the Four Courts. Mellows sang in his inimitable traditional manner,[1] and O'Malley strove hard to control the amusement of the countrymen when Countess Markiewicz recited patriotic poems in her exquisite Ascendancy voice.

On that same day the Executive Committee of the Communist International published its "message to the workers of Ireland" in the English-language edition of *International Press Correspondence*, and it is of interest to note its estimate of the situation.

After prolonged peace negotiations English imperialism is again preparing to coerce the Irish people by force of arms. After all the efforts of the English bourgeoisie to maintain its domination by force of arms had been frustrated by the heroic self-sacrificing defence of the Irish people, it was obliged to come to an understanding with the Irish bourgeoisie. For the semblance of an independent Irish Free State, the representatives of Irish capitalists, Collins, Griffith

[1] For those familiar with the style it will be evoked by the verse, "Come all you brave UNI-ited men."

and Co., sacrificed the friends of the long and successful struggle and received in return the right to exploit the Irish workers together with the English bourgeoisie.

It sympathised with Republican fears of further betrayals, and stigmatised the leaders of Labour as men whose good understanding was vitiated by opportunism. It accused the I.R.A. of deluding itself with phrases. With excusable partiality it handed the future to the young "Communist Party of Ireland".

An important extension of the message was an appeal to the workers of England to perform their duty in frustrating the fresh predatory campaign their rulers were about to launch.

At 2.30 p.m. on 22nd June Sir Henry Wilson, Military Adviser to the six-county administration, was shot dead on the steps of his house in fashionable Belgravia. His assailants were two London Irish Volunteers of pro-Treaty sympathies, Reginald Dunne and Joseph O'Sullivan. They were, needless to say, not the savage desperadoes of the skilfully posed newspaper pictures. This was shown by Dunne's careful choice of the music to be played at the Mass that followed his execution. The blatant prejudice of the judge was a matter of public comment. But the English ruling class is at its ugliest when frightened. Under such circumstances it never forgave anybody its policy had wronged.

There has been endless speculation upon the origin and purpose of the killing. The two Volunteers were acting upon military orders and all roads seem to lead to Collins. A statement recorded in Mr. Rex Taylor's book[1] indicates that the order was conveyed through the Intelligence department of the Volunteers, which Collins still controlled, around 8th June. On 25th May Wilson had led the Tory onslaught on the pact with a vehement speech in Liverpool. In the Commons debates on 31st May, while Collins and Griffith sat in the Distinguished Strangers' gallery, he forced from a reluctant Churchill an undertaking to retain troops in Dublin against the possibility of the declaration of a Republic. His attitude on the constitutional question was so well known that friends tried to dissuade him from addressing meetings in Glasgow. They were afraid he might be shot. It is conceivable that his death arose from some contingency plan prepared for the eventuality that the negotiations should break down with the consequence of war. It might be to stretch things too far to imagine one part of Collins trying to repeat the Phoenix Park incident with which the Invincibles

[1] Rex Taylor, *Assassination*, p. 88.

wrecked Parnell's compact with the British Government. In political terms the shooting must be assimilated to the proposed burning of Belfast and the war on the border, as part of the reaction of a people tortured beyond endurance.

The English ruling class is unrestrained in its anger, but calculating in its revenge. Before the Field-Marshal's body was cold General Macready was summoned by telegraph to London where he was asked whether the Four Courts could be taken by British troops. He replied that they could, but he counselled against it. On that day, 23rd June, Griffith and Cope were in conference with officers of the British and Provisional Government armies over the continued occupation of the Four Courts. It would seem that no decision was arrived at, although the impending military alliance between imperialism and the "Treaty" party was clearly foreshadowed. On the 24th Macready received orders to act. He despatched a special messenger to London and congratulated himself when the orders were rescinded. He had argued that a British attack would unite the two parties, into which Britain had by great cunning and long labour divided the Irish people, and ruin all the Government's work. What seems to have happened is that, possibly from Cope, the British Government received information that the "Treaty" party could be persuaded to act themselves.

The final election results were published on 24th June. No party had an absolute majority, but 94 candidates of the *Sinn Fein* panel had been returned. There were 17 Labour men, 7 Farmers, 6 Independents and 4 Unionists from Trinity College. Only Collins had publicly repudiated the pact. Possibly he was the only leading personality on the "Treaty" side who needed to do so. But when Rory O'Connor seized some boxes of voting forms with the object of checking the "Treaty" party's loyalty to the pact, he found that many second preferences had gone to non-panel candidates. The Republicans had for the most part performed the compact. Their leaders now sat waiting for the summons that never came. The Provisional Government continued in office. The Coalition was forgotten.

If the new *Dail* had met on 1st July, as had been intended, the "Treaty" party would have been represented by 58 deputies and the Republicans by 36. Unionists and Independents would support Griffith in all foreseeable circumstances. In the event of Labour and Farmers joining the Republicans they could only muster 60 votes against 68. The "Treaty" party was thus independent of the Republicans and could afford to brush them aside.

The significance of the election has been much debated. "Treaty"

supporters emphasise that Griffith's party lost only 8 seats while the
Republicans lost 22. Republicans reply that they were working under
the pact, and that panel candidates held 73 per cent of the poll. Others
point to the spectacular success of Labour.

The absence of contests in many western constituencies makes it
difficult to draw conclusions valid for the whole twenty-six counties.
But in Leinster every constituency was contested. The anti-Treaty
party won 5 out of 44 seats. In no case did it top the poll, and where
Labour contested usually came behind Labour. The implication is
plain. As a result of its vacillations it had ceased to carry conviction
in the national field, whereas in the social field it had not distinguished
itself from its opponents. It had provided no compelling reason why the
imposed settlement should not be accepted under duress.

When all contests are taken into account it is seen that the "Treaty"
party won no resounding majorities on first preference votes, except
in the cases of Collins and Griffith with 10,000 and 6,000 majorities
over Labour and Farmer candidates respectively. The largest Labour
majority was Davin's 8,500 over Kevin O'Higgins in Leix–Offaly.
Cathal O'Shannon defeated E. J. Duggan by 7,000 in Louth–Meath,
and the leftwinger Gaffney won by a 4,000 majority in Carlow–
Kilkenny. The only comparable lead by a supporter of the Treaty was
Darrell Figgis' 7,000 in the somewhat exceptional constituency of
County Dublin. Even here Thomas Johnson, the second candidate
returned, had a majority of 1,000 over Gavan Duffy and 3,000 over
Mrs. Pearse.

What then would have happened if Labour had been in a position
to offer more candidates? There seems little reason to doubt that a
number of them would have been returned. Thus one is led to the
conclusion that if, instead of making their pact with the "Treaty" party,
the Republicans had been able in some manner to present a common
front with Labour, involving no more compromise of the national
position than Boland was prepared to accept at Roscommon, the
"Treaty" party might have been deprived of a working majority. This
is, of course, speculation, and serves merely to underline the fact that
Republicans had striven to avoid civil war by compromise with the
enemy instead of by rallying their friends.

Looking back over the years it might seem to a modern observer
that if the lessons of the election had been digested by the men in the
Four Courts, they might possibly at this point have reached the conclusion that the paramount interest now was not so much the preservation of the outward forms of a Republican State, as the preservation

of the revolutionary movement. Perhaps by the establishment of a "patriot opposition" at an appropriate time the struggle might have been continued by other means. But it is the hardest thing on earth to disengage an army in retreat without leading a rout, and the Republicans were given no opportunities for doing so.

On Sunday, 25th June, Mellows made his last public speech, once more at Bodenstown, this time at the *Fianna* commemoration. That evening he decided to seek an accommodation with Lynch, and with McKelvey called on him at the Clarence Hotel to which the officers of the 1st Southern Division had retreated, and remained with him about two hours.

Next day the British Commons met in a frenzy of anti-Irish hysteria. Bonar Law informed Lloyd George and Churchill that they must "answer to the Empire", not for their disastrous Irish policy, but for the fact that it had resulted in the death of one of its instruments. He was told that an ultimatum had been sent to the Provisional Government.

When the army reunification talks had been broken off, the Belfast boycott had been resumed. It was directed by Leo Henderson, a quiet scholarly man who had been secretary to the *Dail* committee on industrial resources. On the day of the Commons meeting Mellows and McKelvey asked him if he could close down the Dublin branch of the Belfast firm of Fergusons, motor dealers, in Baggot Street. Henderson took out a force of Volunteers to raid the premises. There was no intention of commandeering cars for use as transport to the North, though this suggestion has been made. Beggars Bush was quickly alerted. Provisional Government troops under Frank Thornton arrived on the scene and after an engagement Henderson was captured. The new mood by the "Treaty" party was illustrated by their disregarding the terms of the Truce. Henderson was bundled off to Mountjoy like a common criminal.

Mellows and McKelvey called a hasty conference. It was markedly devoid of creative political thinking. The mighty alp of the revolution stood behind them, and all ahead lay in its shadow. O'Malley proposed that an officer of equal rank on the "Treaty" side should be taken as a hostage. They considered possible candidates, including Collins and Mulcahy, finally deciding on General J. J. O'Connell. O'Malley and one companion arrested him at his lodgings and, bringing him to the Four Courts in a motor car, installed him as a military prisoner with the food, drink and tobacco appertaining to his rank. He then telephoned Mulcahy and offered to exchange him for Henderson. Their parochialism, uninventiveness and insensitivity to political mutation soon cost the Republicans dearly.

For now came the day of decision when the issue of dual power must undergo final resolution. British imperialism was in effect threatening a war to impose the "Treaty" settlement. Republicans of all tendencies might therefore dream of a return to the old Anglo-Irish confrontation that had existed before the split. The supporters of the Pact had available for their policy appropriate constitutional forms.

The *Dail* was due to meet on 30th June. After its formal dissolution, its successor (the third *Dail*) would appoint new ministers on 1st July. Six counties might be temporarily lost, but some sort of Republic might still be preserved in twenty-six. Therefore, let the *Dail* be called. Let the new coalition ministry deal with the British ultimatum, and if in face of world opinion there should follow blockade or invasion, let a reunited people face the worst, confident in a fair chance of victory.

There seemed some basis for hope. The British ultimatum had aroused indignation as well as alarm. There was no evidence connecting the occupants of the Four Courts with the shooting of Wilson. The British ministers declined to dislose their secret intimations. Those who had suffered imprisonment for the "German plot" were understandably sceptical.

But this policy, advocated by De Valera and Boland, and supported at least implicitly by Traynor and Lynch, depended on the willingness of Griffith and Collins to work the Pact as it was understood by the Republican side. What if theirs was an alternative policy, in which the trappings of *Dail Eireann* merely dazzled and confused Republicans while the Provisional Government, secure against criticism from the Provisional Parliament, proceeded with the liquidation of the Republic and the establishment of the Free State? Was resistance to this new British intervention possible to men so deeply committed to collaboration? Moreover the path of struggle against the external enemy involved the reanimation of all those social prospects which Griffith had so resolutely smothered. The resumption of the Belfast boycott and the arrest of O'Connell showed that the war-party among the Republicans regarded the Pact as a dead letter. The insult to their deputy Chief of Staff provided the "Treaty" party with a pretext for openly abandoning it. The second *Dail* would not be recalled. Instead the Provisional Government would continue to function as prescribed by the Free State Agreement Act, the provisional parliament being powerless to control it.

It is clear that Griffith and his military advisers gave not a thought to the prospect of resisting the British demand in alliance with the Republicans. They busied themselves ascertaining whether Macready had trench mortars to lend them, and prepared for the meeting with Collins in the afternoon.

In logic, if not in politics, there was a third path in addition to the two outlined. This was that the war-party among the Republicans, who were chipping and sniping at the fittings of the "Treaty" State, should launch a revolutionary offensive and seize power themselves. This would not be proletarian revolution. But without the working class it would seem impossible. It does not appear to have been considered. The war-party was mentally as well as politically wedded to the defensive.

At the Four Courts there seemed to be little apprehension of the serious pass to which things had come. Seamus Robinson told Mellows bluntly that the gauntlet had been thrown down and that he did not propose to spend another night at headquarters. But Mellows insisted that there would be no action against them and that Henderson would be released. Asked to take the precaution of occupying buildings surrounding the Four Courts the Army Council declined on the grounds that to do so would be to take the offensive. Throughout that day came a stream of visitors to whom Mellows betrayed no sign of concern. Here in the Fourt Courts stood the symbol of the Republic. If it was attacked they would resist. If it was defeated, then its defenders would die fighting. His mind seemed set on principles. Practicalities were overshadowed. The conception of taking the offensive, of turning any attack on the Four Courts into a counter-action that would seize power from the "Treaty" party and restore it to the people, was totally absent. The third possible resolution of the dual power was not even considered.

The British military authorities ultimately agreed to lend two pieces of artillery. Armed with this information Griffith, Mulcahy and O'Duffy counted on battering down Collins' objections. They were not vigorously sustained. The others present, O'Sullivan, Tobin, Emmet Dalton, MacManus, Ennis and MacMahon, said little. They knew the cause and recognised the occasion. That evening a Free State officer performed a macabre little ceremony at Beggars Bush. He constructed a wreath of flowers with which in mock solemnity he paraded the barracks square. Asked to explain this act of invultuation he replied that he was performing the funeral rites of the Republic. The decision had been taken. What was left of the Republic was to be destroyed by force. Counter-revolution was now to order an Easter Week in reverse.

CHAPTER EIGHTEEN

EASTER WEEK IN REVERSE

"The defensive is the death of every armed rising."—Karl Marx

ALL rulers are liars and the special "myth of origin" propagated by their official historians in Ireland is that the bourgeoisie came to power amid that "terrible beauty" which, as every schoolboy knows, was born in 1916. The true genesis of that power in the bloody counter-revolution of 1922 is concealed, and, like the Queen of Spain's bottom, presumed devoid of existence. Counter-revolution was simultaneously national and social. The bourgeoisie and their landlord friends were the classes whose immediate interests conformed to the aims of British imperialism, namely the completion of the related systems of Versailles and Washington and the further pursuit of Churchill's fantasy. No treaty could be safe while Ireland contained an independent armed force not committed to it and its bad example encouraged imitation throughout an Empire smouldering with revolt. To the large property-owners within Ireland another aspect presented itself. The existence of a people's army, no matter how reliably it had protected property in the past, involved a principle superior to property. If it could not be suborned it must be suppressed.

June 27th 1922 was one of those fateful days like 23rd April 1916, when the forces of history seem to equip themselves with the passions of human beings. As the leaders of the "Treaty" party screwed up their courage at Beggars Bush, Lynch's officers reported to the Clarence Hotel. In the doomed citadel of the Republic there was little apprehension. Rumours of impending attack were heard, but were disregarded.

In the early evening Lynch and Deasy left the Clarence Hotel for discussions with Mellows and McKelvey. It was after 10 p.m. when they returned. According to Dorothy Macardle the meeting took place at the Four Courts. But it has proved extremely difficult to find anybody to testify to seeing them there. It seems possible that they met elsewhere and that Traynor was present. It is clear that Dorothy Macardle, who describes their leaving the Four Courts after midnight, had postponed the time of the meeting. But that they returned without the slightest sense that an attack was impending, is a certainty. Lynch told his officers that the meeting was fruitful. A promising basis for agreement had been discussed.

What this basis was, is of course a matter of speculation. It suffices to point out that the strategy of each side was to rebuild the alliance against the British by a junction with the "Treaty" party. On whether this could be achieved through compromise, or required rekindling of the war with England, the Republicans were at odds. The revolutionary overthrow of the "Treaty" party seems never to have been considered. Was it utterly excluded by circumstances? If so, a compromise was inevitable. But what compromise, and how to get it? There was little room for manœuvre, and the result of the discussion must have been indefinite, leaving the I.R.A. with no policy and two high commands.

An immediate result of the discussion was that officers of the 1st Southern Division were no longer to be excluded from the Four Courts. One of them, Richard Barrett, Mellows' assistant Q.M.G., immediately left the hotel and returned to his old room. This action was to cost him his life.

In the late evening, while it was still light, two couriers from the Provisional Government forces arrived at the gate of the Four Courts in Chancery Place. One of them, Petit de Mange,[1] handed to Thomas O'Reilly, who was on guard, a message for McKelvey. It was taken in, and a small group of officers met under the dome to consider its contents. It was a demand that the Fourt Courts be evacuated at midnight and that its garrison, whose members were being treated as mutineers, should parade without arms on the far side of the river. The message was sent down to de Mange that there was no reply. Owing to a series of inadvertencies, de Mange did not report to Tom Ennis until approaching midnight. He found his chief pacing the room, convinced he had been taken prisoner.

The first question that the garrison must decide was whether to defend the Four Courts. Nobody suggested accepting Ennis' terms. But a proposal was made to evacuate Dublin and take the field in the country. Mellows was hesitant. He thought the west would fight, and Tipperary. But what of the all-important 1st Southern? Clearly the discussions with Lynch had not touched on the vital contingency.

Mellows felt that the Army Council had created the Four Courts situation and should stay and face the music. It might be unmilitary, but here was the Republic. It was going to be attacked. They should

[1] Dublin-born son of a former *Chef de Cuisine* at the Gresham Hotel.

defend it. Patrick O'Brien was prepared to defend the headquarters. But he must have had little relish for doing so while the headquarters staff, with its constant preoccupation with politics, was on hand. He suggested that Dublin be left to the Dublin men and the Army Council go down country. They could raise a force that would relieve Dublin and thus turn the tables on the Provisional Government. If the Dublin brigade were prepared to turn out at full strength, this might indeed have proved the best plan.

It was decided to remain. Immediately, it was realised that the Four Courts was not in a state of preparedness. O'Malley suggested seizing the Four Courts Hotel, the Bridewell, the Medical Mission, and Patterson's Match Factory to which engineers were already driving a tunnel. But his colleagues objected that this would be to take offensive action. There was evidently a feeling that if the Four Courts were attacked a wave of indignation would sweep Dublin and the Provisional Government might be forced to call in British troops. If, on the other hand, the garrison were to be first in attacking fellow Irishmen, this sympathy would be lost.

O'Malley pointed out that there was no food in the building. He took out a lorry and escort to forage around night bakeries and small shops. He was instructed not to resist arrest. But he intended to disregard his instructions. As a result of this operation some bread, flour and small quantities of provisions were added to the stocks of Belfast boycott biscuits already in the building.

A message was meanwhile sent to the headquarters of the Dublin Brigade. Traynor had inclined to Lynch's side in the Extraordinary Convention, and it was at first feared that he might not respond. But he came in person, and after hearing the intentions of G.H.Q. went to mobilise the Dublin Brigade. The garrison set to work digging trenches behind the gates, and a tunnel was dug under the courtyard, which could be swept by fire. The connections of the various services were cemented down with concrete or molten lead,[1] to make it difficult for the attackers to cut off water or electricity. A mine was laid by the gate.

Already by 11 p.m. there was intense military activity on the side of the Provisional Government. Armoured cars were passing repeatedly down the quays. But the attack which was expected at midnight did not come. According to Calton Younger[2] there was a minor mutiny at

---

[1] Accounts vary on this point. An obvious material would be sulphur, but it is doubtful if it was available unless gunpowder was being made.

[2] *Ireland's Civil War*, p. 313.

Beggars Bush. Petit de Mange was late returning and common sense would demand an ultimatum before the die was cast.

Men of the 5th Battalion of the Dublin Brigade were mobilised and by midnight were busy with picks taken out of the Four Courts, preparing to lay mines outside the gates. The depletion of B Company by transfers to Beggars Bush had been made up by seconding men from the Citizen Army. A number of these had been assisting the 5th Battalion in the manufacture of mine boxes for about a week. These were ordered to report to the Daisy Market at midnight and joined the other mine layers at 12.15. They included Walter Carpenter, Vincent Poole, John Whelan and a man called Wade.

In the early hours Provisional Government troops gathered on Wood Quay and in the surrounding streets. It was here in the territory of the 4th Battalion of the Dublin Brigade that the artillery lent by the British was established. Dr. James Ryan and nurses arrived. They were members of *Cumann na mBan*. Mellows sent to Church Street Priory for Fathers Albert and Dominic, who arrived with a strong escort and gave general absolution to the Catholic members of the garrison.[1] The buildings which O'Malley had wanted occupied were now seized by Provisional Government forces. The most dangerous of these posts were the Four Courts Hotel which was within the actual block comprising the Four Courts buildings, and the Medical Mission which overlooked the main gate in Chancery Place. The garrison was now in a trap.

Soon after 3 a.m. Lancia cars were driven to the gates. The men who were laying mines were ordered at gunpoint to stop working and driven into the Four Courts. The Lancias were then immobilised at the gates to block all egress. At 3.40 a.m. a Free State officer brought an ultimatum signed by Tom Ennis. The garrison was given twenty minutes to evacuate and parade under arrest. Failing compliance they would be attacked. Patrick O'Brien read it to each company separately. The men laughed. Finally at 4 a.m. the officer in charge of the attack, Patrick Daly, telephoned for a reply and was told there was none. The first sign of the attack was a burst of rifle fire. At seven minutes past four there was an explosion. The shelling of the Four Courts had begun with the aid of British artillery.

Sniping from surrounding buildings intensified. Volunteers ascended the dome and returned the fire. There was still a certain desultoriness about the business. "Try not to waste bullets on those

[1] It must be remembered that Carpenter and others were Protestants. Sometimes the story is told as if all were Catholics.

poor fools outside," said Mellows. "We'll need them for the British."
The Provisional Government riflemen took no great pains to hit their
targets. There was no hatred on either side. Even the artillerymen were
in no hurry to learn their trade from the British officer who was supplied
with the eighteen-pounders. There was perhaps a hope that after a
token resistance the garrison would march out covered with glory,
their protest having been made, and then all would be friends again.
But behind the scenes Mulcahy was urging his senior officers to put
behind them the genialities of past comradeship and think only of
service to the State.

It has been pointed out that anti-Treaty forces appreciably out-
numbered those of the Provisional Government in Dublin at this time.
Leaving aside the important question of arms and equipment, the
weakness of the Republican side was the lack of an agreed policy and a
unified command. Lynch's officers at the Clarence Hotel were awakened by the sound of artillery and held an immediate consultation.

Mellows and O'Connor had drafted a proclamation to the people
of Dublin. This was typed by Madge Clifford, and Traynor undertook
to have it printed. While there is evidence that copies of a proclamation were brought into the Four Courts, it is not clear whether
Mellows' text was ever published. The officers at the Clarence Hotel
decided to call together the leaders of the 4th Western Division, who
were at the Exchange Hotel, and others from Vaughans. Brigade
Staff Officers of the Dublin Brigade attended, and Cathal Brugha,
though without military rank, was also present. Possibly the draft
statement from the Four Courts was available as a basis. The well-
known Republican declaration was drawn up by Lynch in Lily
O'Donnell's nursing home in Suffolk Street.

The text ran:

The fateful hour has come. At the dictation of our hereditary enemy
our rightful cause is being treacherously assailed by recreant Irishmen.
The crash of arms and the boom of artillery reverberate in the
supreme test of the nation's destiny.

Gallant soldiers of the Irish Republic stand vigorously firm in its
defence and worthily uphold their noblest traditions. The sacred
spirit of the Illustrious Dead are with us in this great struggle.
"Death Before Dishonour" being an unchanging principle of our
national faith as it was of theirs, still inspires us to emulate their
glorious effort.

We therefore appeal to all citizens who have withstood unflinch-
ingly the oppression of the enemy during the past six years to rally to

the support of the Republic and recognise that the resistance now being offered is but the continuance of the struggle that was suspended by the truce with the British. We especially appeal to our former comrades of the Irish Republic to return to that allegiance and thus guard the nation's honour from the infamous stigma that her sons aided her foes in retaining a hateful domination over her.

Confident of victory and of maintaining Ireland's independence, this appeal is issued by the Army Executive on behalf of the Irish Republican Army.

The first signature was that of Mellows. Then followed those of Rory O'Connor, McKelvey, O'Malley, Seamus Robinson, Sean Moylan, Michael Kilroy, Frank Barrett, Thomas Derrig, Tom Barry, Pax Whelan and Joseph O'Connor. Some of the signatories were not present. Tom Barry was in Cork seeking support for the men in the Four Courts. Seamus Robinson was at home, and Pax Whelan was in the South. The omission of the names of Lynch and Deasy and Peadar O'Donnell has no significance. According to *Poblacht na hEireann*,[1] the omission of three names was due to an error.

The most active courier on the Republican side was Maire Comerford, who braved the bullet-swept streets on her bicycle taking and bringing despatches. One of her first missions was to Traynor whom she believed would be at Suffolk Street. The office was not yet open and she had to wait a considerable time, only to be told that Traynor was at Barry's Hotel. It may be guessed it was mid-morning when she returned to the Four Courts. She was then sent to the Clarence Hotel with a message and asked to bring back a reply. This reply was received with great satisfaction in the Four Courts, and probably contained the news that the Clarence Hotel conference had decided to support them.

But it was to be support within a framework of preconceptions. Lynch and his colleagues decided to return to the South. According to Dorothy Macardle it was agreed "that each section of the I.R.A. should operate in its own locality; the units were not to pass from one Divisional area to another". This was to guarantee the fall of Dublin. At an Army Executive meeting on 16th October Lynch explained the decision as arising from the fact that no central authority of the I.R.A. existed outside the Four Courts. His recollection may have been at fault. On the way to Kingsbridge Station he and Deasy were arrested and brought before Eoin O'Duffy. They were released, some think thanks to their noncommittal replies, others because Mulcahy feared to

---

[1] *War News*, 30th June.

antagonise the 1st Southern Division by holding them. He was satisfied they would not organise the march on Dublin.

At Kingsbridge they found Seamus Robinson on his way to raise Tipperary. Robinson upbraided the Cork men for causing the division of which the Provisional Government had taken advantage. Lynch showed magnanimity. Instead of "you too", he replied "we're all together now". But he tried to dissuade Robinson from bringing back forces to Dublin. He outlined a strategy in which the "Treaty" forces would progressively exhaust themselves on the way south until they finally succumbed on ground chosen by the 1st Southern Division. Robinson was disgusted. It was the way the septs resisted invasion. Each went his way, and Robinson brought his Tipperary men as far as Blessington where they joined up with the South Dublin Brigade.

De Valera was motoring into Dublin when he heard the sound of artillery. At his office he found Brugha, Stack and Robert Brennan. His first instinct was to seek some means of securing a cessation of hostilities. This Brugha would not hear of. He left the room to join the Dublin Brigade. De Valera spent the next two days drafting what he considered acceptable peace terms, though he registered at the mobilisation centre of the 3rd Dublin Battalion.

Traynor made the best of difficult circumstances. He opened headquarters at Barry's Hotel and posted men to positions as fast as they reported. The Council of the Citizen Army met early in the morning and decided to mobilise and attach themselves to Traynor's command as an independent unit. Even the Communist Party of Ireland, under Roderick Connolly and Liam O'Flaherty, started its own engagement. The hall in North Great Georges Street was fortified. Moran's Hotel and Hughes' Hotel in Gardiner's Street were occupied, and shots were exchanged with "Treaty" forces. There was co-operation with the Citizen Army in occupying Findlaters.

Shortage of ammunition slowed the bombardment. General Macready obligingly sent to England for fresh supplies. In particular the "Treaty" forces lacked high explosive shells, and shrapnel made little impression on the robust walls of the great building. It was not until the early hours of Friday morning that a lull seemed to promise the traditional attack at dawn. When bombardment recommenced it was concentrated on a part of the wall in Morgan Place. Finally a breach was made. An assault party entered. Mines were laid to impede its progress by creating obstructions in its path. There was still a reluctance to take life, and the injuries suffered by some of its members resulted from an explosion when an engineer on the Republican side, who could no longer remain awake, fell forward and touched a switch. Hasty barricades were thrown up, but despite the valuable aid of their armoured car, which had been brought into the Four Courts by the Tipperary men, the defenders were slowly pressed back.

On Thursday Traynor had sent a party of thirty Citizen Army men to take over the Hammam Hotel for use as Republican headquarters. He now controlled the row of hotels between Parnell Street and Talbot Street, on the east side of O'Connell Street. The positions in Findlaters and the Gardiner Street hotels were integrated under his command. Countess Markiewicz who had answered the summons of the Citizen Army was at headquarters, together with Brugha and Stack. Communication with the Four Courts was maintained by Maire Comerford. The Dublin brigade held a substantial triangle behind O'Connell Street, but found difficulty in sending reinforcements across the wide thoroughfare covered by armoured cars. The passage was ultimately effected by Citizen Army men armed with "Peter the Painters" who reached the junction of Capel Street. On Thursday Garry Hoolihan had led an unsuccessful attack on the Provisional Government cordon on the north side. A second sortie was contemplated. The Citizen Army men were to create a diversion in the rear of the "Treaty" forces, and thus increase its chance of success

Throughout the morning of Friday the proposed sortie was discussed. The Republicans discussed the use of their armoured car to support a full-scale break out. They would then join Traynor. But this plan had to be abandoned when the water-jacket of its Vickers gun was hit by a stray shot.[1] After a few rounds more the gun grew hot and jammed. At 11.30 a.m. a fire started. A thin wisp of smoke rose on the north side of the building. By noon it had grown to immense proportions covering the whole wall and hiding the dome behind a black pall. As the defenders slowly retreated within the building there were fears for the store of explosives and chemicals in the basement. Efforts were made to remove these, but the fire advanced too swiftly. When it was clear that they could not be saved, Mellows assembled the entire garrison under the dome, where they lay under benches or whatever other protection they could find. At about 12.15 came an ear-splitting explosion which brought down glass, plaster, bricks and woodwork all around. It may be that the fire had reached the explosives. But from the fact that there was one great explosion rather than a succession of smaller ones it is possible that a shell had hit the dump. Newspaper reporters recorded that the ex-

---

[1] It was replaced by a Lewis gun but the nose cap was shot away.

plosion immediately followed a direct hit. Records dating back to the twelfth century were destroyed by the blast and ensuing fire storm.

The explosion undoubtedly shook the morale of the garrison. The Citizen Army men a few hundred yards away were preparing to evacuate when McKelvey sent urgent appeals to Traynor. A truce was arranged while firemen tried frantically to control the blaze. Another truce was agreed upon for the evacuation of the wounded. At 2.15 p.m. came a second explosion. Rory O'Connor told O'Malley of proposals for surrender. Fr. Albert was urging it to save further bloodshed. Mellows resolutely declined to discuss it. "The Republic is being attacked here," he insisted. "We must stand or fall by it. If we surrender now we have deserted it."

Thirty men volunteered for a last desperate sortie to be carried out if the Lancias could be moved from the gates. But others were now clamouring for surrender. McKelvey and O'Connor broached the matter once more. Once more Mellows refused to discuss it. Let those who wanted to surrender do so. Probably some intimation of the division of opinion reached Traynor. A despatch ordering the garrison to make terms was brought in and read out. Its language clearly marked it as a "face-saver". It ran:

> I have gone into the whole situation re your position, and have studied the same very carefully, and I have come to the following conclusion: To help me to carry on the fight outside you must surrender forthwith. I would be unable to fight my way through to you even at terrific sacrifice. I am expecting reinforcements at any moment.
>
> If the Republic is to be saved your surrender is a necessity. As senior officer outside I take it I am entitled to order you to make a move which places me in a better military position. This order will be carried out without discussion. I take full responsibility.

With Mellows still dissenting Fr. Albert was asked to approach the "Treaty" Commandant for terms. The reply was that nothing was acceptable but unconditional surrender. Mellows was seen with his head in his hands, shaking with convulsive sobs as Fr. Albert tried to console him. He recovered and joined O'Malley in destroying every weapon he could lay hands on. The men marched out on to the quays. It was at this point that Mellows became conscious of the demeanour of the ordinary citizens. They were not sympathetic. Nor were they markedly hostile. They tripped on pieces of rubble and cursed the nuisance, interfering with lunch, making them late home from work.

"The workers weren't with us," he confided to Peadar O'Donnell afterwards.

There were about 150 prisoners who were lodged in Jameson's distillery at Smithfield. Some of them discovered an escape route through the manager's house, and informed Mellows. He decided to "stay with the boys". To those who had opposed it the shame of surrender removed the zest from living. Several confessed to being unable to sleep several nights for brooding on it. Forty years later it could still arouse anger, and among those inclined to anti-clericalism the unfortunate intermediary, Fr. Albert, was burdened with unjust blame.

The attack on the North had of course proved a fiasco. A *Cumann na mBan* expedition had left after some hesitation on the Wednesday. They found the anti-Treaty section of the 1st Northern Division confidently awaiting co-operation from the "Treaty" party, and were highly outraged when instead of attacking the British the Provisional Government turned its forces upon themselves, thus frustrating Executive policy simultaneously at the two points where it was in operation.

Meanwhile Lynch had reached Mallow after some obscure adventures in Kilkenny. He drafted a statement to the effect that he had resumed the position of Chief of Staff from Thursday, 29th June. This was published on the following day, by which time he had reached Limerick to begin a week of peace negotiations with the Treaty forces occupying positions in that city. It was made clear that Lynch's policy remained what he had urged at the Convention of 18th June.

At 9 p.m. on Friday, Mellows and his fellow captives were taken to Mountjoy. It was recalled to him that in the expected course of events he would have been attending the last meeting of the second *Dail*. The occasion had been celebrated by the cancellation of the sitting of the Provisional Parliament summoned for 1st July. The announcement was signed jointly by the Cabinet of the second *Dail* and the Provisional Government. There was no British objection to this irregularity.

McKelvey demanded prisoner-of-war status. The officer in charge of the prison replied that O'Duffy's instructions were that "no concessions were to be granted". McKelvey then informed him that the prisoners would refuse to enter the cells. He was told they would be carried. After further discussion the authorities offered an alternative which was accepted. They were to be permitted to spend the night lying on the grass with machine-guns trained on them. Those attempting to move about would be shot. Mellows was appointed Camp

Adjutant and before lying down he wrote an account of what had passed and contrived to smuggle it out. But at midnight members of the Civic Guard appeared. Four men addressed themselves to each prisoner and to the accompaniment of kicks and cuffs the Volunteers were dragged to the cells.

Mellows was placed in D-wing with the other prisoners. Here they met Tom Barry, who had been arrested while attempting to enter the Four Courts disguised as a woman. A group of Volunteers led by MacHenry and McCabe began violent protest next afternoon. Systematic destruction of the cells began. Doors were smashed from their hinges. Mortar was loosened between bricks, and walls were reduced to a condition where prisoners could move from cell to cell. In disturbances in the afternoon a prisoner named Hussy was shot in the leg. All this was more than the regular warders had bargained for and they went on strike. They were replaced by Civic Guards. Prisoner-of-war treatment was then grudgingly conceded by the Provisional Government and operated somewhat capriciously by the prison authorities.

Once having disposed of the garrison in the Four Courts, the Provisional Government could turn its attention to Traynor's positions. Scarcely had the Four Courts fallen when De Valera was in the Hammam Hotel with his peace proposals, while Emmet Dalton outside moved up his eighteen-pounders.

Third parties were anxious to prevent further hostilities. On the initiative of the Labour Party a deputation waited on Griffith and Cosgrave. Griffith described references to homeless civilians as a "red herring". But Cosgrave later intimated that steps would be taken to mitigate hardship. The Women's International League wrote to Griffith asking that Parliament should be summoned. Its President, Mrs. Charlotte Despard, received a curt refusal. She persuaded the Labour Party to attempt to bring about peace in co-operation with the Lord Mayor and the Archbishop of Dublin. These visited the Hamman Hotel and the offices of the Provisional Government. Traynor replied that while only the men in Mountjoy or at Mallow could negotiate on national questions, he would be prepared to order the dispersal of his forces with their arms if the Provisional Government called off its attack. The Provisional Government, however, insisted on the surrender of arms. After a respite of some twenty-four hours fighting was resumed. A last effort of leaders of the Labour Party to convince Mellows, McKelvey and O'Connor, whom they visited at Mountjoy, proceeded to the accompaniment of periodic explosions. The area held by the Republicans was surrounded. Outposts were systematically reduced. Artillery was placed in position to prepare the final assault.

When on Sunday evening, 2nd July, it became clear to Traynor that he was hemmed in on all sides, and that the expected reinforcements were not coming, he resolved if possible to save his army. Leaving small parties to offer ostentatious resistance he gradually evacuated his main forces. In this way he contrived the escape of Stack, De Valera and others.

The main attack on the positions in O'Connell Street opened at 2 a.m. on Monday, 3rd July.[1] Twelve hours later the forces of the Provisional Government held Parnell Square, Talbot Street and Earl Street, and had penetrated into Gardiner's Court. The Republicans had evacuated the Fowler Hall and Hughes' Hotel, but were still holding Moran's Hotel, which was badly damaged. That evening the Gresham was evacuated, the hospital staff being moved to the Granville. Next day the Gresham was partially reoccupied during a lull in the fighting. There were now only seventeen left in the O'Connell Street hotels under the command of Cathal Brugha.

The rear of the Granville was ignited by a stream of oil from Heyte's chemical works in Thomas's Lane, but the fire seems to have been brought under control. The Hammam, however, was blazing furiously and the Gresham was threatened. Traynor sent the order to surrender. Brugha ignored it. A message was sent a second time. But the courier found the gate barred. Finally, on Wednesday evening, Brugha ordered the garrison to leave the Granville but remained himself. Among those who left were Muriel MacSwiney, the widow of the Lord Mayor of Cork, the sister of Kevin Barry, and Art O'Connor. At 7 p.m. firemen saw Cathal Brugha run down the Gresham fire-escape carrying two revolvers. He charged up Thomas's Lane towards Findlater Place. Provisional Government soldiers shouted "halt!" Brugha continued to advance, and fell outside the *Irish Times* store immediately behind the Gresham Hotel. He died in hospital two days later. After the fall of the Republic he had no further use for his life. His tragedy was that for all his boundless loyalty and sublime courage he had not the gift of judging ways and means and adapting them to an end.

On 2nd July the Provisional Government introduced a rigid press censorship, which was later extended to include mail entering the twenty-six counties from external correspondents. In England there were shocked gasps from the Liberals. But the Tories were delighted at the turn of events. They began to look forward to the time when they could dispense with the services of the demagogue who led the coalition and bring reaction into the open. Noble Lords gloated over the destruction in Dublin. What impediment Labour was likely to be was revealed by Mr. J. H. Thomas at Bradford. This gentleman illustrated a principle hundreds of years old, namely that the surest test of a British democrat is his attitude to the Irish question. "The Irish", said Thomas, "were rebelling against a constitution that for the first time gave full liberty to the Irish people." He added, for those who thought a Labour Government might concede at least a few frills to the "full liberty" granted, that an Irish Republic was "something that no political party in this country will concede".

CHAPTER NINETEEN

REPUBLIC WITHOUT GOVERNMENT

ON 29th June Liam Lynch set up temporary headquarters at Mallow. He issued a statement to the effect that from the day he had "taken up duty" as Chief of Staff. This action, taken while McKelvey was still fighting in the Four Courts, was a plain indication that Dublin was not to be relieved.[1] The position of Adjutant-General had been held by Florence O'Donoghue who resigned after the failure of negotiations with Mulcahy. The Executive replaced him with Tom Derrig, who was still at liberty. Lynch seems to have wanted his own men round him. He approached Con Molony, who had signified his intention of retiring from public life, and persuaded him to accept the position. He filled the post creditably and Derrig was happy to serve as his assistant. These preliminaries completed, Lynch moved his headquarters to Limerick, where Deasy and Molony joined him.

At this time, 1st July, Republicans held the whole area south of a line drawn from Waterford to Limerick. The small pro-Treaty enclaves at Listowel and Skibbereen were speedily mopped up. Dublin was still fighting. The South Dublin Brigade together with Robinson's Tipperary men were moving on Blessington only twenty miles outside the city and drawing Provisional Government forces from Kilkenny. The Republicans had an advantage in numbers that was never to recur, especially since the attack on the Four Courts had revolted public opinion. Yet at this time Lynch yielded to the appeals of the Mayor of Limerick and sent Deasy to negotiate with Brennan and O'Hannigan, officers commanding the Provisional Government forces in that city.

His motive has been the subject of much discussion. His biographer, Florence O'Donoghue,[2] held that both sides "still hoped that by limiting the area of conflict some solution of the whole Army problem could yet be found". Con Molony spoke of immobilising 3,000 Provisional Government troops while reinforcements were sent to the

---

[1] On 16th October Lynch spoke of the hostilities that broke out in Limerick, and implied that they had held up an intended advance on Dublin. But Dublin was out of the conflict before battle was joined in Limerick, and Lynch was already hard-pressed. Possibly he was rationalising his early policy in the light of experience.

[2] *No Other Law*, p. 203.

areas around Waterford. But Waterford was in no danger while
Wicklow and Dublin held. Brennan expressed the opinion that Lynch
had been deceived into thinking that the "Treaty" forces in Limerick
were much stronger than they were. But MacManus, sent from Dublin
to investigate and put a stop to the negotiations, recorded that Lynch
held that a compromise in Munster would influence all Ireland and
civil war would be averted. He was indeed pursuing the policy that had
split the Extraordinary Convention.

As to his own motives, Brennan informed Calton Younger[1] that he
had only 200 rifles and deliberately kept Lynch talking, since in any
conflict he would be overwhelmed. Lynch might then link up with the
2nd Western and create the arc around Dublin that Mellows had aimed
at in 1916. MacManus adds the most telling fact of all. Brennan and
Hannigan felt that their troops were not to be relied upon. MacManus
therefore agreed that the negotiations should continue while he sought
arms and reinforcements. Through lack of political judgment Lynch
and his colleagues lost the war in its first week.

The Republican position in Wicklow fell during the first days of July,
and the "Treaty" forces in Kilkenny under their enterprising commander, Prout, were free to tackle the Munster stronghold. Energetic political
measures were taken by the Provisional Government. On 6th July an
appeal was issued inviting recruits to the "regular forces of the Irish
Republican Army". Soldiers demobilised from the British Army, workless and declassed elements flocked to the colours. The Volunteer
nucleus of the "Treaty" army was quickly swamped. While Republicans still hesitated to make war on their former comrades, there existed
no compunction in the reverse direction. This factor contributed to the
gradual embitterment of the conflict.

On 8th July Frank Aiken, Commandant of the 4th Northern
Division, visited Limerick to add his weight to the arguments for peace.
He thought the time was opportune for a general pacification based on
the rejection of the oath of allegiance. His political judgment also was
at fault. Scarcely a week had gone by when, after representing this
opinion to Mulcahy who received him most cordially and asked him to
furnish a memorandum, he was awakened by armed men in the middle
of the night and escorted to Dundalk Jail.

Disillusionment fell swiftly on Limerick. On 9th July Lynch's
despatches outlined plans for dominating the whole area from the
Shannon to Carlow. On the 10th his Headquarters staff retreated from
Limerick, in face of obvious preparations by Provisional Government

[1] *Ireland's Civil War*, p. 362 et seq.

forces, and established themselves at Clonmel. The command was in effect divided into two, O'Malley becoming Assistant Chief of Staff in charge of the Northern and Eastern Divisions. On the 11th the Battle of Limerick began in earnest. Soon after 6 p.m. "Treaty" forces swarmed into the city and began a bitter struggle which lasted over a week.

The Provisional Parliament was to have met on 25th July. On the 13th, after a joint meeting of the Provisional Government and the Cabinet of the second *Dail*, Parliament was prorogued once more. A supreme military council consisting of Collins as Commander-in-Chief, Mulcahy and O'Duffy was constituted. The liquidation of the Republic proceeded. The Supreme Court of *Dail Eireann* was suspended at once, and on the 24th the decree establishing Republican Courts was rescinded "with the concurrence of the *Dail* Cabinet". The British Government made no objection to these curious constitutional expedients, and Churchill let it be known that if ammunition ran short there was plenty more in England, and no need for economy of Irish lives.

One of the appointments made on 13th July was that of Diarmuid O'Hegarty, one of the strong men of the I.R.B., to the military governorship of Mountjoy Jail. Public sympathy for the plight of the prisoners had been growing and causing alarm. Their numbers were increasing as the round-up of "suspects" began. There were protests over food and hygiene, failure to supply tea, towels and disinfectants.

One method of communicating these grievances to the outside world was to shout announcements from windows overlooking the canal bank. Friends of the prisoners, at times press men, used to gather below. On 14th July, after the failure of other measures to end the practice, the authorities announced that prisoners who exposed themselves at the windows would be fired at by soldiers. The shooting began at 3 p.m. At 3.30 p.m. a sheet was suspended from the window announcing that Volunteer Kane and George Plunkett had been wounded. Mellows recognised his mother and the Woods family. With a sudden defiant gesture he flung his legs across the sill and exchanged banter with the younger children. He was dragged inside by his comrades. "What does it matter?" he asked. "They'll shoot me anyway." His impulse was that of Brugha before the Hammam Hotel.

From then on hats on broom-handles and other convenient dummies were poked forth to draw fire. But now it slackened. Part of the guard had mutinied and two lorry-loads were taken away under escort. When Maud Gonne called at the offices of the Provisional Government to protest against the practice of firing on prisoners Griffith declined to see her, but sent out a message that he accepted full responsibility. A week later Tom Barry walked from his cell in a Provisional Government uniform and reached the front gate before he was recognised and carried back into solitary confinement.

There was evidence of demoralisation among the prison staff. The guards were drinking heavily. Revolvers would crack in the small hours after some fancied disturbance. The deputy governor, Patrick O'Keeffe, an old member of *Sinn Fein* who had supported the "Treaty" from admiration for Griffith, was emotionally unequal to the task of acting as jailer to his former comrades. He spent much of his time off duty drinking away the nightmare of his position. He lost dignity with the prisoners when he tried to obliterate a somewhat boisterous kindliness with a species of forced bluster. Even in its prisons the civil war produced strange ambivalences in the minds of its victims of either side. He enjoyed a secret popularity, but little respect.

On 13th July De Valera joined Lynch at Clonmel. Once again his thoughts were on a peace based on compromise. Next day Robert Brennan arrived with Erskine Childers and Dorothy Macardle. They found Lynch pinning flags to a wall-map along the "Waterford Limerick line", and De Valera urging a settlement while they still had something to give away. But who will bargain with weakness? A successful defence of Limerick might have squeezed some small face-saving concession from the Provisional Government. As it was, the very next day, upon a false alarm from Thurles, the entire G.H.Q. scampered incontinently to Fermoy. Brennan left for Cork to act as censor of the *Daily Examiner*. Childers did his best, in face of the sheer inexperience and incomprehension of the staff officers, to organise a publicity department. De Valera remained for the time being in Clonmel, brooding over past events, unable to believe that roads once seemingly open were closed for ever.

After a large portion of its citizens had been reduced to near starvation, Limerick fell on 20th July and Waterford on the 21st. Not unnaturally, the disastrous opening of the civil war led to questioning of Lynch's policy. On 21st July O'Malley wrote to him "Could you give me an outline of your military and national policy, as we are in the dark here." Next day the *Workers' Republic* published its proposals for a complete reappraisal of strategy and tactics. Against Lynch's policy of defensive resistance until the Provisional Government made acceptable concessions, terms upon which the Republicans could bring themselves to participate, the Communist Party of Ireland proposed what meant in effect a second revolution to save the first.

The Editorial ran:

What will attract the masses to support the Republicans? At present they cannot see any benefit in fighting for it! At present the Free State[1] offers them more economic and social advantages. At the moment it seems as if the Labour Party, representative of the masses, can find its salvation in the Free State rather than in the Republic. Once you show the masses that the Republic in Ireland will bring them definite and concrete advantages in their economic and social life, in their day-to-day life, then they will consider that the Republic is "worth fighting for still further after all". But real benefits you must give, not mere sops.

Say boldly and definitely—

Under the Republic all industry will be controlled by the State for the workers' and farmers' benefit.

All transport—railways, canals, etc.—will be operated by the State, the Republican State, for the benefit of the workers and farmers.

All banks will be operated by the State for the benefit of industry and agriculture, not for the purpose of profit-making by loans, mortgages, etc.

That the lands of the aristocracy—who live in luxury in London, and at a distance support the Free State—will be seized and divided amongst those who will and can operate it for the nation's good— among the landless workers, the working farmers, the small farmers. The committees of this class will distribute and decide how the seized land will be worked.

He would be a bold man who would deny that in the state of Ireland in July 1922 such proposals were easier formulated than made good. Nevertheless, here was an attempt to present a comprehensive alternative to the kind of Ireland Griffith was determined to create. It was the reassertion of Connolly's principle that the propertied classes always betrayed the struggle for Irish Independence and that only the working class remained the incorruptible inheritors of the fight for Irish freedom. The petit-bourgeois alliance was dead and gone. It was one major class or the other now. While the Republicans acquiesced in the establishment of bourgeois class power they could face only compromise or defeat.

On 25th July, the day after the Provisional Government forces landed from the sea at Westport, one of the more radical of the Southern Staff officers, Maurice Twomey, presented a memorandum. It was directed ostensibly against a resolution proposed by the Repub-

[1] The Free State was, of course, not due to come into existence till 7th December 1922, but the term was used loosely to designate the Provisional Government and its apparatus.

lican Lord Mayor of Cork at a public meeting on 22nd July. But its trenchant phrases challenged the basis of Republican policy. The resolution had called for the summoning of the second *Dail*, to be followed by a meeting of the third *Dail* (i.e. the Provisional Parliament as seen in terms of the pact) which should then take steps to end the civil war.

Twomey first asked what would prevent a meeting of the second *Dail* from passing a majority vote against the Republicans and then dissolving? He then pointed out that under the pact Republicans had admitted the legitimacy of the third *Dail*, which would undoubtedly refuse to function as the government of the Republic. There was thus no basis for compromise. Hence he criticised the generally accepted notion that the Republicans should wage a purely defensive war on the cry that they had "been attacked". It was said that Republican war aims were to "maintain the Republic and gain control of the army". He demanded some definition of these terms. Where was the Republic? Who was in charge of it? "You cannot very well have a Republic without a government." He proposed as war aims the disbandment of the Civic Guard and of the Provisional Government's army. Truces with these people merely legitimised their existence.

Lynch was unimpressed. He wrote to O'Malley that his aim was to "maintain the existing Republic" and that his means were to be guerrilla warfare. Presumably even Cork City was to be evacuated if attacked. On 26th July Roderick Connolly, President of the Communist Party, visited him at Fermoy. That day there was news that an armoured train had been wrecked at Kingsbridge and that workers had refused to repair it. This revelation of the potentialities of the proletariat influenced Lynch not in the slightest. He had been trained as a small-town shop assistant and such matters were foreign to him. He listened politely to Connolly's proposal that a Republican Government should be set up with Cork City as its capital, that a democratic programme should be published to rally the people, and that in this way the Republic should be saved. To Lynch it was merely a doubtful proposal for "getting Labour behind the Republicans". The vision was absent. He reported the conversation at his staff meeting next day and passed on to things that mattered.

Tipperary Town fell on 30th July. The creamery in those days manufactured condensed milk and had a labour force of several hundred. Under the Republicans the red flag[1] still flew and the Soviet

---

[1] The red flag had flown above the gas works till coal supplies ran out. There was no means of compelling consumers to pay their bills. So much for the anarcho-syndicalist conception of seizing the means of production but not the State.

administered the factory. It was stated in the press that the Republicans set fire to the creamery before leaving the town. This action would of course have been utterly pointless and can be dismissed. It is most likely that the leaders of the Soviet anticipated arrest once the Provisional Government forces occupied the building and determined to destroy all records of their activities. Such was the opinion of the trade union organiser sent to investigate, and the following year the owners took proceedings against the union.

On the day that Tipperary fell, Harry Boland was shot by armed men who burst into his hotel room in Skerries. He died two days later. Carrick-on-Suir fell on 2nd August, Kilmallock on the 5th, and Clonmel on the 8th. There were no Soviets now. But at this time political opposition began to stir once more in Dublin. A "People's Rights Committee" wrote to Collins demanding that the *Dail* should meet to discuss the war. On 7th August the 28th Annual Meeting of the Irish Labour Party and T.U.C. began at the Mansion House.

It was opened by Cathal O'Shannon who appealed to workers not to participate in the fighting. "A plague on both your houses!" was his pithy summary of Labour's policy. The economic consequences of the civil war, unreaped harvests, idle workshops, broken communications, dominated the minds of the delegates. There was indignation at the practice, employed on both sides, of compelling workers at the point of the gun to dig ditches, drive vehicles, or destroy equipment. A foolish statement from O'Malley's Adjutant had been published on 5th August. It was addressed to the trade unions and contained the sentence "organised Labour has up to the present freely co-operated in assisting the 'Free State' and the British Government in their attempt to exterminate the Republican forces". Members of trade unions were informed that those who repaired railways, transported munitions or troops, or restored telegraphic communications would be treated as combatants. Not unnaturally there was considerable indignation.

The main interest of Labour was seen as the securing of peace. There were condemnations of "militarism" on the one hand, and suggestions that fewer Commandant-Generals in the Provisional Parliament would make it a saner gathering. On the other hand, one delegate remarked with flawless logic that if the workers could not decide which of the two contending powers was the legitimate one, and if these insisted on settling matters by force, then they would be best advised to secure arms and enter the arena on their own behalf. There was discussion of whether a country was best off with a regular army, a volunteer army or no army at all. Finally a resolution threatening that if the Provisional

Parliament was not called by 26th August its Labour members would resign their seats was carried unanimously. There was condemnation of the press censorship and the treatment of prisoners by the Provisional Government. It was made clear, moreover, that Labour accepted the "Treaty" not as a voluntary act but under duress. It might seem now, of course, that apart from the all-important issue of partition, all the provisions that the Republicans complained of could be removed by unilateral action within the twenty-six counties. That was possible— once Ireland was back within the framework of imperialism. But this was precisely what the Republicans objected to.

While the T.U.C. was meeting, the struggle in Mountjoy was resumed. There were complaints that putrid meat was being supplied for prisoners' consumption. This was condemned by the health authorities, O'Keeffe's colourful denunciation of the butcher having effected no improvement. Following the incidents at the windows, the prisoners had been moved to C wing. It was decided to try to reach them by tunnelling from a shaft sunk in 28 Innisfallen Parade. The house was entered while its owners were away on holiday. The tunnel was discovered on the night of 10th August and the men outside were arrested. On the same day Cork City fell to Provisional Government troops who had landed at Passage. On the 11th the last permanent strongpoint of the Republicans, Fermoy, was evacuated. The war of positions, which it may be hazarded that Lynch only imperfectly understood, was over. Active service units were organised, about thirty men in each. These lived off the country, but without the universal popular support given their predecessors who fought the Black-and-Tans. Men in prison were frequently refused absolution by chaplains.

On 12th August Arthur Griffith died suddenly of apoplexy, attributed to worry and overwork. He had sought to trade and the devil had made him a robber. The economic dogmata which he had imposed upon patriotism were really no more than prejudices. But they derived from a class, and Griffith mistook them for principles and pursued them with a constancy worthy of principles. When the test of practice revealed their innate irrationality the dilemma tore his brain apart. Not Griffith, but imperialism must be blamed for the result. Childers treated him kindly in the Republican *War News*.

One minor success enlivened Republican gloom. Frank Aiken, who had escaped from jail, gathered fresh forces and recaptured Dundalk on 13th August. He held a meeting in the town square. Resolutions were passed demanding a truce and the summoning of *Dail Eireann*. But his position was insecure. He held the town for three days, after which, like Lynch in the south, he reverted to guerrilla tactics.

When the tunnel from Innisfallen Parade was discovered the prisoners set about digging their own. Communications with the outside world were efficiently organised and under the control of Peadar O'Donnell. Mellows arranged classes for young prisoners who were missing valuable education. Many of these he took himself. He began by proxy to reassemble the organisation of arms importation from Britain and Germany. He opened communication with James O'Donovan, who was interned at the Curragh, and suggested the names of chemists who would work up the supplies of raw materials the Director of Chemicals had left in Dublin. His brother informed him that Briscoe was in America.

The numbness of defeat had worn off. News from outside was eagerly discussed. Mellows and his cell-mate McKelvey held long discussions on past and future policy and tactics. A copy of the *Workers' Republic* was smuggled in. Peadar O'Donnell and Seamus Breslin, both officials of the Irish Transport and General Workers' Union, Eamon Martin and Richard Barrett were drawn in. A group of young workers which included William Gannon and Walter Carpenter used to attend Mellows' lectures and grasped enthusiastically at his hints of a new radical thinking.

On 18th August O'Malley seems to have decided to apply to Mellows for the political guidance that was not forthcoming from Lynch. He asked if he was in touch with events outside, and gave him a survey of the military situation in the areas of his command. In particular he requested a resumé of the army reunification negotiations with which to refute allegations made by the Provisional Government. Before Mellows replied another event shook the foundations of the twenty-six county State. Michael Collins was shot dead in an ambush at *Beal na Blath*, on 22nd August.[1] The men in Mountjoy observed a two-minute silence when a few days later his coffin passed the prison on the way to Glasnevin.

There was much discussion of Collins. According to Peadar O'Donnell,[2] Richard Barrett, who knew Collins well and like Boland expected to be assassinated by him, gave a picture of him which showed him to be, like Griffith, a tragedy of mental limitation. "Without any

---

[1] The mystery of this ambush seems largely factitious. The Republicans knew well the blow they would inflict on the Provisional Government by removing its Commander-in-Chief. They may also have expected the resignation of the Provisional Government, the calling of the *Dail* or a British invasion followed by a united Irish resistance.

[2] *Gates Flew Open*, p. 31.

guidance except his own turbulent nationalism, with the weakness and conspiracy that secret societies breed, he confused the conquest with the mere occupation of the country, with British soldiers and the personal influence of 'undesirables'. He failed to recognise that the military occupation was merely to make the imperial exploitation possible, and so he guaranteed to safeguard the exploiting interests if the soldiers were withdrawn, without recognising that he was thus making himself a bailiff for the conquest. . . . He had emerged from the Tan struggle with the outlook of a 'Fenian Home Ruler' and the code of a tinker swapping donkeys at a fair; he was suspicious of what he was getting, but contented himself that what he was giving was not an honest beast."

In his reply to O'Malley, Mellows intimated that he was in touch with the general situation as far as the newspapers revealed it. He thanked him for the military survey and advised him to keep Frank Aiken up to scratch. He promised the resumé for the next day, and added a note on money and arms. He wanted Cremin to set about selling the big ship, recovering £10,000 outlying for the purchase of arms, and asked O'Malley to make arrangements with Margaret Skinnider and Una Daly. He concluded with a remark explicable only by reference to the death of Collins. "The Free State seems to be a bit groggy these days. Paidin O'Keeffe's view is that the English will be back in a week."

The summary was not, however, completed at this time. Instead, on 26th August Mellows sent out the first of two documents which have always been especially connected with his name. These survive in two versions, the original as addressed to Austin Stack, and the slightly abridged version sent to O'Malley.

The memorandum to Stack ran:

General situation: We are as much in touch with this as the "newspapers" and *Poblacht* and *Bulletin* permit. I am strongly of opinion that the Republican political and military outlook can be co-ordinated. No doubt this has been done but I mention it because during the past six months we suffered badly because responsible officers in their desire to act as soldiers, and because of an attitude towards "politicians" acquired as a result (in my opinion) of a campaign directed towards this end by old G.H.Q., could only judge of situations in terms of guns and men. Even from a military point of view it ought to have been apparent to such men that every situation and advantage—no matter of what nature—should be availed of to gain victory. However I am not going to write an essay on this.

Naturally we are thinking hard here, though the place and atmosphere is not conducive to thought. However, the net result of my cogitations are:

1. A Provisional Republican Government should be set up at once —even if it is unable to function—or to function in a most limited way. This is to be done apart from the question of the *Dail*. The advertisement in today's paper *re* postponement of *Dail* is inserted by Provisional Government. The impression the press and Provisional Government want to create is that the next *Dail* is the "Provisional Parliament" called for by the terms of the Treaty. If at meeting of *Dail* this is not cleared up and it is accepted that it is a "Provisional Parliament" and not the Government of the Republic —then the necessity of a Republican Government is more urgent.

2. The Programme of Democratic control (the social programme) adopted by the *Dail* coincident Declaration of Independence January 1919 should be translated into something definite. This is essential if the great body of workers are to be kept on the side of Independence. This does not require a change of outlook on the part of Republicans, or the adoption of a revolutionary programme as such. The headline is there in the Declaration of 1919. It is already part of the Republican policy. It should be made clear what is meant by it. Would suggest therefore that it be interpreted something like the following which appeared in the *Workers' Republic* of July 22nd last.

Here follow the four points of the Communist Programme (p. 358).

Regarding the last paragraph in above programme—land—it is well to note that the I.R.A. Executive had already taken up the question of the demesnes and ranches and had adopted a scheme for their confiscation and distribution.

This scheme was largely the work of P.J.R.[1] See E. O'M.,[2] Tomas O'Dearg and P.J.R. about this. In view of unprincipled attacks of the Labour Party, and because of the landless and homeless Irish Republican soldiers who fought against Britain, it might be well to publish this scheme in whole or in part. We should certainly keep Irish Labour for the Republic: it will be possibly the biggest factor on our side. Anything that will prevent Irish Labour becoming Imperialist and "respectable" will help the Republic.

As a sidelight on Johnston [*sic*], O'Brien, O'Shannon and Co. it will interest you to know that when they called on us in the Four Courts last May they (particularly Johnston) remarked that no effort had been made to put the Democratic Programme into execution.

[1] P. J. Ruttledge.   [2] Ernest O'Malley.

In our efforts now to win back public support to the Republic we are forced to recognise—whether we like it or not—that the commercial interest, so called, money and the gombeen men are on the side of the Treaty, because the Treaty means Imperialism and England. We are back to Tone—and it is just as well—relying on that great body "the men of no property". The "stake in the country" people were never with the Republic. They are not with it now—and they will always be against it—until it wins. We should recognise that definitely now and base our appeals upon the understanding and needs of those who have always borne Ireland's fight. Even though the decision of the election of 1918 stands; even though the Declaration of Independence remains a fact; even though the election of June 1922 was an "agreed election" at which no issue was put or decided, yet, because of the interpretation put upon it by the Treatyites (and used broadcast by the British) it is essential that the Republic be over again affirmed by the people as soon as possible. When that may be no one can tell, but we cannot look too far ahead. In the meantime the Provisional Republican Government should endeavour to "carry on".

3a. Propaganda. Imperialism. What the rejection of it by Ireland means. What its acceptance by Ireland means. This should be fully explained. What imperialism is, what Empires are—what the British Empire is—its growth. How it exists and maintains itself. Colonies (Irish Free State as a colony)—India, how oppression and possession of it is essential to maintenance of B.E., Money, Trade, Power, etc. (Curzon on India) Extracts Roger Casement's articles on "Ireland Germany and Freedom of the seas", published first in *Irish Review* 1913 or 1914. What Ireland's connection with Imperialism (however much apparent gain) means to her future. No use freeing Ireland to set her up as a State following the footsteps of all the rotten nations of Europe today—what Ireland's rejection of imperialism means etc.

b. Work of the Republic, to show it was—and is—a reality. This is an antidote to the hypocrites who now pretend that it never existed. Some pamphlets have already been published by direction of *Dail* last year, showing how Republic functioned, Courts, land settlement, etc. Decrees. These were sold for 6*d*. each I think. They could be reproduced or used again. The Bulletin published by D/publicity all through war up to signing of Treaty does, I think, contain heaps of dates.

c. Hierarchy. Invariably wrong in Ireland in their political outlook—against people in '98. Frs. Murphy (2), Roche, Herans excommunicated by the then Bishop of Ferns—against Emmet "condoning outrage"—against Young Ireland, "Godless young men", support of Sadlier and Keogh against Fenians: Dr. Cullen,

Bishop Moriarty "Hell not hot enough or eternity long enough", against "Plan of Campaign"—against *Sinn Fein* (early days when it was milk and water) against Irish Volunteers—support England in European war 1914—morally to blame for deaths of thousands of Irish youths in France, Flanders, Mesopotamia, Gallipoli, Macedonia, etc.

Nothing can condone this. European War a hideous holocaust on altar of Mammon; a struggle between Europe for power. Irish Hierarchy blood-guilty. Hierarchy against Easter Rising 1916, denunciation of Pearse, etc. (Pearse the great example of Christian idealism) Hierarchy only opposed conscription when forced to do so by attitude of people. Against I.R.A. during terror. Bishop Cohalan's excommunication decree of December 1920. Hierarchy abandonment of principle, justice and honour by support of Treaty. Danger to Catholicism in Ireland from their bad example—their exaltation of deceit and hypocrisy, their attempt to turn the noble aspect of Irish struggle and bring it to level of putrid politics, their admission that religion is something to be preached about from pulpits on Sundays, but never put into practice in the affairs of the nation, their desertion of Ulster, etc.

"Sceilg"[1] could I think do the above best.

Excuse change of writing. I had to get the above copied by someone else from a letter I am sending to Sighle,[2] lest anything should happen this one. I will close up now, but will continue ideas on propaganda and other things tomorrow.

Regards

L. O. M.

As far as the change in handwriting, the two versions are alike. But in the document sent to O'Malley Mellows' own hand appears only after the words "What imperialism is". He proceeds:

I have given A de S[3] heaps of ideas on propaganda, so won't repeat here.

These are the ideas developed under sub-heading a, b, and c above, and were continued in a further letter Mellows despatched on 29th August:

Continuing mine of the 26th inst. (No. 1) Before doing so however I wish to point out that the matter of establishing a Provisional Republican Government has become imperative because of the probability of the English taking a hand sooner or later. No doubt they will continue to make use of Irishmen as long as the latter can be duped or dazzled by the Free State idea; but even to this there will be an end and then the British will, by using the arguments against

---

[1] J. J. O'Kelly.   [2] Sighle Humphries.   [3] Austin Stack.

Republicans that the F.S. now use, cloud the issue greatly. For the British to calumniate Republicans and belittle their cause by besmirching them is one thing; but for F.S. (and supposed potential Republicans) to do it is another, and different and worse thing. Because the British will not use British arguments to cloak their action but Irish ones "out of our own mouths", etc. Therefore an object—a target—must be presented for the enemy (F.S. or British) to hit at—otherwise it becomes a fight (apparently) between individuals. Hence the necessity of getting the Provisional Republican Government established at once.

Mellows then resumed his discussion of propaganda:

d. Dev's work in America. The time has now come for informing the Irish People what miracles De Valera accomplished there. The attempt to belittle his work for Eire both here and abroad must be defeated. Dealing with America is a stupendous work, and tons of data is needed. But it will be a labour well worth performing. Show how it was the Republic (and the Republic only) that gained such sympathy for us there; that no other cause would have got the slightest hearing—that De V. changed an ignorant and either apathetic or hostile people into genuine sympathisers in two years. He made the name of Ireland respected where it was despised, and the Irish cause an ideal where it had been regarded as political humbug. Fr. Magennis could do a very fine opening chapter describing the state of the Irish movement in America and the attitude generally of America and Americans at the time of Dev's coming.

e. Life of Cathal Brugha. A brief (but not scrappy) account of above would I think do a lot of good. The account in the Bulletin (Catholic) by Sceilg is splendid, but not detailed enough. The underlying idea should be that of "Principle", a word that at one time meant everything to (and conveyed everything of) the I.R.A.

f. Cardinal Mercier; as an offset to their Lordships, a fine pamphlet on the example set for Ireland by Cardinal Mercier—his acts and words—could be written.

g. South Africa. The danger to Ireland of Irish allowing their work to be patterned on example of South Africa. After Treaty of Veer[1] and later formation United South Africa—(all Boers still saying they were Republicans at heart) the real Republicans found an obstacle stood between them and the British—their own. Parallel with Ireland, Smuts and Botha, Collins and Griffith, Cathal Brugha, De Wet, etc. "Five years" fallacy of F. S. Repubs.

4. Courts. Except for Supreme Court, the Repub courts should be maintained. Nothing conveyed proof in America of existence of Republic here so much as the establishment and work of Courts.

[1] Abbreviation: Veereiniging.

5. *Fianna*. We must concentrate on youth—salvation of country lies in this—both boys and girls. *Fianna* never got proper help or encouragement. *Fianna* ideal can save future. The reason for so many young soldiers going wrong is that they never had a proper grasp of fundamentals. They were absorbed into movement and fight—not educated into it. Hence no real convictions.

6. Food Control. Food supply will present a serious problem soon. The obstruction of roads, railways and communications will be intensified. Towns will feel it the worst. Some plan of rationing will have to be thought out and some person (a labour man for preference) put in control. If the Republic is to win out against the Free State and the British, we shall have to face the idea of people suffering many privations. If scheme worked out ahead, it will not be so bad. In fact it would compel a change from present wretched economic outlook and make them rely on their own resources. Many things that are now looked on as necessities would have to be done without—tea, sugar, foreign flour, etc., but oatmeal, oatflour, barley and other wholesome foods would be used. As a matter of fact Ireland has suffered nothing (comparatively speaking) either during Great War or our War. English people (and English women) cheerfully put up with severe deprivations and we Irish think our Cause worth putting up with anything. But do we? Judging by the whines and grumbles one is tempted sometimes to say "certainly not."

7. Communications.
    a. Abroad. Routes and men must be sought out and maintained at all costs for the following: England, Scotland, America, Germany, Belgium, France, Russia, Italy.
    b. Home. Very essential

8. Foreign: India. Isn't the time approaching when we should be in closest touch?

9. Bye-elections. Don't suppose these can take place under present conditions—but we must have our eyes open.

10. Bishops. Can anything be done by a number of clergy coming together?

In the modified version addressed to O'Malley the points relating to Republican Courts, by-elections, *Fianna*, food control, and foreign relations are made in substantially the same terms though in different order. There are added two further sub-sections, one suggesting the immediate drafting of a Republican Constitution, presumably as an alternative to the Free State constitution, and the other headed "Military", which declares the outstandingly important questions to be intelligence, arms and ammunition, communications and England.

In the version of the communication of the 29th addressed to

O'Malley a brief additional passage emphasised the importance of "intelligence, military and political, in Ulster, England and here", arms, communications, the destruction of road and rail links "when British take a hand" and arising out of that, food control.

These documents cannot have been evoked by recent events alone. They draw on the whole of Mellows' experience, his days with the *Fianna*, his knowledge of the writings of Connolly, his vast study of Irish history, and his international outlook formed in America. In his analysis of the character of the proposed Free State he must surely have been one of the first to discuss the new methods of imperial domination which R. Palme Dutt in more recent times christened "neo-colonialism". His insistence on politics, his demand for a return to the masses as the basis of the revolution, for the political education of Republican soldiers, and for the establishment of a new revolutionary government, show him to have been, as Peadar O'Donnell justly remarked, "the richest mind our race had achieved for many a long day".

CHAPTER TWENTY

MINISTER FOR DEFENCE

"The most powerful foe of Labour is capitalistic Imperialism, and in Great Britain capitalistic Imperialism stands or falls by the subjection or liberation of Ireland."—Erskine Childers

ON 26th August the *Dublin Gazette* announced that Mulcahy had taken Collins' place as Commander-in-Chief of the so-called "regular" army. He retained his political appointment in the face of some criticism. As if to celebrate the replacement of the genial gangster by the dedicated tyrant, two prisoners were shot out of hand. They were Martin Conlon, held in custody at Clonmel Town Hall, and John Edwards of Waterford, in Kilkenny Jail. The mercenary riff-raff who had joined up on a six months' contract and expected easy service were now face to face with reality and took out their disillusionment on their victims. On 26th August two *Fianna* boys, Cole and Colley, were murdered in County Dublin. The circumstances were never satisfactorily explained. The torture of prisoners began.

The Provisional Government found it increasingly hard to maintain that it was opposed by no more than a handful of malcontents. On the morning of 30th August 500 prisoners were placed on board the requisitioned channel steamer *Arvonia*, herded below at revolver point, and brought from Limerick to Dublin. They were taken ashore on 2nd September and interned at Gormanstown. Characteristic imperial institutions were being revived in Ireland. The murder gang was accompanied once more by the concentration camp. On 5th September both the *Irish Independent* and the *Freeman's Journal* protested at the intensification of the civil war. An English colonial administrator might have heeded them. He would be paid a salary to have no feelings. Such is the psychology of delegated oppression that the Provisional Government must inject the drug of hatred in order to keep up the deception that it was a free agent.

The sweetness and light dispensed by the newspapers was not entirely void of political purpose. The Labour Party had delivered an ultimatum. It was announced that the Provisional Parliament would meet on 9th September. The Republicans must decide whether and on what terms to participate.

This question was inseparable from that of a military prognosis. There was so little agreement at headquarters that Brigades were consulted. In Cork O'Donoghue and O'Hegarty, forming a so-called "neutral I.R.A.", exercised strong influence for a settlement, if necessary with much more substantial concessions than had been contemplated in May. There seem to have been consultations between "Treaty" and anti-Treaty officers at which peace proposals originating with Alfred O'Rahilly of the University were discussed. Deasy communicated the opinion that the two armies should "fuse" on the basis of recognising the "absolute independence" already won—in a word the acceptance of the "Treaty".

Lynch was displeased. Although Rory O'Connor wrote from Mountjoy warning against his peace-making proclivities, he had learned by experience that compromisers often finished with nothing gained. He had a discussion with De Valera who was intent on visiting Cork. De Valera felt that the military struggle was doomed to end in defeat. Lynch believed it was possible by means of raids, destruction of communications and disruption of administration to make government by the "Treaty" party impossible. Then they would compromise. De Valera left for Cork in what Lynch described as a bad humour.

De Valera was determined on a last effort to secure the implementation of at least some part of the pact. He received encouragement in Cork, and proceeded to Dublin. He met Mulcahy secretly on 6th September. On that day Mellows sent O'Malley his summary of the negotiations. He seems to have assumed that Republicans would attend the assembly, but left it to the discretion of those outside to choose the deputy who would challenge Mulcahy. De Valera met with a blank refusal to take a single step towards meeting his wishes. The terms were the "Treaty" and nothing less. Next day De Valera reported to *Cumann na Poblachta* the failure of this attempt at negotiations. He made the point that the Second *Dail* had not met to dissolve itself and therefore was not dissolved, and that the assembly that was to meet on the 9th did not pretend to be *Dail Eireann*. He proposed abstention, except for two deputies, whose inevitable exclusion would demonstrate that the Provisional Parliament was not *Dail Eireann*.

On 8th September *Cumann na mBan*, having held a meeting to discuss the universal rumours of peace, addressed a resolution to O'Malley. They took the precaution of sending a copy to Mellows in Mountjoy. The women's organisation had borne the brunt of the political struggle since the attack on the Four Courts. The names of Madge Clifford, Una Daly, Sighle Humphries, Bridget Mullane, Anna Kelly, Maire Comerford and Eileen McGrane are merely examples from the large body of gifted women who handled correspondence, kept lines of communication open and performed a hundred and one almost impossible tasks with tireless devotion. The resolution made the demand that in the event of the Army Executive opening peace negotiations, *Cumann na mBan* should be represented at them. Never was a demand more justified. O'Malley, however, preferred not to deal with it and referred it to Lynch. There were no peace negotiations. The principle was not decided. When ultimately the war was brought to a close the women were not consulted.

The Provisional Parliament duly opened. Ginnell attended but not O'Mahoney. A Gilbertian comedy was enacted. Before signing the roll Ginnell enquired whether it was *Dail Eireann* he had come to. He was told to ask no questions until the *Ceann Comhairle*[1] (the term used in the *Dail*) had been elected. He remained while Professor Hayes was voted to this elevated position. Then he asked again. He was told that his question could not be answered because the *Ceann Comhairle* had been elected and he had not signed the roll. The Parliament was referred to as *An Dail*.[2] Many of the procedural forms of *Dail Eireann* were retained. So much or so little had the strength of Republican sentiment achieved. But Ginnell was forcibly ejected.

Cosgrave, who was elected "President of the *Dail*", announced his policy and appointed his Ministry. The first consisted of implementing the "Treaty" and establishing the Free State. The second was composed of members of the Provisional Government to whom were added the survivors of the *Dail* Cabinet. E. J. Duggan and Finian Lynch were ministers without portfolio. The inclusion of these colourless individuals provoked queries. It was explained that they were members of the Provisional Goverment and under the Free State Agreement Act could not be removed even by the "Parliament to which the Provisional Government was responsible". Would Lloyd George have intervened if they had been dropped? Probably not. His own government was obviously not long for this world. But the forms of transition devised in London became shibboleths. They could not be departed from without risk to class interests within Ireland. The purpose of British policy, blunderingly conceived and executed as it was, had been to create a political garrison in Ireland to replace the military whose position had become untenable. This object was now accom-

---

[1] Literally "Head of the Council"—Speaker.   [2] Literally "The Assembly".

plished. Out of the revolutionary movement itself had been selected and moulded a political party whose existence was bound up with retaining intact the British system of law, politics and social relations. The old colonial relationship was preserved in a new form.

Mellows understood this in sharp terms of social interests. Others saw only the inessential symbol, the oath of allegiance to the foreign king. The mass of people of small means felt cheated but were not sure how. It could not be expected that Republicans would find it easy to agree on a policy. That offered by Mellows had the advantage that it alone could lead in the direction of a united Ireland by appealing to the workers of the Belfast area over the heads of the lambeg-drumming demagogues who were fooling them. Rory O'Connor sent out his recipe on 12th September. He begged O'Malley to "beware of the compromising mind of the diplomat", and suggested the burning down of Provisional Government departments, for example the Customs or Department of Local Government. "Cosgrave can be easily scared to clear out", was his opinion, and he offered as evidence the allegation that under the terror Cosgrave had lost his nerve and spent seven weeks with a priest in Manchester while he recovered it.

O'Connor's approach to the threatened postal workers' strike was characteristic. It was not a question of supporting the workers in their struggle against wage reductions, but of availing of the confusion to seize the mails from scab postmen, or if Civic Guards were used, to capture their arms. He was in touch with Mrs. Childers who proposed far more ferocious "progaganda by the deed". She proposed the placing of bombs in London Tubes. If Mellows showed himself in what might be called the "Jacobin" tradition of Fenianism, derived from Tone through Lalor, O'Connor could be quoted as an example of the "Blanquist" tendency. His temperament was entirely artistic despite his high engineering qualifications. He was an ardent musician and chess-player, yet in politics his mind was dominated by his emotions.

Both Mellows and O'Connor were, in their ways, offensivists still. But the defensivists of the south were presented by De Valera with three choices, sketched in a memorandum sent to *Cumann na Poblachta* on 13th September. The first was that the Republican Party would declare itself the "legitimate *Dail*". Presumably there would then proceed the long work of securing adhesion to it. The second was that the Army Council "take control" and assume responsibility for continuing the struggle. The political party should cease to operate publicly since it was permitted no legal opportunities. The third was that a joint council be established.

The debate that now occupied the Republican movement took up precious time and energy but could not be avoided. A group of women in Glasgow who were publishing an uncensored edition of *Poblacht na hEireann*[1] wrote in strong support of a radical programme. The workers and small farmers could not be expected to come out and fight for the Republic when they were "sick and spiritless from long deferred hopes and empty promises". Now that the postal workers and building workers were on strike against wage reductions, the Republicans should declare themselves. "If the workers of Ireland were ardently Republican you could snap your fingers at the Green-and-Tans and their bosses."

Lynch read Mellows' summary of the army negotiations. They were somewhat critical of himself, but he showed no resentment. "I fear his ideals prevent him from seeing the same military outlook as others at times," was his sole comment. He urged that Mellows should be consulted over all decisions to be taken, and asked for a copy of the social programme. Of De Valera's propositions he remarked, "The army has its mind made up to total separation from England; I do not think this also can be said of the party." Lynch was hardening as the struggle grew more difficult, thus establishing his status as a hero. He saw no virtue in calling together the Republican members of the second *Dail*.

On 18th September the Free State Constitution Bill was introduced in the Provisional Parliament, now generally known as "the *Dail*", but, as has been explained, having little in common with the revolutionary *Dail Eireann*. Under pressure from Tom Johnson the Ministry disclosed that a number of clauses in the Bill were not subject to modification as the British had insisted that they were essential to the fulfilment of the "Treaty". The position was thus that if *Cumann na Poblachta* deputies had taken their seats and by some means secured a majority the government would have disregarded the wishes of the House. That they could do so without fear was provided for in the stipulation that they were irremovable until *after* the Constitution was adopted.

At this time the Volunteers were able to operate in fairly large columns and could occasionally occupy small towns temporarily. The political situation was improving. The oppressiveness of the Provisional Government was being felt on the economic front. *Cumann na mBan* had approached Hanna Sheehy-Skeffington, who undertook to address propaganda meetings in O'Connell Street and to write a series of articles in the American press based on Mellows' summary of the negotiations. The weakness of the Republican position was that the

[1] Now generally spoken of as *An phoblacht*.

policy of trying to make "government" impossible made a number of the legitimate activities of the civil population impossible as well. It was against this weak spot that the Provisional Government proposed to strike.

They were assisted by a chance occurrence. O'Malley responded to Lynch's request for a copy of Mellows' policy document. A copy was made. But in the course of despatch it was captured on the person of Miss O'Connell,[1] finding its way to officials who realised its value as propaganda. It was published across the greater part of a page of the *Irish Independent* on 21st September. A column of comment accompanied the reproduction. With rare astuteness the writer did not pretend that Mellows and his colleagues had embraced Communism. They were accused of pretending to embrace it in order to win the suffrages of the workers who were to be used as "political cannon fodder" for the Republican cause. He had indeed struck a real deficiency in the programme, the absence of any appeal to the workers' own organisation, as if the emancipation of the workers need not be the task of the workers themselves. The guerrilla warfare being resorted to was, according to the *Irish Independent*, aimed at ruining the propertied classes in order to find means of bribing the propertyless. Clearly such a plan invited strong action by those who wanted peace, work and reconstruction.

The political offensive against the Republicans was well prepared. On 27th September Mulcahy asked for emergency powers. He wanted the power to establish military Courts. These were to have the power to try persons charged with aiding or abetting an attack on the forces of the Provisional Government, with damaging property, or being in "unauthorised possession" of arms or ammunition. There was also an "anything else" clause. In order to take a good broom to all wisps of rebellion the Bill authorised military Courts to try any person committing a breach of "any general Order or Regulation made by the Army authorities". Rory O'Connor had been accused of planning a military dictatorship. Here it was with a vengeance. Tom Johnson said so, but was not heeded. The measure was passed after O'Higgins made an extraordinary speech, the only recognisable purport of which could be that the Bill was intended to catch Erskine Childers. Its two most sinister provisions were that military Courts would sit *in camera* and could impose sentences of death or deportation as well as imprisonment.

But to what part of the globe could an Irish Government deport

---

[1] O'Malley's despatch. Eamon Martin's recollection is that a copy was seized from the saddlebag of Charles Murphy's bicycle. Possibly this was another copy.

Irishmen? England came to the rescue. The old hen consented to billet
one chicken on another. The Provisional Government negotiated with
Churchill with a view to transporting the leaders of the opposition to
St. Helena or Seychelles. On 3rd October came the next stage in the
offensive. A conditional amnesty was offered to all Republicans
prepared to hand in their arms and abjure their allegiance by 15th
October. With scarcely an exception they treated the offer with
contempt.

The evidence of rising sympathy in the country heartened the men in
Mountjoy. Whereas in July the Provisional Government forces had
been hailed in many a town they captured as the harbingers of peace,
now it was the turn of the Republicans to be cheered when on rare
occasions they were able to take possession. This fact was noted by the
Provisional Government and added urgency to their campaign of
repression. Mellows' social programme had not been received as the
authorities who published it had hoped. The people did not believe it
was Communism, and even if it was they were not to be frightened
from their needs by a word.[1] Mellows wrote to America asking Sceilg
to bring back the books that he had left with Kirwans. Hope pre-
dominated in the long letter he sent to Sean Etchingham on 3rd
October, as the following extracts will show:

Dear Patsy,
You have been in my thoughts since that fatal day when the
thunder of Churchill's guns against the Four Courts ushered in the
new British regime. I would like to write much of my thoughts to
you now—thoughts some sad, some gay—but circumstances
forbid. . . . All is not lost. On the contrary the existence of the
Republic was never so plain to see else why all this effort to crush it?
I wish to God I were out. Haven't felt such energy for years. The
rest here has done me good, even though for a time our treatment
makes me blush for the fair name of Irishmen. . . . I will never forget
the feeling of humiliation when we were dragged into Mountjoy
and thrown into the cells. At the hands of the English I would have
felt proud to be so honoured (as I felt when the "peelers" brought
me up in handcuffs from Gorey in 1915) but to experience this at the
hands of one's fellow-countrymen was degrading. . . . I don't see
that any step (except surrender) could have been taken by Republicans that would have prevented Civil War. I have therefore nothing
to regret; nothing to be sorry for. It was bound to come so long as
the idea of surrender of the Republic and acceptance of "common

[1] It must be clearly understood that there was no widespread fear of Communism
among Irish workers in 1922. Much evidence on this point could be adduced if necessary.

authority" obtained. . . . The birds in the bush are talking about an island! What ho! My merry men! Luff, luff a little, helmsman. The *Poblacht* says St. Helena, the *Observer* opines the Saltees. The latter would suit my delicate constitution. . . . Of course you saw the publication given my hastily written outline of ideas that fell into their hands. The effort to brand it "Communism" is so silly. I only referred to the "Worker" because it had set forth so succinctly a programme of constructive work that certainly appealed to me. The publication of ideas on propaganda made me wonder. . . .[1]

The proposal for the establishment of a Republican Government was taken up by Fr. Dominic who wrote to O'Malley impressing its urgency. Throwing into question the whole basis of Republican tactics since the Treaty he argued "I think it is high time to proclaim a Provisional Government of the Republic. It should have been done in January; it was imperative in July; it is of the utmost urgency now. Every hour is of importance. We are without a government—nothing more in the eyes of the world than murderers and looters." He added that it was the destitution in Dublin that was driving men whose families were starving to join the Provisional Government's army.

According to Peadar O'Donnell,[2] the publication of Mellows' policy statement, and the great significance obviously attached to it, had a sharp reaction within Mountjoy. "By common impulse a surge towards escape welled up and swallowed every other activity in the jail." There had already been two tunnels discovered, and one attempt to escape with the aid of "Treaty" soldiers, two of whom were sentenced to seven years' imprisonment for their part in the affair. The boldest plan yet was conceived. It was to smuggle into the jail enough guns to enable the prisoners to shoot their way out. About this time Mellows started the production of a prisoners' magazine which he named the "Book of Cells". In it Peadar O'Donnell made his debut as a writer.

The plan was due for execution on 8th October. "When the gate was

---

[1] In this letter Mellows makes reference to a delicate subject which is worth a brief explanation. He refers to himself and Etchingham as the "two deserted". During his stay at Athenry he had become interested in a bright musical girl prominent in *Cumann na mBan*. His proposal of marriage was accepted after the Rising and the engagement ring was brought from the U.S.A. by Eamon Corbett. Mellows met her on several occasions after his return. But her interest seems to have waned. About the time of the civil war she returned his ring, which he had with him in Mountjoy. The saddest part of the story Mellows, who seems to have blamed her, never knew. The opinion of medically qualified persons who knew her at this time is that she was suffering from incipient schizophrenia. Etchingham had remained a bachelor following some disappointment in his youth, and it is to this Mellows was referring.

[2] *The Gates Flew Open*, Chapter 11, p. 62.

opened by the military police in the morning", O'Donnell writes,[1] "the selected orderlies would go into the circle as usual, but instead of taking up the tea cans and bread they would prod revolvers into the policemen's ribs and order 'Hands up', and get the keys of the gates." Once the keys had been obtained the prisoners' Commanding Officer, Cooney, who would be disguised in the uniform of a Provisional Government Army officer, would make for the guardroom, and secure the switchboard. From the guardroom, prisoners now armed with rifles, would man the Lancia which stood outside. The guard on the main gates would be ordered to open them. If they flung their keys beyond reach, the keys obtained in the guardroom would be tried. Failing this a mine was available to blow the gates. Bill Gannon and Thomas O'Reilly were to pick off the crew of a machine-gun post on the roof of the porch. The break-out was under the leadership of Richard Barrett.

Unfortunately, when covered with the revolvers the police failed to put up their hands like Christians. They danced around in a panic. A sentry noticed this and raising his rifle fired a warning shot. There was no means of halting the firing. Sentries on the platforms and military police were shot down. Among the prisoners Peadar Breslin was killed and another was wounded. O'Keeffe had the prisoners walking round the ring all day without food. Meanwhile the police and military wrecked every cell, smashed Mellows' violin and stole the watch given him by Mrs. Woods. O'Keeffe was much blamed for the events of the day. But his motive appears to have been to allow the guards to work off their feelings on the prisoners' possessions while he kept the prisoners from bodily harm in the compound.

With extraordinary courage Cooney left his comrades and approaching O'Keeffe told him that he took complete responsibility for the attempted escape. When the prisoners were allowed back to the wreckage in their cells Mellows called a meeting to consider how to protect Cooney. Those present were O'Donnell, Barrett and Rory O'Connor. It was agreed that Mellows should inform O'Keeffe that the prison council as a whole was responsible. Apparently there were no serious reprisals. Cooney was soon back in charge. And another tunnel was being made.

Two days after the attempted break-out the Irish bishops met at Maynooth and issued the much discussed joint pastoral condemning resistance to the Provisional Government, and declaring that the Republican oath could not be regarded as binding. Two days later the

[1] *The Gates Flew Open*, p. 69.

"regular" army authorities issued a proclamation that military Courts would begin to function on 15th October. Not by any means all the secular clergy accepted the principle that it was a priest's duty to pry into the politics of those who made confession to him. There was, however, a tendency of prison chaplains to use their influence in favour of the powers that existed. For some time the prisoners in Mountjoy were denied the sacraments. Some suffered in silence. Others became bitterly anti-clerical, even professing atheism, sometimes in that politically sterile form that sees, if not God's will, at least the clergy's will in every wrong that affects the body politic. Mellows was among those who said nothing. He was a devout Catholic, deeply versed in church doctrine, and knew that what the bishops had done would yet be repudiated. It was, but too late.

At length it was clear that the Republican movement could delay its policy decisions no longer. The Army Executive met at Ballybeacon, County Tipperary, on 16th and 17th October. Nine members were present on the first day, namely Lynch, O'Malley, Moylan, Barry, Deasy, Robinson, O'Connor (3rd Bn. Dublin), Derrig and Frank Barrett. On the 17th Pax Whelan joined them. Lynch reviewed the sequence of events from the attack on the Four Courts, and Barry and Deasy reported on the recent meeting with the Provisional Government officers Ennis and Russell. They had suggested a peace settlement on the basis of the disbandment of both armies, the abolition of the post of the Minister of Defence and a police force modelled on the Canadian system. It was strange that such utopian proposals were discussed seriously. On the second day Con O'Malony, who had expressed the view that "democratic politics are not for us" in relation to Mellows' draft, proposed "that the Army Council be instructed to negotiate terms of peace such as will not bring this country into the British Empire". This, together with the proviso that the final decision rested with the Executive, was unanimously adopted.

The same officer, with Seamus Robinson's support, then moved a further resolution, "that this Executive calls upon the former president of *Dail Eireann* to form a government which will preserve the continuity of the Republic. We pledge this government our whole-hearted support and allegiance while it functions as the government of the Republic and we empower it to make an arrangement with the Free State Government, or with the British Government, provided such arrangement does not bring the country into the British Empire. Final decision on this question to be submitted to the Executive." This motion was carried with one dissentient.

The Mellows proposals were not discussed. The aim of the war was still not total victory, but an acceptable compromise. Hence, though it might involve as adventurous guerrilla actions as could be devised, it was still politically defensive. The government was to be established, but it was to be a shadowy formality, the army Executive reserving to itself separate negotiating powers and final decision. A third resolution called upon De Valera to form the government. Finally those members of the Executive who were in prison were formally replaced, McKelvey by Frank Aiken, O'Connor by Con Maloney, O'Donnell by Lehane and Mellows by Sean MacSwiney.

On 25th October the final stages of the Free State Constitution Bill were taken. On the same day members of the second *Dail* met secretly. A communique which had been agreed with the Army Council was issued next day. It ran:

Dail Eireann, Parliament and Government of the Republic met yesterday in secret session, the former Deputy Speaker presiding. A clerk of the House was appointed.

The resolution followed:

WHEREAS the Speaker and other appointed Executive officers in disregard of their duty and in open disobedience to the mandamus[1] of the Supreme Court, have refused to summon Dail Eireann, the duly elected Parliament of the Republic,

and WHEREAS (these) have joined in a traitorous conspiracy and armed revolt, pretending to establish a so-called "Free State" and a Provisional (partition) Parliament . . . destroy the independent sovereignty of the nation and the integrity of its ancient territory

THEREFORE we . . . call on the former President Eamon De Valera to resume the Presidency and to nominate a Council of State . . . (and resolve) that Eamon De Valera be hereby appointed President of the Republic and Chief Executive of the State

(and) that the following, nominated by the President, be hereby appointed Council of State, Austin Stack, Robert Barton, Count Plunkett, J. J. O'Kelly, L. Ginnell, S. T. O'Kelly, Sean O'Mahoney, Mrs. O'Callaghan, Mary MacSwiney, P. J. Ruttledge, Sean Moylan and M. P. Colivet

[1] Secured by Mrs. Tom Clarke just before the Court was dissolved.

(and) that pending the next meeting of the Dail we hereby empower the Council of State to sanction such ministers and Executive Officers as the President may nominate and may have the Council's approval.

Two days later the Army Council on behalf of the "custodians of the Republic" confirmed this decision.

In a sense Mellows had attained his first objective. A political standard was planted to which Republicans could rally. But two months had been lost. The military position of the Volunteers had immeasurably worsened. It was becoming necessary for Republicans to drop all inherited legalisms and grasp the position before them with their sober senses, to estimate which classes were still interested in Irish independence, what their requirements were, and how they could be rallied. Mellows' social programme had sketched out a policy which would revive the alliance of 1916, between offensivist Fenianism and the socialist working class, as the centre of national resistance. Without this programme the revival of *Dail Eireann*, belated, in part artificial, and oriented towards the re-establishment of the petit-bourgeois alliance that had achieved so much but which was now shattered, could only seal the division between Republicanism and Labour, and imprison its members in their own house. The Russian Bolsheviks answered the "second Kornilov plot" by seizing power without waiting for the "uncertain voting of November 7th". What would have been their position if, having failed to do so, they had found themselves trying to re-establish the Council of Soviets in the midst of a bloody terror directed by a "constitutional" monarchy having "soviet" ministers? The comparison is not too wild for consideration.

The Provisional Government was desirous of making haste. Its Parliament was induced to pack its bags, while the military authorities spent a fortnight restoring law and order. During this spell of military absolutism, against which Tom Johnson protested eloquently but without effect, Republicans began the attempt to collect taxes on behalf of *Dail Eireann*. On 3rd November Stack and De Valera issued a proclamation repudiating Provisional Government debts. It was decided to prepare for publication a full account of the London negotiations which had been hidden from the people at the time. Erskine Childers was brought from the south to undertake the work.

Childers called at his cousin's house at Annamoe, Co. Wicklow, and was there on the night of 11th November. In the small hours the military raided it. Childers was arrested and found in possession of a Colt automatic, which he had not used, and which was a souvenir given him by Michael Collins. The news of his capture was well-blazoned. Winston Churchill was addressing a meeting in Dundee. Determined to miss no opportunity of smearing the working class with the barbarous vulgarity of his own, he expressed delight at the taking of the "murderous renegade" and added "Such as he is may all that hate us be."

Childers was not yet dead. He was on trial for his life. No doubt his judges were illuminated by Churchill's wishes. The charge was possession of arms. The trial took place on 17th November, *in camera*. On that day four prisoners, one a boy of eighteen, were executed for the same offence. Kevin O'Higgins, with frankness Churchill would never have permitted himself in his own Parliament, explained that the purpose was to create a precedent for the execution of Childers. Childers was found guilty and sentenced to death. Against his inclinations, since he had refused to recognise the Court, he agreed to appeal in order to facilitate the issue of a writ of *habeas corpus* to which could be joined eight prisoners whose names were being withheld.

Meanwhile De Valera selected his cabinet and on 13th November submitted it to the Army Council for approval. He appointed Austin Stack Minister for finance, P. J. Ruttledge for Home Affairs, Sean T. O'Kelly for Local Government, for Economic Affairs Robert Barton and for Defence Liam Mellows. Until Mellows could effect his escape it was agreed that Defence documents should be issued by De Valera and countersigned by Liam Lynch. De Valera explained that but for his arrest he would have nominated Childers as Secretary to the Cabinet and Director of Publicity. On the 17th a proclamation was issued declaring the Provisional Government illegal and its adherents rebels against the Republic.

The writ of *habeas corpus* which had been applied for on behalf of Childers and the others was refused on 23rd November, but permission to appeal was granted. Notice was served on the military authorities. They had learned something from the executioners of Wolfe Tone. Next morning Childers was taken to Beggars Bush. Parallel with the carriage in which he was conveyed was a tender which contained his coffin. The journey was enlivened by the insults of the guard. He was shot at dawn while his appeal was pending.

Three other prisoners were executed on account of an alleged street ambush, and Mulcahy, anxious to rebut charges of inhumanity, assured the Provisional Parliament that "we provided for these men all the spiritual assistance that we could, to help them in their passage to eternity". Since he also provided all the material assistance, what more could they want?

What state of mind lay behind this drivelling piety? Hysteria? Intellectual and moral bankruptcy? It is interesting to speculate. The certainty is that the members of the Provisional Government were no longer themselves. Action makes the man, and they were now little more than the physical embodiment of British policy in Ireland.

The policy of ruthless slaughter evoked its natural reaction among the Republicans. On 28th November a note was sent to the Speaker of the Provisional Parliament. It began, "The illegal body over which you preside has declared war on the soldiers of the Republic and suppressed the legitimate Parliament of the Irish nation." The note warned of the serious consequences that would follow the further maltreatment of prisoners. Two days later indignation had risen further. A list of deputies who had voted for the "murder Bill" was issued with instructions that they were to be shot on sight. Houses of such were to be burned to the ground, together with those of members of murder gangs and of active supporters of the Provisional Government. A clarification issued next day provided that fathers must not be held responsible for the actions of their children.

Bonar Law had replaced Lloyd George as Prime Minister of England. So long would Lloyd George's guarantee have lasted. On 20th November, when the London Parliament assembled, the new Premier introduced two Bills, the Irish Free State Constitution Bill and the Irish Free State (Consequential Provisions) Bill. These received their second readings on 27th November. Only one member of Parliament protested that the Bills derived from a treaty "based upon coercion and signed under duress". He was Shapurji Saklatvala, member for Battersea (North). The attitude of most Labour members was non-committal. They were largely men of parochial interests. The form of development of the Irish struggle was beyond their experience and incomprehensible to them. They could not understand that it was still their duty to fight British imperialism even though some of the former leaders of national liberation were now in league with it. That the fight against British imperialism is above all a British responsibility they had not even begun to understand.

Mellows had been working hard on social questions in expectation of escape. He had filled exercise books with plans for the improvement of Dublin in such a way as to facilitate the work and enjoyment of the common people. He had prepared a thesis on the role of the Labour Party, part of which was subsequently published by Frank Gallagher, himself in Mountjoy since 11th October. It included such passages as

Labour played a tremendous part in the establishment and main-tenance of the Republic. Its leaders had it in their power[1] to fashion that Republic as they wished—to make it a workers' and peasants' Republic. By their acceptance of the Treaty and all that it connotes—recognition of the British monarchy, the British Privy Council, partition of the country and subservience to British capitalism, they have betrayed not only the Irish Republic but the Labour movement in Ireland and the cause of the workers and peasants throughout the world.

It is a fallacy to believe that a Republic of any kind can be won through the shackled Free State. You cannot make a silk purse out of a sow's ear. The Free State is British-created, British controlled and serves British imperial interests. It is the buffer erected between British capitalism and the Irish Republic.

If the Irish people do not control Irish industries, transport, money and the soil of the country, then foreign or domestic capitalists will. And whoever control the wealth of a country and the processes by which wealth is attained control also its government.

The document reached Gallagher on 4th December. Mellows' mind was ranging widely over the problems raised by the new phase of imperialist domination in Ireland. Gallagher noted that he had been instructed to "hurry out" and guessed that a new tunnel was under construction.

The Free State Constitution Act received the Royal Assent on 5th December. Timothy Healy, the man whose sharp tongue had hounded Parnell to his ruin, was appointed Governor-General. He took office next day when the Free State finally came into existence. It was he who officially summoned its Parliament, a gathering devoid of all festivity.

All members took the oath of allegiance to the Crown of England, but Tom Johnson read a statement signed by all Labour members indicating that they did so under protest and without prejudice to future action. The sole gain was that the Free State Government was now responsible to Parliament and could be removed by it. The Republican deputies did not attend. To do so would be to abandon *Dail Eireann* they had so recently revived. What would have happened if they had decided to follow the lead of Labour as De Valera did four years later, taking the oath under protest, while maintaining that the assembly was not the national parliament of the Irish people? They would probably have been arrested before they crossed the threshold and their appearance would have been exhibited as proof of apostasy. They were in no mood to try the experiment.

[1] Mellows here overlooked their exclusion from *Dail Eireann*.

On 7th December both houses of the six-county Parliament presented an address to the King of England praying that the powers of the Parliament of the Irish Free State should "no longer" be exercised in Northern Ireland. To find out what power ever had been exercised there by the Free State would be a suitable puzzle for a linguistic philosopher. On the same day Sir James Craig repudiated the Boundary Commission. The policy of the "Treaty" party lay in ruins together with the country they had imposed it on. On this day two deputies who had voted for the "murder Bill", Sean Hales and Patrick O'Malley, were shot while leaving a hotel on Ormond Quay, Dublin. Hales died. The Republicans were held to blame.

That evening the Free State Cabinet met. Frightened angry men debated their course of action. Mulcahy is said to have proposed the execution of four leading Republican prisoners as a reprisal. According to one account, no names were mentioned. Eoin MacNeill seconded. Kevin O'Higgins was revolted by the proposal. But he was the only one shocked into sanity, and the others soon persuaded him. When Joe McGrath arrived it was O'Higgins who persuaded him. The order was issued by Mulcahy, and it is usually held that it was he who selected or approved the selection of the victims. He was, of course, no more guilty than the other members of the Cabinet.

The men chosen were O'Connor, McKelvey, Barrett and Mellows. On what basis was the choice made? One man was taken from each province, it has been said. But who represented Connacht? Mellows was so unmistakably a Leinster man that nobody would seriously consider him in this connection, unless he was paying a belated penalty for his part in 1916. Again, if the choice was made on grounds of prominence, Barrett was virtually unknown. The intellect of a "dangerous man" belonged only to Mellows and Barrett, the others were able but not outstanding. But all were I.R.B. men who had left the fold, and above all, they knew too much. Mellows knew the revolutionary movement from its inception and was in the midst of all the unity negotiations. O'Connor knew the intrigues that surrounded the Plunkett Convention and the unification of *Sinn Fein*, and more embarrassing still, the campaign in England. McKelvey knew of the relations with the North. And finally, Barrett had been close to Collins and was familiar with the affairs of "the squad". Already Childers had carried to the grave his unrivalled knowledge of the "Treaty" negotiations. Who can deny that when those four tongues were silenced the world became much safer for "official history"?

CHAPTER TWENTY-ONE

SHOT AT DAWN

THE mood in the prison was of tempered optimism. The establishment of the Free State, releasing their minds from the fetters of false hope, forced Republicans into the future. Popular disillusionment could not be far off. Mellows stayed up till well after midnight as a stream of visitors came to his cell. At 3 a.m. he was wakened. He was ordered to collect his property and move to another cell. He was not alarmed. He assumed that he was to be transferred to another prison, or perhaps to a concentration camp. He gathered up his belongings. After arrival at the new cell he was told he would be shot at dawn.

He asked for a priest. The prison chaplain came to see him. From the first it was clear that the bishops' pastoral hung between him and absolution. The chaplain stood by the letter of the pronouncement, and asked for a recantation. This Mellows indignantly refused to give, and told the priest he preferred to die without the sacraments. It was in the next few hours that he wrote his two letters, one to his mother, the other to the Hearns in Westfield. The letters are simple and dignified, and show a self-control that is quite astonishing. For a devout Catholic to face death without intermediary is to stake eternity on the judgment of one moment. It is the bravest thing he can do.

He wrote first to his mother.

My dearest mother,
The time is short and much that I would like to say must go unsaid. But you will understand; in such moments heart speaks to heart. At 3.30 this morning we (Dick Barrett, Rory O'Connor, Joe McKelvie and I) were informed that we were to be executed as "reprisal". Welcome be the will of God, for Ireland is in his keeping despite foreign monarchs and treaties. Though unworthy of the greatest human honour that can be paid an Irishman or woman, I go to join Tone and Emmet, the Fenians, Tom Clarke, Connolly, Pearse, Kevin Barry and Childers. My last thoughts will be on God and Ireland and you.

You must not grieve, mother darling. Once before you thought you had given me to Ireland. The reality has come now. You will bear this as you have borne all the afflictions the cause of Ireland brought you—nobly and bravely. It is a sore trial for you, but that great courageous soul of yours will rejoice, for I die for the truth. Life is only for a little while, and we shall be reunited hereafter.

I would write to Barney separately, but, alas! he is not at home. That he will be brave I know; that he will persevere until the wrong is righted and the shadow of shame is lifted from our country I do not doubt. May God bless and protect him and give him courage, fortitude and wisdom necessary to adhere to truth and honour and principles. Through you I send to him my fondest love.

Through you I also send another message. It is this: Let no thought of revenge or reprisals animate Republicans because of our deaths. We die for the truth. Vindication will come, the mists will be cleared away, and brothers in blood will before long be brothers once more in arms against the oppressor of our country—Imperialist England. In this belief I die happy, forgiving all, as I hope myself to be forgiven.

The path the people of Ireland must tread is straight and broad and true, though narrow. Only by following it can they be men. It is a hard road but it is the road Our Saviour followed—the road of Sacrifice. The Republic lives; our deaths make it a certainty.

I had hoped that some day I might rest in some quiet place—beside grandfather and grandmother in Castletown, not amidst the worldly pomp of Glasnevin, but if it is to be the prison clay it is all the sweeter, for many of our best lie there.

I send my love to Aunts Maggie, Julia, Jane and Annie, all my cousins in Wexford, Dublin, Clare and Armagh.

Tell Patsy also I send my love, and Father Feeney and Father McGuinness.

Go to Mrs. Pearse. She will comfort you. I intended writing to Mrs. Woods and family, but time prevents me doing so. Give my love to them all.

I have had the chaplain to see me. It is sad, but I cannot agree to accept the Bishops' Pastoral. My conscience is quite clear, thank God. With the old Gaodhals I believe that those who die for Ireland have no need of prayer.

God bless, protect and comfort you,
                    Your loving son,
                         Willie.

His letter to the Hearns is dated 4.30 a.m. 8th December.

Dear John and Mrs. Hearn,
    The time draws short. An hour ago I was informed that I was to

be shot at eight o'clock this morning—as a reprisal. Well, I shall die for Ireland—for the Republic; for that glorious Cause that has been sanctified by the blood of countless martyrs throughout the ages; the cause of Human Liberty. The Republic stands for truth and honor—for all that is noblest in our race. By Truth and Honor—by Principle and Sacrifice alone will Ireland be free. That this is so —that this is immutable—I am prepared to stake all my hopes of the hereafter.

Ireland must tread the path Our Redeemer trod. She may shrink, as indeed she has shrinked[1]—"Put away this Chalice"—but her faltering feet will find the road again, as indeed she is already finding it. For that road is plain and broad and straight; its signposts are unmistakable. It is the road on which Wolfe Tone, and Emmet and Mitchel, and the Fenians, and Tom Clarke, Pearse, Connolly, Kevin Barry, Terry MacSuibhne and Childers were the guides.

I have no regrets, for the future of Ireland is assured. The Republic is assured and before long all Irishmen, including those now unhappily in arms against the Republic, will be united against Imperialist England—the common enemy of Ireland and of the world.

To you and Mary I send my love. I know your prayers will be offered for me, though, with the old Gaedhals[1] I share the belief that those who die for Ireland "have no need of prayer".

God bless you all,
With affectionate regards,
Liam O'Maoiliosa[1]
In mBêurla, Liam Mellows.

To John J. and Mrs. Hearn,
9, High Street,
Westfield.

From the reference to dying without need of prayer, which occurs in both letters, and seems to have been remembered from Pearse's oration at Bodenstown, it is clear that he had not come to an understanding with the chaplain. This supposition is supported by the evidence of another priest.

Fr. Piggott was a chaplain at Wellington Barracks, and a convinced if not fanatical supporter of the Free State. He sat up late on the night of 7th December, only retiring when it was clear that no further accretions of slack would revive the fire. He was worried at the mood of the "Treaty" party. Already there had been ten executions and he feared more.

[1] So spelled.

The telephone rang. He was asked to dress and await a further message. This he did. The message came in the shape of two Crossley tenders to escort him to Mountjoy. He complained that the prison was outside his sphere of duty. Fr. MacMahon was there. But he was assured that Fr. MacMahon had sent for him at the request of Rory O'Connor with whom the Mountjoy chaplain was having great difficulty.

He spent two hours with Rory O'Connor. Then came a knock at the door. Would he see Mellows? He went in to Mellows who had in his hand the paper he had been requested to sign. "Look at this!" said Mellows. It was clear that no useful discussion was possible and he returned to O'Connor, nevertheless expecting Mellows to send for him. But Mellows did not. Mass was said. Litanies were recited. O'Connor, Barrett and McKelvey had Communion, but Mellows did not. The men were blindfolded. The Governor stood to attention. Everybody waited on everybody else. Fr. Piggott persuaded the Governor to uncover Mellows' eyes while he spoke to him. He asked if he would make confession. "There is no time," was the reply.

"You can wait a little longer," the priest told the Governor. He took Mellows into a cell and arranged to hear his confession. Treaties and political recantations were forgotten about. Fr. Piggott asked Fr. MacMahon to go into the chapel to obtain the Viaticum. He failed to return. Fr. Fennelly appeared and he asked him to stay with Mellows while he looked for Fr. MacMahon. He heard knocking. Fr. Mac-Mahon was locked in the sacristy which he must pass through to leave the chapel. The problem now was to find the Deputy-Governor, O'Keeffe, who held the key. He was found, hopelessly drunk. He had spent the night deadening his senses before the nightmare that had engulfed him. Told that Fr. MacMahon was locked in the sacristy he hiccupped "What the blashted hell does he want doing in there?" Finally the keys jingled and Fr. MacMahon was let out.

Fr. Piggott heard Mellows' confession and administered the last rites of the Catholic Church. Mellows handed him a crucifix with the request that it should be taken to his mother. They returned to where the other three were waiting. As all four moved off to the place of execution, Barrett started to sing "The top of the Cork Road". Fr. Piggott walked between Mellows and O'Connor. As the two were led off Mellows called to the others "Slan libh, boys." Those were not the last words he spoke. The firing squad was tense for the occasion and tenser for the delay. The greater part of the volley went wide, and

Mellows' last words were a piteous appeal for the *coup de grace*. Nine revolver shots were fired before the four men were dead.

The execution took place at about 9 a.m. Mellows' last message was delivered to Eamon Martin by a prison officer. It was written at 7.30 a.m. and ran:

> To my dear comrades in Mountjoy. God bless you, boys, and give you fortitude, courage and wisdom to suffer and endure all for Ireland's sake.
>   An poblacht Abu!
>   Liam O Maoiliosa (Liam Mellows)

8th December is the day of the "Feast of the Immaculate Conception". The Free State authorities had offered a grave affront by ordering executions on such an occasion. Prisoners rose early so as to hear Mass at 7.30 a.m. They found the doors of the chapel closed, and were told the service would be delayed at least an hour. Some returned to bed. Others talked and joked by the door. They guessed the priest had fallen suddenly sick. Then the jail seemed suddenly filled with military policemen. In A wing a warder lost his head and fired two warning shots. Rumours flew. The Governor had been assassinated. The tunnel had been discovered and four men taken to Tintown. Another attempted break-out had been forestalled. There was a wave of excitement, with shouts and cat-calls from prisoners still in their cells.

Suddenly the commotion was quelled. The chapel was opened and the men filed in. Clearly it had been used already. An altar-boy stood with face white as parchment. The realisation of what had happened swept like an icy gust through the gathering. Fr. Fennelly appeared in a state of intense agitation. He remained kneeling as he made the effort to compose himself. Then with voice shaking he said, "Let us offer this Mass for four of your comrades who went before their God ten minutes ago." Some of the prisoners refused to kneel. There were sobs and some curses. When Fr. MacMahon arrived to give an account of what had happened there were bitter rejoinders. More anti-clericalism was generated in that five minutes than in a previous generation. The prison was a place of desolation all day, and there was little sleep the night following.

The executions shocked Ireland and the world. No notice was posted outside the prison. Mrs. Woods, who called to deliver a parcel for Tony, remarked only the uneasy haste with which it was taken from her by the soldier at the gate. She heard rumours of O'Connor's execution from the conductor of the Donnybrook tram. A few minutes later newsboys were shouting stop-press. And the four names were there to be seen. Mr. and Mrs. Woods went to Mount Shannon Road where the house was full of neighbours. A soldier had brought the last letter.

It was decided to make an effort to secure the body. Mr. and Mrs. Woods set off to Mountjoy with Mrs. Mellows. They met Maud Gonne and Mrs. Despard who were on their way from the prison. These turned again and added their request. When it was refused all repaired to Mount Shannon Road to consider what was to be done. At this point Fr. Piggott appeared with the crucifix. He had to listen to many bitter reproaches. They thought he had refused Mellows absolution and would not give him time to explain. Mr. Woods then drove the four women to the house of the Governor-General at Chapelizod. The place bristled with defences. At length an ex-British soldier whose parents lived in Donnybrook agreed to take in a message. The reply was that "His Grace" could not intervene. An approach to Gearoid O'Sullivan was no more fruitful. It is said, however, that when Maud Gonne and Mrs. Despard succeeded in interviewing the Archbishop of Dublin, they secured a promise that if there were further executions of innocent prisoners he would denounce the government. Half a loaf was better than no bread. Mellows' death was not registered by the authorities until the following March. They could not even spell his name correctly.

The *New York Nation* described the executions as "murder, foul and despicable, and nothing else". Dr. Maloney must have regretted his flirtation with the "Treaty". The Labour Party sharply protested in the Free State *Dail*. The most telling indictment came from the family of the deceased T.D., Sean Hales. These repudiated the Mountjoy murders in a letter of dignified protest which they sent to the press. Their action was the more generous since Sean Hales was not an embittered Free Stater, and they could with reason have expected that he would not be the first to be made an example of. They wrote:

> We view with horror and disgust the execution of the four Irishmen Richard Barrett, Liam Mellowes [*sic*], Joseph McElvey and Rory O'Connor as a reprisal for the death of our dearly beloved brother, and we think it a criminal folly to believe that such methods will end the strife in our land; and we are of the opinion that reprisals on either side will only increase the bitterness and delay the reconciliation that all patriotic Irishmen long and pray for, and also that the

sole testimony of a British Officer is a very insufficient proof of how
he met his death.

Signed   Robert Hales (Father)
          Margaret Hales (Mother)
          Liam Hales (Brother)
          Domhnal Hales (Brother)
            Italian Consul, Genoa, Italy
          Margaret Hales (Sister)
          Elizabeth Hales (Sister)

Per Liam Hales,
   Knocknacurra, Ballinadee,
   December, 1922

The Hales family prophesied truly. The Mountjoy murders sealed
the divisions between Free State and Republican as nothing else had
done. If, as Blythe and others have argued, they ended the Republican
policy of "Shoot at sight", they also ended the possibility of compromise. The civil war dragged on for another five months. Millions
of pounds were spent. Thousands of acres were let go waste. Debts
were piled up and jails and concentration camps crammed with
prisoners. The price of counter-revolution was that neither in the six
nor the twenty-six counties could the government survive a return to
normal conditions.

The war ended without a decision. The Republicans dumped arms
and went home. The era of neo-colonialism began, with its assault on
working-class standards and stultification of the national economy,
until these things brought their own inevitable reaction and the forces
of progress regrouped for a new epoch of struggle. It was the greatness
of Mellows that he, more clearly than any in the Republican movement, grasped the fundamentally plebeian nature of the Irish national
struggle. Its essential components are the working class and the
revolutionary petite-bourgeoisie of town and country. Only from time
to time does the main body of the big bourgeoisie enter into alliance
with these, and such alliance is invariably fraught with hesitations and
indurability.

Mellows' thought failed to reach Connolly's in one important
respect, namely in regard to the question of class leadership. To
Connolly the leadership, not merely the participation, of the working
class was to be desired. Hence his immense stress on the role of the mass
organisations of the workers themselves. But the Irish revolution did
not develop in such a way as to give the workers the leadership.
Mellows was too close to it for easy analysis of this circumstance. He

foreshadowed the great struggles of the thirties when workers and Republicans joined to repulse fascism. His principle was temporarily forgotten in the forties, to be rediscovered by Republicans in the sixties. It is therefore right that Irish people should remember Mellows, and because he stood for this principle honour his memory today.

Much less than Connolly was Mellows involved in British affairs. It is noteworthy, however, that never once, in speech or writing, did he fail to distinguish between British imperialism and the British people. His internationalism is attested repeatedly. His insistence, therefore, that the chain of responsibility for the series of events which led to his execution led away back through the renegade Welshman to the system of imperial plunder based in England, should be taken to heart by all British democrats. It was the compulsion of the Government of Ireland Act that decided the rules of the game thereafter to be played in Ireland, the compulsion of the "Treaty" that established its agents in power. The results are therefore the concern of the British people. And when Irish people ask for solidarity in mitigating their severity, or setting the axe to the root of the whole system, British democrats should respond. In so doing they will pay belated respects to the great revolution that was strangled on their doorstep, by their ruling class, and help to build up a new alliance which will help them, too, when they wish it, to escape from the clutches of one of the most corrupt imperialisms the world has ever known.

INDEX